Using Smart©

Andrew N. Schwartz

Que™ Corporation
Indianapolis, Indiana

Library of Congress Catalog No.: 85-63881
ISBN 0-88022-229-8

90 89 88 87   8 7 6 5 4

Interpretation of the printing code: the rightmost double-digit number is the year of
the book's printing; the rightmost single-digit number, the number of the book's
printing. For example, a printing code of 87-4 shows that the fourth printing of the
book occurred in 1987.

Screen reproductions in this book were created by means of the PRINT SCREEN
program from DOMUS Software, Ltd., Ottawa, Ontario, Canada.

Dedication

To Debbie

   Michael

      Julie

         . . . and Snoops

Product Development Director
David F. Noble, Ph.D.

Editorial Director
David F. Noble, Ph.D.

Managing Editor
Gregory Croy

Production Editor
Bill Nolan

Editors
Gail S. Burlakoff
Katherine Murray

Technical Editors
Anne Fuller
Jeanne Saalfrank

Cover designed by
Listenberger Design Associates

Composed in Garamond and Que Digital
by Que Corporation

About the Author

Andrew N. Schwartz received his B.A. from Amherst College and his M.B.A. from the Amos Tuck School of Business Administration at Dartmouth College. He is president of his own computer consulting and development company in St. Louis, Missouri. The firm specializes in data base management and information analysis applications. Previously, he was a consulting manager for Tymshare, Inc., a computer services company.

Mr. Schwartz is vice president of the St. Louis Users' Group for the IBM PC and a member of the Independent Computer Consultants Association.

Mr. Schwartz has written several articles for *PC Magazine,* including a feature on the Smart System. He is a frequent contributor to computer publications in the St. Louis area.

Foreword

This is a practical book.

This is a business-oriented book.

This book is based on day-to-day use of the Smart System with my clients and in the management of my own business. In this book, I have included actual examples of business applications, which I hope you will be able to relate to your own business needs.

In this book, you will find the instructions necessary for using Smart, tips for using it successfully, and cautions for avoiding pitfalls. I have written the book as if I were sitting at your elbow, guiding you along the way as your understanding of Smart deepens.

Use this book to learn how to develop your initial applications. Refer to it again as your applications mature. (The Index will help you put your finger on specific topics, and the Table of Contents is designed to help you locate information on specific commands.) As your needs grow, use this book to learn about other Smart application modules and how you can make the best use of them in the management of your business.

Smart is a powerful system. This book will help you navigate through Smart's many features and commands so that you can make full use of all the Smart System's capabilities.

Table of Contents

Trademark Acknowledgments

Que Corporation has made every attempt to supply trademark information about company names, products, and services mentioned in this book. Trademarks indicated below were derived from various sources. Que Corporation cannot attest to the accuracy of this information.

1-2-3 and Symphony are registered trademarks of Lotus Development Corporation.

Above Board is a trademark of Intel Corporation. Intel is a registered trademark of Intel Corporation.

Ashton-Tate, dBASE, dBASE III, and Framework are registered trademarks of Ashton-Tate Company.

DIF, Lotus, 1-2-3, and Symphony are registered trademarks of Lotus Development Corporation.

Dow Jones News/Retrieval is a registered trademark of Dow Jones and Company, Inc.

IBM is a registered trademark of International Business Machines, Corporation. IBM PC XT and TopView are trademarks of International Business Machines Corporation.

Microsoft is a registered trademark of Microsoft Corporation.

Netware and Novell are registered trademarks of Novell, Inc.

PRINT SCREEN is a registered trademark of DOMUS Software, Ltd.

Smart is a copyright of Innovative Software.

The Source is a service mark of Source Telecomputing Corp., a subsidiary of The Reader's Digest Association, Inc.

WordStar is a registered trademark of MicroPro International Corporation.

Acknowledgments

I would like to acknowledge the contributions of:

Stan Christ of Innovative Software

Robert Wells

My many clients who are using Smart and who have contributed their ideas and suggestions during the development of this book

Introduction

What Is Smart?

The Smart system is an integrated software product containing today's most-needed business applications:

> Data Base Manager
> Spreadsheet
> Word Processor
> Communications
> Time Manager

Unlike other integrated programs that have smaller modules "shoehorned" into a dominant one, Smart's modules are powerful enough to stand alone. Each module, in fact, can be purchased separately. If you need only the Data Base Manager, you can purchase that module and skip the Spreadsheet and Word Processor modules. The Communications Module and the Time Manager are included with the basic system.

If you need two of the three modules, however, it makes sense to buy the entire system. Each module is capable of standing alone as a full-featured product, but the real beauty of the system is in the integration of the modules—their capability of sharing data.

Other stand-alone packages on the market today allow the importing and exporting of data to and from other programs, but the process is usually time-consuming and cumbersome. With Smart, the data flows smoothly, and one application can span several modules. Consider this example:

> You have made your final sale for the month, and you need to analyze the results and send them to headquarters. You initiate the Data Base Manager and begin the application. The sales figures are aggregated by product class and automatically sent to the Spreadsheet.

> Further calculations, comparing the monthly performance figures to the previous year and to budget, are performed in the Spreadsheet. A graph is produced and included in the memo to the sales manager. The relevant portions of the worksheet then are sent to the Word Processor, where they

are combined with a pre-defined memo to form a complete memo for headquarters. The memo and the original worksheet then are sent to the Communications module. With no action on your part, the Communications module transfers the data to headquarters after 10:00 p.m.

This scenario not only is possible with Smart, but it can be performed completely without operator intervention under Smart's powerful Project Processing language. This degree of integration is completely impossible with the stand-alone products on the market, such as Lotus 1-2-3®, dBASE III®, and WordStar®.

Smart, introduced in the summer of 1984, is relatively new to the microcomputer software market. Version 2.0 was released in 1985; Version 3.0, on which this book is based, was introduced in the spring of 1986.

Who Should Use this Book?

If you are just now purchasing Smart, you need this book. *Using Smart* provides many examples, explanations, tips, and cautionary notes that cannot be covered in the software manuals. In each section, a single model is used to demonstrate the use of each command in constructing and using an application. In the Spreadsheet section, for example, a financial model is built "from the ground up" and finally integrated with spreadsheets from other divisions within the same company.

Efficient ways of working with Smart, as well as inefficient methods to avoid, are highlighted in this book. A product with the depth of Smart sometimes has "quirks" or undocumented features; these are noted in *Using Smart*. Having this book at your elbow as you build your applications can save you many hours of frustration.

If you already own Smart, you can also use this book. You'll learn ways to improve your application designs for more efficient processing. When I showed drafts of this book to some of my clients, I got the reaction "So *that's* how that works!"

If you have gotten into just one or two of the modules, you already know how frustrating it can be to have to learn the product on your own. Let *Using Smart* help you explore the other modules. I wrote this book as though I were standing over your shoulder, showing you how to do what you want to do.

If you are considering purchasing Smart, you can use this book to discover whether Smart is the product for you. If you find that it is, this book will give you a head start on the development of your applications.

Do you still need the manuals? Yes, absolutely. This book is not intended to take the place of the reference manuals. Many setup, configuration, and other one-time instructions that cannot be covered here are covered in the manuals. The manuals also include reference tables and information on error messages that are not covered in *Using Smart*.

What you *will* find in this book are clear explanations of the commands and features, complete with examples and references to other commands. The chapters are designed so that related commands are grouped together, and the entire book is thoroughly indexed so you can find subjects quickly and easily.

An Overview of Smart

The Smart system consists of three primary application modules (Spreadsheet, Word Processor, and Data Base Manager), two additional modules (Communications and Time Manager), the Project Processing language, and the functions and standards necessary to make these parts into an integrated whole. If you need only a spreadsheet or data base manager, you may want to purchase the appropriate Smart module separately. But if you need two or more of the applications—and *especially* if you need to use them together—the complete Smart system is an outstanding choice.

What makes the Smart system different? Spreadsheets, word processors, and data base programs have been around for a number of years, and by "hook or by crook," many of us have managed to pass data from one to another. After all, you could always summarize numbers in dBASE®, write them to an external file, and read them into 1-2-3.

If you are trying to use existing stand-alone packages to put together your own "integrated" system, however, you'll have several problems to overcome. Creating your own system can be

> *Cumbersome:* The field sizes don't match, data types differ, and record and field formats vary. Sometimes you need quotation marks around a field (single or double?), and sometimes you don't. Sometimes a blank space is the right delimiter, but at other times you need to use a comma. In still other cases, the data must be in a "fixed" format.

Time-consuming: By the time you figure out how to transfer the data, you might as well have retyped it. For repetitive tasks, you may want to figure out how to pass the data, but for smaller, one-time jobs, the time spent may not be worthwhile. Not only do you have to take the time to figure out how to do the job, but then you have to sit there and babysit the job. There is no good way to move from one separate application to another, performing various tasks automatically in each package and then passing control to another package. (The task is impossible if the procedure must make decisions on the next package to use, depending on the outcome of the current job.)

Expensive: You can spend twice as much buying separate packages to accomplish what the Smart system will do.

Totally impossible: Print a graph from 1-2-3 in the middle of a Wordstar file? Automatically log on to your mainframe computer at 2:00 a.m., download a data file, read the data to your data base, aggregate it, and produce a report? Perhaps. But what if the report is to be produced only when sales in the eastern division exceed sales in the western division by 10 percent? What then?

Other attempts have been made to produce "integrated" packages. Originally, 1-2-3 was to be a 3-in-1 piece of software: a spreadsheet, a word processor, and a data base. The program succeeded as a spreadsheet, but serious word-processor and data-base users looked elsewhere.

Then came Symphony® and Framework®. Symphony is an outstanding spreadsheet, and Framework is a fine word processor, but the other applications in these programs are "shoehorned" into the primary structure. Users who want a full-featured data manager, for example, do not choose Symphony for that purpose.

The fact that Smart offers the major modules as separate software items that can be integrated has many advantages, but perhaps some disadvantages as well. One plus is that because the modules are separate, they are not constrained by the restrictions of the others. For example, a spreadsheet has fixed boundaries (rows and columns), and a data base should not be constrained by these boundaries, as is the data base capability of 1-2-3.

In Smart, however, because you can use only one module at a time, you may be at a disadvantage if you need to pass small bits of data from the Data Base Manager, for example, to the Spreadsheet. (If you use an operating system with windowing capabilities, you can have two or more modules active at once. Smart provides direct support for the TopView™ operating environment.)

In most cases, however, using only one module at a time is no problem, because you ordinarily use just one for a while and then move on to another one. Moving from one module to another takes only a few seconds and is even faster if you have a hard disk.

An Overview of the Smart System Modules

As you know, the Smart system is made up of three primary application modules (Spreadsheet, Word Processor, Data Base Manager) and two additional modules (Communications and Time Manager). The following pages briefly introduce each module, describing their capabilities and uses.

The Smart Data Base Manager

The Smart Data Base Manager is a relational data base that allows you to look up data in as many as 24 files simultaneously. (A virtual device driver allows as many as 100 files to be open at one time.) Files in the Data Base Manager can be defined either as fixed or as variable length, depending on your needs. You can declare up to 15 key fields, called *keys*, for a file, which are used to change the order in which you view or print a file. A key field can also be used to perform fast searches; you can find a specific record in a file of 20,000 in just a second or two.

Several different field types are available: alphanumeric, numeric, date, time, Social Security Number, phone, sequential, and inverted name (in which the field is sorted on the last word in the field). An alphanumeric field can be as long as 1,000 characters, with a total of 4,096 characters in the record. One record can have as many as 255 fields.

File definition is easy and straightforward; a file of 20 fields can be defined in 10 or 15 minutes. You can set passwords for the entire file or for particular custom screens. Fields can be defined as input fields or calculated from the contents of other fields.

You can create as many as nine custom screens for a given file. A custom screen can display just a portion of a file, and fields can be defined as *read-only* or *mandatory*. (A read-only field is displayed on the screen but cannot be changed. A mandatory field must be entered and cannot be left blank.) One screen can have as many as 15 pages.

There are several different ways of reporting from the Data Base Manager. You can use the Print command when you just want the output without anything fancy. The Report command produces formal reports. The Table format lists the fields in column format; the Form format can be used to print reports on preprinted forms. You can use a combination of the two to print complex reports, by joining two files. For example, an invoice is usually a combination report, in which the heading portion is the Form and the detail below is the Table.

A Query command is used to select a subset of the records for viewing or processing. For example, after the records are initially selected, you don't have to screen through the data base to repeat the selection each time you produce a report. Even if you change the order temporarily, you can still return to the original subset.

The Smart Spreadsheet

The Smart Spreadsheet has every feature you would expect in a top-notch spreadsheet package, plus some additional features that make it an outstanding program. The maximum size of a single worksheet is 9,999 rows by 999 columns; the spreadsheet can handle such a large worksheet because it ignores blank cells. Each cell can contain numbers of up to 15 significant digits, as many as 99 characters of text, or formulas containing up to 1,000 characters. Several formats for date fields are also available. For faster calculations, the Spreadsheet supports the 8087 and the 80287 coprocessor chips.

Windows abound in the Smart Spreadsheet; you can have as many as 50 windows on the screen at one time! A window can contain a different view of the same worksheet or display an entirely different worksheet. Formulas within the Spreadsheet module can reference other worksheets; this is a good feature for consolidating worksheet data.

The Graphics command in the Spreadsheet is so powerful that it could have been created as a stand-alone module. You can create two- and three-dimensional bar charts; line and scatter plots; plots that are combinations of bars, lines, and scatters; and pies and "cakes" (3-D pies), too. Want a high-low chart? No problem.

You can output your graph in several forms. With the appropriate monitor, you can display the graph on the screen, of course. Color monitors work just fine, but the Spreadsheet's support for the EGA (Enhanced Graphics Adaptor) and the Hercules™ graphics card provides even greater resolution. A variety of printers are supported for dot-matrix printing of your graph; some examples are provided later in this book. If your printer is not exactly the same as one of the directly supported devices, you can alter the printer-control codes to conform to your printer's specifications.

Many popular plotters are supported, such as those from Amdek, Calcomp, Hewlett-Packard, and Houston Instruments. For slide presentations, the Polaroid Palette system is supported.

In addition to displaying, printing, and plotting your graphs, you can insert them in the body of documents you produce with the Word Processor module.

The Smart Word Processor

The Smart Word Processor can handle files as large as you can create, because you can swap portions of the document out to disk. As many as 50 windows can be created, permitting simultaneous viewing or "cut-and-paste" operations from one document to another.

The speed of the Word Processor is impressive. Paragraphs are reformatted automatically as you insert or delete text. You don't have the annoying cursor delay that sometimes occurs with other word processors.

The screen display of the Word Processor is visually oriented. Any of Smart's 12 fonts can be indicated with different colors on a color monitor, or you can actually display the font itself in graphics mode. Even on a monochrome monitor, the status line always tells you the font of the current character.

One feature I particularly like is the ability to incorporate a graph in the body of a document. After a graph is saved to a file in the Spreadsheet, you can position the graph in your document, specify the size, and print it on your dot-matrix printer in enhanced mode. (Before you print, you can also edit the graph, adding your own words or lines.)

The Smart Communications Module

The Communications module is used to transmit and receive files from another computer. Files can be sent and received either in text mode or under the error-correcting Xmodem protocol. With the proper modem, you can dial the phone number of the other computer or answer an incoming call.

Under the control of Smart's Project Processing, you can initiate fully automated transmission sessions, complete with password protection and error correction. Your computer may be configured to act as the "satellite" that sends data to a host computer or as the host that other computers call. Password protection is available here, too.

The Smart Time Manager

The Time Manager module is an electronic calendar. Separate calendars can be maintained for different individuals or functions. Tasks and specific meetings, along with explanatory notes, can be entered for a given day. You can print complete calendars for a week or a month at a time.

The calendars are built-in and perpetual. If you want to enter your employees' birthdays for the next five years, for example, you can do so. Changing data is easy; if a meeting is rescheduled, you just change the date, and the entry is automatically moved to the proper calendar page.

Common Features of the Smart Modules

Certain features are common throughout the Smart system. Once you have learned these common features in one module, you can use them in the others, as well. The common features are referenced in each section of this book, but they deserve to be highlighted here also.

Confidence Levels

The Smart system has several different levels of operation, depending on how familiar you are with the commands and features. Confidence levels 1, 2, and 3 list the commands of the current module on the two command lines at the bottom of the screen. An example is shown in figure I.1. You can press the corresponding number key to switch to another command list or press the slash (/) key to advance to the next list.

```
10       ----------------------------------------------------------------
11  Tax........  11.8  12.0  12.1  12.2  12.4  12.5  12.6  12.8  12.9  13.1
12  Net Income.  12.8  13.0  13.1  13.2  13.4  13.5  13.7  13.8  14.0  14.1
13       ----------------------------------------------------------------
14  EPS......  0.04  0.04  0.04  0.04  0.04  0.04  0.04  0.04  0.04  0.04
15  --------------------------------------------------------------------
16     Average       Gr Prof      Sales        G&A        Intst      Tax
17     Shares:       Rate %       Grow %    Expense:    Expense:    Rate%
18     350,000         42           11         2.8         2.2        48
```

```
Command list 1:  Autohelp  Blank  Copy  Delete  Edit  Find  Goto  Help  Insert
                 Move  Name  Print  Report  Scroll  Vcopy
Worksheet: canada      Loc: r1c1                 FN:       Font: Standard
AUTOHELP - remove/restore help line at bottom of screen (toggle)
```

Fig. I.1. *Command List 1.*

The default confidence level of each module can be established by means of the Parameters command. Level 3 shows all the available commands; you should begin at that level. Levels 1 and 2 do not display all the commands. If you are building the system for someone else, you may want to use one of these lower confidence levels for them.

Levels 4 and 5 do not display a command line at all; they just show the word *Command:* on the first line below the window. You must enter the command on your own. Of course, you won't use these levels until you are familiar with the commands, but using these confidence levels can greatly accelerate the operation of the system. Level 4 displays the command as soon as you have typed enough characters for Smart to recognize the command; you then press Enter to begin execution of the command. If you are in level 5, execution begins as soon as Smart recognizes the command.

Quick Keys, Macro Keys, and Project Processing

If you don't want to use the command menus, you can use the quick keys associated with most of the common commands. Quick keys are built into the Smart system and consist of either a function key (F1 through F10) or a key combination using the Control key (Ctrl) or the Alternate key (Alt). Commands common to each module usually have the same quick key; for example, the Load command is Alt-L in every module. You'll find some exceptions, however. The discussion of each command lists the quick key. Quick keys, the commands, and their functions are listed also in Appendix A.

Two special quick keys deserve mention here. The F1 key provides Help at any time. If you are looking for a brief description of a command or its options, press F1. The F10 key is used throughout the Smart system to indicate that you are finished with your work and want to save the file. If you are defining a report, building a project file, entering data, or defining a query, use the F10 key to save your work and return to the previous command level. If you want to exit *without* saving, press the Escape (Esc) key.

To create your own quick key where one does not exist or to simplify repeated execution of a series of commands, you can define a Macro key. Select an unused keystroke combination—try it first to make sure it is not already used for something—and select the Macro Define command. Then enter the keystrokes you need. Definitions can be stored in a file for retrieval in a later session; you can load them automatically by specification in the Parameters command. Macros can contain up to two lines of keystrokes.

Project Processing is another way to execute Smart commands. At the simplest level, a project file can contain any Smart command that you could enter from the keyboard. Thus, a project file can store more commands than a Macro key. More importantly, the Project Processing facility is actually a language that can be used to automate completely a complex or repetitive process. Full prompting, menu display, error checking, file handling, testing, branching, and run-time parameter substitution are available in Project Processing. You can also begin the execution of another project file either in the same module or in another module.

Windows are common throughout the Smart system. Initially, only one window is displayed. Use the Split command to create other windows (dividing the screen either horizontally or vertically) and the Zoom command to cause the current window to fill the whole screen temporarily. The permissible number of windows varies from module to module.

In most cases, when you are prompted to select a file, field, screen, or other item choice, you are presented with a pop-up menu (see fig. I.2.). You can respond to a pop-up menu in several ways. The easiest way is to use the cursor-control keys to move the arrow to the desired selection and then press Enter. You can also type the name of the selection in response to the prompt on the command line. If a field number is shown (as in the Data Base Manager) you can type either the number or the name of the field. If you have the option of specifying a new name (such as the name of a new worksheet), you just type the name.

When the Smart system displays a list of files for the pop-up menu, only those files in the current subdirectory are displayed in the menu. If you want the pop-up menu to show the contents of another subdirectory, you enter the path and the file specification — \ *mydata* \ *.db*, for example — and then press F5. If you know the name of the file you want from the other subdirectory, you either specify the path and file name (and drive, if it differs from the current drive) or change the subdirectory through the file New-Directory command.

The control of file names for display in the pop-up menu is accomplished by means of file extensions. Each file extension in the Smart system has a special meaning. For example, .DOC files are Word Processor document files, and .WS files are Spreadsheet worksheets. Refer to Appendix B for a complete list of the file extensions used in Smart.

```
              1        2     3     4     5     6     7     8     9    10    11
 1     ████████████          CANADIAN DIVISION
 2                   Jan   Feb   Mar   Apr   May   Jun   Jul   Aug   Sep   Oct
 3   Net Sales..   70.6  71.2  71.9  72.6  73.2  73.9  74.6  75.3  75.9  76.6
 4   Gross Prof.   29.7  29.9  30.2  30.5  30.8  31.0  31.3  31.6  31.9  32.2
 5               -------------------------------------------------------------
 6   G&A Exp....    2.8   2.8   2.8   2.8   2.8   2.8   2.8   2.8   2.8   2.8
 7   EBIT.......   26.9  27.1  27.4  27.7  28.0  28.2  28.5  28.8  29.1  29.4
 8   Int Exp....    2.2   2.2   2.2   2.2   2.2   2.2   2.2   2.2   2.2   2.2
 9   EBT........   24.7  24.9  25.2  25.5  25.8  26.0  26.3  26.6  26.9  27.2
10               ------------------------------------- -----------------------
11   Tax........   11.8  12.0  12.1  12.2  12.4  12.5  12.6  12.8  12.9  13.1
12   Net Income.   12.8  13.0  13.1  13.2  13.4  13.5  13.7  13.8  14.0  14.1
13               -------------------------------------------------------------

 ═▶ BILLS        BUDGET84      BUDGET85       BUDGET86      CANADA
    COMPINT      DEPSAL        DOMESTIC       DOMGRAPH      FORMULA
    INTALL       INTNATL       INTRNATL       JUSDEMO       LOAN
    MATDEMO2     PERSON        SLRYPLAN

Enter worksheet name:
load
Worksheet: canada      Loc: r1c1                    FN:        Font: Standard
LOAD - load a worksheet into the current window
```

Fig. I.2. *A pop-up menu.*

Smart Enhancements for Version 3.0

Although you'll find many enhancements in Smart Version 3.0, two of them deserve special mention.

Beginning with Version 3.0, a multi-user version of Smart is available. Although this product has the same functions as the single-user version, the multiuser product is priced and packaged separately. Multiuser Smart runs under the Novell 4.60 NetWare, Advanced NetWare, and any DOS 3.10-compatible network, including PCNET and Apricot Point 32.

Smart now supports the expanded memory specification, operating under either the Lotus/Intel/Microsoft or the AST/Ashton-Tate/Quadram implementations. If you have one of these boards, Smart uses them in two ways. Standard memory is expanded to the maximum (about one megabyte). Any additional memory is used for paging, to allow for creation of larger spreadsheet and Word Processor documents. You can find out the amount of memory available by pressing Ctrl-@.

Getting Started with Smart

Getting started with Smart can be divided into three separate
operations: (1) physically installing the programs on your hard disk
or floppy disks, (2) configuring your system after installation, and (3)
daily initiation of Smart sessions.

Installing the Program

Fortunately, the Install program on the Communications disk
makes the installation of Smart easy. Execute this program from drive
A: and answer the questions. A complete guide to installation is
found in the Smart Start Guide. You are prompted when to insert
each disk in your floppy dive.

I strongly recommend that you install Smart on a hard disk,
although that is not mandatory. Operation of the system is faster (10
times as fast as reading from a floppy disk) and easier (you don't
have to change floppies). You can work with larger files, such as data
bases larger than the capacity of a floppy disk, and a greater number
of files. Some features, such as the Spellchecker in the Word
Processor, are awkward to use with a floppy-based system.

Configuring the Program

The primary configuration commands you need to use are the
Parameters and Configure commands. The Parameters command is
found in each of the applications modules, and Configure is located
on command list 3 of the main menu. The options in the Parameters
command are covered in the appropriate sections of this book. Most
of the settings of the main-menu Configure command are determined
during installation. You should, however, execute Configure to make
the following decisions:

Time Format	(AM/PM or 24-hour)
Date1 Format	(99-mmm-99, 99 mmm 99, or 99.mmm 99)
Date2 Format	(99-99-99, 99/99/99, 99.99.99, or 99/99-99)
Date Style	(MMDDYY, DDMMYY, or YYMMDD)

Currency Symbol and symbol location

Decimal Separator

Thousands Separator

Division by zero result (Zero or Error)

Printer Port Location (and settings if you use a serial printer)

Characters per line default

Lines per page default

Paging file path (if other than default)

Applications data paths (other than default)

Your choice of an application path depends on how you want to initiate Smart on a day-to-day basis.

Beginning a Smart Session

I have found it best to load all the Smart programs in a separate subdirectory (\Smart, for example), make the data directory the current directory (cd \mydata), set the path to find the Smart programs (path \smart;\ ) and begin the session. Operating this way does not require setting or changing any of the applications data paths in the Configure command of the main menu.

The simplest way to begin a Smart session is to type *Smart* and press Enter. The main menu is then displayed, as shown in figure I.3.

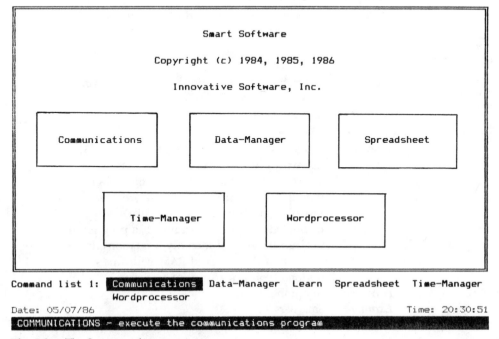

Fig. I.3. *The Smart main menu.*

After you are comfortable with the Smart system, you may want to initiate an application module directly, without going through the main menu. If you add one of the following letters after the Smart command, you can enter the desired module:

s   Spreadsheet
w   Word Processor
d   Data Base Manager
c   Communications
t   Time Manager

To go directly to the Word Processor, for example, you enter

smart w

at the DOS prompt.

You can select several other options when you enter the Smart system. They are explained in the following list.

Option: Execute a project file after entering Smart
Format: -p(project file name)
Example: Smart -pinvoice

Option: Set a data path for files accessed from main menu
Format: -d(path)
Example: Smart -dmydata

Option: Do *not* use the installed 8087 or 80287 coprocessor
Format: -n
Example: Smart -n

Option: Issue the following command after entering Smart
Format: -a(command)
Example: Smart -aload

Option: Reserve a number of K (kilobytes) of RAM for use with the DOS access mode. (The DOS access mode is initiated by typing Ctrl-O in any module. A secondary command processor is invoked, and you can execute all DOS commands and run programs. If a program does not run because of memory limitations, increase the size of the reserved RAM with this -r option. Type *exit* to return to Smart.)
Format: -r(number)
Example: Smart -r48

Option:	Designate a disk I/O driver. If you are using Smart on a network, this option is used to identify the network driver file. If you are not operating on a network, you may need this option to be able to open more than 14 files at one time, typically in the Data Base Manager. If you need to increase the number of files to a maximum of 100, the file used is VIRTUAL.DVR, and the format of the option is -fvirtual.
Format:	-f(filename)
Example:	Smart -fnet_3pl
Option:	Do *not* use expanded memory.
Format:	-e
Example:	Smart -e
Option:	Use expanded memory but do *not* use disk paging.
Format:	-x
Example:	Smart -x
Option:	Use expanded memory but do not go beyond normal memory.
Format:	-y
Example:	Smart -y

The last three options affect the usage of the Expanded Memory capabilities available with any of the supported Expanded Memory boards. If you have one of these boards, the Smart system uses memory up to the maximum (1 megabyte) to work with even larger spreadsheets or documents. Unless you have specific reasons for doing so, you should not have to use these last three options.

You can use any of these options with the other options. If you tend to use the same set of options repeatedly, you may want to create a batch file to enter the commands.

Conclusion

The Smart system provides integration of the most necessary applications in today's business environment:

    Data Base Manager
    Spreadsheet
    Word Processor

Communications
Time Manager

Each of the primary modules is powerful enough to stand alone, providing the full features you would expect from a complete package. The full benefits of Smart are truly realized when the modules are used to complement each other.

The major sections of this book are devoted to each of the modules. In each section, I cover the features of the module, the types of appropriate applications, operation of the commands, and tips for efficient usage. You will discover that once you know how to use it, Smart will help you accomplish your computing tasks quickly and easily.

Part I

The Smart Data Base Manager

Chapter 1

Introduction to the Smart Data Base Manager

The Smart Data Base Manager is designed for easy, efficient storage and reporting of detailed data. Depending on the amount of disk space available, the Data Base Manager can store information about 999,999 employees or 999,999 inventory items.

Data storage in the Smart Data Base Manager is separate from the reporting procedures, allowing you to create reports that vary widely in both form and content. Data entry can be customized for different users of an application, allowing for several levels of responsibility in maintaining portions of a file and differing levels of security. As data is entered, it can be checked for validity or used to calculate new data items.

You may sometimes have difficulty in deciding whether to use the Data Base Manager or the Spreadsheet for a given application. If your applications include large lists of items that are constantly being added and deleted, if much of the data is alphabetic, or if you need several different reporting formats, you probably need to use the Data Base Manager. If, on the other hand, your application is smaller, is primarily numeric, and involves modeling and "what if" analysis, you might be better off using Smart's Spreadsheet module.

Both data bases and spreadsheets have advantages, but each has its place in the right application. This section of *Using Smart* presents concepts of the Smart Data Base Manager and methods for making it work for you. Specific examples demonstrate its use and should solidify your understanding of the ways in which data bases can meet your computing needs.

Data Base Concepts

Reviewing a few basic data base concepts will help you to understand the Smart Data Base Manager.

Files

Data in a data base is stored in *files*, in much the same way that data in your office is stored in file cabinets. For example, a file cabinet drawer is used to store your company's personnel records. You probably label each drawer to indicate its contents. You will give files in the Smart Data Base Manager names such as PERSON or INVOICE.

Records

If you think of the file cabinet in data base terms, the file drawer is a *file*, and each piece of paper in the drawer is a *record* within that file.

Fields

A record within a file stores different pieces of information about an employee: first name, last name, city, state, telephone number, department, etc. On a personnel form, these pieces of information might be entered on separate lines or portions of lines. In a data base, these individual lines are called *fields*. Each record in a file will probably have several fields. Each record in a Smart Data Base Manager file can have as many as 255 fields.

Fixed versus Variable-Length Fields. When you look at any form, such as an employee record, each field usually has the same amount of space in every record. Although some people have longer last names than others, the form generally has space for the longest. But the field size for BIRTHDATE certainly does not have to vary from individual to individual. If one record's fields are the same size as the corresponding fields for the next record, they are called *fixed-length fields*.

But what if the amount of data you want to store varies greatly from record to record? What if, for instance, your personnel application form asks applicants to write a paragraph telling why they are applying for the job. Some applicants write more than others. What do you do then?

One method of dealing with this problem would be to establish a fixed-length field that is as long as the longest answer you expect to get. This certainly would work, although you probably would waste a good deal of space.

The Smart Data Base Manager provides *variable-length fields* as the solution to this problem. As you will see in the following chapters, when you create a file, you have the choice of defining it as either a fixed-length or a variable-length file. Although variable-length files have the advantage of saving space, they generally take longer to read and write than do fixed-length files.

Whatever the format, fixed or variable, the Smart Data Base Manager has a maximum record length of 4,096 characters, or *bytes*, per record. You usually can think of a byte as equivalent to a letter, such as *A* or *B*; however, because of the way your computer stores numbers internally and the way the Smart Data Base Manager uses them, numbers usually take less space in memory.

Key Fields. As you enter data in your data base, each record is stored *sequentially*, immediately after the previously entered record in the file. Although this may be acceptable if you always want to look at data in this order, usually you want also to look at your data in other ways. You may want your file of employees listed in order by last name, not necessarily in the order in which they were hired.

Although the Smart Data Base Manager can sort your data into a particular order, based on the contents of one or more fields, you may decide that the order of one field is always important. In your employee data base, for example, you may want to be able to switch rapidly to looking at the list in alphabetical order.

To accomplish this quick switch in the Smart Data Base Manager, you define one or more *key fields*. By defining a key field, you establish a list that is always maintained in order by the contents of that field and contains the field's internal record number. Although you don't see it, this hidden list of record numbers exists; you use it when you use the Order command to list the records of your file by the contents of a key field.

Screens

Screens in the Smart Data Base Manager are used to display on your monitor one or more fields from a record in your data base. When you call up (or *LOAD*) a file, you must specify which screen is

to be used if you have created a custom screen. There are two basic
types of screens in the Smart Data Base Manager.

The Standard Screen

Every file you create has a standard screen (see fig. 1.1). Although
the standard screen is not fancy, you can use it to perform many
Data Base Manager functions.

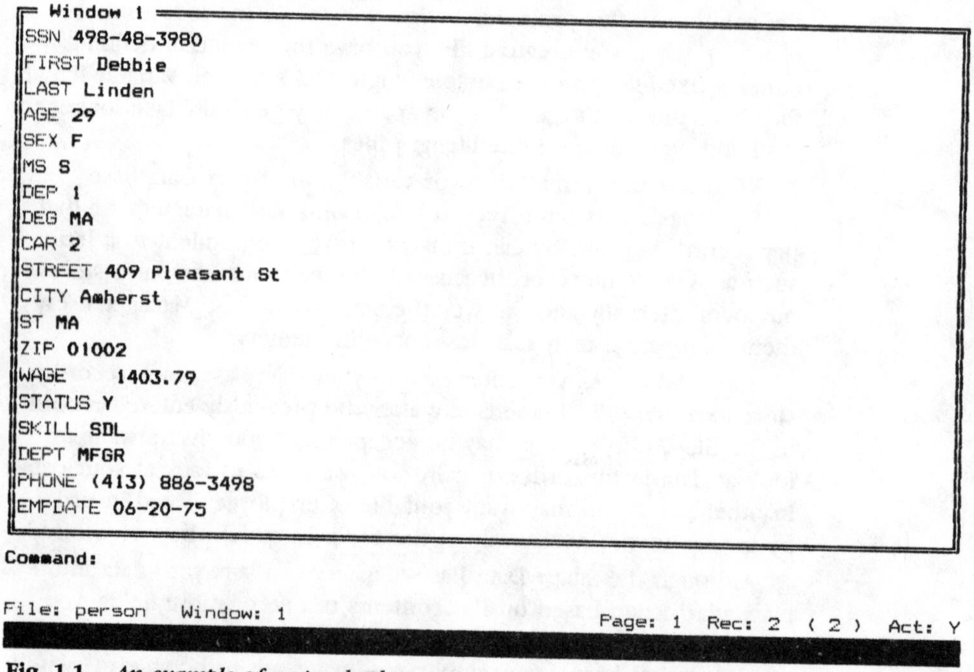

```
╔═ Window 1 ═══════════════════════════════════════════════════╗
║ SSN 498-48-3980                                               ║
║ FIRST Debbie                                                  ║
║ LAST Linden                                                   ║
║ AGE 29                                                        ║
║ SEX F                                                         ║
║ MS S                                                          ║
║ DEP 1                                                         ║
║ DEG MA                                                        ║
║ CAR 2                                                         ║
║ STREET 409 Pleasant St                                        ║
║ CITY Amherst                                                  ║
║ ST MA                                                         ║
║ ZIP 01002                                                     ║
║ WAGE    1403.79                                               ║
║ STATUS Y                                                      ║
║ SKILL SDL                                                     ║
║ DEPT MFGR                                                     ║
║ PHONE (413) 886-3498                                          ║
║ EMPDATE 06-20-75                                              ║
╚══════════════════════════════════════════════════════════════╝

Command:


File: person    Window: 1
                                          Page: 1  Rec: 2  ( 2 )  Act: Y
```

Fig. 1.1. *An example of a standard screen.*

Custom Screens

In addition to the standard screen provided for every file, you also
can create one or more *custom screens* (see fig. 1.2). Custom
screens allow selection and positioning of fields, special instructions,
range checking, and password protection.

Data Types

Your data bases can have eight types of fields, each with a
different use.

Alphanumeric

Alphanumeric fields (often called "alpha" fields) can contain any
characters except double quotation marks. You use this type of field

```
┌─ Window 1 ═══════════════════════════════════════════════════


              EMPLOYEE MAILING ADDRESS MAINTENANCE
              ═══════════════════════════════════════


       SSN: 498-48-3980

       LAST NAME: Linden        FIRST: Debbie

       STREET ADDRESS: 409 Pleasant St

       CITY: Amherst       STATE: MA  ZIP CODE: 01002

       PHONE NUMBER: (413) 886-3498




Command:

File: PERSON    Window: 1                    Page: 1  Rec: 2  ( 2 )  Act: Y
```

Fig. 1.2. *An example of a custom screen.*

for names, addresses, product descriptions, codes, and (sometimes) numbers. You cannot perform any calculations with a number that is stored in an alpha field.

Numeric

Numeric data fields can contain numbers with or without decimal places. Typically, you set up a numeric field to store a value such as a pay rate, a price, or a quantity that you want to use in a calculation. In the example in figure 1.1, WAGE is a numeric field.

Date

The Smart Data Base Manager has a special format for storing dates, because they occur frequently in data base applications. Dates can be printed in any of several formats, without disrupting the proper sorting sequence. You won't run into situations in which "Apr 85" comes before "Jan 85." Special functions for adding and subtracting dates are explained in the chapter on functions in Part V. In the example in figure 1.1, EMPDATE is a date field.

Time

Like the Date data type, Time needs special handling for printing, sorting, and calculating. Time can be displayed in either a 12-hour or a 24-hour format.

Counter

This data type can contain a sequential counter, which is maintained by the Smart Data Base Manager. For instance, if you want the system to automatically maintain invoice numbers for you as you enter each invoice record, you use the counter data type.

Social Security Number

In your personnel data base, you could, of course, set up a nine-character alpha field to store Social Security Numbers (SSNs). But the Social Security Number is a special data type in the Smart Data Base Manager because SSNs appear frequently in data bases and because it is useful to enter and print them in the format XXX-XX-XXXX. In the previous example (fig. 1.1), the SSN field is of the Social Security Number data type.

Phone

For the same reasons that it has an SSN data type, the Smart Data Base Manager has a special data type for telephone numbers. The Phone format displays an input "mask" that already contains the parentheses and the dash, making the number easier to read. Phone numbers are displayed and printed in reports in the format (000) 000-0000. In figure 1.1 the field called PHONE is of the Phone data type.

Inverted Name

Instead of having one data base field for a first name and another for a last name, you can have one field of the Inverted Name type. Such a field allows you to keep first and last names in the right order in your data base, but to sort on the last name. For example, a field that contains *Michael Davis* sorts by the last name, *Davis*.

Physical versus Logical Order

As mentioned previously, records you enter into a data base file are maintained in sequential *physical* order: in the file, each record follows the one previously entered. When you first call up (or Load) a data base file from your disk, the records are in this physical order.

However, you don't always want to look at your file in sequential order. The order in which a file is viewed or processed can be changed in two ways so that, instead of looking at that file in its physical order, you can see its records arranged in a *logical* order that is based on a set of rules. The Smart Data Base Manager can change rapidly from one order to another because the data itself may not have to be sorted. Instead, the data can be rearranged on the screen or in your report.

Key Order

You know from the preview of the "key" concept that you can order your file by the contents of a previously established key field. As you will learn in Chapter 3 ("Creating Files"), you can define a key field when you create a file or you can add or delete a key field later.

Index Order

Certain functions in the Smart Data Base Manager create index files, which also can be used to change the file's logical order. For instance, if you decide to sort your file on a field that is not a key field, you create an index that is used to change the order of the file.

Data Base Size Limitations

Although the Smart Data Base Manager can handle large files and has the capacity for any data base that is appropriate for a microcomputer, you should be aware of certain size limitations:

1. Maximum number of records is 999,999.
2. Maximum number of bytes per record is 4,096.
3. Maximum number of fields per record is 255.
4. Maximum length of an alphanumeric field is 1,000 bytes.
5. Numeric fields can be from 2 to 18 characters. (Remember, however, that the decimal point and the minus sign of a negative number each consume one space.)
6. A counter field has six digits.

Working with the Data Base Manager

Certain techniques will make your job easier and more enjoyable as
you work with the Data Base Manager.

Identifying Fields

In using the Smart Data Base Manager, you are often asked to
specify the field to which a command applies. You may need to do
so for the Sort command, a calculation, the Report command, or any
other command that calls for identification of fields. You can identify
fields in several ways.

You can always use the number of the field. The first field you
define when you create your data base (Lastname, for example) is
field 1, the next field you set up is 2, and so on. This method
obviously is quick and easy, particularly because the pop-up menu
shows the field numbers.

However, you don't use the field numbers if you are defining a
standard procedure that will be used repeatedly. The number of a
field changes if you add another field before it. For instance, if you
add an SSN field before your ZIP field (which is field number 6), ZIP
becomes field number 7. If your standard procedure definition refers
by number to the ZIP field, the procedure definition must then be
changed.

For standard procedures, you should use the field name or a
unique abbreviation. If you enter a field name and later add another
field, the Smart Data Base Manager will usually reference the correct
field. In interactive prompts, using either a field name or unique
abbreviation is acceptable, as is using field numbers.

Instead of typing a field's number or name, you can move the
arrow within the pop-up menu in order to point to the appropriate
field; then you press the F6 function key. The number of the field is
entered for you. It is followed by a semicolon, which is the separator
character in a list of fields.

Separating Field References

If more than one field is specified in a list of fields, use the
semicolon (;) to separate individual fields. To specify a range of
fields, use the vertical bar (|) to indicate a from-to condition (see
figs. 1.3 through 1.6 for examples of field references).

```
╔═ Window 1 ══════════════════════════════════════════════════════════╗
║SSN 239-87-8876                                                       ║
║FIRST Michael                                                         ║
║LAST Davis                                                            ║
║AGE 61                                                                ║
║SEX M                                                                 ║
║MS M                                                                  ║
║DEP 1                                                                 ║
║DEG MBA                                                               ║
║CAR 2                                                                 ║
║STREET 180 Lewis Ave.                                                 ║
║CITY Covington                                                        ║
║ST LA                                                                 ║
║ZIP 70433                                                             ║
║╔═ Available fields ═════════════════════════════════════════════════╗║
║║ ═► k   1 SSN        2 FIRST      k   3 LAST        4 AGE            ║║
║║        5 SEX        6 MS             7 DEP         8 DEG            ║║
║║        9 CAR       10 STREET        11 CITY       12 ST            ║║
║║       13 ZIP       14 WAGE          15 STATUS     16 SKILL         ║║
║║       17 DEPT      18 PHONE         19 EMPDATE    20 PCT           ║║
║╚════════════════════════════════════════════════════════════════════╝║
╚══════════════════════════════════════════════════════════════════════╝
```

[1:5

F6 will select the current field

File: person   Window: 1   Page: 1 Rec: 3 (3) Act: Y

WRITE - write data in ASCII, DIF, M-SYLK, SMART or text format

Fig. 1.3. *Select fields 1 through 5.*

```
╔═ Window 1 ══════════════════════════════════════════════════════════╗
║SSN 239-87-8876                                                       ║
║FIRST Michael                                                         ║
║LAST Davis                                                            ║
║AGE 61                                                                ║
║SEX M                                                                 ║
║MS M                                                                  ║
║DEP 1                                                                 ║
║DEG MBA                                                               ║
║CAR 2                                                                 ║
║STREET 180 Lewis Ave.                                                 ║
║CITY Covington                                                        ║
║ST LA                                                                 ║
║ZIP 70433                                                             ║
║╔═ Available fields ═════════════════════════════════════════════════╗║
║║ ═► k   1 SSN        2 FIRST      k   3 LAST        4 AGE            ║║
║║        5 SEX        6 MS             7 DEP         8 DEG            ║║
║║        9 CAR       10 STREET        11 CITY       12 ST            ║║
║║       13 ZIP       14 WAGE          15 STATUS     16 SKILL         ║║
║║       17 DEPT      18 PHONE         19 EMPDATE    20 PCT           ║║
║╚════════════════════════════════════════════════════════════════════╝║
╚══════════════════════════════════════════════════════════════════════╝
```

[1:13;18

F6 will select the current field

File: person   Window: 1   Page: 1 Rec: 3 (3) Act: Y

READ - read ASCII, fixed, or SMART files

Fig. 1.4. *Select fields 1 through 13, plus field 18.*

```
╔═ Window 1 ═══════════════════════════════════════════════════════╗
║SSN 239-87-8876                                                    ║
║FIRST Michael                                                      ║
║LAST Davis                                                         ║
║AGE 61                                                             ║
║SEX M                                                              ║
║MS M                                                               ║
║DEP 1                                                              ║
║DEG MBA                                                            ║
║CAR 2                                                              ║
║STREET 180 Lewis Ave.                                              ║
║CITY Covington                                                     ║
║ST LA                                                              ║
║ZIP 70433                                                          ║
╠═ Available fields ═══════════════════════════════════════════════╣
║  ══▶ k    1 SSN         2 FIRST     k   3 LAST         4 AGE      ║
║           5 SEX         6 MS            7 DEP          8 DEG      ║
║           9 CAR        10 STREET       11 CITY        12 ST       ║
║          13 ZIP        14 WAGE         15 STATUS      16 SKILL    ║
║          17 DEPT       18 PHONE        19 EMPDATE     20 PCT      ║
╚══════════════════════════════════════════════════════════════════╝
[1:6;dept
F6 will select the current field
File: person    Window: 1                    Page: 1  Rec: 3  ( 3 )  Act: Y
   PRINT - print the current file, page or record
```

Fig. 1.5. *Select fields 1 through 6, plus field DEPT.*

```
╔═ Window 1 ═══════════════════════════════════════════════════════╗
║SSN 239-87-8876                                                    ║
║FIRST Michael                                                      ║
║LAST Davis                                                         ║
║AGE 61                                                             ║
║SEX M                                                              ║
║MS M                                                               ║
║DEP 1                                                              ║
║DEG MBA                                                            ║
║CAR 2                                                              ║
║STREET 180 Lewis Ave.                                              ║
║CITY Covington                                                     ║
║ST LA                                                              ║
║ZIP 70433                                                          ║
╠═ Available fields ═══════════════════════════════════════════════╣
║  ══▶ k    1 SSN         2 FIRST     k   3 LAST         4 AGE      ║
║           5 SEX         6 MS            7 DEP          8 DEG      ║
║           9 CAR        10 STREET       11 CITY        12 ST       ║
║          13 ZIP        14 WAGE         15 STATUS      16 SKILL    ║
║          17 DEPT       18 PHONE        19 EMPDATE     20 PCT      ║
╚══════════════════════════════════════════════════════════════════╝
[ssn!age;phone
F6 will select the current field
File: person    Window: 1                    Page: 1  Rec: 3  ( 3 )  Act: Y
   BROWSE - displays records in a tabular format
```

Fig. 1.6. *Select fields SSN through AGE, plus field PHONE.*

Although you can specify individual, consecutive fields by entering their numbers or names separated by semicolons, using the vertical bar (|) can be quicker and more accurate. Furthermore, if you have many fields to specify, the prompt line may not be long enough for you to list the fields individually. A field list can contain a maximum of 80 characters.

Moving the Cursor

Mastery of the cursor-control keys can make using the Smart Data Base Manager easy, quick, and enjoyable. On the standard IBM keyboard, some of the keys on the numeric keypad also are cursor-control keys (see fig. 1.7). (On the keyboards of other computers, the cursor-control keys may be located in another position. Consult your computer manual if you have any doubts.)

Fig. 1.7. *Keyboard cursor-control keys.*

The Num Lock key is used to control the functions of the numeric keypad. Num Lock is a toggle: you press it once to use the number functions of the keys, and press it again to use the cursor-control functions. On the standard IBM PC and XT keyboards, there is nothing to indicate which of these modes is active. On the IBM Personal Computer AT, a Num Lock light indicates that you are in numeric mode; if the light is off, you can use the keys to move the cursor.

Let's look at the cursor-control keys and how they work in the Smart Data Base Manager. These keys have consistent "meanings" that may vary slightly, depending on which command you are executing.

Used alone, the arrow keys generally move the cursor one space (the ← and → keys) or one line (the ↑ and ↓ keys). The movement is nondestructive; if you are in Update mode, for instance, you do not destroy the contents of a field by moving the cursor over it. In

Browse mode, the right- and left-arrow keys shift one field at a time, allowing you to view additional fields that may be off the edge of your screen. If you want to move the cursor by only one character-space at a time in Browse mode, use the Ctrl key along with the appropriate arrow key.

The Ctrl-Home and Ctrl-End key combinations move the cursor to the beginning and end of a file, respectively. In other words, Ctrl-Home (holding down the Ctrl key and pressing the Home key) moves the cursor to the first logical record of the file. Similarly, the Ctrl-End combination moves the cursor to the last logical record. Note that this movement is relative to the *logical* order of records (their order according to the key or index field), not the *physical* order (the order in which records were entered). Of course, if your file is in sequential physical order, Ctrl-End moves the cursor to the last physical record in the file.

The page-movement keys, PgUp and PgDn, move through the file or from one screen to another. If you are in Browse mode, PgUp moves up through your file one page at a time. (A page is defined as the amount of data that can be displayed on your screen at one time.) If the program is in Enter mode and you have a multiple-page screen, PgUp moves up to the previous page of that screen, if there is one. PgDn moves in the opposite direction.

In addition to the cursor-control keys, two function keys deserve mention here because their use is similar, in some cases, to that of the ↑ and ↓ keys. The F5 key goes to the previous record in your data base and the F6 key goes to the next record. You can use these function keys in addition to the ↑ and ↓ keys, both in and out of Browse mode. If you are not in Browse mode, you can use only the F5 and F6 keys to go to the previous or next record.

Conclusion

This chapter reviews basic concepts of data bases in general, and of the Smart Data Base Manager in particular. A knowledge of the structure of data base files and of the types of data they contain is important for a solid understanding of the ways in which you will be able to create files. For further information on creating files, see Chapter 3.

Chapter 2

Handling Data Files

When you start the Smart Data Base Manager, you have a "blank slate" because you have neither loaded any files to work with nor indicated what you want to do. To work with files, you must first provide the file names and specify the screens to be used in processing. Load and Activate, commands that you use for working with data files, are discussed in this chapter.

The Smart Data Base Manager can handle files containing thousands of records, but your computer's internal memory cannot hold that many. This is one of the big differences between Smart's Data Base Manager and the program's Spreadsheet module. The Spreadsheet reads the contents of all columns and rows into RAM and therefore cannot handle files as large as those handled by the Data Base Manager. The Data Base Manager reads groups of records from the disk into an internal buffer (an area of memory set aside for file data), thus handling huge files in small increments.

The Load command opens the file, sets up appropriate buffers for reading and writing, and reads some records from the file into the buffer. The size of buffer space is governed by the *files* statement in your CONFIG.SYS file.

Ordinarily, the Smart system (working within DOS) can have open only 14 files at a time, even if you specify

files = 20

in your CONFIG.SYS file. If you find that you need to work with a greater number of files, you should use the virtual file driver capability, which permits simultaneous use of as many as 100 files. To use this capability, start your Smart Data Base Manager session by typing

SMART D -fvirtual

to load the driver file VIRTUAL.DVR; this file must be in the same directory as the Smart programs. (You cannot use the virtual file driver if you are operating Smart on a network.)

As you move through your file, reading and writing records, Smart flushes and refills the buffer as needed to make room for additional records. Some records that you have entered or updated may therefore be changed on your disk, and some still may reside in the buffer area in RAM. If you were to lose power to your computer, you would lose only those changes still in the buffer, not those already written to disk. The Save command, discussed in this chapter, addresses this potential problem.

Loading Files (4–Load, Alt-L)

The Load command is found on command list 4 (see fig. 2.1); you can also execute it by pressing the Alt-L quick key. The function of this command is to open and prepare a data base file for processing and to display it in the current window.

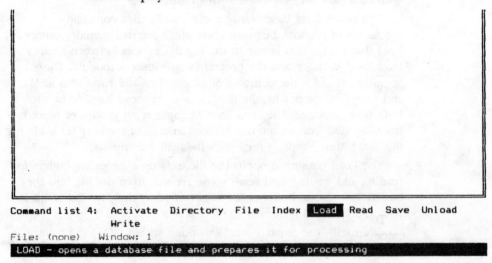

```
Command list 4:  Activate  Directory  File  Index  Load  Read  Save  Unload
                 Write
File: (none)    Window: 1
 LOAD - opens a database file and prepares it for processing
```

Fig. 2.1. *The Load command.*

The Load command displays a pop-up menu of files available in the current subdirectory. You can point to a file by moving the arrow in the menu, or you can respond to the prompt by typing the name of the file (see fig. 2.2).

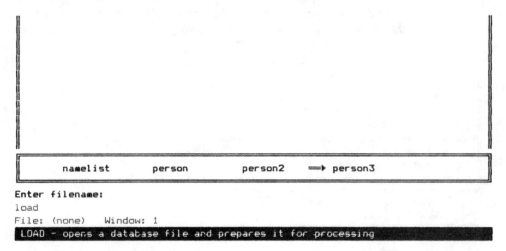

```
        namelist         person         person2   ==> person3

Enter filename:
load
File: (none)    Window: 1
LOAD - opens a database file and prepares it for processing
```

Fig. 2.2. *Enter a file name to load.*

Smart supports subdirectories, so you can enter the path and name of a file that is not in the current subdirectory. For example, you might enter

\bill\invoice

to load the file called *invoice* that is in the *bill* subdirectory. Because Smart automatically displays the names of files in the current subdirectory only, most users find that the following steps make working with the Smart Data Base Manager easier:

1. Change directory to location of data files:

    CD \BILL

2. Set Path to location of Smart programs:

    PATH \SMART;\

3. Enter SMART:

    SMART D

To display the files in another subdirectory, at the prompt to enter a file name you first supply a path and a file specification, then press the F5 key. A specification for data base files might be:

\account*.db

Then you can use the cursor keys to choose a file. (Refer to
Appendix B for a complete list of file extensions used in the Smart
system.)

If you have created screens other than the standard screen, Smart
prompts you, after you enter the file name, to select a screen for use
with this file. Again you see a pop-up menu. As shown in figure 2.3,
you select a screen by moving the arrow pointer. You *cannot* type in
the name of a screen that is not shown.

```
┌─ Screens for file person3 ══════════════════════════════════════
│    ═➤standard                              newhire
│      salary
```

```
Enter screen name:
load person3 screen
File: (none)   Window: 1
 LOAD - opens a database file and prepares it for processing
```

Fig. 2.3. *Select a screen for the file.*

If the screen has been protected with a password, you are now
prompted to enter it (see fig. 2.4). The password, which is not
displayed, is masked by asterisks (*) as you type.

```
Enter the screen password:
load person3 screen salary
File: (none)   Window: 1
 LOAD - opens a database file and prepares it for processing
```

Fig. 2.4. *Enter the screen password.*

Note that if you assigned a password to the file when it was created, you must enter that password when you select the standard screen. Any user can load (without supplying a password) alternative screens for that file which are *not* "passworded." If you want total protection against unauthorized access to your files, you must assign passwords not only to the files but also to each screen.

After three incorrect attempts at entering the correct password, the Load is aborted. Do *not* forget your passwords; there is no way to discover what they are or to circumvent this security.

When a file is loaded, the first record—in physical, not logical order—is displayed in the current window. (Refer to the preceding chapter if you need to review the concept of physical versus logical order.) If you want to work with your file in a different order, use the Order command. Refer to Chapter 5, "Arranging Data," for a discussion of that command.

Although you may not load the same file and screen twice, the Smart Data Base Manager can load the same file with *different* screens. This capability becomes useful if you have more than one window displayed on your screen and you need to view simultaneously different portions of a single file. To keep records synchronized between two windows, use the Link command (see the section on "Using Windows" in Chapter 4).

What if a file is already loaded in the current window when you load a different file? The old file, which remains active, is removed from the current window; the newly loaded file now resides in the window. (To verify that the old file is still active, you can use the Index command to view a list of all active files.) You can return to the old file by using the Goto command or the F4 key (see Chapter 4).

Be careful when you return to the old file, however. You will find that it is again in sequential order, even if you ordered it previously by a Key or an Index. Be sure to change the order again, if necessary.

Activating Files (4-Activate)

If you want to make a file active but do not want to disturb the file in the current window, use the Activate command from command list 4. The effect of this command is the same, and the prompts are identical to those of the Load command except that the file itself is not displayed in any window. When you need to view the file, you must use the Goto File command or the F4 function key.

If there is no file in the current window, the Activate command operates like the Load command, displaying the first physical record.

If you are beginning a job that involves many "passworded" files, you may find it useful to activate all of them at the outset so that you get the entry of passwords out of the way. You can then use the Goto File command to move from file to file.

Unloading Files (4–Unload, Alt-U)

When you finish working with a file, you should unload it. Unloading is not absolutely necessary, but, because each active file consumes a portion of available RAM, failure to unload may result in slower processing or a message indicating that you are out of memory.

The Unload command is on command list 4, as are the Load and Activate commands. The quick key for Unload is Alt-U.

When you execute the Unload command, you are given the choice of unloading All, a File, or a Screen (see fig. 2.5). If you select All, every active file and screen is unloaded. Any records that may be in the internal buffers are written to the disk files, and the files are closed. If several windows are open, however, they remain visible on the screen. Use the Close command to close them. Typically, you use the Unload All command if you are finished with one application and ready to start another. If you use the Quit command to exit the Smart Data Base Manager altogether, all files are unloaded automatically.

```
CAR 2
STREET 546 Olive Hill
CITY Oak Park
ST IL
ZIP 60301
WAGE     834.52
STATUS A
SKILL CKP
DEPT ACCT
PHONE (312) 439-8760
EMPDATE 10-01-59

Select option:  All  File  Screen
unload
File: person3   Window: 1              Page: 1  Rec: 1  ( 1 )  Act: Y
 UNLOAD - deactivate a database file
```

Fig. 2.5. *The Unload command options.*

If you select the Unload File command, the pop-up menu displays the names of open files. To select the file you want to unload, you use the cursor keys to move the arrow, and then you press Enter (see fig. 2.6). You may *not* type the name of a file. Any file can be unloaded, whether or not it is in the current window.

```
STREET 546 Olive Hill
CITY Oak Park
ST IL
ZIP 60301
WAGE      834.52
STATUS A
SKILL CKP
DEPT ACCT

   ══▶ namelist        person3

Select database filename:
unload file
File: person3   Window: 1                    Page: 1  Rec: 1  ( 1 )  Act: Y
UNLOAD - deactivate a database file
```

Fig. 2.6.   *Unloading a file.*

To unload only one screen of a file, select the Unload Screen command. A pop-up menu then displays the active screens for the file in the *current* window (see fig. 2.7). Select the screen to unload by moving the cursor and pressing Enter. Note that if you want to unload the screen for a file that is not in the current window, you must first display the file in the current window or use the Goto command to go to the window in which that file is displayed.

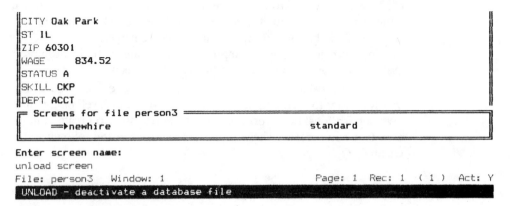

```
CITY Oak Park
ST IL
ZIP 60301
WAGE      834.52
STATUS A
SKILL CKP
DEPT ACCT
 ┌─ Screens for file person3 ══════════
     ══▶newhire                         standard

Enter screen name:
unload screen
File: person3   Window: 1                    Page: 1  Rec: 1  ( 1 )  Act: Y
UNLOAD - deactivate a database file
```

Fig. 2.7.   *Unloading a screen.*

If you use the Unload Screen command and only one screen is active, the Smart Data Base Manager proceeds to unload the file in the current window without prompting you for the name of the screen to unload.

After you execute the Unload command, the current window remains blank. Use the Goto File command to display another file and screen in that window.

Saving Files (4–Save, Alt-S)

The Smart Data Base Manager continually writes to disk as you enter new records or update existing records. But several records in the internal *buffer* (as previously mentioned) may not have been written to disk. To ensure that these records are written out and that your file is 100 percent safe on disk, use the Save command. For instance, if you will be away from your computer for a few minutes and plan to continue from your "stopping place," you should use the Save command to write your file to disk.

The Save command is found on command list 4; its quick key is Alt-S. This command has no options; execute it, and all currently active files are written to disk. No part of your current application is changed in RAM or on your screen.

Conclusion

This chapter introduces the commands used to make a file active (Load and Activate), to deactivate a file (Unload), and to ensure that a file is written to your disk (Save). The Load command not only activates a file but also displays it in the current window. If a file has multiple screens, you are prompted to select one. You are prompted also to enter any passwords that protect the screens or files.

If you are using files that someone else has developed, you need to know how to load and activate them. If you are developing your own applications, however, you need to know how to create your own files and screens. These topics are covered in the following chapter.

Chapter 3

Creating Files

If you are designing your own data base instead of using one that someone else has created, you must know how to create files and define data fields.

A file, as I mentioned in the preceding chapter, is a collection of related records that you treat as a group. Each record, in turn, consists of a group of data items stored in *fields*. The fields also are treated as a group. For example, a file of personnel information might contain one record for each employee, and each record might store information such as Last Name, First Name, Address, etc. If you have a file for invoice information, you might use one record for each invoice, and the fields would include Invoice Number, Date, Customer Number, and Amount.

The first part of this chapter explains how to create both new files and files that are similar to existing ones. The second part deals with the creation of data-maintenance and display screens.

Creating a File (1–Create, Alt-C)

No matter what kind of data items your file will contain, take a few minutes to write down as many data items as you can think of. You can save some time if you define all your fields at the outset. (Later in this chapter, you will learn how to add fields to a file.)

After you have a good idea of the contents of your file, select the Create command from command list 1 (see fig. 3.1). The Quick Key for Create is Alt-C.

```
STREET 18 Worcester St
CITY Beaumont
ST CA
ZIP 92223
WAGE    1004.56
STATUS 2
SKILL CLSP
DEPT SALE
PHONE (916) 475-4228
EMPDATE 06-15-75
```

Command list 1: Autohelp Browse Create Delete Enter Find Goto Help
                 Print Query Report Scroll Update
File: person   Window: 1   Page: 1 Rec: 10 (10) Act: Y
CREATE - creates a new file or screen

Fig. 3.1. *Command list 1: Create.*

Figure 3.1 shows the Create command in Command list 1. To create a file, select File from the option list:

> Select option: File Screen

You then are prompted to enter a new file name. The file name can have a maximum of eight characters and must follow the DOS file name conventions. You should select a name that is easy to recognize, because you will use the name frequently while using your application.

For most files used in the Smart System, you do not provide a file extension. Smart automatically assigns an extension of .DB to a data base file; screens are contained in files with an extension of .DBS. (For a complete list of the Smart file extensions, refer to Appendix C.)

Be sure to select a file name that is not currently in use. If you try to use the name of an existing file, the Smart Data Base Manager will not detect the error immediately, but will continue with the file definition prompting sequence. Only at the end of the sequence will the error be displayed.

Making a File of Fixed or of Variable Length

The next prompt asks whether the file is to be fixed-length or variable-length (see fig. 3.2). As was discussed in the introduction to

Smart's Data Base Manager, the fields in each record of a *fixed-length file* are of the same length as the corresponding fields in every other record. For example, if the length of the Firstname field is 12 characters in record 1, the length is 12 characters in record 2. If you establish a file as fixed-length, you should try to make the fields long enough to accommodate the longest data item. You will probably use fixed-length files most of the time.

```
STREET 18 Worcester St
CITY Beaumont
ST CA
ZIP 92223
WAGE     1004.56
STATUS 2
SKILL CLSP
DEPT SALE
PHONE (916) 475-4228
EMPDATE 06-15-75
```

```
Select option:  Fixed-Length  Variable-Length
create file person4
File: person   Window: 1                    Page: 1  Rec: 10  ( 10 )  Act: Y
 CREATE - creates a new file or screen
```

Fig. 3.2. *Selecting Fixed-Length or Variable-Length.*

A variable-length file is useful in some cases. If the amount of data to be stored in some alphanumeric fields varies greatly, for example, you may want to use a variable-length file. An example of such a file is a personnel application file in which you want to record applicants' responses to questions. Some applicants might write long answers, and others might write short answers.

You should not create all files as variable-length, however, because of the Smart Data Base Manager's file-access methods. Smart can process fixed-length files much faster than variable-length files.

Using a Password

The next prompt concerns whether the file has a password (see fig. 3.3). Actually, this prompt is misleading; you really are choosing whether the *standard screen* is to have a password. As was pointed out in the last chapter, you can load a screen that has no password and the screen can display all or part of a file that is protected by a password.

```
║STREET 18 Worcester St
║CITY Beaumont
║ST CA
║ZIP 92223
║WAGE    1004.56
║STATUS 2
║SKILL CLSP
║DEPT SALE
║PHONE (916) 475-4228
║EMPDATE 06-15-75
```

```
Select option: █No-Password█ Password
create file person4 fixed-length
File: person   Window: 1                    Page: 1  Rec: 10  ( 10 )  Act: Y
█CREATE - creates a new file or screen█
```

Fig. 3.3. *Password options.*

If you want absolute security for your file, you should assign a password to the file and all its screens. Passwords must be four characters in length, and they are *case sensitive.* (In other words, if the original password is in uppercase letters, you must enter the password the same way.) Don't forget your password; if you do, you will not be able to use the file.

Remember, too, that a password prevents only unauthorized access to a file through the Smart system. The password does not prevent the accidental erasure of the file itself.

Specifying New or Existing (Matching/Similar)

If you are creating a file for the first time, it is a New file (see fig. 3.4). If the file already exists and you are creating a variation of it, you should choose Matching or Similar. These options are discussed later in this chapter.

When you select the New option, the file-definition screen is displayed (see fig. 3.5). You use this screen to define each data field in your file.

Defining a New File

The file-definition screen has two main areas: the definition area, at the top of the screen; and the control area, in the lower portion of the screen. The definition area has five columns in which information

```
‖STREET 14 Spring St.
‖CITY Hartford
‖ST CT
‖ZIP 06101
‖WAGE     887.23
‖STATUS 1
‖SKILL BSMP
‖DEPT ACCT
‖PHONE (203) 739-3095
‖EMPDATE 07-23-45
```

Select option: **New** Matching Similar
create file person4 fixed-length no-password
File: person   Window: 1   Page: 1 Rec: 11 (11) Act: Y
CREATE - creates a new file or screen

Fig. 3.4. *File-creation options.*

```
┌═ Creating file ══════════════════════════════════════════════
‖          Fld No │ Title        │ Type │ Length │ Running Total
‖                 │              │      │        │
‖                 │              │      │        │
‖                 │              │      │        │
‖                 │              │      │        │
‖                 │              │      │        │
‖                 │              │      │        │
‖                 │              │      │        │
‖                 │              │      │        │
‖                 │              │      │        │
‖                 │              │      │        │
‖                 │              │      │        │
‖                 │              │      │        │
```

F3 Calc fld   F7 Insert field   F10 Exit   PgUp Prev page   Home First entry
F4 Del calc   F8 Delete field   Esc Abandon   PgDn Next page   End Last entry
Title can be up to 16 characters long

CREATE - creates a new file or screen

Fig. 3.5. *The file definition screen.*

is entered about each field. The five columns in the definition area
are *Fld No* (Field Number), *Title, Type, Length,* and *Running Total.*

Field Number

Fld No is the abbreviation for Field Number. The Smart Data Base Manager assigns a sequential number to each field in the file. This number may be used at a later time in the operation of the Smart Data Base Manager to select a field for some commands. You will usually want to use the field name for standard routines, however, such as reports or query definitions.

You should define calculated fields after defining any fields that are used in the calculation. The order of definition of other fields does not matter. However, if you put the frequently-used fields at the beginning of the file, less time and effort is required to select them from pop-up menus and to maintain them in standard screens.

Title

The title of a field in the Smart Data Base Manager can be a maximum of 16 characters in length. Because you use field names frequently, you should try to select names that are short enough to be typed easily, but long enough to describe the contents of the fields. Remember that on reports and custom screens you can always include a more informative description of the field contents; the field name is primarily for your use.

Try to keep the names as short as the fields themselves, if possible. For instance, *EMPDATE* is a good name for a field containing the date on which an employee joined the company, because a date field is 8 characters in length. In Browse mode, the names of fields are used as column headings; if the field names are longer than the fields, the names are shortened (or *truncated*). The longer field name EMPLOYEE-DATE thus would appear as EMPLOYEE.

When you use the Print command, the complete field name is used as the column title, and the width of the column is adjusted to the length of the title or the field width, whichever is longer. If a considerable amount of space is used for extra columns, the amount of data you can fit on one page may be limited.

Field Types

Type indicates the type of the current field. The eight field types are:

Alphanumeric (A): An alphanumeric field contains text information: letters, numbers, or both. Any special characters except double quotation marks (″) can also be used. In some instances, you might want only numbers in the field, such as a ZIP code or department code, or if leading zeros are important. You cannot, however, perform calculations on the data in an alphanumeric field.

Numeric (N): Only numeric information may be contained in a numeric field. Other accepted characters are the decimal point (.), the plus sign (+), and the minus sign (-). Generally, you use this data type for calculations.

Date (D): Date fields provide capabilities not only for storage and correct sorting capabilities, but also for special formatting and calculating. You select the formats for storage and display of dates by selecting the Configure command from the main menu. Usually, you select these formats when you install the Smart system.

Counter (C): A counter field contains a sequential record count, which is maintained by the Smart Data Base Manager. The count may begin at 1 or may be initialized through the Utilities Alter-count command. For example, you might use a Counter field to maintain invoice numbers in an accounts-receivable file or to keep application numbers in a personnel-applicant flow system.

Time (T): A time field, like a Date field, has a special format and a special use. You should use the Configure command at the main menu to establish your time display convention; options are AM/PM format (04:06:23P) and 24-hour format (16:06:23). The Smart system has special functions for time calculations.

SSN (S): The special format for the Social Security Number places the dashes (-) in the correct locations, as in 488-37-4780. You do not have to enter the dashes in the field; the system does that for you.

Phone Number (P): Like the SSN field, the Phone Number field has a special format for phone numbers. The format is: (999) 999-9999. In either Enter or Update mode, you do not type the parentheses or the dash; you just type the numbers. There is no error checking for valid area codes, however. If you need error checking, you can use the Link command, which is discussed in the next chapter.

Inverted Name (I): Instead of keeping separate fields for first name and last name, you can define one field as an inverted name type. For instance, an inverted name such as *Debbie Linden* can be sorted by *Linden* rather than by *Debbie*.

Field Length

Each field type has length restrictions:

Field Type	*Length Restrictions*
Alphanumeric	1000 characters maximum per field.
Numeric	Two characters minimum, 18 characters maximum. When you specify the size of numeric fields, *numeric precision* means the number of positions to the right of the decimal point. You may specify from 0 to 8 positions. The decimal point takes one position, so be sure to allow enough room. For example, a percent field with 2 positions to the right of the decimal should be defined as N6.2 to allow for 100 percent (100.00).
Date	Automatically set at 8 characters.
Counter	Automatically set at 6 characters.
Time	The field length is set at 9 characters if you are using the AM/PM format, or 8 characters if you are using the 24-hour format.
SSN	Automatically set at 11 characters.
Phone	Automatically set at 14 characters.
Inverted Name	Maximum of 1000, but only the first 100 characters are considered in a sort.

The total length of all fields in a record may not exceed 4096 characters. When you specify the length of the fields in the file definition, the number of remaining characters is displayed in the control area of the screen, and you are reminded of the length considerations.

Running Total

You may need sometimes to find the total of values in a certain numeric field for all records in the data base. For instance, if you have a file containing invoices, you may want to find the total of outstanding balances. You can define the field with a *Y* in the Running Total column, and the total figure is available through the File-Specs Running-Totals command. A special function allows you to use that value in project processing.

Figure 3.6 shows a completed file-definition screen. Note that the field called WAGE has a type of *N2,* indicating that the field is numeric and has two decimal places. The total length is 10, and seven places (10 minus 2 minus 1) remain to the left of the decimal point.

```
╒═ Creating file ═══════════════════════════════════════════════
║       Fld No │ Title        │ Type │ Length │ Running Total
║          .1  │ Lastname     │  A   │   15   │
║           2  │ Firstname    │  A   │   10   │
║           3  │ SocSecNo     │  S   │   11   │
║           4  │ PhoneNo      │  P   │   14   │
║           5  │ JobNo        │  A   │    4   │
║           6  │ Wage         │  N2  │   10   │      N
║           7  │ AppSeq       │  C   │    6   │
║           8  │ Appdate      │  D   │    8   │
║           9  │ Apptime      │  T   │    9   │
║          10  │ Rating       │  NO  │    2   │      N
║          11  │ Offer        │  N2C │   10   │      N
║
╘════════════════════════════════════════════════════════════════
F3 Calc fld   F7 Insert field   F10 Exit      PgUp Prev page   Home First entry
F4 Del calc   F8 Delete field   Esc Abandon   PgDn Next page   End  Last entry
Title can be up to 16 characters long
```

CREATE - creates a new file or screen

Fig. 3.6. *Completed File Definition Screen.*

Take a close look at field number 11, OFFER. Notice the letter *C* after the field type *N2.* The C indicates that the OFFER field is calculated every time the record is entered or updated.

You use the function keys F3 and F4 to establish or delete field calculations. To create a calculated field, you define the field in the usual fashion, and then move the cursor back to the field and press F3. The Formula Editor screen appears, and you can then enter any legitimate formula. The formula can contain field names, constants, or functions (see fig. 3.7). A calculated field should be defined after you have defined any fields used in the calculation.

The formula for the OFFER field (fig. 3.7) divides the contents of the RATING field by 100, adds 1, and multiplies the result by the value in the WAGE field. Thus if RATING is 4, OFFER is 1.04

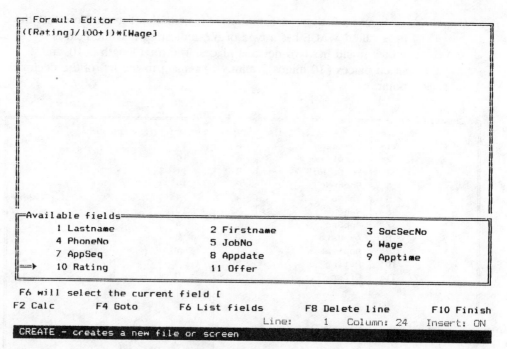

```
┌─ Formula Editor ═══════════════════════════════════════════════════════╗
║((Rating]/100+1)*[Wage]                                                   ║
║                                                                          ║
║                                                                          ║
║                                                                          ║
║                                                                          ║
║                                                                          ║
║                                                                          ║
║                                                                          ║
║                                                                          ║
║                                                                          ║
║                                                                          ║
║                                                                          ║
║                                                                          ║
║                                                                          ║
║                                                                          ║
┌─Available fields═══════════════════════════════════════════════════════╗
║      1 Lastname          2 Firstname          3 SocSecNo                 ║
║      4 PhoneNo           5 JobNo              6 Wage                      ║
║      7 AppSeq            8 Appdate            9 Apptime                   ║
║ ══➤  10 Rating          11 Offer                                         ║
╚══════════════════════════════════════════════════════════════════════════╝

   F6 will select the current field [
   F2 Calc        F4 Goto        F6 List fields        F8 Delete line        F10 Finish
                                     Line:      1    Column: 24    Insert: ON
   CREATE - creates a new file or screen
```

Fig. 3.7. *Formula Editor screen for calculated field.*

multiplied by WAGE. Although you can use a field number in the a formula, I recommend using the actual name of the field. The formula will then be easier to understand when you display it. (The File-Specs Calculated-Fields command is used for that purpose.) Also, the field numbering sequence will be altered if you later create a similar file and insert additional fields at the beginning of the record.

When you are using the Formula Editor, pressing the F6 function key causes the field names to be displayed in a pop-up menu. If you use the cursor to identify fields, the system inserts the field numbers but not the field names. In addition to the normal mathematical calculations (+, −, *, /), you may use any of the Smart functions. Refer to the chapters on functions for complete descriptions of their use.

You can include as many as 1,900 characters in the formula for a calculated field; however, this limit may be less if the formula contains many IF. . .THEN. . .ELSE logic statements. Although you can extend your calculation statements beyond the 80 characters on the screen, you will actually be able to define longer calculations if you stay within the screen boundaries. If you use sets of IF. . .THEN. . .ELSE statements, the ELSE must be on a separate line.

Be careful not to create a field calculation that references itself. This type of reference is called a *circular reference*. Because calculations are actually performed twice (upon entry and exit), a circular reference will double the value of the field. An example of a circular reference would be one in which a field to contain year-to-date sales is defined with the following calculation:

[ytdsales] + [sales]

When you have finished defining the field calculation, press F10 to return to the file-definition screen. You can then continue to define any additional fields. Notice that the validity of the calculation's syntax is checked at this time, but the field names are not checked until you indicate that you're finished with the file definition. If the syntax of a calculation is incorrect, you can fix the calculation by pressing F3 again.

Press F10 to complete the file definition. To verify that you are through defining the file, you must answer the question:

Are you finished defining the file (y/n)

Once you have finished defining a file, you cannot change the definition or add another field. You can, however, create a file similar to this one and make any necessary changes in the new file. (If you have data in the old file, use the Utilities Restructure command to transfer the date.) To avoid having to retrace your steps, you should try to include all necessary fields when you first define the file.

Key Fields

After you press *Y* (not Enter), you see the prompt:

Do you want to define a key field (y/n)

In many cases, key fields can be useful time-savers. In other cases, they are mandatory. Defining a key field allows you to quickly rearrange the records in the file according to the sorting sequence of the values in the key field(s). If you define a key field, the Smart Data Base Manager maintains a *key file*, which contains the order of the records according to the value in the key field(s). For more information about key fields, see Chapter 1.

Suppose, for example, that you frequently view your applicant file in order by last name; when duplicate last names exist, the records are ordered by first name. You could establish a key field to keep the records in that order. As applicants come through the door, you add their information to the file in sequential order, and the Smart Data

Base Manager maintains the list in order by the key fields. You use the Order command, which is discussed in Chapter 5, to change the order of viewing the file.

You can define up to 15 key fields, but you need to be selective. The more key fields you define, the slower your system will run when you enter and update records in the data base. The system runs more slowly when you define many key fields because Smart must maintain a separate file for each key field. If you often need to locate records quickly by the Lastname field, you probably need a key field. If, on the other hand, you view the file in order by the Wage field only once a month, you may want to use the Sort command instead of defining a key field. (The Sort command is discussed in Chapter 5.)

Some commands work faster if you have a key field. Under certain conditions, the Find command makes very good use of the key field. If you plan to link one file to another by a common field, the field in the second file *must* be a key field.

```
┌─ Creating file ════════════════════════════════════════════════
│         Fid No │ Title          │ Type │ Length │ Running Total
│           1    │ Lastname       │  A   │   15   │
│           2    │ Firstname      │  A   │   10   │
│           3    │ SocSecNo       │  S   │   11   │
│           4    │ PhoneNo        │  P   │   14   │
│           5    │ JobNo          │  A   │    4   │
│           6    │ Wage           │  N2  │   10   │      N
│           7    │ AppSeq         │  C   │    6   │
│           8    │ Appdate        │  D   │    8   │
│           9    │ Apptime        │  T   │    9   │
│          10    │ Rating         │  NO  │    2   │      N
│          11    │ Offer          │  N2C │   10   │      N
│
┌─Available fields══════════════════════════════════════════════
│═▶  1 Lastname          2 Firstname           3 SocSecNo
│    4 PhoneNo           5 JobNo               6 Wage
│    7 AppSeq           8 Appdate             9 Apptime
│   10 Rating          11 Offer
└────────────────────────────────────────────────────────────────

 F6 will select the current field [lastname;firstname
 Enter major key followed by minor keys

 CREATE - creates a new file or screen
```

Fig. 3.8. *Defining key fields.*

First you need to indicate the key field and any secondary keys. In figure 3.8, the key field is the Lastname field, and the secondary key field is Firstname. Designate key fields by typing either the field names or numbers on the prompt line, with colons (:) as separators. Alternately, use the cursor keys to move the cursor to a field and the F6 key to enter the field number on the prompt line. Press Enter after you have designated the key fields.

When a key field is defined, the system defaults to a full field ascending order organization (see fig. 3.9). In some applications, however, you may need to use descending order. For example, if you have a file that stores employee job histories, you may want to have a major sort on employee number in ascending order, and on the job history date in descending order.

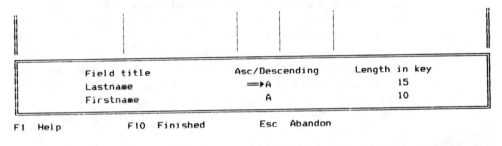

Field title	Asc/Descending	Length in key
Lastname	⟹A	15
Firstname	A	10

F1 Help   F10 Finished   Esc Abandon

CREATE - creates a new file or screen

Fig. 3.9. *Key sort order and length definition.*

After you have selected the key fields, you press F10 to complete this process. You are then asked:

Do you want to define another key field (y/n)

If you do, press *y* and repeat the process. If you don't define all your key fields at this time, don't worry; you can add key fields later by using the Key Add command. You can always delete unnecessary keys with Key Delete.

If you don't want to create any additional key fields, press *n* to return to the command list. The creation of your file is now complete.

Creating a Matching File

You can use the Create command to create a file that matches an existing file. You may decide to do so if, for example, you want to keep the records for one division in one file and the records for another division in another file. The command sequence for creating a matching file from an existing file (also called the *source* file) is the same as for creating a new file, except that you select Matching rather than New.

After you select Matching, you see a pop-up menu containing the names of the active files. Use the cursor keys to move the pointer to the correct file name and press Enter. Note that the *source* file must be active; you cannot enter the file name from the keyboard.

The file you create can differ from the source file in a few ways. You can change from fixed- to variable-length fields, for example. You can also change the password of the file. If you select No-Password and the source file is protected with a password, your destination file will have the same password as the source file. If you select Password, the password of the source file is used even though you are prompted to enter a new password. If the source file is not protected, you can specify a password for the Matching file. You then are prompted for a password, but it has no effect; the file is not protected by password. To cancel password protection or to add a password, use the Create File . . . Similar command sequence, instead of Create File . . . Matching.

You need to define a different set of key fields for your new file, because the original keys from the source file are not carried over to the destination file. The custom screens from the source file are carried to the matching file, however, and are available automatically. The passwords for custom screens are also copied to the new file. You cannot change these passwords.

If you want to change custom-screen passwords or layouts, you must create a similar file and then create similar screens.

Creating a Similar File

Although you can use Create File . . . Matching to make some minor changes to a file structure copied from the structure of an existing file, you cannot make any changes to the fields themselves. As your application grows, you may want to add additional data fields to a file, change the format or length of some fields, or delete unnecessary fields.

Using the Create File . . . Similar command sequence, you can base the structure of a new file on an existing file. In a similar file, all the same fields are defined, but you can add and delete fields, change the names or formats of fields, or define calculated fields.

Remember, you may not directly change the structure of an existing file; you must create a file that is similar to the existing file, make your changes, and then use the Utilities Restructure command to transfer the data.

When you execute the command sequence Create File . . . Similar, a pop-up menu appears, displaying the names of the active files. To select the name of the source file from this menu, use the cursor keys to move the cursor to the file name and press Enter. You cannot select the file by typing its name.

If the source file is protected by password, you must supply the password, even if the new file is not to be protected. From this point forward, the procedure is the same as creating a new file with the Create File . . . New command.

If you already have data in the source file, you may want to move the data to the new file. Use the Utilities Restructure command to copy the contents of the old file to the new one. (Refer to Chapter 12 for more information on the Utilities Restructure command.)

Creating a New Screen

Just as the Create File command sequence is used to create a new file or one that is similar to an existing file, the Create Screen command sequence is used to create custom screens for data entry and display. You can have a maximum of nine custom screens for any one file, in addition to the standard screen.

To create a screen, make sure the file you are working with is active (the file does not have to be in the current window). Then proceed to Command list 1, and select Create Screen (see fig. 3.10). You then are prompted to enter the name of the new screen (see fig. 3.11).

Screen names can have a maximum length of 20 characters. If you want your screen to be protected by a password, you can select Password at the next prompt. Remember that in order to make a file truly secure, you should protect both the file and the custom screens. If a file is protected and the custom screens are not, anyone can access the file and the data on the custom screens.

Don't forget that passwords are *case sensitive*. In addition to knowing the password, you must know whether the password is to be entered in upper- or lowercase letters. When you first type the password while creating the file, the password is displayed on-screen.

```
STREET 546 Olive Hill
CITY Oak Park
ST IL
ZIP 60301
WAGE      834.52
STATUS A
SKILL CKP
DEPT ACCT
PHONE (312) 439-8760
EMPDATE 10-01-59
```

Select option: File Screen
create

File: person3   Window: 1   Page: 1 Rec: 1 (1) Act: Y
CREATE = creates a new file or screen

Fig. 3.10. *Creating a screen.*

```
STREET 10 Dennis Drive
CITY Winnfield
ST LA
ZIP 71483
WAGE     1544.00
STATUS 1
SKILL AMFD
DEPT MKTG
PHONE (318) 729-5060
EMPDATE 10-01-85
```

Enter the new screen name:
create screen

File: person3   Window: 1   Page: 1 Rec: EOF (13) Act: Y
CREATE = creates a new file or screen

Fig. 3.11. *Entering the new screen name.*

From that point on, whenever you load the file and enter the password, it is masked with asterisks (****).

After you select your password choice, you are prompted to indicate whether the screen is New or Similar to an existing screen for this file or any other file. The New option is used to create a brand new screen (see fig. 3.12).

The Similar option is a powerful feature that takes advantage of previously created screens. You can use this command if you are developing an application and want to change the contents or appearance of an existing screen, or if you have executed the Create File . . . Similar command sequence and have changed the fields in

```
STREET 10 Dennis Drive
CITY Winnfield
ST LA
ZIP 71483
WAGE    1544.00
STATUS 1
SKILL AMFD
DEPT MKTG
PHONE (318) 729-5060
EMPDATE 10-01-85
```

```
Select option: New  Similar
create screen address no-password
File: person3   Window: 1                    Page: 1  Rec: EOF  ( 13 )  Act: Y
CREATE - creates a new file or screen
```

Fig. 3.12. *Selecting Create Screen . . . New.*

the new file. Remember that the Create File . . . Similar does not
carry the screens forward to the new file.

Issuing the Create Screen . . . New command calls up the screen-
creation editor (see fig. 3.13). Initially, the design area of the
screen editor is blank. In figure 3.13 I have entered several fields and
some text.

```
PERSONNEL DATABASE - ADDRESS CHANGES


    Last Name:r_____   First Name:r_____
    Social Security Number:r_____


   ┌──────────────────────────────────────────┐
   │ Street Address:_____           │
   │ City:m_____  State:m_  Zip Code:m____ │
   │                                          │
   │ Telephone Number:_____          │
   └──────────────────────────────────────────┘
```

```
F1 Help       F3 Ins w/o ttl F5 Prior fld  F7 Ins fld  AF7 E-status F9 Clr Page
F2 Next Menu F4 Box/Line    F6 Next fld   F8 Del fld  AF8 Range    F10 Exit
   Field 6 MS  Length 1              Pg:1  Ln:1  Ps:1       IO:#
   CREATE - creates a new file or screen
```

Fig. 3.13. *The screen editor.*

The screen is divided into several parts: the design area, at the top of the screen; the control area, which displays function-key information; and the status line, which contains information about the current screen.

The status line shows the name of the field that is currently available for insertion, the length of the field, the page number of the current screen, and the line-and-column position of the cursor. The IO indicator, which shows # in this example, indicates the order of prompting of the fields. The IO:# indicator signifies that the user is prompted to enter data in the fields in the order of their appearance in the data file. Press Alt-F3 to change the indicator to IO:P if you want the user to enter data in the order of the fields' appearance on screen.

Creating a Similar Screen

To create a screen that is similar to an existing screen, use the command Create Screen . . . Similar. You are prompted to provide a name for the new screen and to enter password information. You must then specify the source file and the source screen, if more than one screen is active. The source screen must be active, but it does not have to be in the current window.

The screen-creation editor then is invoked; Smart has done as much of the work for you as possible. Any matching fields are in place; all text and boxes are correctly positioned. Any fields that existed in the old screen but do not exist in the new one are dropped from the screen. You may then proceed to change the fields, alter the text, and change editing characteristics to fit the requirements of the new screen.

Using the Function Keys

The function keys are used to control the entry, placement, and validity checking of text and data on the screen. Table 3.1 explains use of the function keys in screen creation.

Table 3.1
Function Keys

F2	Changes the control-area menu.
F3	Inserts a field without the standard title. The inserted field is listed on the status line. Use F3 if you have inserted your own field-identification text.
F4	Draws a box or a line on the screen. Position the cursor at the upper left corner of the box, then press F4. Move the cursor to the lower right corner, and press Enter. The box in the example was drawn with this feature.
F5	Makes the previous *available* field available for insertion, based on the order of the fields in the file.
F6	Advances to the next available field for insertion. The field name shown in the status line changes.
F7	Inserts a field with the standard title. Use this key if you do not write your own field-identification text on the screen.
F8	Deletes a field, making it *available* again for insertion.
F9	Clears the current page. Other pages of the same screen are not affected.
Alt-F7	Selects edit status for the current field. Move the cursor to a field and press Alt-F7 to select the edit status for that field. Selections are:
	r Read only. The field appears on the screen, but cannot be changed.
	m Mandatory. Data must be entered in the field.
	Press Alt-F7 again to return to optional entry mode.
Alt-F8	Provides range checking. The value entered for the field must fall within a specified range. You are prompted for the upper and lower ends of the range.
	Any range that you check must be continuous. For example, you might want to make sure that an applicant is between the ages of 18 and 65. If you want to check a discontinuous list, such as state abbreviations or department codes, use the Lookup command. Lookup not only validates entries

	against another file, but may also retrieve values from that file for insertion in the current file.
Alt-F3	Changes input order. The default prompting order is based on the order of the fields in the file. If you prefer to prompt in screen order, press Alt-F3. The last item on the status line changes from *IO:#* to *IO:P*.
Alt-F4	Erases a line or a box. This feature works the same as F4, but erases an existing line or box.
Alt-F5	Inserts a new line. The rest of the screen moves down.
Alt-F6	Deletes the current line.

A field can be inserted only once on a screen. As you select fields for insertion by using either F3 or F7, the fields are removed from the list of available fields. You can view the list of available fields by pressing F5 or F6; the field names then appear on the status line.

If your data base is too large for all the fields to fit on one screen, or if you have a large quantity of text or instructions, you can create additional pages. Each screen can have as many as 15 pages. Use PgDn and PgUp to move from page to page.

When screen creation is completed, press F10. As you can see in figure 3.14, Smart reminds you that not all the fields have been inserted if you select only some of the fields on the screen.

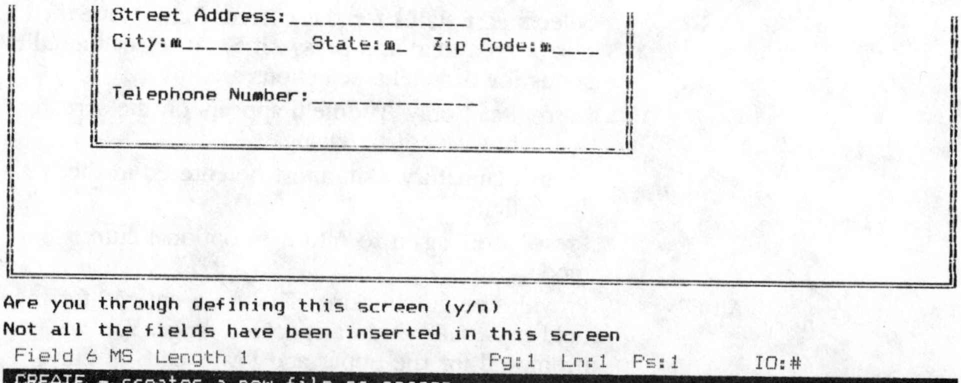

```
 ║  ║ Street Address:_____     ║                  ║
 ║  ║ City:m_____   State:m_  Zip Code:m____ ║           ║
 ║  ║                                     ║                  ║
 ║  ║ Telephone Number:_____    ║                  ║
 ║  ║                                     ║                  ║
 ║  ╚═════════════════════════════════════╝                  ║

Are you through defining this screen (y/n)
Not all the fields have been inserted in this screen
   Field 6 MS  Length 1                 Pg:1  Ln:1  Ps:1      IO:#
   CREATE - creates a new file or screen
```

Fig. 3.14. *Exiting screen creation.*

If you have created screens you no longer need, use the Utilities Erase Screen command sequence to delete them. The Utilities command is found on Command list 2.

Conclusion

The Create File and Create Screen commands are of primary importance if you are building your own application. Both files and screens may be protected by password to provide security for sensitive applications. Files and screens may be built from scratch, or may be created as variations of existing files and screens.

Chapter 4

Viewing Files

Although some applications rely heavily on manipulation of files and printed reports, many others are more screen-oriented. In such applications, viewing the file on the screen is most important. This chapter discusses the primary ways of viewing screens, switching between them, and viewing different portions of your files.

In the preceding chapter, you learned how to create files; you learned also that a standard screen is created for each file you create. That chapter also showed you how to create custom screens, which can provide additional text information and editing features.

When you load a file and a screen, they are placed in the current window and you see the file's first sequential record. A screen shows you one record at a time. To view other records, you use the F6 key to view the next record and the F5 key to view the previous record. The Ctrl-Home key addresses the first record of a file; Ctrl-End addresses the last.

Screens containing many fields or a great deal of text may occupy more than one page. You can use the PgDn key to display the next page for the same record and PgUp to display the previous page.

Using the Browse Command (1–Browse, Alt-B)

Seeing many records at one time is frequently desirable. If you are looking for the record of a particular individual or customer, for example, you may want to view an entire page of records and to change the view page by page. You can do this with a Data Base Manager feature called Browse mode.

The Browse command is found on command list 1 (see fig. 4.1); the quick key is Alt-B. Use this command to view all the fields in Browse mode; use the Browse Off command or press Alt-B again to toggle back to "normal" viewing.

```
CITY Winnfield
ST LA
ZIP 71483
WAGE     1544.00
STATUS 1
SKILL AMFD
DEPT MKTG
PHONE (318) 729-5060
EMPDATE 10-01-85


Command list 1:  Autohelp  Browse  Create  Delete  Enter  Find  Goto  Help
                 Print  Query  Report  Scroll  Update
File: person    Window: 1                    Page: 1  Rec: EOF  ( 13 )  Act: Y
  BROWSE · displays records in a tabular format
```

Fig. 4.1. *Selecting the Browse command.*

The entire window in Browse mode is filled with as many records and fields as the window will hold (see fig. 4.2). Note that the column headings are the field names, some of which are truncated because the fields themselves are shorter than their names. For example, although the name of the fourth field is AGE, only AG shows because the width of the field is two digits.

When you enter Browse mode, the status line does not change. The arrow on the left side of the screen points to the current record; the same record remains current as in normal mode. You can move the arrow up to the previous record by pressing F5 or ↑ key, or down to the next record by pressing F6 or ↓ key.

Browse mode can be useful for selecting records that need further processing. To change an employee record, for example, you move the cursor arrow to the employee's name and then execute the Update command, which is explained in Chapter 8. At the conclusion of the Update command, the screen remains in Browse mode.

The PgUp and PgDn keys work differently in Browse mode than they do in "normal" mode. PgUp scrolls up one window page; PgDn

```
 ═ Window 1 ═══════════════════════════════════════════════════════════
    SSN           FIRST       LAST        AG S M DE DEG CA STREET           CITY
    345-98-7593 Rosanna     Ronaldo     51 M M 3  BA  2  546 Olive Hill    Oak Park
    498-48-3980 Debbie      Linden      29 F S 1  MA  2  409 Pleasant St   Amherst
    239-87-8876 Michael     Davis       61 M M 1  MBA 2  180 Lewis Ave.    Covington
    208-23-0300 Julius      Karenski    41 M D 0  PhD 1  18 Olive St.      Louisvill
    887-63-5498 Jeff        Harris      34 M M 4  BA  5  1201 Horton Rd.   Lyndhurst
    598-44-5922 LeAnne      Markus      48 F W 1  MBA 1  14 Crumpet Ave.   Alamosa
    876-33-0989 Marilyn     Lester      55 F M 4  AB  3  6 Greenville St   Yarmouth
    987-65-7653 David       Marzetti    47 M D 0      1  20 Grayln Dr.     Wilmingto
    387-59-8374 Charles     Steffans    25 M M 2  BS  2  44 Center Drive   Brunswick
    498-34-5998 Paula       Bernstein   30 F S 3  MA  3  18 Worcester St   Beaumont
    776-39-8763 Alfred      Adelson     60 M M 0  BA  1  14 Spring St.     Hartford
    345-54-2287 Ellen       Aliakbari   35 F S 0      1  2171 University   Westfield
 ══▶198-03-3024 Howard E.   Peters      18 M S 0      1  10 Dennis Drive   Winnfield




```

Command:

File: person   Window: 1   Page: 1 Rec: EOF (13) Act: Y

Fig. 4.2. *Information displayed in Browse mode.*

scrolls down. If you are at the top of a file, PgUp moves the pointer
to the first record of that file.

The Home and End keys move the pointer to the first and last
displayed records. Ctrl-Home and Ctrl-End move to the first and last
records in a file respectively.

Sometimes a file contains more fields than can be viewed at one
time on the screen. In such cases, you can use → to scroll one field
to the right and ← to scroll one field to the left. To scroll one
character at a time, use the Ctrl-→ and Ctrl-← key combinations.

If your file contains several large fields, you may want to toggle to
"alternate" Browse mode, in which each field is displayed 14
characters wide. In this mode, fields longer than 14 characters are
truncated; shorter fields are expanded. Use Alt-F4 to toggle on and
off this "alternate" Browse mode.

To view only a few fields or to change the order in which they're
displayed, execute the Browse Fields command (see fig. 4.3) to view
a pop-up menu of field names. Use the cursor-control keys to move
the arrow to a field, and press F6 to select that field. Press Enter
when you have selected all the fields you want. You also can type the
field names or numbers, separated by semicolons, on the prompt line.

```
STREET 14 Spring St.
CITY Hartford
ST CT
ZIP 06101
WAGE     887.23
STATUS 1
SKILL BSMP
DEPT ACCT
PHONE (203) 739-3095
EMPDATE 07-23-45
```

```
Select option:  All  Fields  Off
browse
File: person    Window: 1                    Page: 1  Rec: 11  ( 11 )  Act: Y
  BROWSE - displays records in a tabular format
```

Fig. 4.3. *Selecting the Browse Fields option.*

Using Windows

So far, we have considered the monitor's screen to be identical to the file screen. But the Smart Data Base Manager, as well as other modules, can display multiple *windows* simultaneously. This powerful feature is used to view several files concurrently, linking them by a common field, or to display different portions of one file. If you need to see more data than a small window is able to display, you can Zoom the current window at any time so that it fills the monitor screen.

Splitting the Screen (3–Split, Alt-H and Alt-V)

The Split command, found on command list 3, is used to create these additional windows on your monitor screen (see fig. 4.4). There are two quick keys for Split: Alt-H splits the screen horizontally, and Alt-V splits it vertically.

After selecting the Split command you select one of two options, Horizontal or Vertical (see fig. 4.5).

Then move the cursor to the upper left corner of the location you have chosen for the new window, and press Enter (see fig. 4.6). With the window border displayed, a new screen split horizontally must contain at least three lines. A new screen split vertically must contain at least 13 character spaces.

```
= Window 1 =
SSN 198-03-3024
FIRST Howard E.
LAST Peters
AGE 18
SEX M
MS S
DEP 0
DEG
CAR 1
STREET 10 Dennis Drive
CITY Winnfield
ST LA
ZIP 71483
WAGE    1544.00
STATUS 1
SKILL AMFD
DEPT MKTG
PHONE (318) 729-5060
EMPDATE 10-01-85
```

```
Command list 3:  Border  Close  Link  Paint  Split  Unlink  Zoom

File: person    Window: 1                      Page: 1  Rec: EOF   ( 13 )  Act: Y
  SPLIT - split the current window into two windows
```

Fig. 4.4. *The Split command.*

```
STREET 10 Dennis Drive
CITY Winnfield
ST LA
ZIP 71483
WAGE    1544.00
STATUS 1
SKILL AMFD
DEPT MKTG
PHONE (318) 729-5060
EMPDATE 10-01-85
```

```
Select option:  Horizontal  Vertical
split
File: person    Window: 1                      Page: 1  Rec: EOF   ( 13 )  Act: Y
  SPLIT - split the current window into two windows
```

Fig. 4.5. *The Split command's Horizontal and Vertical options.*

The result, shown in figure 4.7, is a new window containing the current file and screen. Notice that the window number is displayed in the upper left corner of the window border. In previous examples

```
STREET 10 Dennis Drive
CITY Winnfield
ST LA
ZIP 71483
WAGE    1544.00
STATUS 1
SKILL AMFD
DEPT MKTG
PHONE (318) 729-5060
EMPDATE 10-01-85
```

```
Move cursor to new window border and press Enter:
split vertical
File: person    Window: 1                    Page: 1  Rec: EOF  ( 13 )  Act: Y
 SPLIT - split the current window into two windows
```

Fig. 4.6. *Identifying a new window area.*

of the Smart Data Base Manager, in which only one window was
displayed, this window number was unimportant. But with multiple
windows on the screen, observing these numbers is important
because several commands require window numbers.

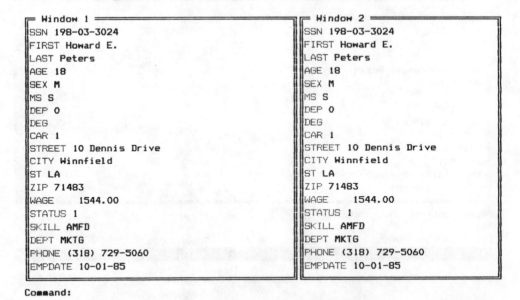

```
= Window 1 =                           = Window 2 =
SSN 198-03-3024                        SSN 198-03-3024
FIRST Howard E.                        FIRST Howard E.
LAST Peters                            LAST Peters
AGE 18                                 AGE 18
SEX M                                  SEX M
MS S                                   MS S
DEP 0                                  DEP 0
DEG                                    DEG
CAR 1                                  CAR 1
STREET 10 Dennis Drive                 STREET 10 Dennis Drive
CITY Winnfield                         CITY Winnfield
ST LA                                  ST LA
ZIP 71483                              ZIP 71483
WAGE    1544.00                        WAGE    1544.00
STATUS 1                               STATUS 1
SKILL AMFD                             SKILL AMFD
DEPT MKTG                              DEPT MKTG
PHONE (318) 729-5060                   PHONE (318) 729-5060
EMPDATE 10-01-85                       EMPDATE 10-01-85
```

```
Command:

File: person    Window: 1                    Page: 1  Rec: EOF  ( 13 )  Act: Y
```

Fig. 4.7. *Result of using the Split command.*

Notice also that the current window number appears in the screen's status line. In figure 4.7, the current window is number 1. If you use the Goto command to go to window 2, the current window number indicated on the status line will change to 2. All status-line information refers to the current window.

Although the new window initially shows the same file as does the current window, you usually want to have a different file in the new window. To display a different file, you can either go to the window and use the Load command to load another file or use the Goto command to display an active file. (The Goto command is discussed later in this chapter.)

In the example shown in figure 4.8, the DEPT file has been loaded in window 2. Note that Browse mode has been initiated so that all records are displayed. You can invoke Browse mode in one window without affecting any other window.

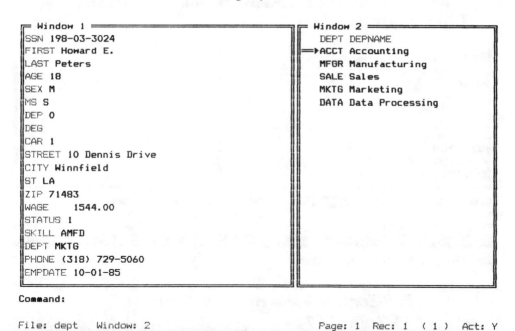

Fig. 4.8. *Two windows with separate files.*

You can now display as many as 25 windows per monitor screen. The more windows you add, however, the smaller they are and the less you can see. In many cases, multiple windows are convenient; in other cases, they are mandatory for using certain commands. Among the commands for which windows are mandatory are Link, discussed later in this chapter, and Lookup, discussed in Chapter 8. Furthermore, some forms of the Report command require multiple windows, as do the Relate and Transactions commands.

Closing Windows (3–Close, Alt-W)

You know that you can add windows with the Split command. You can remove them with the Close command, which is found on command list 3 (see fig. 4.9). The quick key for Close is Alt-W. When you Goto a window that you want to close and then execute the Close command, that window is closed and adjacent windows are expanded to fill the remaining screen space. If only one window is active, you cannot close it. Even though the window is closed, the file that it displayed remains active. But be careful, because the order of the file reverts to *sequential*. (Refer to the Order command in Chapter 5.)

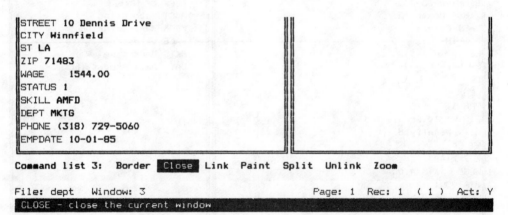

Fig. 4.9. *Selecting the Close command.*

Full-Screen Viewing of a Window (3–Zoom, F7)

With many small windows or a window that contains many fields, you may not be able to see everything you need. To create a full-screen display of a window, select the Zoom command from command list 3 (see fig. 4.10). The quick key, which toggles the Zoom display and the normal display, is F7; there are no options to the Zoom command. The window that you want to change must be the current window.

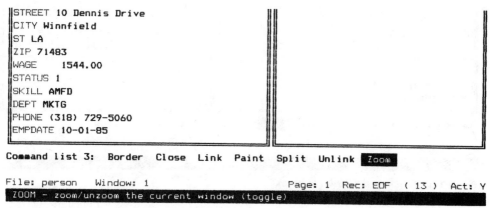

```
STREET 10 Dennis Drive
CITY Winnfield
ST LA
ZIP 71483
WAGE    1544.00
STATUS 1
SKILL AMFD
DEPT MKTG
PHONE (318) 729-5060
EMPDATE 10-01-85
```

Command list 3:   Border   Close   Link   Paint   Split   Unlink   Zoom

File: person   Window: 1   Page: 1 Rec: EOF (13) Act: Y
ZOOM - zoom/unzoom the current window (toggle)

Fig. 4.10.   *Choosing the Zoom command.*

Although most commands may be executed while a window is "zoomed," you can neither split nor close the window. To execute these commands, you must use Zoom again to return to the multiple-window display.

Linking Two Windows (3-Link, Unlink)

In the previous examples, there has been no relationship between the windows on the screen. The windows could have shown related or unrelated data. Frequently, however, relationships exist between the data in different windows.

The Link command is used to join two windows whose files share a common field. The linking fields in both files must be of the same data type, and the linking field must be a key field in the "link-to" file. As shown in figure 4.10, the PERSON file and the DEPT file both contain a DEPT field. The Link command can be used to display in window 2 a record whose DEPT field matches the DEPT field of the record in window 1.

Before using the Link command, you must order the file in the link-to window by the linking key field—in this case, the DEPT field of the DEPT file. (See the next chapter for information about the Order command.)

You begin execution of the Link command from the window of the "link-from" file (window 1, the PERSON file, in this example). After you select Link from command list 3 (see fig. 4.11), Smart prompts you to supply the number of the link-to window (see fig. 4.12). When you enter that number and press Enter, a pop-up menu of available fields appears across the bottom of the screen.

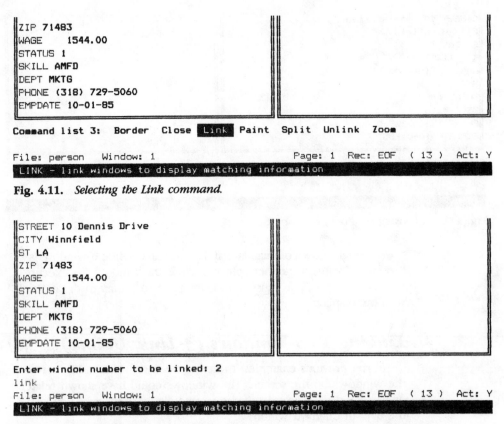

Fig. 4.11. *Selecting the Link command.*

```
STREET 10 Dennis Drive
CITY Winnfield
ST LA
ZIP 71483
WAGE    1544.00
STATUS 1
SKILL AMFD
DEPT MKTG
PHONE (318) 729-5060
EMPDATE 10-01-85

Enter window number to be linked: 2
link
File: person    Window: 1                    Page: 1   Rec: EOF   ( 13 )   Act: Y
LINK - link windows to display matching information
```

Fig. 4.12. *The prompt for the window number.*

Next, you are prompted to establish the link by selecting a field from the file in the current window. You select the DEPT field (see fig. 4.13). (Although the field names in this example happen to match, fields do not always need to have the same name in both files.)

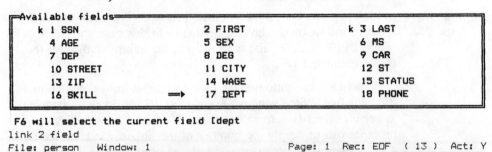

Fig. 4.13. *Selecting the field to link from.*

As a result of using the Link command, the department record displayed in window 2 matches the department of the record in window 1. As shown in figure 4.14, the arrow in window 2 now points to the MKTG Marketing record.

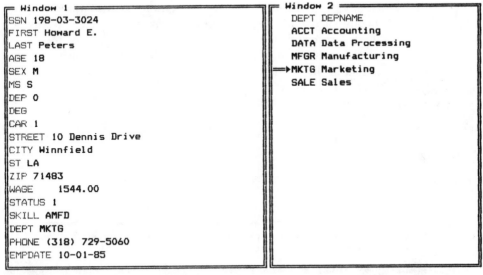

```
╔══ Window 1 ════════════════╗  ╔══ Window 2 ═══════════════════╗
║SSN 198-03-3024             ║  ║  DEPT DEPNAME                 ║
║FIRST Howard E.             ║  ║  ACCT Accounting             ║
║LAST Peters                 ║  ║  DATA Data Processing        ║
║AGE 18                      ║  ║  MFGR Manufacturing          ║
║SEX M                       ║  ║═➤MKTG Marketing              ║
║MS S                        ║  ║  SALE Sales                  ║
║DEP 0                       ║  ║                              ║
║DEG                         ║  ║                              ║
║CAR 1                       ║  ║                              ║
║STREET 10 Dennis Drive      ║  ║                              ║
║CITY Winnfield              ║  ║                              ║
║ST LA                       ║  ║                              ║
║ZIP 71483                   ║  ║                              ║
║WAGE    1544.00             ║  ║                              ║
║STATUS 1                    ║  ║                              ║
║SKILL AMFD                  ║  ║                              ║
║DEPT MKTG                   ║  ║                              ║
║PHONE (318) 729-5060        ║  ║                              ║
║EMPDATE 10-01-85            ║  ║                              ║
╚════════════════════════════╝  ╚═══════════════════════════════╝

Command:

File: person   Window: 1              Page: 1  Rec: EOF  ( 13 )  Act: Y
```

Fig. 4.14. *The result of linking files.*

As you change the record in the current window, the matching record in window 2 automatically changes according to the value in the DEPT field of the record in window 1. If there is no match between the two files, the program issues a warning beep.

Unfortunately, only one link may be active from a file at one time. The introduction of another link overrides any previous link. Instead of linking two different files, you can link two windows that contain the same file; these windows can display different fields. In this case, the file does not have to be in key order by the link field; any field may be linked to synchronize the two views.

To remove a linkage, execute the Unlink command (command list 3).

Using the Goto Command (1-Goto, F4)

The Goto command, found on command list 1 (see fig. 4.15), has three functions. It can be used to change the current window, to change the active file displayed in the current window, or to display a different record from the current file. The quick key for the Goto command is F4. Each of the functions of the Goto command is discussed in this section.

```
STREET 20 Grayln Dr.
CITY Wilmington
ST NC
ZIP 28401
WAGE      901.45
STATUS 2
SKILL GNX
DEPT ACCT
PHONE (704) 472-0042
EMPDATE 10-30-85
```

Command list 1: Autohelp Browse Create Delete Enter Find `Goto` Help
                        Print Query Report Scroll Update
File: person   Window: 1   Page: 1 Rec: 8 (8) Act: Y
  GOTO - goto a file, a window, or a record

Fig. 4.15. *Selecting the Goto Command.*

Displaying a Different File (Goto File)

The Goto File command (see fig. 4.16) changes the file displayed in the current window, provided that the file is active. If the file is not active, you must first load it (loading a file also displays it).

```
STREET 14 Spring St.
CITY Hartford
ST CT
ZIP 06101
WAGE      887.23
STATUS 1
SKILL BSMP
DEPT ACCT
PHONE (203) 739-3095
EMPDATE 07-23-45
```

Select option: `File` Record Window
goto
File: person   Window: 1   Page: 1 Rec: 11 (11) Act: Y
  GOTO - goto a file, a window, or a record

Fig. 4.16. *Selecting Goto File.*

In response to the Goto File command, you are prompted for the name of the file to be displayed (see fig. 4.17). You cannot type the file name; instead, you must use the cursor to point to a name in the menu, and then press Enter.

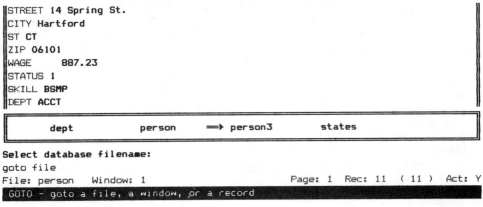

```
STREET 14 Spring St.
CITY Hartford
ST CT
ZIP 06101
WAGE      887.23
STATUS 1
SKILL BSMP
DEPT ACCT
```

```
        dept            person    ==> person3        states
```

```
Select database filename:
goto file
File: person    Window: 1                    Page: 1  Rec: 11  ( 11 )  Act: Y
GOTO - goto a file, a window, or a record
```

Fig. 4.17. *Selecting a file.*

If the file has more than one active screen, a pop-up menu prompts you to select a screen (see fig. 4.18). Note that the Goto File command may be used to switch to another screen for the same file. By selecting a different screen for the current file, you can change screens while keeping active the current file in the window.

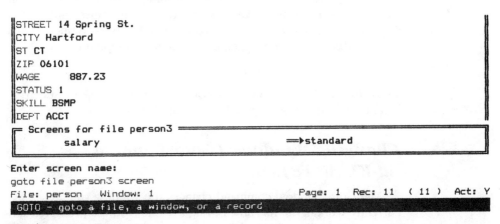

```
STREET 14 Spring St.
CITY Hartford
ST CT
ZIP 06101
WAGE      887.23
STATUS 1
SKILL BSMP
DEPT ACCT
= Screens for file person3 =
        salary                      ==>standard
```

```
Enter screen name:
goto file person3 screen
File: person    Window: 1                    Page: 1  Rec: 11  ( 11 )  Act: Y
GOTO - goto a file, a window, or a record
```

Fig. 4.18. *Selecting a screen.*

Displaying a Different Record (Goto Record)

The Goto Record command is used to display a different record of the current file. Of the three options for the Goto Record command (see fig. 4.19), Rec-Number is used most often, because you probably use the quick keys F5 and F6 to go to the next and previous records. When you use the Rec-Number option, you must supply a *logical* record number, which is based on the order of the file according to a key field or an index file, rather than a *sequential* number.

```
STREET 14 Spring St.
CITY Hartford
ST CT
ZIP 06101
WAGE      887.23
STATUS 1
SKILL BSMP
DEPT ACCT
PHONE (203) 739-3095
EMPDATE 07-23-45




Select option:  Next   Previous  Rec-Number
goto record
File: person   Window: 1                    Page: 1  Rec: 11  ( 11 )  Act: Y
GOTO - goto a file, a window, or a record
```

Fig. 4.19. *Selecting the Rec-Number option.*

You can answer the Goto Record Rec-Number command prompt with an *absolute* record number such as *150* or with *relative* numbers such as *+5* or *-75*. (The plus sign means that you want to advance a given number of records; the minus, that you want to skip back.) You can use quick keys for this relative movement: Alt-F5, to skip back a certain numbers of records, and Alt-F6 to advance. When you press either of these quick keys, you are prompted to

Enter number of records to skip:

To go to the Next or Previous record, use either the Goto Record command or the more accessible F5 and F6 function keys.

Changing Windows (Goto Window, Alt-F7, Alt-F8)

The Goto Window command changes the window you are currently working in. As shown in figure 4.20, you are prompted for the number of the window that you want to go to. The status line then indicates the new window and file.

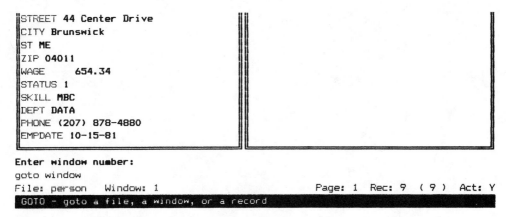

STREET 44 Center Drive
CITY Brunswick
ST ME
ZIP 04011
WAGE   654.34
STATUS 1
SKILL MBC
DEPT DATA
PHONE (207) 878-4880
EMPDATE 10-15-81

Enter window number:
goto window
File: person   Window: 1   Page: 1 Rec: 9 (9) Act: Y
GOTO - goto a file, a window, or a record

Fig. 4.20. *Changing from one window to another.*

Use the Alt-F7 and Alt-F8 quick keys to go to the previous window or the next. If only two windows are open, you can use either key to toggle between them.

Conclusion

So that you can work easily with your data, the Smart Data Base Manager provides several useful ways for viewing data. Using either the default standard screen or a custom screen, you can display simultaneously all the fields for one record. The screen can hold as many as 15 pages.

Browse mode can be used if you want to view several records at the same time; you can find and select a record more easily than if you were to search through your file record by record. In Browse mode, you can select only the fields you want to see and arrange them in an order that is best for you.

Using the Smart Data Base Manager's windowing capabilities, you can display multiple files simultaneously; you can also link files, relating one to another. Simultaneous display of files is frequently useful; it is mandatory for certain commands that are described in other chapters of this book.

Chapter 5

Arranging Data

The order in which data is entered in your file is probably not the order in which you intend to view it forever. Instead of always viewing your list of employees in the order in which they were hired, you may want to arrange the records in order by the employees' last names, for example, or by department code. You can put the records in sequence according to the values in virtually any field or combination of fields in the file. The Key and Sort commands play a major role in helping you view your data in various orders. The Order command is also instrumental in this process.

You learned about keys in Chapter 3. A file was created in that chapter, and key fields were added during file creation. But remember that I also said that keys could later be added to a file. As this chapter explains, one of the functions of the Key command is adding key fields to an existing file. The Key command also has other functions, as you shall see.

Remember, too, that you don't need a key field in order to view your data in a sequence other than that of the physical (sequential) record order. You can sort the file at any time and use the resulting index to put the records of the file in the new sequence. The functions of the Key and Sort commands are very similar, but you'll notice some differences. Each command has advantages and disadvantages, which are discussed in this chapter.

Using the Key Command (2-Key, Alt-G)

The concept of a key should be familiar to you. If not, you may want to consult Chapter 1. Designating a key field or a group of key fields indicates that Smart is to maintain a permanent reference file that keeps track of each record in an order determined by the contents of the key field. Whenever you exit the Enter or Update command by pressing F10, Smart prompts you to indicate whether you want to update the keys. If you press *y*, Smart updates the permanent index to reflect the additions to the file.

```
STREET 546 Olive Hill
CITY Oak Park
ST IL
ZIP 60301
WAGE        878.75
STATUS Y
SKILL CKP
DEPT ACCT
PHONE (312) 439-8760
EMPDATE 10-01-59
```

```
Command list 2:  File-Specs  Key  Lookup  Order  Relate  Sort  Transactions
                 Utilities
File: person   Window: 1                         Page: 1  Rec: 1  ( 1 )  Act: Y
 KEY - add, delete, organize or update key fields
```

Fig. 5.1. *Selecting the Key command.*

Because the key files are maintained as you go along, you can switch quickly from one key-field order to another. For a complete discussion of this process, see the section on "Using the Order Command" later in this chapter. The Key command is found on command list 2 (see fig. 5.1). The quick key is Alt-G. The four main options of the Key command are Add, Delete, Organize, and Update (see fig. 5.2).

Adding Keys (Key Add)

As its name implies, the Key Add command is used to add a key to an existing file. Any field can be used as a key field, although usually key fields contain discrete values such as department names, last names, or Social Security numbers rather than continuous values such as wages, ages, or numbers of dependents. Select Key Add, and

```
┌─────────────────────────────────────────────────────────────────┐
│STREET 546 Olive Hill                                             ║
│CITY Oak Park                                                     ║
│ST IL                                                            ║
│ZIP 60301                                                       ║
│WAGE        878.75                                              ║
│STATUS Y                                                        ║
│SKILL CKP                                                       ║
│DEPT ACCT                                                       ║
│PHONE (312) 439-8760                                           ║
│EMPDATE 10-01-59                                               ║
└─────────────────────────────────────────────────────────────────┘

Select option: ▐Add▌ Delete  Organize  Update
key
File: person    Window: 1                        Page: 1  Rec: 1  ( 1 )  Act: Y
▐KEY - add, delete, organize or update key fields                           ▌
```

Fig. 5.2. *The Key command options.*

you see the pop-up menu of fields. In figure 5.3, I am adding a key
for last name and first name, creating a compound key field. After
these key fields are created, a lowercase *k* is displayed next to the
LAST field on key-related menus. The *k* indicates that the field is a
major key. Notice that the SSN field is designated a major key in
figure 5.3.

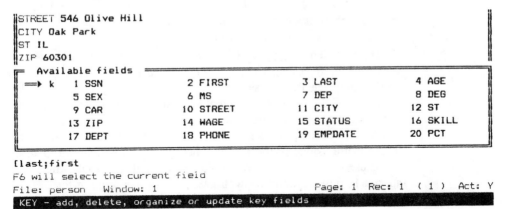

```
┌─────────────────────────────────────────────────────────────────┐
│STREET 546 Olive Hill                                            ║
│CITY Oak Park                                                    ║
│ST IL                                                           ║
│ZIP 60301                                                      ║
│┌─ Available fields ═══════════════════════════════════════════┐│
││ ═▶ k   1 SSN          2 FIRST        3 LAST         4 AGE    ││
││       5 SEX          6 MS           7 DEP          8 DEG     ││
││       9 CAR         10 STREET      11 CITY        12 ST      ││
││      13 ZIP         14 WAGE        15 STATUS      16 SKILL   ││
││      17 DEPT        18 PHONE       19 EMPDATE     20 PCT     ││
│└──────────────────────────────────────────────────────────────┘│
└─────────────────────────────────────────────────────────────────┘

[last;first
F6 will select the current field
File: person    Window: 1                        Page: 1  Rec: 1  ( 1 )  Act: Y
▐KEY - add, delete, organize or update key fields                           ▌
```

Fig. 5.3. *The fields available with Key Add.*

Select the key field(s) from the pop-up menu by using the cursor
keys to point to the field and pressing F6; or simply type the field
names or numbers on the prompt line. After you press Enter to
complete the selection of the key field (or fields), you see the menu
for designating the sorting sequence and key lengths (see fig. 5.4).
Notice that the default sorting order is always Ascending (A) and the
default key length is the full length of the field.

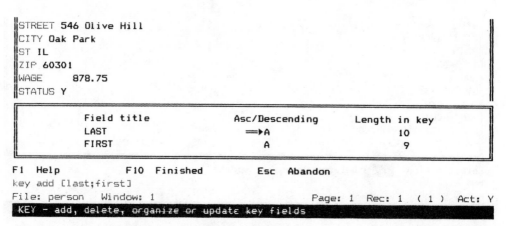

```
STREET 546 Olive Hill
CITY Oak Park
ST IL
ZIP 60301
WAGE      878.75
STATUS Y
```

Field title	Asc/Descending	Length in key
LAST	⇒A	10
FIRST	A	9

```
F1  Help              F10  Finished          Esc  Abandon
key add [last;first]
File: person   Window: 1                    Page: 1  Rec: 1  ( 1 )  Act: Y
KEY - add, delete, organize or update key fields
```

Fig. 5.4. *Key Add Sorting sequence and key length.*

If you want to arrange your key entries in Descending sequence, press *D* to overwrite the A. The D designates descending order. (Smart uses collation-table sorting techniques to make uppercase and lowercase identical key-field contents appear together. Some other programs use a sorting technique based on ASCII values. With those techniques, all uppercase characters appear before any lowercase characters; *XYZ*, for example, appears before *abc*.) A descending sequence is particularly useful if you have a date field and you want to see the most recent record first.

The field lengths appear in the third column of the menu, as shown in figure 5.4. Usually, the default field length is appropriate for the key-field length; occasionally, however, you many want to use just a portion of the field as the actual key. Do so only if the key field is very long, and you are sure you can get the proper sort sequence by using just a part of the field as the key. You will be able to save time in the maintenance of the key and also decrease the amount of disk space used by the key reference file. Be careful if you take this approach, however, and be well aware of the contents of the field. For example, if you shorten a last-name key to six characters, you cannot guarantee that *Andersen* will appear before *Anderson*.

To change the length of the key, use the → key to move the cursor to the third column of the menu, and the ↑ or ↓ to point to the proper field. Type the new value you want to use as the key length.

The Smart system has a maximum limit of 100 characters per key field, and 500 characters total for all keys.

Press F10 to complete the Key Add process. The program then sorts the keys and returns to the command menu. At this time, however, the records in the file are not in order by the key field. You must use the Order command to accomplish that.

Updating Keys (Key Update)

Chapter 8 shows you that after you have used the Enter command, Smart prompts you to indicate whether you want to update the key fields if your file has keys. Smart does not update the keys as you enter each new record; the program updates them in a group after you finish using the Enter command. If you plan to enter more records, you may want to postpone updating the keys. Before you can access the new records in the key order, however, you must update the keys by selecting Key Update or by answering *y* to the prompt for updating the key fields. The two choices have the same function.

You may not need to update keys at the completion of an Update procedure. Of course, if you have changed a field that is a part of a key, you'll need to update the keys so that they are in the right order. When you change only nonkey fields, however, you don't have to update the keys, even though you are prompted to do so. The list of records in the key file remains valid if the key fields are unchanged. If you decide not to update the key fields, the Smart system may display the following warning message when you try to execute some commands, such as the Report command:

```
File contains un-updated records. Continue (y/n)
```

You may safely ignore this message, although it is disconcerting.

In some circumstances, you are not reminded to update your keys. You still must update them, however, to succeed in using Smart's key capabilities. The Transactions command and Project Processing facility do not update keys; you must either manually perform the Key Update commands or include the command statement in the Project file. Other commands that do not remind you to update the keys are Utilities Restructure, Read, and Relate.

Rebuilding Keys (Key Organize)

The Key Organize command is used to rebuild key index files if they have been erased or damaged. You have the option of organizing All or One of the key index files. If you select One, you are prompted to identify the selected field. You should have to execute this command only if you receive a system message instructing you to do so.

Erasing Keys (Key Delete)

If you want to erase a key, use the Key Delete command. Simply identify the appropriate field on the pop-up menu, and then press Enter. There are no options to select. The more key fields you have, the longer a Key Update process will take. You should therefore keep the number of keys to a minimum.

Using the Sort Command (2–Sort, Alt-J)

Sorting a file is similar to using a key to arrange records. There are some significant differences, however.

Some commands require not only that the file be in a specific order, but also that the order be established through the use of a key field. For example, the Link command requires a key field, because the index file is used in record selection. The Query Count command also requires the use of a key, even though only one file is involved. Remember, too, that when you order a file by means of a key, *all* of the records are available, but in the order specified by the key field.

Updating an index key with the Sort command requires a different procedure than is needed with other commands. Remember that when using the Enter or Update commands, you update the keys by responding *y* to the prompt

Do you wish to update the keys now (y/n)

Although the Sort command creates an index, you cannot update this file without executing the Sort command again. The key index addresses all records in a file; and the Sort command operates within the current view of the file.

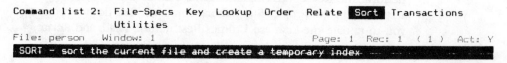

Fig. 5.5. *Selecting the Sort command.*

The Sort command is found on command list 2 (see fig. 5.5). The quick key is Alt-J. After you select Sort from the command list, four main options are displayed (see fig. 5.6). These options are Define, Now, Predefined, and Undefine.

```
Select option:  Define  Now  Predefined  Undefine
sort
File: person    Window: 1                          Page: 1  Rec: 1  ( 1 )  Act: Y
  SORT - sort the current file and create a temporary index
```

Fig. 5.6. *The Sort command options.*

Creating Sort Definitions (Sort Define)

The Sort Define command is used to define sorting conditions. As with other Define commands, the definition is stored in a file for later use. After you select Sort Define, a pop-up menu displays the names of the existing sort definition files. You then identify an existing file, or enter a file name to create a new one.

From this point, defining the sort is just like using Key Add (see figs. 5.3 and 5.4). Although the Key Add command creates the index file, the Sort Define command merely creates the sort definition file. You then use the Sort Predefined command to perform the sort and create the index file.

Performing a Sort and Creating an Index (Sort Predefined)

To sort your file, first select the Sort Predefined command, and then identify the sort definition file you want to use. You must also enter a name for the index file that will store the results of the sort. You can reuse an existing index file name if the file is not currently in use. The message sorting... appears on the command line while the file is being sorted.

Bear in mind several points about the sorting process. The Sort command will operate *within* the current order of the file. If you have ordered your file so that only 10 percent of the records are in the current view, Smart sorts only those records. In such a case, it is probably faster to execute the Order command first to limit the view to 10 percent of the records, and then to execute the Sort command so that fewer records will be sorted.

You may not need to use the Sort command at all if the desired result is a portion of a file that has already been put in order by one of the keys. First, order your file by the key field, and then perform the Query . . . Index command sequence. Finally, use the Order . . . Index command. The file remains in the original order of the key. (The Query command is covered in Chapter 11, and the Order command is covered later in this chapter.)

Let's say that you want to create an alphabetical list of individuals living in Massachusetts. One way to accomplish this task would be to follow this sequence of steps:

1. Query to identify the Massachusetts individuals.
2. Order to select the subset, using the index.
3. Sort by Lastname.
4. Order to establish the alphabetical sequence.

If you already have Lastname as a key field, however, a faster method would be to

1. Order by the key of Lastname.
2. Query to identify the Massachusetts individuals.
3. Order to select the subset, using the index.

Notice that you don't have to perform the Sort. The alphabetical sequence created by the Order Key command is maintained throughout the process.

The Sort Predefined command does not order the file; you must use the Order command to rearrange the view of the file. Because the Order command does not re-sort the file, you can switch to the new order very quickly. If you don't add new records or change the values in the fields used in defining the sort, you can rapidly switch back and forth from Order Key to Order Sequential to Order Index.

If you add new records that might be included in the Sort view, you must remember to execute the Sort command again. The Sort Index command differs from the Key commands in that Smart does not automatically prompt for an update when records are added or changed.

Sorting without Sort Definitions (Sort Now)

If you need to sort a file immediately and you don't want to store the definition, use the Sort Now command. With one major exception, using Sort Now is the same as using Sort Define. The exception is that the Sort Define command permits a mix of ascending- and descending-order fields if you specify a multiple-field sort. The Sort Now command, however, requires that all fields be sorted in either ascending or descending order (see fig. 5.7).

Smart uses *collation-table sorting techniques* to ensure that upper- and lowercase words are sorted together. In a conventional sort by ASCII values, all words in uppercase letters come before any words in lowercase.

When you have selected the fields, you are prompted to choose an ascending or descending sorting order. After you answer this prompt, the file is sorted and an index is created.

```
CAR 1
STREET 10 Dennis Drive
CITY Winnfield
ST LA
ZIP 71483
WAGE    1544.00
STATUS 1
SKILL AMFD
DEPT MKTG
PHONE (318) 729-5060
EMPDATE 10-01-85



Select option: Ascending  Descending
sort now ind] fields [last;first]
File: person   Window: 1                    Page: 1  Rec: EOF  ( 13 )  Act: Y
SORT - sort the current file and create a temporary index
```

Fig. 5.7. *The Sort Now command sequencing options.*

Erasing Sort Definitions (Sort Undefine)

If you have created Sort definitions that you no longer need, you can erase them with the Sort Undefine command. A pop-up menu displays the names of the sort definition files in the current subdirectory.

Using the Order command (2–Order)

Smart Data Base Manager files are physically created in sequential order; each new record is appended to the file in a position immediately following the previous record. Every time a file is loaded, the program defaults to this same sequential order.

In several chapters of this book, the *physical* order of a file is compared to the *logical* order. The Order command is used to change the logical order of a file so you can view or process the records in a sorted or selected order. The Order command also is used to reset the program to a sequential file view.

The *logical order* of a file may refer to two different conditions. In the first condition, the file is ordered by the contents of one or more fields. For example, you can establish an order by ZIP code for a mailing list. In the second condition, the Order command is used to select a set of records for viewing. An example of this usage might be "all the records for individuals living in Ohio, Maine, and Kansas." Both order conditions can exist simultaneously.

When you order a file, you do not physically rearrange the records on the disk. Whether you use a key field or a specifically created index, the Order command is used to change the way a file is displayed or made available for processing. You can order a file quickly because the sorting to create or maintain the index or key has already been done.

Arranging a File (Order)

The Order command, which is found on command list 2 (see fig. 5.8), establishes the logical order of a file. You can establish the order of a file with three different command sequences: Order Sequential, Order Key, and Order Index (see fig. 5.9).

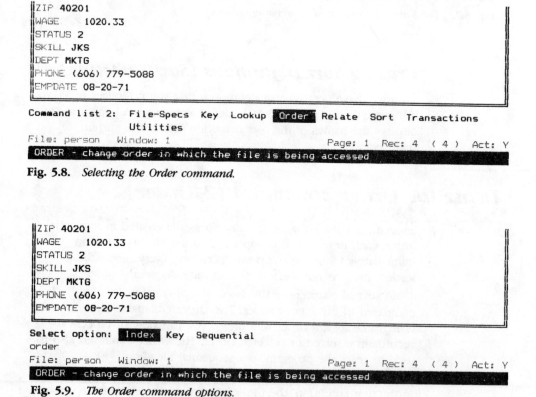

Fig. 5.8. *Selecting the Order command.*

Fig. 5.9. *The Order command options.*

Changing to Original File Order (Order Sequential)

Order Sequential changes the order of the file to the original sequential (physical) order and makes all the records available for viewing or processing. Use this command to reset the order of the file after it has been changed by either of the other two Order options. When you originally load a file or use the Goto command to display one in the current window, the file is in sequential order.

Setting the Order by Key Fields (Order Key)

To set the order of the file by any of the key fields, use the Order Key command. A pop-up menu of field names appears, and you select the appropriate field from that menu (see fig. 5.10). Use the cursor keys to point to the key field and press Enter. You can also type the field name or number on the prompt line. Notice that the key fields are preceded by the letter *k*. After the file has been ordered by a key field, all records in the file are available in the key order. As figure 5.11 shows, the status line changes to reflect the key order.

```
┌─Available fields══════════════════════════════════════════════════════┐
│    k 1 SSN              2 FIRST           ══▶ k 3 LAST                  │
│      4 AGE              5 SEX                 6 MS                      │
│      7 DEP              8 DEG                 9 CAR                     │
│     10 STREET          11 CITY              12 ST                      │
│     13 ZIP             14 WAGE              15 STATUS                   │
│     16 SKILL           17 DEPT             18 PHONE                     │
└───────────────────────────────────────────────────────────────────────┘

 F6 will select the current field [
 order key
 File: person    Window: 1                      Page: 1  Rec: 4  ( 4 )  Act: Y
 ORDER - change order in which the file is being accessed
```

Fig. 5.10. *Selecting the order of the Key.*

```
┌──────────────────────────────────────────────────────────────────────┐
│WAGE      887.23                                                        │
│STATUS 1                                                                │
│SKILL  BSMP                                                             │
│DEPT  ACCT                                                              │
│PHONE (203) 739-3095                                                    │
│EMPDATE 07-23-45                                                        │
└──────────────────────────────────────────────────────────────────────┘

Command:

File: person    Key: 3    Window: 1                 Page: 1  Rec: 1  ( 11 )  Act: Y
```

Fig. 5.11. *The Order key status line.*

Creating an Ordering Index (Order Index)

A key field establishes a permanent reference file that can be used to order a file, but you can also create temporary index files through the Sort and Query commands. These temporary index files, just like the key reference files, are lists of record numbers in the order in which the records are to be displayed and processed. Unlike key files, however, index files are not automatically updated when you add records to a file or change field values. Index files must be re-created as needed.

When you use Order Index, a pop-up menu is displayed (see fig. 5.12); it shows the names of the index files in the current subdirectory.

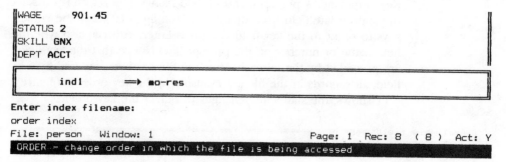

```
WAGE       901.45
STATUS 2
SKILL GNX
DEPT ACCT

        ind1        ==> mo-res

Enter index filename:
order index
File: person   Window: 1                    Page: 1  Rec: 8  ( 8 )  Act: Y
ORDER - change order in which the file is being accessed
```

Fig. 5.12. *Using the Order Index command.*

The Sort command creates an index that is used to arrange the file in order by the contents of one or more fields. These fields are usually *not* key fields. Thus, even though ZIP is not a key field, you can Sort the file by the ZIP field, create an index, and then Order the file by that index.

The Query command creates an index of selected records based on a set of criteria provided when you issue the command. You could use Query to select the records of the individuals in Ohio, Maine, and Kansas, by testing on the ST (State) field.

As figure 5.13 shows, the status line changes to reflect the index order.

The effect of using Order commands is cumulative, because each command works on the result of the previous command. For instance, if you want an alphabetical list of all individuals in Missouri, you first Order the file by the key field LAST to put the list in alphabetical order. Then use Query to select the Missouri residents.

```
WAGE    1453.75
STATUS 2
SKILL ZOBY
DEPT MKTG
PHONE (617) 873-0979
EMPDATE 09-05-75
```

Command:

File: person   Index: mo-res   Window: 1   Page: 1   Rec: 1   (7)   Act: Y

Fig. 5.13. *The Order index status line.*

Finally, Order the file again by the index created from the Query command.

You can use successive Query commands to narrow the subset of available records even further. In Chapter 11, "Using the Query Command," you will learn how to enter multiple screening conditions simultaneously.

Here's a hint for more efficient processing: If you are performing a "sort and select" combination and you have a key field for the sort, first use Order Key, then Query, and finally another Order command. If you were to execute the Query command first, you would have to sort the data by the key field because Order Key resets the status of the file to make all records available.

If you need to sort by a nonkey field, you can save time by executing Query and Order Index first. In this way, you will have fewer records available after using the Query command, and the sort will run more quickly.

Remember that the order of a file is changed back to sequential if you use the Goto command to view another file in the same window. You must Order the original file again if you return to it. If you need to alternate between files, you should create a second window so that both files are available in their respective orders.

Conclusion

The ability to arrange your data in a logical way is vital to the management of data bases. The capability to display and process records in an order other than the one in which they are entered is one of the hallmarks of a data base management system.

The Smart system can sort your data into the order you need whenever you need it. The program also can maintain key files that allow you to reorder your file without having to perform a sort. Whether you use a Sort command or a Key command is your decision. You need to consider how often you need to rearrange the file, how quickly you need to switch from one order to another, how much disk space is available, and how long the Update process will take. Keys can be added and deleted as necessary, so you can change your decision if the requirements of your application change.

The Order command is essential for establishing the order in which a file is processed or viewed and selecting a subset of records that meet certain criteria. The Key reference files are maintained by the Smart Data Base Manager throughout the execution of Enter and Update commands. The Order Key command is used to rearrange the file according to these keys. You create temporary index files in Query and Sort, which are then used in Order Index. The Order Sequential command resets the file view to its original physical order.

Chapter 6

Locating Data

You know now that when you are looking for the record of a
specific employee in your personnel file, you can use the Browse
command to display 18 records on the screen at one time. You can
then advance manually through the file until you find the record you
want. If the employees are listed in alphabetical order by last name,
finding a specific person is certainly easier. The computer, however,
is doing little to help you in your search.

But what if the file contains several thousand records? What if the
search pattern is complex, and you are trying to find records of
employees earning less than $875?

Selecting Records with the Find Command (1–Find, F3)

You use the Find command to search through your file and display
records that meet specified conditions, or *criteria.* You can
search for records containing values that are equal to the criterion
you specify, records containing values that are greater than or less
than your criterion, or records that simply contain the search value
in a specified field. You can search the whole file, search forward
from the current record, or even search backward through the file.
There are options for handling upper- and lowercase differences and
whole-word conditions.

Although some of the options work only on alphanumeric fields, the Find command operates on all types of data fields. As shown in figure 6.1, the Find command is on command list 1; the quick key is the F3 function key.

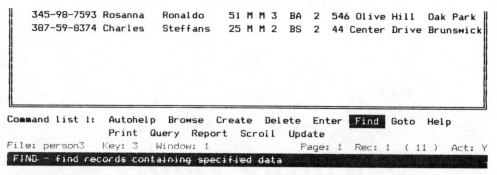

| 345-98-7593 Rosanna | Ronaldo | 51 M M 3 | BA | 2 | 546 Olive Hill | Oak Park |
| 387-59-8374 Charles | Steffans | 25 M M 2 | BS | 2 | 44 Center Drive | Brunswick |

Command list 1:   Autohelp Browse Create Delete Enter Find Goto Help
                   Print Query Report Scroll Update
File: person3   Key: 3   Window: 1   Page: 1   Rec: 1   (11)   Act: Y
FIND - find records containing specified data

Fig. 6.1. *Selecting the Find command.*

Selecting Field Names

When you execute the Find command, a pop-up menu of field names is displayed (see fig. 6.2). Use the cursor-control keys to move to the desired search field. You can press F6 to select the current field, or simply press Enter; you can also type on the prompt line the field name or number. Ordinarily you select only one field; you might select more than one field, however, if your search applies to several fields simultaneously. In such a case, you would find the record in which any of the fields matches your search condition.

Available fields
⟹ k 1 SSN   2 FIRST   k 3 LAST
   4 AGE   5 SEX   6 MS
   7 DEP   8 DEG   9 CAR
  10 STREET   11 CITY   12 ST
  13 ZIP   14 WAGE   15 STATUS
  16 SKILL   17 DEPT   18 PHONE

 F6 will select the current field [last
find
File: person3   Key: 3   Window: 1   Page: 1   Rec: 1   (11)   Act: Y
FIND - find records containing specified data

Fig. 6.2. *A list of fields.*

Using Logical Operators in a Search

When you have selected a field, you are shown a menu of logical operators you can use to match your search value against the file contents (see fig. 6.3).

```
345-98-7593 Rosanna    Ronaldo     51 M M 3  BA  2  546 Olive Hill   Oak Park
387-59-8374 Charles    Steffans    25 M M 2  BS  2  44 Center Drive Brunswick




Select option:  Equal  Greater-Than  Less-Than  Partial
find [last]
File: person3   Key: 3   Window: 1                    Page: 1  Rec: 1  ( 11 )  Act: Y
FIND - find records containing specified data
```

Fig. 6.3. *Selecting a logical-operator option.*

You select the Equal option to search for field contents that match exactly what you supply in your search criterion. If you are looking for the record of a particular employee, for example, you use the Equal option to match the employee's name.

Select Greater-Than or Less-Than if you are searching for a record with a field value that is either greater than or less than the value you supply. Even though the records need not be in order by the contents of the field to be searched, you will see that the search is faster if they are.

You use the Partial option if you are searching for a word or a string of characters that is somewhere within a field. The Partial option would find *mouth* in the CITY field containing *Yarmouth* or *5* in an AGE field containing *35*. Although this option works with numeric fields, it is most applicable to alphanumeric fields.

Entering Your Search Criterion

After you select a logical search operator, you are prompted to enter your search criterion. You now type the value or string of characters for which you are searching (see fig. 6.4). Do not use quotation marks, even if there is a leading space or a space in the middle of the string. However, if your search criterion includes a *trailing* space, you must enclose the string *and* the space in double quotation marks (*"*):

"Boston "

```
Enter the information to find:  Harris
find [last] equal
File: person3   Window: 1                        Page: 1  Rec: 1  ( 1 )  Act: Y
 FIND · find records containing specified data
```

Fig. 6.4. *Enter the information to find:*

Selecting Additional Options

After you enter the search criterion, you are prompted to enter additional option specifications (see fig. 6.5). Press the initial letter of each option that you want to use; options can be used in combination and can be entered in any order. Press Enter after you have indicated which options you want to use.

```
Enter options:
find [last] equal Harris options
B Backward  G Global  I Ignore case  W Whole words only
 FIND - find records containing specified data
```

Fig. 6.5. *The search options.*

The *Backward* option searches from the current record back to the beginning of the file. The *Global* option always searches from the beginning of the file. If you specify neither of these, the search will begin with the current record and proceed toward the end of the file.

The *Ignore case* option causes Smart to disregard the case of both the field's contents and the search criterion. Thus you do not have to remember whether you entered names or other alphanumeric data in upper- or lowercase.

The *Whole words only* option finds records in which the search string is an entire word—that is, a word with either a blank or a field terminator at both ends. For example, if an employee lives on Green street, you can search for a whole word and find *Green;* with that search criterion, however, you will not find *Greenville* street. (In this example, you also should use the Find Partial option because there probably is a house number in front of *Green*, and the field therefore will contain several words.)

After you have selected the search options, the system begins looking through the file to find the first record that meets your search criterion. If a record is found, it is displayed and the message shown in figure 6.6 appears.

```
┌─ Window 1 ═══════════════════════════════════════════════════════════════
│   SSN         FIRST      LAST      AG S M DE DEG CA STREET           CITY
│   345-98-7593 Rosanna    Ronaldo   51 M M 3  BA  2  546 Olive Hill   Oak Park
│   498-48-3980 Debbie     Linden    29 F S 1  MA  2  409 Pleasant St  Amherst
│   239-87-8876 Michael    Davis     61 M M 1  MBA 2  180 Lewis Ave.   Covington
│   208-23-0300 Julius     Karenski  41 M D 0  PhD 1  18 Olive St.     Louisvill
│═▶887-63-5498 Jeff        Harris    34 M M 4  BA  5  1201 Horton Rd.  Lyndhurst
│   598-44-5922 LeAnne     Markus    48 F W 1  MBA 1  14 Crumpet Ave.  Alamosa
│   876-33-0989 Marilyn    Lester    55 F M 4  AB  3  6 Greenville St  Yarmouth
│   987-65-7653 David      Marzetti  47 M D 0      1  20 Grayln Dr.    Wilmingto
│   387-59-8374 Charles    Steffans  25 M M 2  BS  2  44 Center Drive  Brunswick
│   498-34-5998 Paula      Bernstein 30 F S 3  MA  3  18 Worcester St  Beaumont
│   776-39-8763 Alfred     Adelson   60 M M 0  BA  1  14 Spring St.    Hartford
│   345-54-2287 Ellen      Aliakbari 35 F S 0      1  2171 University  Westfield
│   198-03-3024 Howard E.  Peters    18 M S 0      1  10 Dennis Drive  Winnfield
│
│
│
│
│
│
└─────────────────────────────────────────────────────────────────────────
Data found in [LAST], continue search (y/n)
find [last] equal Harris options
File: person3   Window: 1                      Page: 1  Rec: 5  ( 5 )  Act: Y
FIND - find records containing specified data
```

Fig. 6.6. *A record is found.*

If this is not the record you want, press *y* to continue the search. (Do not press Enter.) If additional records meet the criterion, Smart displays the next record found and prompts you to indicate whether you want to continue. But if this is the last record that meets the condition, the message shown in figure 6.7 is displayed.

If you choose not to continue the search, press *n* (refer to fig. 6.6); the current record is again displayed. When you choose to continue a search and no more matching records are found, the current record is the one that was current before you began the Find command; it is *not* the last record found. If you need to repeat the Find command, use the Alt-R quick key, which repeats the most recent Find command even though there may be other intervening commands.

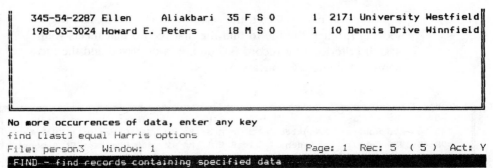

```
   345-54-2287 Ellen      Aliakbari  35 F S 0     1  2171 University Westfield
   198-03-3024 Howard E. Peters      18 M S 0     1  10 Dennis Drive Winnfield
```

```
No more occurrences of data, enter any key
find [last] equal Harris options
File: person3   Window: 1                        Page: 1  Rec: 5  ( 5 )  Act: Y
FIND -- find records containing specified data
```

Fig. 6.7. *No more occurrences of data.*

Searching Quickly in Binary Search Mode

As a default, the Find command searches record-by-record through the file, beginning at the position you specify. Each record is matched to the search criterion (or criteria). This kind of search can be compared to thumbing card-by-card through a random stack of index cards, looking for the record of an employee with a specific Social Security number. Under the proper conditions, however, the system will do a *binary search*. This is the fastest search mode possible in Smart. The conditions for a binary search are

1. The field on which you want to search must be the major field of a key. (Note that, as shown in fig. 6.2, key fields in the pop-up menu are marked with a *k*.)

2. The file must be ordered by this key field.

3. The search must apply to a single field.

4. You must use the Equal option.

5. You cannot use the Ignore case or Whole word options.

If you have a large file or if you need to find records quickly, this is by far the best technique to use. If you need to find inventory quantities quickly, for instance, you can find an inventory record in a few seconds by searching on the part-number field of your inventory records, even if thousands of parts are listed in your data base. The search might take 15 to 20 minutes if it were performed without this binary search technique, depending on the amount of data in each record and the type of hardware you are using.

If the system finds an exact match, the first matching record is displayed and the message shown in figure 6.8 appears.

```
     345-98-7593 Rosanna    Ronaldo    51 M M 3  BA  2  546 Olive Hill  Oak Park
     387-59-8374 Charles    Steffans   25 M M 2  BS  2  44 Center Drive Brunswick
```

```
Data found, displaying first occurrence - press any key to continue
find [last] equal Davis options
File: person3  Key: 3   Window: 1                 Page: 1  Rec: 4  ( 3 )  Act: Y
FIND - find records containing specified data
```

Fig. 6.8. *The first occurrence message.*

If an exact match is *not* found, the system stops at the first record whose contents most closely match your criterion. If the search string matches the leftmost part of a field's contents, the record containing that field is displayed, and the Find operation terminates. In figure 6.9, for instance, the search string is *Peter;* the system has found the record for Howard E. Peters. This feature saves you the time involved in typing a complete name for the search. If a partial match is found in the leftmost portion of the field, the search

```
= Window 1 =
    SSN          FIRST       LAST       AG S M DE DEG CA STREET           CITY
    776-39-8763 Alfred      Adelson    60 M M 0  BA  1  14 Spring St.     Hartford
    345-54-2287 Ellen       Aliakbari  35 F S 0      1  2171 University  Westfield
    498-34-5998 Paula       Bernstein  30 F S 3  MA  3  18 Worcester St  Beaumont
    239-87-8876 Michael     Davis      61 M M 1  MBA 2  180 Lewis Ave.   Covington
    887-63-5498 Jeff        Harris     34 M M 4  BA  5  1201 Horton Rd.  Lyndhurst
    208-23-0300 Julius      Karenski   41 M D 0  PhD 1  18 Olive St.     Louisvill
    876-33-0989 Marilyn     Lester     55 F M 4  AB  3  6 Greenville St  Yarmouth
    498-48-3980 Debbie      Linden     29 F S 1  MA  2  409 Pleasant St  Amherst
    598-44-5922 LeAnne      Markus     48 F W 1  MBA 1  14 Crumpet Ave.  Alamosa
    987-65-7653 David       Marzetti   47 M D 0      1  20 Grayln Dr.    Wilmingto
==>198-03-3024 Howard E.   Peters     18 M S 0      1  10 Dennis Drive  Winnfield
    345-98-7593 Rosanna     Ronaldo    51 M M 3  BA  2  546 Olive Hill   Oak Park
    387-59-8374 Charles     Steffans   25 M M 2  BS  2  44 Center Drive Brunswick
```

```
Data not found, displaying closest match - press any key to continue
find [last] equal Peter options
File: person3  Key: 3   Window: 1                 Page: 1  Rec: 11  ( 13 )  Act: Y
FIND - find records containing specified data
```

Fig. 6.9. *Display of the closest match.*

operation stops on the next record. A search for Petrofsky, for example, will stop at Ronaldo.

Conclusion

You can use the Find command to search through your file in logical order to locate records that satisfy your criteria. Although you can search visually, the Smart Data Base Manager often performs the task faster and more accurately, especially if the file is very large. For rapid access, you can initiate an extremely fast *binary search* under certain conditions.

Chapter 7

Handling Multiple Files

Most of the examples so far have involved only one file. But you may recall that in Chapter 4, "Viewing Data," you learned about handling windows with the Link command. This chapter explains how to use multiple files with Smart.

The Smart Data Base Manager offers several ways of handling multiple files. You can choose the method that fits your needs. If you need to create a new file from two existing files, for example, you use the Relate command. If you need to move data or to post activity from one file to another, you use the Transactions command. And if you have created a new file that is similar but not identical to an existing file and you need to transfer the data to the new file, you can use the Utilities Restructure command.

The examples in later chapters often build on multiple-file interactions. You will learn, for instance, that the Report command can display data from two linked files in the same report. The Utilities Concatenate command appends one file to another. With the Lookup function, you can draw data from one file and insert it in another while entering data or updating the data base.

Using the Relate Command (2–Relate, Alt-N)

Use of the Link command is an example of joining two files. Each file remains a separate entity with its own structure and data, even though the files share a common field. But some Smart commands require that data from several files be stored in one physical file. In such a case, you use the Relate command, which is found on command list 2 (see fig. 7.1). The quick key is Alt-N.

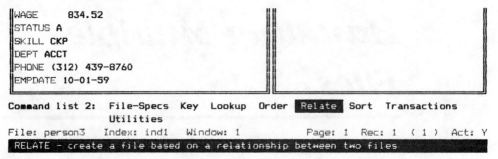

```
WAGE      834.52
STATUS A
SKILL CKP
DEPT ACCT
PHONE (312) 439-8760
EMPDATE 10-01-59


Command list 2:  File-Specs  Key  Lookup  Order  Relate  Sort  Transactions
                 Utilities
File: person3    Index: ind1    Window: 1              Page: 1  Rec: 1  ( 1 )  Act: Y
RELATE - create a file based on a relationship between two files
```

Fig. 7.1. *Selecting the Relate command.*

The Relate command can define four different types of relations between two files. The most common relation is one in which you have two files, and you want to create a new file containing all records that match a common field. For example, you may want to create a file that uses data from the personnel file and the *names* of the departments from the department file. (The DEPT field of the personnel file contains only abbreviations for the department names.) This is called an *intersect* relation. The relation types are summarized as follows:

The *Intersect* relation creates new records only when the linking field matches in the two files.

The *Not-Intersect* relation creates new records only when no match is found. For example, you may want to create a file of all employees who are not listed in a particular department and of all the departments that have no employees.

The *Subtract* relation can be used to create records from the second file that do not match records in the first file. For example, you may want to create records for departments that have no employees.

The *Union* option creates records for all conditions, regardless of whether there are matching departments or employees.

Defining Relationships (Relate Define)

Unlike many of the commands discussed thus far, the Relate command has so many options that you must create a definition before you can use the command. The advantage of creating a definition is that later you can edit and reuse the definition. The Relate command is frequently used in day-to-day, repetitive applications, so you will want to be able to store the definitions.

Before you begin, make sure that both files and the appropriate screens are loaded. The file in the current window (DEPT), which is called File 1 in this example, should be ordered by the key field you plan to use as the linking field. In this example, the linking field is DEPT. File 2 does not have to be loaded in a window.

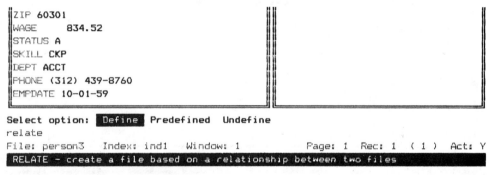

```
ZIP 60301
WAGE       834.52
STATUS A
SKILL CKP
DEPT ACCT
PHONE (312) 439-8760
EMPDATE 10-01-59
```

```
Select option: Define  Predefined   Undefine
relate
File: person3   Index: ind1   Window: 1            Page: 1  Rec: 1  ( 1 )  Act: Y
RELATE - create a file based on a relationship between two files
```

Fig. 7.2. *The Relate Define option.*

When you select Relate Define (see fig. 7.2), you are prompted to enter the name of the definition. If you have already defined other relations, you will see a pop-up menu showing the names of the relations. To create a new definition, type a new name and press Enter. To edit an existing definition, either type the name or use the cursor keys to highlight the selection. You then see the following prompt:

Enter relate definition file name:

You are then prompted to enter the name of the file to be used as File 2. If you have more than one active screen, you are also prompted for the name of the screen. In the example, *person3* is File 2 (see fig. 7.3).

```
         dept          ==> person3
```

Select database filename:
relate define deprel1 file
File: dept   Key: 1   Window: 1   Page: 1 Rec: 1   (1)   Act: Y
 RELATE - create a file based on a relationship between two files

Fig. 7.3. *Selecting the data base file name.*

The relate definition screen (fig. 7.4) is used to specify the linking fields and to specify from both files the data fields that are to be carried to the new file.

```
 Relate Definition

     File 1: dept
     Link fields [dept]
     rel. fields [depname]

     File 2: person3
     Link fields [dept]
     rel. fields [1:5]
```

Available fields
==> k 1 SSN   2 FIRST   k 3 LAST
     4 AGE   5 SEX   6 MS
     7 DEP   8 DEG   9 CAR
    10 STREET   11 CITY   12 ST
    13 ZIP   14 WAGE   15 STATUS
    16 SKILL   17 DEPT   18 PHONE

 F6 will select the current field [1:5
File 2 relate fields

 RELATE - create a file based on a relationship between two files

Fig. 7.4. *The Relate Definition screen.*

The linking fields in both files happen to be named DEPT. The fields could have different names, but the fields must have the same data type and length. The data is taken from DEPNAME in File 1 and

from fields 1 through 5 from File 2. Use the ↑ and ↓ keys to move
between field definition inputs. You can display a pop-up menu of
the fields in the appropriate file by pressing F7. Fields are specified
by using the cursor keys to move the cursor to the name of the
desired field in the pop-up menu. You can then press F6 to insert
the field number on the prompt line, or simply press Enter. In the
example shown in figure 7.4, I typed the field names for the first
three fields so that my definition would be easier to read. Note that I
specified fields 1 through 5 by typing *1|5* on the prompt line.

When you are finished creating the definition, press F10 to save it
and return to the command list.

Specifying Relation Type (Relate Predefined)

After the relation definition is saved, you select the command
sequence Relate Predefined to use the definition. A pop-up menu
appears, showing the names of the relation definitions in the current
subdirectory (see fig. 7.5).

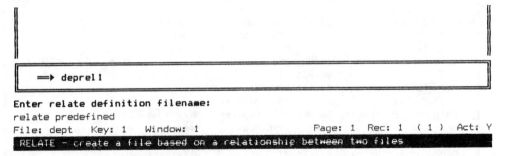

```
 ⟹  deprel 1

Enter relate definition filename:
relate predefined
File: dept   Key: 1   Window: 1               Page: 1  Rec: 1  ( 1 )  Act: Y
 RELATE - create a file based on a relationship between two files
```

Fig. 7.5. *Selecting a Relate definition file name.*

Next, select one the four relation types (see fig. 7.6). For this
example, select Intersect to create a file of employees who are
working for valid departments. Remember that Intersect does not
create a record where there is no match.

After selecting the option, you see the following prompt:

Enter the new file name:

You cannot enter the name of an existing file. Use the Utilities Erase
File command to erase any file whose name you want to use again.

The Relate command is executed in two steps. The structure of
the file is created first, and then the data is added. You can observe

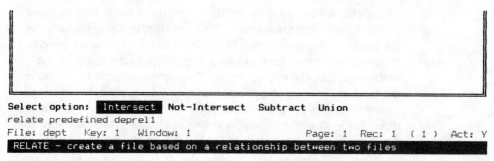

Fig. 7.6. *Relation options.*

this process if you watch closely, but both steps take place without your intervention. The number of records written is displayed briefly on completion of the process. The new file is bound by the same restrictions on number of fields and total record length that limit any other file in the Smart Data Base Manager. Figure 7.7 shows the file created by the Relate command.

```
┌─ Window 1 ────────────────────────────────────────────────────────────┐
│   DEPT DEPNAME          SSN           FIRST      LAST       AG S        │
│ ═►ACCT Accounting       345-98-7593 Rosanna    Ronaldo     51 M        │
│   MFGR Manufacturing    498-48-3980 Debbie     Linden      29 F        │
│   SALE Sales            239-87-8876 Michael     Davis       61 M        │
│   MKTG Marketing        208-23-0300 Julius     Karenski    41 M        │
│   ACCT Accounting       887-63-5498 Jeff       Harris      34 M        │
│   SALE Sales            598-44-5922 LeAnne     Markus      48 F        │
│   MKTG Marketing        876-33-0989 Marilyn    Lester      55 F        │
│   DATA Data Processing  387-59-8374 Charles    Steffans    25 M        │
│   SALE Sales            498-34-5998 Paula      Bernstein   30 F        │
│   ACCT Accounting       776-39-8763 Alfred     Adelson     60 M        │
│   MFGR Manufacturing    345-54-2287 Ellen      Aliakbari   35 F        │
│   MKTG Marketing        198-03-3024 Howard E.  Peters      18 M        │
│                                                                        │
│                                                                        │
│                                                                        │
│                                                                        │
│                                                                        │
│                                                                        │
└────────────────────────────────────────────────────────────────────────┘

Command:

File: deplist    Window: 1                     Page: 1   Rec: 1   ( 1 )   Act: Y
```

Fig. 7.7. *New file created by the Relate command.*

The Intersect option creates records only when there is a match in linking fields, but the Not-Intersect option creates records only when there is *no* match. Figure 7.8 shows a file created with the Not-Intersect relation. The file contains records for all individuals who do *not* work for a valid department (ADMN is not in the DEPT file) and all departments that have *no* employees (the MDSE department).

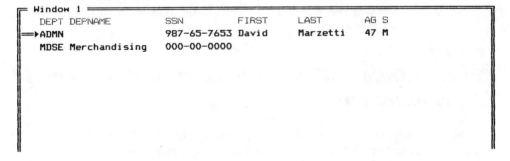

Fig. 7.8. *Files found as a result of Not-Intersect relation.*

To get a list of the employees not currently assigned to a valid department (line 1 of fig. 7.8), use the Subtract option. The result is shown in figure 7.9.

```
┌─ Window 1 ═══════════════════════════════════════════════════════════
│   DEPT DEPNAME          SSN            FIRST      LAST       AG S
│═▶ADMN                   987-65-7653 David        Marzetti   47 M
│
│
│
│
│
│
```

Fig. 7.9. *The files displayed as a result of the Subtract relation.*

The Union option extracts all records from both files, regardless of a match on the key field. This relation is a combination of the Intersect and the Not-Intersect relations (refer to figures 7.7 and 7.8).

Although File 2 need not have a key field and need not be ordered by the linking field, you can speed up the Relate process by ordering the file. The file must be in a window, however, before you can order it. (Remember that if a file is not in a window, it reverts to sequential order. See Chapter 5 if you need to review the use of the Order command.) If you don't want to see File 2 on the screen, you can always Zoom File 1.

If the linking fields are key fields in both files, the Relate command works faster if File 1 is the smaller of the two files. Use the Query command to limit the number of records available in File 2; this will also speed the process. Again, remember to load the file in a window first.

Copying Data with the Transactions Command (2–Transactions, Alt-T)

The Transactions command is used to post data from one file to another. Typically, you have a master file and a transaction file. You might post daily or weekly transactions from a transaction file to reflect activity during the period. For example, the master file could be an inventory file, and the transaction file could contain the individual sales records, which show the item number and the quantity sold (or returned). At the end of the day or week, the Transactions command is used to subtract the quantity sold from the inventory file in "batch" mode. (If you have designed your system so that the inventory is debited immediately from the master file as each sale is made, you would not need the Transactions command to update the on-hand inventory file.)

Like the Relate command, the Transactions command is used with two files that share a linking field. Linking fields must be of the same type and length, but they need not have the same name.

The field sending the data is called the *source,* and the field receiving the data is called the *destination*. One file is called the *driver* file, and the other file is called the *driven* file. The driver file contains those records that cause a transaction to take place. The needs of your application determine which file is which. In the sales-transactions example, the file of sales records is the driver file because you want the master file to be updated for each sale. When you select Transactions Predefined, the driven file must be in key order by the linking field, and both the source file and the destination file must be in active windows. The command can be executed from either window.

You can post the transactions to either file depending on the needs of your application. In this example, you could post the quantities from the sales record file to the master file by subtracting the quantity sold. On the other hand, you might want to produce a profitability analysis report, showing the profit margins for the items sold. In that case, you could post the current item cost and selling price to the sales file and then multiply by the quantity sold during the interval. You could then use that data in the report.

The Transactions command is found on command list 2, and the quick key is Alt-T (see fig. 7.10).

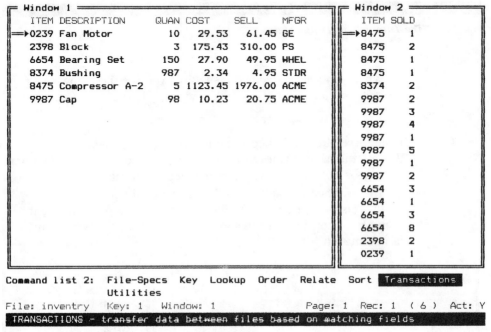

Fig. 7.10. *Selecting the Transactions command.*

Creating a Transaction Definition (Transactions Define)

When you have selected the Transactions command, you have three options: Define, Predefined, and Undefine (see fig. 7.11). The first step is to define a new transaction. You may also edit an existing transaction definition (with the Define option), but you can change only the fields and the actions. You cannot change the source and driver designations.

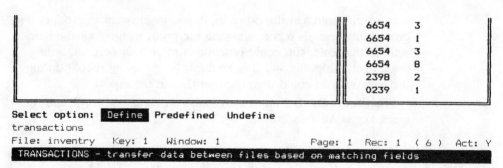

Fig. 7.11. *The Transactions Define option.*

When you select Transactions Define, you see the following prompt:

Enter transaction definition filename:

If you have already defined some transactions, a pop-up menu displays the names. You can choose a predefined transaction by using the cursor keys or by typing a transaction file name.

You are then prompted to select a source file name (see fig. 7.12). This is the name of the file that is the source of data for the Transaction command. In this example, the SALES file is the source of information.

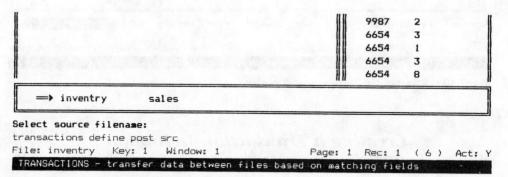

Fig. 7.12. *Selecting the source file name.*

Next, select S-Driver or D-Driver to indicate whether the destination file (D-Driver) or the source file (S-Driver) is the driver (see fig. 7.13). Think of the *driver* file as the one causing the transaction to be initiated. In this case, the source file (SALES) is the driver file, because the sale of a product initiates the inventory reduction. You must remember the exact sequence of command selections and keyboard entries because if you later want to edit the definition, you must enter it in exactly the same way.

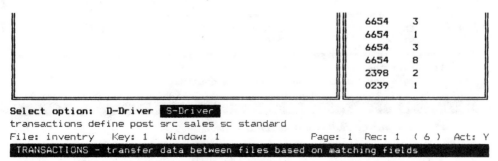

```
                                                          6654    3
                                                          6654    1
                                                          6654    3
                                                          6654    8
                                                          2398    2
                                                          0239    1

Select option:  D-Driver  S-Driver
transactions define post src sales sc standard
File: inventry   Key: 1   Window: 1              Page: 1  Rec: 1  ( 6 )  Act: Y
TRANSACTIONS - transfer data between files based on matching fields
```

Fig. 7.13. *Selecting destination/driver or source/driver.*

Select the field from the source/driver file that is to be used as the linking field in the transaction (see fig. 7.14). In this case, the source/driver field is the ITEM field; the item number is in both the source file and the destination file. If your destination file were the driver file, the prompt would ask for the linking fields in the source/driven file.

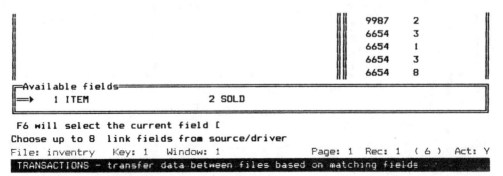

```
                                                          9987    2
                                                          6654    3
                                                          6654    1
                                                          6654    3
                                                          6654    8
 Available fields
  ➔    1 ITEM                    2 SOLD

F6 will select the current field [
Choose up to 8 link fields from source/driver
File: inventry   Key: 1   Window: 1              Page: 1  Rec: 1  ( 6 )  Act: Y
TRANSACTIONS - transfer data between files based on matching fields
```

Fig. 7.14. *Selecting the source/driver link fields.*

The next step is to choose a linking field from the destination/driven file (see fig. 7.15). Only one field can be chosen; in this example, the field is ITEM. Note that the ITEM field is a key field, as it must be if the source file is the driver file.

The transaction definition screen, shown in figure 7.16, is used to enter the fields used in the transaction and to specify the action that is to take place. To add an action, move the pointer to the

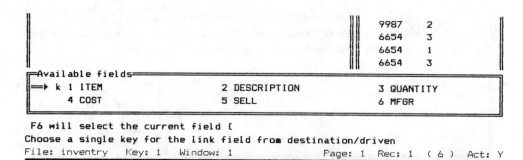

Fig. 7.15. *Selecting the destination/driven link field.*

appropriate destination field and press F7. For this example, we are going to update the QUANTITY field.

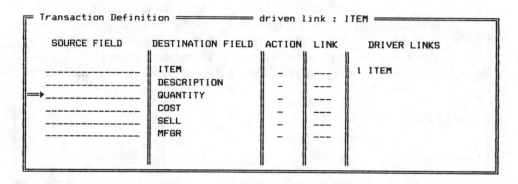

Fig. 7.16. *The Transaction definition screen.*

After you press F7, a menu at the bottom of the screen displays the fields from the source file that can be used in the transaction (see fig. 7.17). This example uses the SOLD field, which contains the quantity sold.

```
┌─Available fields════════════════════════════════════════════════════╗
│       1 ITEM              ══▶    2 SOLD                               ║
└──────────────────────────────────────────────────────────────────────╝
```

F6 will select the current field [

File: inventry   Key: 1   Window: 1   Page: 1 Rec: 1 (6) Act: Y
TRANSACTIONS - transfer data between files based on matching fields

Fig. 7.17. *The source file fields.*

Figure 7.18 shows that after you indicate the source file field, the
system displays the name of the field on the definition screen, and
the cursor flashes on the ACTION field. Possible actions are Move
(M), Add (A), and Subtract (S); no other actions are possible. In this
case, you want to subtract from the inventory quantity on hand, so
you enter *S* for Subtract.

```
┌═ Transaction Definition ═══════════════ driven link : ITEM ═══════════┐
│                                                                       │
│    SOURCE FIELD    DESTINATION FIELD  ACTION  LINK    DRIVER LINKS     │
│                                                                       │
│    _____ ║ ITEM          ║   _  ║  ___ ║  1 ITEM           │
│    _____ ║ DESCRIPTION   ║   _  ║  ___ ║                   │
│    SOLD             ║ QUANTITY      ║   _  ║  ___ ║                   │
│    _____ ║ COST          ║   _  ║  ___ ║                   │
│    _____ ║ SELL          ║   _  ║  ___ ║                   │
│    _____ ║ MFGR          ║   _  ║  ___ ║                   │
│                                                                       │
│                                                                       │
└───────────────────────────────────────────────────────────────────────┘
```

Enter M for move or A for add or S for subtract

File: inventry   Key: 1   Window: 1   Page: 1 Rec: 1 (6) Act: Y
TRANSACTIONS - transfer data between files based on matching fields

Fig. 7.18. *Selecting an action.*

If more than one field from the source file is to be used in a
transaction with a field from the destination file, you can use F3 to
copy the definition line for the destination field. Move the pointer to
the line in question and press F3.

Figure 7.19 shows the completed screen. If you want to indicate other fields on the transaction definition screen, repeat the process; otherwise, press F10 to end.

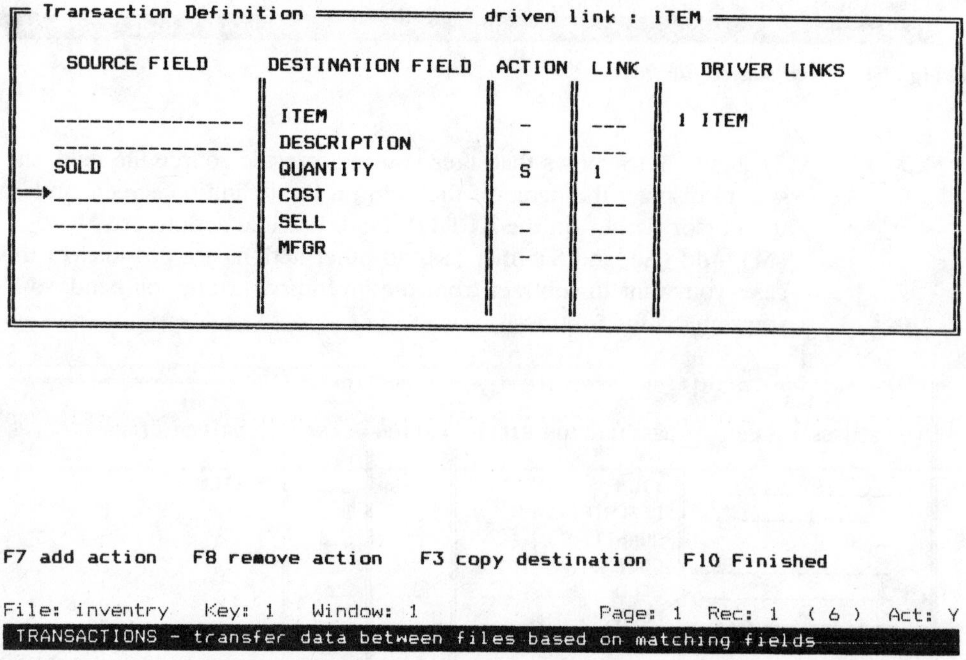

```
 ┌─ Transaction Definition ═══════════ driven link : ITEM ══════
 │
 │      SOURCE FIELD      DESTINATION FIELD   ACTION  LINK    DRIVER LINKS
 │
 │    ─────────────────  │ ITEM           ││  -  ││  ─── ││  1 ITEM
 │    ─────────────────  │ DESCRIPTION    ││  -  ││  ───
 │     SOLD              │ QUANTITY       ││  S  ││  1
 │ ═▶ ─────────────────  │ COST           ││  -  ││  ───
 │    ─────────────────  │ SELL           ││  -  ││  ───
 │    ─────────────────  │ MFGR           ││  -  ││  ───
 │
 └──────────────────────────────────────────────────────────────
```

```
 F7 add action    F8 remove action    F3 copy destination    F10 Finished

 File: inventry   Key: 1    Window: 1              Page: 1   Rec: 1  ( 6 )  Act: Y
 TRANSACTIONS - transfer data between files based on matching fields
```

Fig. 7.19. *The completed Transaction definition screen.*

Smart now prompts you to indicate whether you want to use the entire file each time. If you want the SALES file to be started from scratch for each sales period, press *y*.

The final prompt asks whether you want to delete the records in the driver file if a match is found. To ensure that transactions are not counted twice, press *y*. The records are not removed from the file; they are only deactivated.

Using a Predefined Transaction (Transactions Predefined)

After you have defined a transaction, you can use the definition with the Transactions Predefined command. Before you execute the command, however, be sure that you have displayed both files in windows and that the driven file is ordered by the key field so that the key field can be used as the link in the transaction. Either window can be the current window.

When you select Transactions Predefined, you are prompted to enter a transaction definition file name. A pop-up menu is displayed, showing the names of the files in the current subdirectory (see fig. 7.20). You can enter the name of a file in a different directory if you supply the file path.

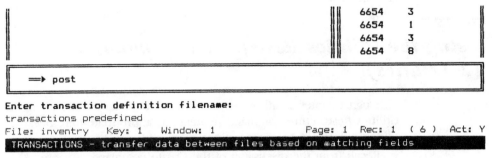

```
                                                    6654    3
                                                    6654    1
                                                    6654    3
                                                    6654    8

     ➡ post

Enter transaction definition filename:
transactions predefined
File: inventry    Key: 1    Window: 1              Page: 1  Rec: 1  ( 6 )  Act: Y
TRANSACTIONS - transfer data between files based on matching fields
```

Fig. 7.20. *Entering the Transaction definition file name.*

If you want an audit trail, select Audit from the next option list. An audit report prints one record from the driver file per line, showing the record number, the linking field, and the record number in the driven file. If no match is found for a record in the driver file, this fact is indicated on the report. You can send the report directly to the printer or to a file. An example is shown in figure 7.21.

If you do not select an audit, execution of the command begins immediately. The status of the work in progress is displayed on the status line, but that information is not retained at the completion of the procedure.

```
Transaction: post       Date 11-12-85  Source: sales     Destination: inventry
-------------------------------------------------------------------------------

Driver Record: 1        Link field: 8475        Driven Record: 1
Driver Record: 2        Link field: 8475        Driven Record: 1
Driver Record: 3        Link field: 8475        Driven Record: 1
Driver Record: 4        Link field: 8475        Driven Record: 1
Driver Record: 5        Link field: 8374        Driven Record: 2
Driver Record: 6        Link field: 9987        Driven Record: 3
```

Fig. 7.21. *A report printed with Audit Print.*

Removing a Transaction Definition (Transactions Undefine)

If you no longer need a transaction definition file, you may undefine it by the Transactions Undefine command. A pop-up menu displays the names of the files in the current directory. Use the cursor key to indicate the name of the definition to Undefine and press Enter. The command executes immediately, without any double check.

Using the Utilities Restructure Command (2–Utilities)

Although Chapter 12 discusses the Utilities commands, discussing the Utilities Restructure command sequence is appropriate here because of its similarity to the Transactions command.

Recall from the discussion of the Create command (Chapter 3) that when you have to change the format of a file, you select Create Similar to bring up the basic structure of the file so that you can change it. The Create Similar command creates the new file for you, but the data remains in the original file. The Utilities Restructure command is used to move the data from one file to another.

To use the Utilities Restructure command, you need to have both files active; the new file must be in the current window. The Utilities command is found on command list 2 (see fig. 7.22).

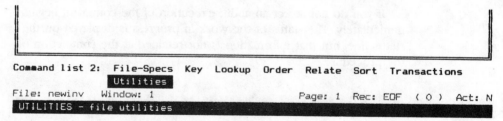

Fig. 7.22. *Selecting Utilities from command list 2.*

Several Utilities options are then displayed (see fig. 7.23). Only the Restructure option is discussed in this chapter. The rest of these options are discussed in Chapter 12.

After you select Restructure, you are prompted for the name of the active file to be used as the source (see fig. 7.24). The

```
Select option:   Alter-Count  Concatenate  Duplicates  Erase  File-Fix
                   New-Password  Purge  Restructure  Totals-Recalc
File: newinv     Window: 1                       Page: 1  Rec: EOF  ( 0 )  Act: N
UTILITIES - file utilities
```

Fig. 7.23.   *Choosing the Utilities Restructure option.*

```
      ⟹ inventry        newinv        sales

Select source filename:
utilities restructure
File: newinv     Window: 1                       Page: 1  Rec: EOF  ( 0 )  Act: N
UTILITIES - file utilities
```

Fig. 7.24.   *Selecting the source filename.*

active file is the "old" file whose structure was copied with the Create . . . Similar command. Move the cursor to the name of that file and press Enter. You cannot type the name of the file.

The restructure definition screen shows the fields from both files and matches like fields from both files (see fig. 7.25). In this example, all fields have been matched between the source and the destination file, with the exception of the new field LEADTIME. Nothing can be done about this new field; you must later fill in the data with the Update, Transactions, or Query commands.

If you have changed a field name, however, the system cannot determine that the contents of the field should be transferred. To indicate this, move the pointer to the source field with the blank name and press F7 to insert a field. A pop-up menu is displayed, showing the names of the fields from the source file. When you select a field, its name is inserted on the definition screen.

The field names are checked at the time of entry, but data types are never checked. Moving the contents of an alphanumeric field to a numeric field will result in a zero value. Moving contents of a numeric field to an alphanumeric field causes the numeric value to be stored as an alphanumeric value; this is one way to change

```
┌─ Restructure Definition ════════════════════════════════════════════════════╗
║   Field              Source field                    Dest. field             ║
║ ══▶    1             ITEM                             ITEM                     ║
║        2             DESCRIPTION                      DESCRIPTION              ║
║        3             QUANTITY                         QUANTITY                 ║
║        4             COST                             COST                     ║
║        5             SELL                             SELL                     ║
║        6             MFGR                             MFGR                     ║
║        7             ────────────────                LEADTIME                 ║
╟──────────────────────────────────────────────────────────────────────────────╢
║                                                                              ║
║                                                                              ║
║                                                                              ║
║                                                                              ║
║                                                                              ║
║                                                                              ║
╚══════════════════════════════════════════════════════════════════════════════╝

F1  Help           F7 Insert a field        PgUp Prev group   Up arrow    Prev line
F10 Finished       F8 Delete field          PgDn Next group   Down arrow  Next line
Source inventry    Destination newinv
UTILITIES - file utilities
```

Fig. 7.25. *The Restructure Definition screen.*

numeric data to alphanumeric data. If the source file is ordered by an
index, only those records available are entered in the new file.

Conclusion

The Smart Data Base Manager uses the key-field method to share data
among files. The Relate command is used to combine data from two
files; you can then combine the resulting file with a third, if
necessary.

The Transactions command is used to post data from a
transactions file to a master file by adding, subtracting, or overlaying
values. Batch-oriented applications can be developed with this
command. An audit trail can be printed or stored in a disk file.

You use the Utilities Restructure command when you have
created one file that is similar to another and you want to transfer
data to the new file. This command is easy to use because the Smart
Data Base Manager recognizes matching names.

Chapter 8

Entering and Deleting Data

No matter how well you have designed your data base and its screens, it isn't going to be useful if it doesn't contain data. This chapter discusses entering data from the keyboard. You will learn how to enter data into a file and how later to update the data. You'll also learn about the Lookup command, which is used to extract data from another file when you are entering or updating data and to perform validity checks so that you can be sure your data is correct. This chapter also introduces the Delete command and the Utilities Purge command sequence; both are used to remove records from the data base.

Entering Data (1–Enter, Alt-E)

The Enter command is found on command list 1. The quick key is Alt-E (see fig. 8.1).

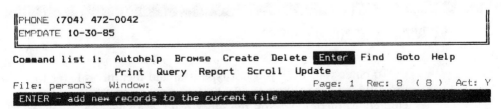

```
PHONE (704) 472-0042
EMPDATE 10-30-85

Command list 1:  Autohelp  Browse  Create  Delete  Enter  Find  Goto  Help
                 Print  Query  Report  Scroll  Update
File: person3   Window: 1                    Page: 1  Rec: 8  ( 8 )  Act: Y
 ENTER - add new records to the current file
```

Fig. 8.1. *Selecting the Enter command.*

When you select the Enter command, you immediately see an input representation of the screen that is in the current window. If the screen is a standard screen, it is used as the Enter template. Alternatively, a custom screen loaded in the current window is used as the template.

Figure 8.2 shows the standard screen template for the personnel file, and figure 8.3 shows a new-employee data-entry screen. Notice that the text in both screens—the field names in the standard screen and the explanatory labels in the custom screen—remains as it was originally designed. The difference is that the data-entry screens have no data. Underscores show the placement of data in alphanumeric and numeric fields; some special field types, such as SSN, Date, and Phone, are shown filled with zeros. The cursor appears as a flashing solid block, highlighting the first field to be filled according to the order of field entry for the screen. More about that later.

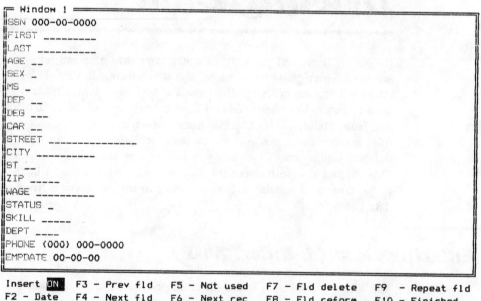

Fig. 8.2. *A template for a standard screen.*

To enter your data, you just type it in and then press Enter to move the cursor to the next field. Alphanumeric text is accepted as entered. Numeric fields, on the other hand, can take only numbers. If you enter in a numeric field a character that is not a number, the

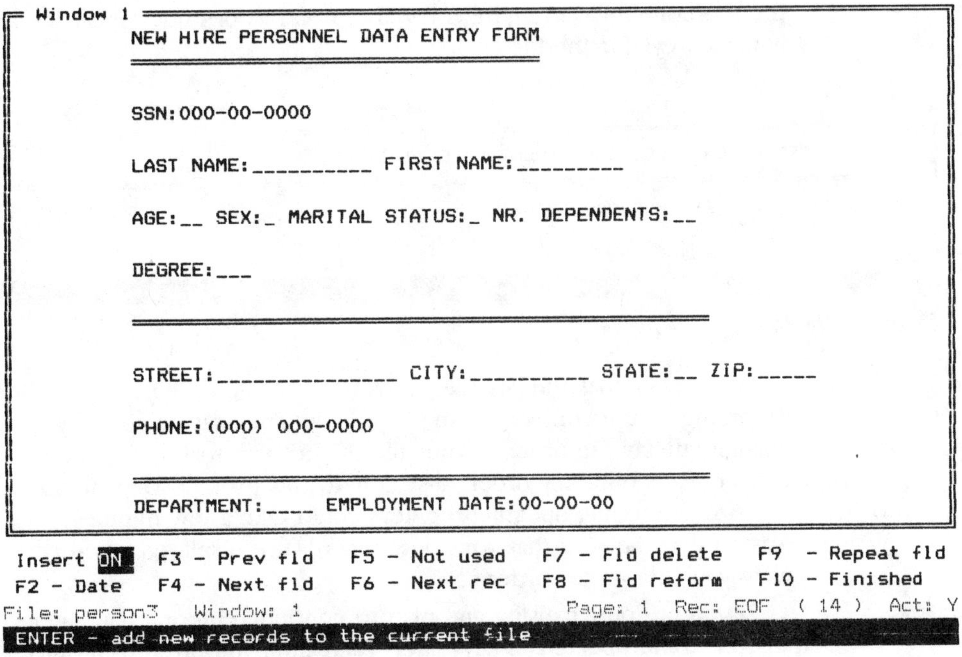

```
╔═ Window 1 ═══════════════════════════════════════════════════╗
║    ┌────────────────────────────────────────────────────────┐ ║
║    │  NEW HIRE PERSONNEL DATA ENTRY FORM                     │ ║
║    │  ══════════════════════════════════                     │ ║
║    │                                                         │ ║
║    │  SSN:000-00-0000                                        │ ║
║    │                                                         │ ║
║    │  LAST NAME:_____ FIRST NAME:_____              │ ║
║    │                                                         │ ║
║    │  AGE:__ SEX:_ MARITAL STATUS:_ NR. DEPENDENTS:__        │ ║
║    │                                                         │ ║
║    │  DEGREE:___                                             │ ║
║    │                                                         │ ║
║    │  ══════════════════════════════════════════════        │ ║
║    │                                                         │ ║
║    │  STREET:_____ CITY:_____ STATE:__ ZIP:_____ │
║    │                                                         │ ║
║    │  PHONE:(000) 000-0000                                   │ ║
║    │                                                         │ ║
║    │  ══════════════════════════════════════════════        │ ║
║    │                                                         │ ║
║    │  DEPARTMENT:____ EMPLOYMENT DATE:00-00-00               │ ║
║    └────────────────────────────────────────────────────────┘ ║
╚══════════════════════════════════════════════════════════════╝
Insert ON   F3 - Prev fld   F5 - Not used    F7 - Fld delete   F9  - Repeat fld
F2 - Date   F4 - Next fld   F6 - Next rec    F8 - Fld reform   F10 - Finished
File: person3   Window: 1                    Page: 1  Rec: EOF  ( 14 )  Act: Y
ENTER - add new records to the current file
```

Fig. 8.3. *A template for a custom screen.*

computer beeps at you. Similarly, only numbers can be entered in the SSN and Phone fields. Dates are checked for validity; the system does not let you enter an invalid date. In fields that have special formatting features, such as SSN, Date, and Phone, the cursor automatically skips over the formatting characters; all you do is enter the numbers.

To speed data entry, answer *yes* at the prompt

Automatic return on full field:

on the Parameters command list. Enabling this option causes the cursor to proceed to the next field after you have entered all the characters in a field. When you have filled the last field on your screen, the program automatically displays the next screen if you have enabled this option. Similarly, if your screen is longer than one page, the program automatically proceeds to the next page.

You don't have to fill the screen completely if you do not need to or if some fields are designated as not mandatory. To go to the next record, press F6. If you do fill the screen, Smart displays another blank entry template.

When you are through entering data, press F10 to return to the command level. If you have defined keys for your file, you will see the prompt shown in figure 8.4. (The prompt does not appear if you have no keys for the file.)

```
DEPARTMENT:ACCT EMPLOYMENT DATE:11-16-85

Do you wish to update keys now (y/n)


File: person3   Window: 1                      Page: 1  Rec: EOF  ( 14 )  Act: Y
ENTER - add new records to the current file
```

Fig. 8.4. *The Update Keys prompt.*

Remember that the key files keep track of each record in your file according to the contents of the key fields. This feature allows you to change quickly the order of your file. If you plan to use a procedure that depends on a key order, answer *y* to this prompt. Depending on the size of the file, updating the keys could take a few minutes. Answer *y* to be sure that your new records are displayed when you view your file in key order.

If you are only pausing and plan to continue entering data later, answer *n* and update the keys later. Each time you finish using the Enter or Update command, you are prompted for key update information. You can select the Key Update command when you decide to update the keys.

In Enter mode, you can use the cursor and function keys to change your data before you proceed to the next record. The function keys are shown in the control area at the bottom of the screen (refer to figs. 8.2 and 8.3).

Some items in the control area deserve special attention. The insert-mode status is highlighted in the upper left corner of the control area. In figures 8.2 and 8.3, insert mode is on. To turn it off, press the Ins key. This key is probably most important when you are using the Update command. Depending on how you need to update your data, you may find it more convenient to have Insert mode on or off. Even in the Enter command, however, you may go back and correct any entries before you proceed to the next record.

The F2 key can be used to enter the current system date in a date field. (But make sure you set the correct system date and time when you start the computer.) Pressing Alt-F2 enters the current system time in a Time field.

The F8 key can be used to reform the entries in a large, multiline alphabetic field, correcting the spacing and creating a better-looking display or report. Pressing F9 fills the current field with the contents of the same field in the previous record. You will find this key most helpful when there is a great deal of similarity between records. It's a real time-saver.

The Ctrl-L key combination performs a Lookup in manual mode. (The Lookup command is discussed later in this chapter.)

Remember that the Create Screen command can be used to designate certain fields on a custom screen as *read only* or as *mandatory*. Because a read-only field is bypassed when you issue the Enter and Update commands, a read-only field would be of little value with the Enter command. If you make a field mandatory, however, you must enter data in that field. If you neglect to enter data in a field designated as mandatory, you will get an error message. This field type can be used with both the Enter and Update commands.

An error message will also be displayed if you try to enter data that is outside a range you have specified. A field range may be specified when you create a custom screen. For a review of this topic, refer to Chapter 3 on "Creating Files."

Updating Data (1–Update, Alt-I)

After a record has been entered in a file, you can change the contents of that record with the Update command. (The record can be entered either manually with the Enter command or by the system with one of the data loading commands, such as Utilities Concatenate, Read, or Relate.) The Update command is found on command list 1, and the quick key is Alt-I.

```
        DEPARTMENT:ACCT EMPLOYMENT DATE:07-23-45

Command list 1:  Autohelp  Browse  Create  Delete  Enter  Find  Goto  Help
                 Print  Query  Report  Scroll  Update
File: person3    Window: 1                    Page: 1  Rec: 11  ( 11 )  Act: Y
UPDATE - allows editing of the current record
```

Fig. 8.5. *Selecting the Update Command.*

The Update command is very similar to the Enter command, with one exception: the data is already there. You use the same editing keys with Update that you use with Enter. Notice that insert mode is off in figure 8.6; any text you type will overwrite the contents of the field.

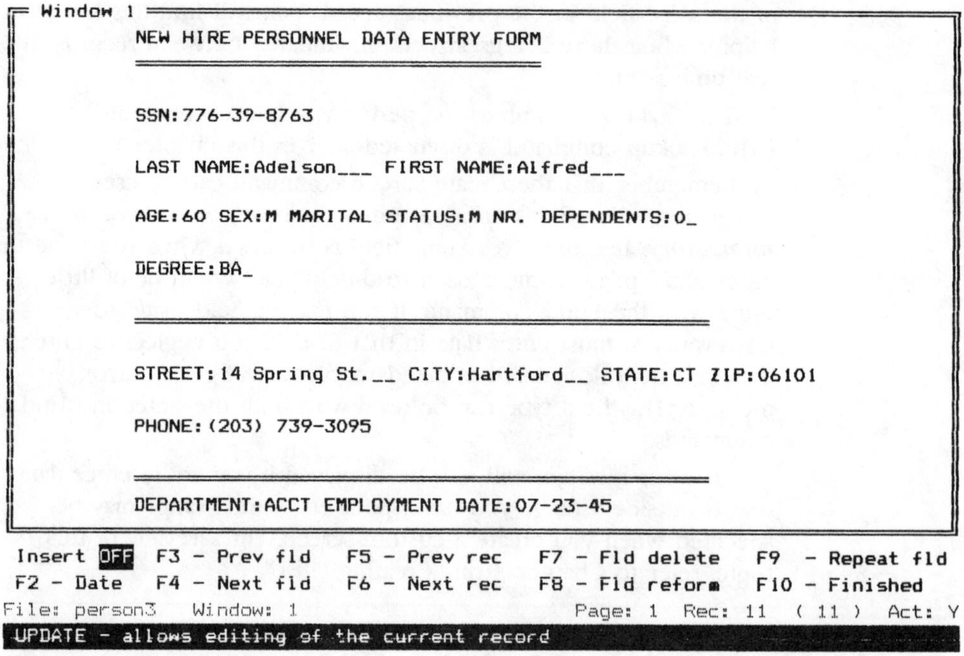

```
┌─ Window 1 ──────────────────────────────────────────────────────┐
│                                                                  │
│       NEW HIRE PERSONNEL DATA ENTRY FORM                         │
│       ══════════════════════════════════                         │
│                                                                  │
│                                                                  │
│       SSN: 776-39-8763                                           │
│                                                                  │
│       LAST NAME: Adelson___ FIRST NAME: Alfred___               │
│                                                                  │
│       AGE: 60 SEX: M MARITAL STATUS: M NR. DEPENDENTS: 0_        │
│                                                                  │
│       DEGREE: BA_                                                │
│                                                                  │
│                                                                  │
│       ══════════════════════════════════                         │
│                                                                  │
│                                                                  │
│       STREET: 14 Spring St.__ CITY: Hartford__ STATE: CT ZIP: 06101 │
│                                                                  │
│       PHONE: (203) 739-3095                                     │
│                                                                  │
│                                                                  │
│       ══════════════════════════════════                         │
│                                                                  │
│       DEPARTMENT: ACCT EMPLOYMENT DATE: 07-23-45                │
└──────────────────────────────────────────────────────────────────┘
Insert OFF  F3 - Prev fld   F5 - Prev rec   F7 - Fld delete   F9  - Repeat fld
F2 - Date   F4 - Next fld   F6 - Next rec   F8 - Fld reform   F10 - Finished
File: person3    Window: 1                    Page: 1 Rec: 11 ( 11 ) Act: Y
UPDATE - allows editing of the current record
```

Fig. 8.6. *The Update screen.*

One additional function key is available with the Update command
that is not available with the Enter command. That is the F5 key,
which is used to go to the previous record; you cannot return to the
previous record with the Enter command. In both commands,
pressing F6 causes the next record to be displayed.

When you use the Enter command, you are always adding records
to the physical end of the file. The Update command, however,
operates in the order you have established for the file. The order can
be based on a key or an index from the Query or Sort command;
records can also be updated in the order in which they were
entered. The order of the file can be changed to make using the
Update command as easy and quick as possible.

Press F10 to terminate the Update command, and the key update
prompt is displayed. If you have changed a key field and plan to
execute a command that will use the keys, you should update the
keys. If you plan to immediately use Update or Enter again, you can
postpone updating, if you like. It's good practice to make sure that
your keys are updated before you quit a session or unload a file. This
prevents you from forgetting to update and later discovering that
your key files do not work correctly. There is no permanent damage

or loss of data if you do forget. Simply execute the Key Update command the next time you load the file.

Extracting and Checking Data with the Lookup Command (2-Lookup)

The Lookup command in the Smart Data Base Manager is used to extract data from another file based on a matching field in both files. The command also is used to validate the accuracy of a field in the current file. For instance, you might want to retrieve the name of the department based on the department code, or just ensure that the department code is valid.

The Lookup command is found on command list 2 (see fig. 8.7). There is no quick key.

```
     DEPARTMENT:MKTG EMPLOYMENT DATE:10-01-85


Command list 2:  File-Specs  Key  Lookup  Order  Relate  Sort  Transactions
                 Utilities
File: person3   Window: 1                    Page: 1  Rec: EOF  ( 13 )  Act: Y
LOOKUP - automatically retrieve data from other files
```

Fig. 8.7. *Selecting the Lookup Command.*

The Lookup command has five options: Define, Index, Load, Remove, and Undefine (see fig. 8.8). Before you can proceed with any other option, you must first Define the lookup you plan to perform.

```
     DEPARTMENT:MKTG EMPLOYMENT DATE:10-01-85


Select option:  Define  Index  Load  Remove  Undefine
lookup
File: person3   Window: 1                    Page: 1  Rec: EOF  ( 13 )  Act: Y
LOOKUP - automatically retrieve data from other files
```

Fig. 8.8. *The Lookup Options.*

In the following example, which uses an abbreviated employee file, we will perform a lookup from that file into the DEPT file, which contains the department names. The lookup procedure will retrieve the department names based on the department code. The current screen must be the destination screen; the source file must be active, but it does not have to be displayed in a window until the lookup is actually performed. The screens are shown in figure 8.9.

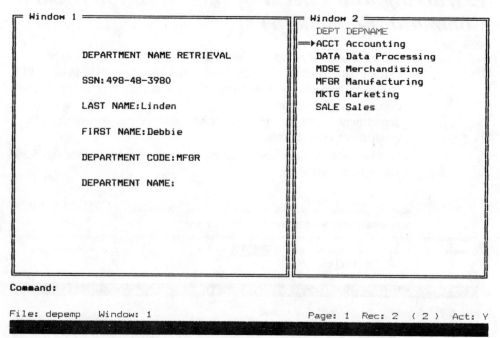

```
┌─ Window 1 ═══════════════════════╗┌═ Window 2 ══════════════════════
│                                  ║│    DEPT  DEPNAME
│                                  ║│══▶ACCT  Accounting
│   DEPARTMENT NAME RETRIEVAL      ║│    DATA  Data Processing
│                                  ║│    MDSE  Merchandising
│   SSN: 498-48-3980               ║│    MFGR  Manufacturing
│                                  ║│    MKTG  Marketing
│   LAST NAME: Linden              ║│    SALE  Sales
│                                  ║│
│   FIRST NAME: Debbie             ║│
│                                  ║│
│   DEPARTMENT CODE: MFGR          ║│
│                                  ║│
│   DEPARTMENT NAME:               ║│
│                                  ║│
│                                  ║│
└──────────────────────────────────╝└─────────────────────────────────

Command:

File: depemp    Window: 1                    Page: 1  Rec: 2  ( 2 )  Act: Y
```

Fig. 8.9. *An example of the Lookup command.*

Creating a Lookup Definition (Lookup Define)

The first step is to define the Lookup. Provide a name for the definition. If you have already defined other lookups, you can edit an existing definition; or you can create a new one by entering a new name. After you have entered the name, a pop-up menu appears, prompting you for the name of the field in the destination file that will be used as the linking field (see fig. 8.10). Here I have selected the DEPT field by typing its name on the prompt line. You can also select a field by moving the cursor to the appropriate field and pressing Enter.

Now specify the source file, from which the data will be extracted (see fig. 8.11). Move the cursor to the name of the file to be used and press Enter. Then specify the linking field in the

```
┌─Available fields════════════════════════════════════════════════════════╗
│    1 SSN                        2 FIRST                       3 LAST      │
│══▶  17 DEPT                     18 DEPNAME                                │
└──────────────────────────────────────────────────────────────────────────┘
```
```
F6 will select the current field [dept
lookup define deptlook link
File: depemp    Window: 1                              Page: 1  Rec: 2  ( 2 )  Act: Y
 LOOKUP - automatically retrieve data from other files
```

Fig. 8.10. *Specifying the destination file linking field.*

source file in the same way you specified the linking field in the destination file.

```
┌──────────────────────────────────────────────────────────────────────────┐
│        depemp       ══▶ dept              person3                         │
└──────────────────────────────────────────────────────────────────────────┘
```
```
Select source filename:
lookup define deptname link [dept] file
File: depemp    Window: 1                              Page: 1  Rec: 2  ( 2 )  Act: Y
 LOOKUP - automatically retrieve data from other files
```

Fig. 8.11. *Specifying the source file.*

The Lookup definition screen is displayed next, showing all the possible destination fields in the right column and open entries in the source field column. To specify the name of the source field, move the cursor to the position opposite the destination field, and press F7 to display the names of the fields in the source file. Select the appropriate source field from the pop-up menu. The result is shown in figure 8.12.

If more than one field in the destination file is to be filled with data from the source file, you can enter multiple fields by repeating the procedure. When you are finished, press F10 to return to the command level.

Loading a Lookup Definition (Lookup Load)

After you finish using the Lookup Define command, you must select Lookup Load before you can actually use the lookup definition (see fig. 8.13).

The pop-up menu displays the names of lookup definitions. You can either select a name from the list or type the name. If you are retrieving data from several files simultaneously during an Enter or Update operation, several Lookup definitions can be loaded.

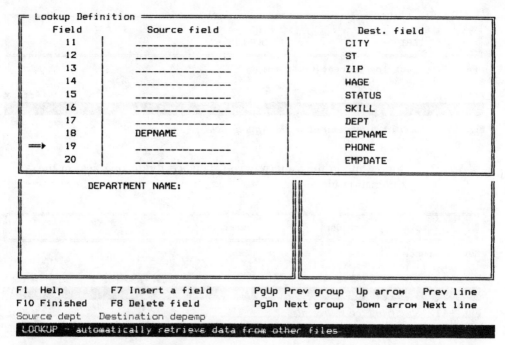

Fig. 8.12. *The Lookup Definition screen.*

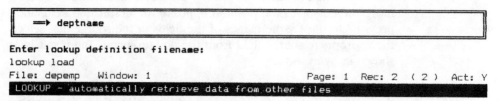

Fig. 8.13. *Using the Lookup Load command.*

Displaying Lookup Definitions (Lookup Index)

In the Update and Enter operations, the number of lookup procedures you have defined is displayed on the status line. With other commands, however, you will see no evidence that the Lookup Load command was successful. You can use Lookup Index to list the active Lookup definitions. Lookup Index displays the name of the Lookup definition, the source file name, the destination file name, and the numbers of the linking fields.

Using Lookups

The source file does not need to be in a window when you use Lookup Define. Before you use the source file, however, it must be displayed in a window and ordered by the key linking field. The destination file must be in the current window. Figure 8.14 shows an update screen that uses Lookup to retrieve the department name from the DEPT file. Notice that Lookups: 1 appears on the command line.

```
┌─ Window 1 ════════════════════════════════════════════════════════╗
║                                                                    ║
║       DEPARTMENT NAME RETRIEVAL                                     ║
║                                                                    ║
║       SSN:498-48-3980                                               ║
║                                                                    ║
║       LAST NAME:Linden____                                          ║
║                                                                    ║
║       FIRST NAME:Debbie___                                          ║
║                                                                    ║
║       DEPARTMENT CODE:MFGR                                          ║
║                                                                    ║
║       DEPARTMENT NAME:Manufacturing__                              ║
║                                                                    ║
║                                                                    ║
║                                                                    ║
║                                                                    ║
║                                                                    ║
╚════════════════════════════════════════════════════════════════════╝
 Insert  OFF   F3 - Prev fld   F5 - Prev rec   F7 - Fld delete   F9  - Repeat fld
 F2 - Date    F4 - Next fld   F6 - Next rec   F8 - Fld reform   F10 - Finished
 File: depemp Lookups: 1 Mode: AUTO              Page: 1  Rec: 2  ( 2 )  Act: Y
 UPDATE - allows editing of the current record
```

Fig. 8.14. *Using the Lookup command with Update.*

When you use Enter or Update, the status line shows the number of Lookup definitions in effect and indicates whether the Lookup is automatic (AUTO) or manual (MAN). In automatic mode, the system automatically performs the lookup procedure; in manual mode, you must press Ctrl-L to perform the lookup procedure. AUTO is Smart's default mode; you can, however, toggle between the two modes by pressing Ctrl-A.

In either case, when the lookup is performed, the system compares the contents of the linking field to the source file, retrieves the contents of the specified field from the source file, and enters the data in the appropriate field of the destination file. An error message is displayed if the system cannot find a match in the source file. If this happens, return to the link field and correct the entry. Then go on to the next field to bypass the lookup procedure.

You can also use the Lookup command simply to validate an entry without retrieving information. For example, if you just want to make sure that the department codes are correct, but you do not want to copy the department names over, simply skip the step of specifying the fields in the Lookup definition screen. If the department code you have entered does not exist in the source file, you will get an error message.

Removing Lookup Definitions (Lookup Remove)

An extensive data-entry procedure may use several lookup definitions. Because lookup definitions take up memory space, you should remove the definitions when you no longer need them. To erase a lookup definition, select Lookup Remove and use the cursor to highlight the name of the definition that is not needed for the current session. This command removes lookup definitions from memory but leaves them on the disk; to erase them from the disk, use Lookup Undefine.

Erasing Lookup Definitions (Lookup Undefine)

If you want to erase a lookup definition permanently, use the Lookup Undefine command. Unlike Lookup Remove, which just removes the definition for the duration of the session, Lookup Undefine erases the definition from the disk.

Deleting Records

You may no longer carry a particular product, or an employee may have left the company. In such a case, you want to delete from your file the record that no longer applies. By physically purging deleted records, you will not only save disk space, but you may also find that your application runs faster. In the Smart Data Base Manager, deleting a record flags it for deletion but does not physically remove it from the file. The rightmost symbols on the status line indicate the delete status of the current record. *Act: Y* indicates that a record is active; *Act: N* means that a record is not active—in other words, that it has been marked for deletion.

Marking Records for Deletion (1-Delete, Alt-D)

The Delete command is found on command list 1 (see fig. 8.15); the quick key is Alt-D.

```
DEPT SALE
PHONE (303) 797-5939
EMPDATE 10-30-65


Command list 1:  Autohelp  Browse  Create  Delete  Enter  Find  Goto  Help
                 Print  Query  Report  Scroll  Update
File: person    Window: 1                        Page: 1  Rec: 6  ( 6 )  Act: N
 DELETE - deletes or activates the current record (toggle)
```

Fig. 8.15. *Selecting the Delete command.*

The Delete command changes the status of the current record from active to deleted or from deleted to active. Although most Data Base Manager commands ignore a deleted record, some do not. The Report and Transactions commands skip over deleted records, but the Print command prints them. The Order command does not automatically disregard deleted records either, but you can use the Query command to create an Index that excludes deleted records. To find out how to create such an index, refer to Chapter 11.

Removing Marked Records (2-Utilities Purge)

The Delete command only marks a record for deletion, but the Utilities Purge command physically removes deleted records from the file. Before using this command, you must unload the file. Because the file is totally rewritten, you may want to *back up* (make a copy of) your file before beginning this process, just in case anything goes wrong. The fastest way to copy the file is to use the File Copy command on command list 4. Remember to copy both the .DB and .DBS files. The Utilities command is found on command list 2, as shown in figure 8.16.

Although a separate chapter is devoted to the Utilities command, reviewing the use of the Utilities Purge command with the Delete command is appropriate here. When you select the Utilities Purge

```
DEPT ACCT
PHONE (312) 439-8760
EMPDATE 10-01-59
```

Command list 2:   File-Specs Key Lookup Order Relate Sort Transactions
                         Utilities
File: person   Window: 1   Page: 1 Rec: 1 (1) Act: Y
UTILITIES - file utilities

Fig. 8.16. *Selecting the Utilities command.*

```
DEPT ACCT
PHONE (312) 439-8760
EMPDATE 10-01-59
```

Select option: Alter-Count Concatenate Duplicates Erase File-Fix
                 New-Password Purge Restructure Totals-Recalc
File: person   Window: 1   Page: 1 Rec: 1 (1) Act: Y
UTILITIES - file utilities

Fig. 8.17. *Selecting the Utilities Purge command.*

book	inventry	newinv	⇒ person2	sample
depemp	invsave	newsal	person3	states
dept	namelist	person	sales	

Enter filename:
utilities purge
File: person   Window: 1   Page: 1 Rec: 1 (1) Act: Y
UTILITIES - file utilities

Fig. 8.18. *Selecting a file from the Utilities Purge file menu.*

command (see fig. 8.17), a pop-up menu displays the names of files in the current subdirectory of your disk. Even though you cannot purge active files, their names are still displayed in the menu (see fig. 8.18).

If you select an active file, expect to see the following message:

Error - file must be unloaded before doing purge

If the message appears, simply unload the file and execute the command again.

If the file is unloaded, execution of the command continues; the system double-checks you by asking:

Do you have a backup of this file (y/n)

To make a backup of the file, use Smart's File Copy command or the COPY command at the DOS level. Although the system does not require a backup file, having one may make you feel more comfortable. In either case, answer *y* to proceed with the purging of deleted records.

Note that when deleted records are purged, key files are erased from the disk. When you reload the file, you must perform Key Update or Organize to re-create the key files. Any index files that you may have created still exist, however; they are invalid now because all the record numbers have changed. You can safely erase these index files with the File Erase command (remember to specify the extension .IDX).

You can also use the Query command to force records to be active or deleted, depending on the selection criteria. Refer to Chapter 11 for further information on this process.

Conclusion

To enter data "by hand," use the Enter command; to change existing data, use the Update command. Later chapters will cover methods for moving data into a file from other sources, either external files or other modules within the Smart system.

The Lookup command retrieves data from other files for entry into the the current file. Lookup not only saves you a significant amount of time, but also can be used to validate data entry in order to ensure that the data is as accurate as possible.

Deleting records is a two-step process in the Smart Data Base Manager. First, records are marked for deletion with the Delete command (or Replace Delete, in the Query command). Next, and less frequently, you use the Utilities Purge command to physically remove deleted records from your file and to "free up" disk space. Because the Delete command simply marks records for deletion, they can be undeleted, if necessary, before you perform a purge.

Chapter 9

Producing Reports

In most computer applications, you must be able to produce reports from your files. If you are the only one using the system, you may need only screen displays or simple reports. But if other people or other companies need to see data from your system, you will need not only screen displays and elementary reports but also formal reports.

The Smart Data Base Manager can produce both quick reports in a standard format, with few "bells and whistles," and formal reports in a wide variety of formats you design. The Print command is used to produce those simple "quick" reports, which get information on paper rapidly and easily. The Report command starts the formal reporting procedure, in which you can produce reports in many different formats; you can even join two files to produce a combined-file report.

The Report command directs output to the screen, to the printer, or to a file (for transmission to another computer, perhaps). But the Print command directs output only to the screen or to the printer.

Using the Print Command (1–Print, Alt-P)

The Print command is found on command list 1 (see fig. 9.1); the quick key is Alt-P.

```
DEPT ACCT
PHONE (614) 776-3398
EMPDATE 07-01-70
```

Command list 1: Autohelp Browse Create Delete Enter Find Goto Help
                 Print Query Report Scroll Update
File: person3   Window: 1   Page: 1 Rec: 5 (5) Act: Y
PRINT - print the current file, page or record

Fig. 9.1. *Selecting the Print command.*

The Print command is used for quick reporting from a file when
you don't need a fancy format or when your primary goal is to
produce a report quickly and easily. The Print command's three
main options are used for printing several records from a file, the
current page of the current file, or all pages of the current record
(see fig. 9.2).

```
DEPT ACCT
PHONE (614) 776-3398
EMPDATE 07-01-70
```

Select option: File Page Record
print
File: person3   Window: 1   Page: 1 Rec: 5 (5) Act: Y
PRINT - print the current file, page or record

Fig. 9.2. *The Print command options.*

Printing Several Records (Print File)

The most common use of the Print command is to print several
records from a file; select the Print File command sequence for this
purpose (refer to fig. 9.2). If you want the fields listed across the
page with one record per line, select the Report option (see fig.
9.3). (Do not confuse this with the Report command, which is
discussed later in this chapter.)

```
DEPT ACCT
PHONE (614) 776-3398
EMPDATE 07-01-70
```

Select option: List Report
print file
File: person3   Window: 1   Page: 1 Rec: 5 (5) Act: Y
PRINT - print the current file, page or record

Fig. 9.3. *Selecting the Print File Report format.*

A pop-up menu appears, from which you select the names of the fields to be printed. Select the field names in the usual manner: by using the pointer and the F6 key, or by typing the names or numbers of the fields. Enter the fields in the order (left-to-right) in which you want them to appear on the report. Then choose whether the output is to go to the screen or to the printer (see fig. 9.4). The Print command cannot direct output to a disk file; use the Report command if you need that feature.

```
DEPT ACCT
PHONE (614) 776-3398
EMPDATE 07-01-70


Select option: Screen  Printer
print file report [1¦3]
File: person3   Window: 1                    Page: 1  Rec: 5  ( 5 )  Act: Y
PRINT - print the current file, page or record
```

Fig. 9.4. *The Print output options.*

If you direct output to the printer, be sure your paper is positioned so that the print head is at the top of a page; Smart does not issue a form-feed command when printing begins. A form-feed command is issued when printing is finished, and the paper advances until the print head is at the top of the next page.

Field names are used as column headings. The column width is either the field width or the field name, whichever is longer. To print as much as possible on a page, when you create the file try to make field names no longer than the field width, and make the field widths as short as possible. Both the screen and the printer display automatically "wrap around": fields that won't fit on the first line are printed on the next line. The result can be difficult to read. (The printer's line width is governed by the Configure settings on Smart's main menu.)

If output is directed to the screen, you can control the display's scrolling speed by typing a number between 1 and 10 (1 is the slowest and 10, represented by 0, is the fastest). The default scrolling rate is 5. To make the scrolling pause, press any key; press any key again to cause scrolling to resume.

To cancel the screen's scrolling or the printer's printing, press Ctrl-Z. On the screen, the print procedure is canceled immediately. On the printer, you are prompted to:

Enter C to cancel; Enter R to resume (c/r)

This feature lets you pause without having to reprint the whole report if you need to change or adjust the paper.

Figure 9.5 shows the output from the Print File Report . . . Printer command.

```
SSN          FIRST      LAST
--------------------------------------
345-98-7593  Rosanna    Ronaldo
498-48-3980  Debbie     Linden
239-87-8876  Michael    Davis
208-23-0300  Julius     Karenski
887-63-5498  Jeff       Harris
598-44-5922  LeAnne     Markus
```

Fig. 9.5. *Result of the Print File Report . . . Printer command.*

If you have to print many fields or if the fields are long, you may want to use the List option instead of the Report option. The List option prints the fields one below another, as shown in figure 9.6.

```
Records #: 11  Act: Y
LAST: Adelson
FIRST: Alfred
SSN: 776-39-8763
DEPT: ACCT
WAGE: 887.23

Records #: 12  Act: Y
LAST: Aliakbari
FIRST: Ellen
SSN: 345-54-2287
DEPT: MFGR
WAGE: 997.66

Records #: 10  Act: Y
LAST: Bernstein
FIRST: Paula
SSN: 498-34-5998
DEPT: SALE
WAGE: 1004.56
```

Fig. 9.6. *The output from the Print File List . . . Printer command.*

Note that the physical record number and the active flag (Y/N) are printed. All records, even those that have been deleted, are printed in logical order. To eliminate deleted records, use the Query command to create an index, then order your records by that index. The Print command starts printing at the first record in the logical sequence and continues through the last record. At the end of the procedure, whichever record was current before the printing began is still current.

Printing All Pages of the Current Record (Print Record)

If you want to print information from the current record only, use the Print Record command to print all the pages of the current record. Three pages are printed on one sheet of paper, and the system then begins printing on a new sheet. All fields are printed; there is no field selection.

The Print Record List command sequence prints fields in a list format, in which each field appears below the previous one. The fields are displayed in the order in which they appear on the screen, but the output does not reflect the screen format (see fig. 9.7). Even if the current record is deleted, it appears on the printout. Remember that you can tell the active status of a record by the *Act:Y* or *Act:N* indicator on the command line. (For a complete discussion of deleted records, refer to Chapter 8.)

```
Records #: 4  Act: N
SSN: 208-23-0300
FIRST: Julius
LAST: Karenski
AGE: 41
SEX: M
MS: D
DEP: 0
DEG: PhD
CAR: 1
STREET: 18 Olive St.
CITY: Louisville
ST: KY
ZIP: 40201
WAGE: 1020.33
STATUS: 2
SKILL: JKS
DEPT: MKTG
PHONE: (606) 779-5088
EMPDATE: 08-20-71
PCT: 1.6
```

Fig. 9.7. *Result of the Print Record List command.*

The Print Record Screen command sequence provides a printout that reflects the screen format. Two options are available: *All* and *Data*. Selecting All causes everything shown on the screen to be printed: the text, any boxes or lines, and the data itself. (The printout, as shown in figure 9.8, is an approximation of the graphics displayed on your screen.) Choosing Data causes Smart to print only the data, without any boxes, lines, or labels.

```
PERSONNEL DATABASE - ADDRESS CHANGES
----------------------------------------


Last Name:Ronaldo      First Name:Rosanna
Social Security Number:345-98-7593

+-------------------------------------------+
| Street Address:546 Olive Hill             |
| City:Oak Park     State:IL  Zip Code:60301 |
|                                           |
| Telephone Number:(312) 439-8760           |
|                                           |
+-------------------------------------------+
```

Fig. 9.8. *Result of Print Record Screen All command.*

Printing the Current Page of the Current Screen (Print Page)

The Print Page command works like the Print Record command, except that it prints only the current page of the current screen instead of all pages. The Print Page All option prints text, graphics, and data; Print Page Data prints data only.

Using the Report Command (1-Report)

As you have seen, the Print command is quick and easy to use. Its disadvantages are that it lacks flexibility in formatting, is capable of handling only one file, and includes deleted records in the printout. The Report command overcomes these drawbacks. This command can be used to produce formal, complex reports; however, report definitions can be much more complex than those for the Print command. The Report command is found on command list 1 (see fig. 9.9).

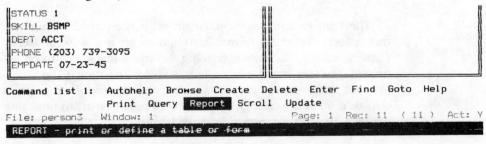

Fig. 9.9. *Selecting the Report command.*

With the Report command, you can produce two basic types of reports. The first type, called a *table*, is similar to the output produced by the Print File Report command: each detail line of the report represents a record from the file, and data fields are aligned in columns. The advantages of using the Report Table command sequence are that you can supply your own column headers (other than the column names), specify the column spacing, supply report headers and footers, and control column breaks. You can include calculations in the report, as well. Wide fields can be wrapped around within a shorter specified width.

The other basic type of report is called a *form*; in this type, a record's individual fields can be positioned at specified locations on the page, as if you were printing on a preprinted form. Each record of the data base is represented by one *page* of the report, rather than by one detail line.

Using the Report command, you can also define reports that combine elements of these two report types; you can split the page so that the top portion is a form, and the bottom portion a table, or vice versa. Data in the two portions of a combination report can come from *two different files* that are linked by a common field. To print an invoice, for instance, you might make the top portion of the report a form, with data coming from the customer file, and print the invoice line-items in table format at the bottom of the report, with data coming from the sales file. The linking key would be the customer number.

Figure 9.10 shows the report that is used as an example in this chapter. Although this report is not complicated, it serves to illustrate the important features of the Report command. The data in the top portion of the report comes from the DEPT file, which contains the department codes and names; the data in the bottom portion comes from the PERSON3 file, which contains all the detail information about your employees. The key field, which ties the two files together, is the DEPT code.

As you can see, one page is devoted to each department. The name of the department is printed in the heading of the report, along with some titles and a date. The bottom portion of the report prints selected data fields for each employee in the department. Customized column headings are provided, as well as a total of wages by department.

The first set of options for the Report command includes *Define* a new report (or edit an existing definition), *Print* the report (based

```
                    ABERDEEN MANUFACTURING CORPORATION
                            Department Listing

                        Department:   Accounting
                              11-18-85


         LAST            FIRST                   EMPLOYMENT
  DEPT   NAME            NAME      SSN           DATE        WEEKLY PAY  HOME PHONE
  ------------------------------------------------------------------------------
  ACCT   Adelson         Alfred    776-39-8763   07-23-45       887.23  (203) 739-3095

         Harris          Jeff      887-63-5498   07-01-70       576.22  (614) 776-3398

         Ronaldo         Rosanna   345-98-7593   10-01-59       834.52  (312) 439-8760

                                                              ----------
                                                  Total         2297.97
                                                              ==========
```

Fig. 9.10.   *A combination report.*

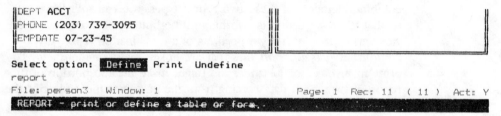

Fig. 9.11.   *The Report Define, Print, and Undefine options.*

on a predefined definition), or *Undefine* a report (see fig. 9.11).
Reports must be defined before they can be printed.

Select Report Define to begin definition of a report. If you are
defining a new report, type its name at the prompt. If you are
revising a report, use the cursor keys to move the arrow to the
report name, and then press Enter. You can define a new report or
revise an existing one only for a file that is currently loaded. If you
are defining a combination report, make sure that both files and their
appropriate screens have been loaded.

Defining the Report Page

As shown in figure 9.12, a prompt in the control area reminds
you to select the Page option first.

The page-definition screen has three main sections: the first (see
fig. 9.13) defines the overall layout of the page; the others pertain to

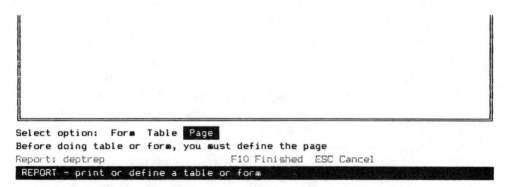

Select option: For**m** Table `Page`
Before doing table or for**m**, you **m**ust define the page
Report: deptrep   F10 Finished ESC Cancel
`REPORT - print or define a table or form`

Fig. 9.12. *The Report Define Form, Table, and Page options.*

Page Definition
➡ Page length (in lines): `66`
   Page **w**idth (in characters): `80`
   Page nu**m**bers: Left Right Center Left-right Right-left `No-numbers`
   Start page nu**m**ber: `1`

   Lines per inch: `6` 8
   Characters per inch: `10` 12 17

Fig. 9.13. *The report page layout options.*

table and form specifications. You can specify a table, a form, or both on one page of the report.

The page-definition screen defines the characteristics of a page. Note that all options are set initially to certain common values. These values, called *defaults*, are used unless you supply new values. The "normal" page length (66 lines) and width (80 characters) have been set. You can change the numbers by typing over them: move the cursor arrow to the appropriate line, and retype the value. By pressing the space bar or the cursor keys, you can move the highlighted block for the page number to an appropriate location.

Most of the options are self-explanatory. The *Start page number* value, however, may be misleading. That value indicates the number that will be placed on the first printed page. By entering a *3*, for example, you do not bypass the text that would ordinarily be printed on the first two pages; the page number will appear as *3* on the first page. Page numbers are printed at the bottom of the page. The Left-right and Right-left options are useful if you are printing a report that will be bound in book format.

Specifying Form and Table Layout

In this sample report, I am defining both a form and a table. Figure 9.14 shows my definitions for the form; figure 9.15 shows definitions for the table. The cursor keys are used to move the highlighted block to indicate whether a form is on the page.

To make changes or entries on this screen, use the ↑ and ↓ to move the cursor to a new line. If the entry on the line is a value, type the value and press Enter, which keeps the cursor on the current line, or ↓, which completes the entry and advances the cursor to the next line. If the line calls for selecting from a menu choice, use →, ←, or the space bar to move the highlighted block.

Next, you define which portion of the full page will be devoted to the form or table. The default layouts place the upper left corner of the "printable" space at line 1, column 1, and the lower right corner at line 63, column 80 (refer to fig. 9.14). In this sample report, I have allocated the first 5 lines to the form, and indicated (refer to fig. 9.15) that I want to start the table portion in line 7 and let it continue through line 63.

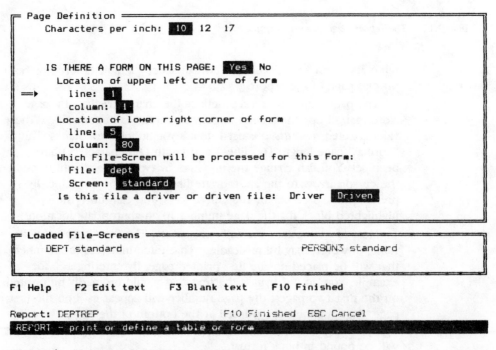

Fig. 9.14. *The report form layout specifications.*

```
┌─ Page Definition ═══════════════════════════════════════════════════┐
│                                                                      │
│     IS THERE A TABLE ON THIS PAGE: ▓Yes▓ No                          │
│        Location of upper left corner of table                        │
│  ══▶    line: ▓7▓                                                     │
│         column: ▓1▓                                                   │
│        Location of lower right corner of table                       │
│           line: ▓63▓                                                  │
│           column: ▓80▓                                               │
│        Which File-Screen will be processed for this Table:           │
│           File: ▓person3▓                                            │
│           Screen: ▓standard▓                                         │
│        Is this file a driver or driven file: ▓Driver▓ Driven         │
│        Double space body of table:  Yes ▓No▓                         │
│        On combination reports:                                       │
│           Start table overflow at top of page: ▓Yes▓ No              │
│                                                                      │
└──────────────────────────────────────────────────────────────────────┘
┌─ Loaded File-Screens ═══════════════════════════════════════════════┐
│     DEPT standard                          PERSON3 standard          │
│                                                                      │
└──────────────────────────────────────────────────────────────────────┘

F1 Help    F2 Edit text    F3 Blank text    F10 Finished

Report: DEPTREP                      F10 Finished  ESC Cancel
REPORT -- print or define a table or form
```

Fig. 9.15. *The table layout specifications.*

You must specify both a file and a screen to be used as a source for your report. Note that my report uses two different files; the form data comes from the DEPT file, whereas the table data comes from the PERSON3 file. Although I have specified standard screens, you can specify a custom screen. Because specification of the screen's name is case-sensitive, be sure to type the name of the screen exactly as it appears in the screen selection menus.

It is easy to choose which file will be the *driver* and which the *driven* if there is only one file in the report: that file must be the *driver*. By designating a driver file, you ensure that, for every record in the file, one line (for a table) or one page (for a form) appears on the report. In this example, I have designated the PERSON3 file as the driver (see fig. 9.15) to ensure that every employee is listed in the report. If I wanted to ensure that every department were listed in the report, I would make the DEPT file the driver.

Note that two additional questions appear at the bottom of figure 9.15. If you want the table portion of the report to be double-spaced, indicate double-spacing by moving the highlighted block.

The option about overflow applies only to combination reports. If your table information contains more records than will fit the physical page length, do you want to start the next page immediately at the top of the next paper, or do you want to skip down a number of lines to compensate for the form? Note that this option does not let you repeat the form data on the overflow pages.

When you have finished defining the page, press F10 to save your page-specification options.

Defining a Form

If your report includes a form, select Form from the list of options shown in figure 9.12; the form-definition screen is then displayed (see fig. 9.16).

```
┌─ Form Definition ═══════════════════════════════════════════════
│ ABERDEEN MANUFACTURING CORPORATION
│ Department Listing
│
│                         Department:   [depname]
│                                       today
│
│
│
│
│
│
│
│
│
└─────────────────────────────────────────────────────────────────
┌─ Options ═══════════════════════════════════════════════════════
│
│
│
│
│
│
│
└─────────────────────────────────────────────────────────────────
Select option:  Calculated  Field  Label  Page-Number  Text
                Duplicate  Edit  Move  Remove
Report: deptrep        Line 1    Col 1            F10 Finished   ESC Cancel
 REPORT - print or define a table or form
```

Fig. 9.16. *Defining a form.*

The types of information you can enter on a form are text, fields, labels, and calculations. In the screen shown in figure 9.16, the company name and report title were entered as text fields, as was the word *Department*:. The actual name of the department was entered as a field to be printed at the time the report is run.

When you select a data type, the system prompts you to designate the area in which to insert data. You first position the cursor at the upper left corner of the area, and then select Text, Field, or Calculated. Then you move the cursor to the lower right corner of the area, press Enter, and type the text. Finally, press F10. Several text entries can be entered in the same area, but fields and calculations should each have their own areas. A label definition may contain several fields; labels are covered later in this chapter. The areas may not overlap.

Specifying Information Types

Text information is typed from the keyboard and may be entered in either upper- or lowercase. After entering the text, press F10 to exit; a prompt then asks you to specify how the text will be justified:

    Justify: Left Right Center

The text doesn't shift position on the screen as a result of your selection; instead, the result takes effect when the report is printed. (If you refer to the printout shown in fig. 9.10, you'll see that the first two lines of the definition shown in fig. 9.16 are centered.)

Field information comes directly from the data base and is printed on the form. After you define the area, you select a field from a pop-up menu. You can select justification options just as you do for a text entry.

The area for a field can be defined, either intentionally or accidentally, as smaller than the field itself. You therefore are given the option of specifying display of an error message during printing if the information in the field is larger than the area. Selecting *Yes* at the *Flag on overflow* prompt causes the error message to be printed if the condition exists; otherwise, the printing continues without an error message.

For a numeric field, you can specify the number of decimal places (precision 0 to 8), commas (Yes or No), currency sign (Yes or No), and percentage sign (Yes or No). You can have negative numbers indicated by a leading minus sign, parentheses, or the word *credit*. You can also choose to suppress printing of negative numbers.

If you use the Report command to print checks, you should use the check-protection option to fill the field's empty left portion with asterisks (****250.00, for example).

A calculated field is also defined in an area. You can include any data base fields, constants, and functions in the calculation. The source fields do not have to be numeric; you can also perform any legitimate function on date, time, or alphanumeric data.

Page numbers can be positioned with the Page-Number option. (This is *not* the same option that appears on the page-definition screen in fig. 9.13. Although both options may be specified, you probably would use only one.) You can choose to define a string of text to accompany the page number, as in *Page Number: *. The page number replaces the asterisk when the report is printed. You can choose to justify the page number within the area and to flag the overflow.

The Label option is used primarily for mailing labels. You can specify several fields in one area, with one list of fields per line. Use semicolons between the field names; a maximum of four field names may be specified per line.

To use this option, you define the area with the maximum number of lines and columns needed to contain all your data. Then press F6 to get a pop-up menu listing the fields. You select a field list from this menu and press Enter. The cursor automatically advances to the next line.

There are two main advantages to using the Label option for printing mailing labels. If a particular line contains no data, a blank line is not printed; instead, the remaining lines are moved up, producing a better looking label.

Furthermore, if you have label stock with two or three labels across the page, you can process the corresponding number of records simultaneously. After you define the fields in the label area, finish the process by pressing F10. A pop-up menu displaying label options then appears; an important option is

> Obtain the next record before processing this label : Yes No

For the first label on the left, you should answer *No*; answer *Yes* for subsequent labels to the right. Depending on your printer's characteristics, the label-printing process may be faster if you can handle label stock that is "2 up" or "3 up." (Use the Duplicate command to simplify copying your label-area information.) You define one set of labels across the page; you do not define them all the way down the page. Set your page length (fig. 9.13) and lower right corner of the form (fig. 9.4) to match the height of one label.

Restrictions do apply, however. Fields cannot be formatted individually with the Label option, and you have a maximum of four fields per line within a label area.

Moving, Removing, and Editing Information

Some of the options on the form-definition screen involve the entry of information to be printed; other options help you create and edit these entries. The Move command is used to move information from one location on the form to another. Position the cursor at the appropriate area and select Move from the menu. Then move the cursor to the upper left corner of the new area and press Enter.

The Remove command is used to delete information *and the area* from the form. Position the cursor on the area and select Remove. Note that there is no double-check on this operation; when you execute the command, the area vanishes.

The Edit command is used to change the contents of an information area. If it is a text area, you can insert and delete characters. If it is a field area, you can change the name of the field and the display options. If it is a calculation, you can edit the calculation and change the display options.

Defining a Table in a Report

The third subcommand on the Report menu is Table, which is used to initiate definition of the table portion of a report. Figure 9.17 shows the main menu of the Table subcommand.

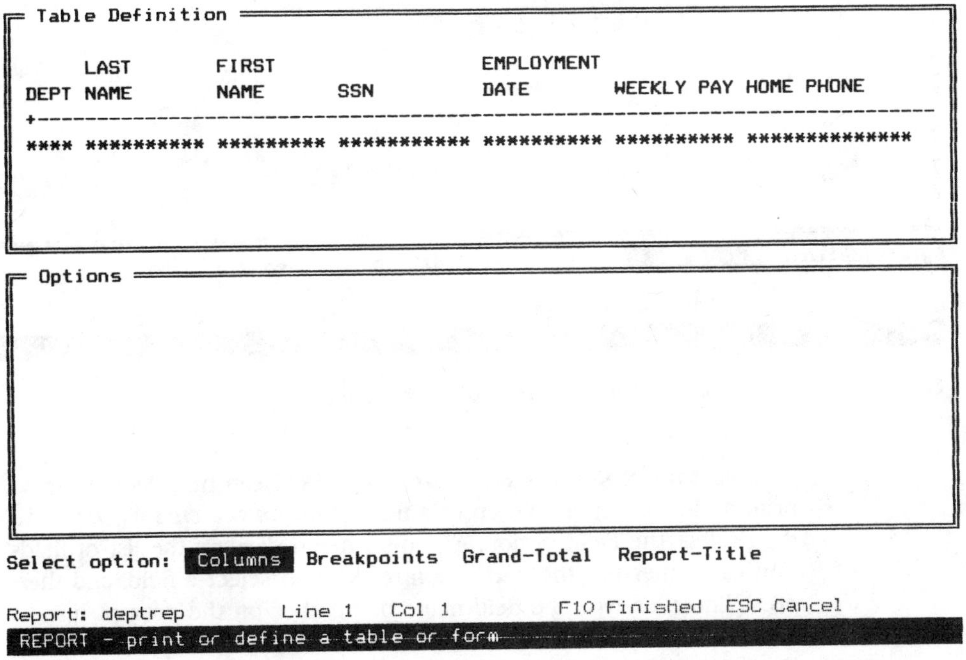

```
┌─ Table Definition ═══════════════════════════════════════════════════════┐
│                                                                            │
│         LAST        FIRST                EMPLOYMENT                         │
│  DEPT  NAME         NAME      SSN        DATE       WEEKLY PAY HOME PHONE   │
│   +-------------------------------------------------------------------------│
│                                                                            │
│  ****  **********  *********  ***********  **********  **********  ************** │
│                                                                            │
│                                                                            │
└────────────────────────────────────────────────────────────────────────────┘
┌─ Options ══════════════════════════════════════════════════════════════════┐
│                                                                            │
│                                                                            │
│                                                                            │
│                                                                            │
│                                                                            │
│                                                                            │
└────────────────────────────────────────────────────────────────────────────┘
Select option: █Columns█ Breakpoints  Grand-Total   Report-Title

Report: deptrep        Line 1   Col 1          F10 Finished  ESC Cancel
REPORT - print or define a table or form
```

Fig. 9.17. *The report table definition screen.*

Initially, the two windows in this table-definition screen are blank; figure 9.17 shows the completed entries for production of a report. As the menu at the bottom of the figure shows, you can specify four major categories of items within a table definition: Columns, Breakpoints, Grand-Total, and Report-Title.

Specifying Table Columns

Like the form specification, the table-columns specification contains information items (Fields, Calculations, or Text) and operations (see fig. 9.18).

```
┌─ Table Definition ═══════════════════════════════════════════════════════════════
│
│        LAST          FIRST
│        NAME          NAME                    EMPLOYMENT
│   DEPT NAME          NAME        SSN         DATE        WEEKLY PAY HOME PHONE
│   +----------------------------------------------------------------------------
│
│   **** *********** ********** *********** ********** ********** ***************
│
│
└────────────────────────────────────────────────────────────────────────────────

┌─ Options ════════════════════════════════════════════════════════════════════════
│
│
│
│
│
│
│
│
│
└────────────────────────────────────────────────────────────────────────────────
Select option: ▐Calculated▌ Field  Text  Edit  Move  Remove

Report: deptrep          Line 1   Col 1            F10 Finished   ESC Cancel
 REPORT -·print or define a table or form
```

Fig. 9.18. *Selecting options from the table columns menu.*

Selecting Fields for a Report. Any field can be selected for printing in the report. To enter a field, *position the cursor first* and then select the Field option. A pop-up menu displays the list of fields. You can either use the cursor-control keys to select a field, and then press Enter, or type the field name or number on the prompt line. After you select a field, a secondary menu displays the options for the field display (see fig. 9.19).

```
 ┌─ Table Definition ═══════════════════════════════════════════════════════
 │
 │        LAST          FIRST                    EMPLOYMENT
 │   DEPT NAME          NAME         SSN         DATE         WEEKLY PAY
 │   +─────────────────────────────────────────────────────────────────────
 │
 │   **** ********** ********* *********** ********** **********  █
 │
 │
 └──────────────────────────────────────────────────────────────────────────
 ┌─ Field Options ══════════════════════════════════════════════════════════
 │        Column Width  14
 │        Heading Lines
 │           Line 1:
 │   ═►     Line 2:  HOME PHONE
 │        Heading Justification:  Left   Right   Center   None
 │
 │        Precision:  0
 │        Field Justification:  Left   Right   Center
 │        Commas:  Yes  No
 │
 └──────────────────────────────────────────────────────────────────────────
 F1 Help     F2 Edit text     F3 Blank text     F10 Finished
 Field-name: PHONE
 Report: deptrep          Line 1    Col 61          F10 Finished  ESC Cancel
 REPORT - print or define a table or form
```

Fig. 9.19. *The field options menu.*

Compare the many field options listed here to the lack of options for the Print command. With the Report command, you have many options for controlling the appearance of the report. You can specify a column width, for example; the default is either the field size or the field name, whichever is longer. If the name is longer than the field, you can shorten the column width and select heading lines that fit within the new width.

Keeping in mind the column width, you can select heading lines as needed. Two lines of headings can be selected. Options for justifying the headings are Left, Right, Center, and None.

You can specify precision and insertion of commas for a numeric field, as well as currency, percent, and negative-value formats (see fig. 9.20). The actual contents of the field can be justified Left, Right, or Center.

If a column width in the table is set to a value less than the field size, the width of the field contents may possibly exceed the width of the column. In the section on form definition, you saw that you could choose either to issue a warning (flag) or to truncate the field in case of an overflow. In the table definition, however, you choose

```
┌─ Table Definition ═══════════════════════════════════════════════════════════
│
│        LAST        FIRST                    EMPLOYMENT
│  DEPT  NAME        NAME        SSN          DATE        WEEKLY PAY
│  +---------------------------------------------------------------------------
│
│  ****  **********  *********  ***********  **********  ***********  ▌
│
│
│
└─────────────────────────────────────────────────────────────────────────────
```

```
┌─ Field Options ══════════════════════════════════════════════════════════════
│        Heading Justification:  Left  Right  Center  None
│
│ ══▶  Precision:  0
│        Field Justification:  Left  Right  Center
│        Commas:  Yes  No
│        Currency sign:  Yes  No
│        Percent sign:  Yes  No
│        Negative number format:  Minus  Parenthesis  Credit  Reject
│        If text overflows:  Truncate  Wrap
└─────────────────────────────────────────────────────────────────────────────
```

F1 Help   F2 Edit text   F3 Blank text   F10 Finished
Field-name: PHONE
Report: deptrep   Line 1   Col 61   F10 Finished   ESC Cancel
REPORT - print or define a table or form

Fig. 9.20. *Selecting more field options.*

either to truncate or to wrap the field contents. If you choose the Truncate option, the field contents are "chopped off" at the end of the space allocated for the field. If you select the Wrap option, the "field contents are printed on multiple lines within the column, with a maximum of 10 lines of wrap. Wherever possible, the system breaks the lines between words.

Inserting Calculations in a Report. If you choose to insert a calculated data item, the calculation can contain any valid field name, constant, or function. The calculation can be performed on numeric, alphanumeric, date, or time data. The options are the same as for field selection. A calculated-field formula can be up to 255 characters long. Although the system accepts a formula that exceeds the 80-column screen boundary, you will be able to enter the maximum 255 characters if you break lines before they reach the edge of the screen. If you have a series of *if . . . then . . . else* statements, you should place each *else* on a separate line.

Entering Text in a Report. You can enter a maximum of 60 characters of text, or *literals*. Options for justification of a text entry are Left, Right, and Center.

Editing, Moving, and Removing Table Definitions. As in the form definition, you can perform certain operations as you define a table.

If you select Edit from the menu to edit fields, calculated entries, or text, you can change the options, headings, and contents. To move a field, you must *first* position the cursor anywhere within the field and then select the Move option from the menu. Then position the cursor where you want the leftmost character of the field contents to appear, and press Enter. (If a field is already located there, that field and any others to the right automatically will be moved to the right.)

To remove a field, position the cursor on the field and select the Remove option. Be sure that this is what you want to do; there is no double-check with this command.

Defining Breakpoints

After all your columns have been specified, you can define your breakpoints. By defining breakpoint options, you specify the action to be taken when the contents of a field (typically a sort field) in the current record are different from those of the same field in the previous record.

You can specify any or all of five output lines for the breakpoint; the breakpoint line can consist of a blank line, a single underscore, a double underscore, the printing of results, or none of these.

Specifying Breakpoint Options. Refer to the sample report in figure 9.10; note that the processed records of three employees in the accounting department are followed by a single underscore, a total value, a double underscore, and a page break. Compare these results to the specifications shown in figure 9.21 for the breakpoint output lines.

The result on the report, which is labeled *Total,* can be changed by specifying a different kind of result calculation. If you choose a different result calculation, you probably should change the label that will be printed on the result line. (The option for a result is chosen after you finish defining the result of the report; I'll discuss those options when we reach that point.) I have also chosen to skip to a new page after the break so that the report for each department begins on a new page.

Figure 9.22 shows that printing of duplicate field entries is suppressed. This means that the abbreviation of that department is printed only once on each page, since all individuals on one page belong to the same department. (The department code, *ACCT,* is printed to the left of the name of the first employee listed.)

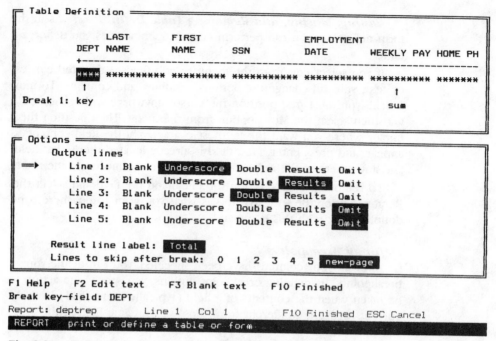

Fig. 9.21. *Defining the report's breakpoint options.*

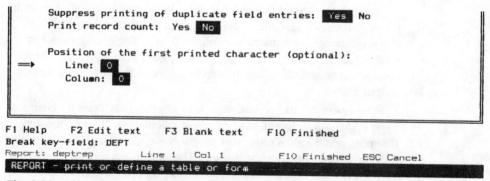

Fig. 9.22. *Continuing to define a report's breakpoint options.*

An optional record count can be printed. You can specify the exact line and column location of any results, in case there are areas specified at the bottom of a page for totals, such as totals on an invoice. (If paper has advanced past the specified location for that data, it is printed in the correct spot on the following sheet.)

Press F10 to save the options. If you have selected the Results option for a breakpoint, move the cursor so that it points at the field which will be used as the source of the result, and then indicate the type of operation by pressing one of the following function keys:

F3 Sum
F4 Average
F5 Minimum
F6 Maximum
F7 Clear the selection

In figure 9.23, the WAGE field (labeled *WEEKLY PAY*) is the source of the calculation. A sum calculation is specified for the sample report. Several numeric fields can be specified in results selection, but any field can be specified only once for each breakpoint. If you need both the minimum and maximum, for instance, you must specify another breakpoint for the same field.

```
┌─ Table Definition ══════════════════════════════════════════════════════════
│
│              LAST        FIRST                  EMPLOYMENT
│         DEPT NAME        NAME       SSN         DATE         WEEKLY PAY HOME PH
│         +--------------------------------------------------------------------
│
│         **** ********** ********* *********** ********** ********** *******
│              ↑
│ Break 2: key
│
└─────────────────────────────────────────────────────────────────────────────

┌─ Options ═══════════════════════════════════════════════════════════════════
│
│
│
│
│
│
│
│
│
└─────────────────────────────────────────────────────────────────────────────
Use cursor and function keys to enter break columns
F3 sum  F4 average  F5 minimum  F6 maximum F7 clear
Report: deptrep        Line 1    Col 50         F10 Finished  ESC Cancel
 REPORT - print or define a table or form
```

Fig. 9.23. *Specifying the source for a calculation.*

Editing Breakpoint Specifications. You can edit the specifications for the breakpoints. After you select the Edit option, use the F3 and F4 keys to indicate the breakpoint field. You *cannot* change the type of result in a breakpoint while editing; you must remove the breakpoint and later add it again.

Specifying Grand Totals

Like the Breakpoints option, the Grand-Total option is used to specify results at the end of a report. The option specifications are the same as those for Breakpoints, except that the text *Grand Total* identifies the results of the calculations. Only numeric fields may be specified. Although you can specify several fields, the only result available is *sum*; the *average*, *minimum*, and *maximum* options are not available.

Defining a Report Title

Up to this point, you have been looking at the contents of a report; you also need a heading and, possibly, a footing to identify and explain your report. A form report probably does not need a heading, because you usually specify all text in the body of the report. But a table report usually needs a heading.

Figure 9.24 shows that you can specify as many as 3 lines of headings to appear at the top of every page, and 3 lines of footings at the bottom. The headings and footings themselves can be left-justified or centered, but both must follow the same pattern.

```
╔═ Title Definition ══════════════════════════════════════════╗
║     Heading                                                  ║
║                                                              ║
║  ⟹   Title Justification:  Left  [Center]                    ║
║        Line 1:  █                                            ║
║        Line 2:  █                                            ║
║        Line 3:  █                                            ║
║        Blank Lines After Heading:  0 [1] 2  3                ║
║                                                              ║
║                                                              ║
║     Footing                                                  ║
║                                                              ║
║        Line 1:  █                                            ║
║        Line 2:  █                                            ║
║        Line 3:  █                                            ║
║        Blank Lines Before Footing:  0 [1] 2  3               ║
║                                                              ║
║                                                              ║
║     Date in heading:  Alpha-date  Numeric-date [No-date]     ║
║     Lines to enclose report:  Yes [No]                       ║
╚══════════════════════════════════════════════════════════════╝
 F1 Help     F2 Edit text     F3 Blank text     F10 Finished

 Report: deptrep          Line 1    Col 1          F10 Finished   ESC Cancel
 REPORT - print or define a table or form
```

Fig. 9.24. *Defining the report's title.*

You can separate the heading or footing from the body of the report with 0 to 3 blank lines. You can specify no date, an alpha date (in the format "May 25, 1969"), or a numeric date (in the format "8/20/71"). The date, which is printed on the last line of the titles, is always right-justified. You can also specify an optional horizontal line of dashes to enclose the report. This line is printed below the heading and above the footing.

No report title is specified for this sample report because it is a combination report; the form portion supplies the heading. If a heading were specified, it would appear after the form and before the table section.

As usual, you press F10 to save the title definitions. If all other definitions are complete, press F10 to return to the command list.

Printing the Report (Report Print)

After a report is defined, you use the Report Print command to print it. In response to this command, a pop-up menu of available report definitions is displayed. After you select which report to print, another menu prompts you to select the output destination (see fig. 9.25).

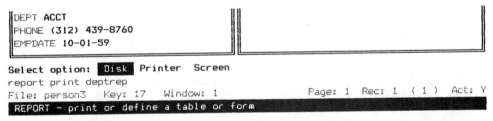

Fig. 9.25. *Selecting a destination for the Report Print command.*

If you choose Printer, your printer automatically begins printing your report; choose Screen to display the report on your monitor. You can press Ctrl-Z to halt the display; pressing *C* then cancels the display, and pressing *R* resumes it. You control the scrolling rate by pressing a number from 1 to 10 (1 is slowest and 10 is fastest; 0 represents 10 for this purpose). Pressing the Esc key cancels the printing, Ctrl-Z gives you the opportunity to cancel or resume, and any other key causes the display to pause.

If you select Disk, you are prompted for an output file name. Provide a standard DOS file name, but do *not* supply an extension. Smart will automatically append the extension .PRT to the file name. If the file already exists, you are asked if you want to continue.

Erasing a Report Definition File (Report Undefine)

To erase a file containing a report definition, use the Report Undefine command. Be careful: the system does not ask you to confirm your decision.

Conclusion

The two primary methods for printing data from the Data Base Manager are the Print command and the Report command. The Print command is used for quick, easy reports that do not require special formats or options. The Report command is used for formal reports with exacting requirements. The Report command options are extensive; by mastering them, you can produce outstanding printed output. Chapter 32, covering Project Processing, discusses other methods of specifying printed output.

Chapter 10

Interfacing Files

Many Data Base Manager applications are entirely self-contained; there is no need to interface with files outside the module. In a self-contained system, you use the Enter command to enter data in files; any output is in the form of reports from the Print or Report commands.

However, if you need to be able to read data from a file and store it in your Data Base Manager file, or if you need to write data to another system, the information in this chapter is important. Generally, the process of reading data from an external DOS file is called *importing;* the process of writing, *exporting.* Data can be imported from three different types of files that may derive from sources other than Smart; data can be exported to five destinations. In addition to the Read (import) command and the Write (export) command, you can use the Send command to send data from the Data Base Manager to one of the other Smart modules.

Using the Send command to transfer data directly to another module is a major part of the significance of an integrated system like Smart. If you purchase three separate software packages to perform data base management, word processing, and spreadsheet processing, passing data from one package to another will take time and work. You will have to "write out" the data, exit the package, run a conversion routine (if one exists), enter the destination package, and finally "read in" the data. The Smart system, however, automatically handles formatting the data and transferring it to the new module; you don't have to worry about it.

Reading (Importing) an External File

The Read command is used to import data from one of three types of external DOS files for storage in the Data Base Manager file in the current window. As records are read from the *external* file, new records are created in the *internal* Data Base Manager file. An external file may come from another program (such as BASIC) or another package (such as dBASE), or it may even be "downloaded" from your company's mainframe computer. The file may even come from the Smart system itself.

Samples of the three types of external files (called *ASCII*, *Fixed*, and *Smart* files) are shown in figures 10.1, 10.2, and 10.3. These three examples contain data that can be read into the SSN, LAST, AGE, WAGE, PHONE, and EMPDATE fields of the PERSON file.

ASCII Files

ASCII files are *comma delimited:* commas separate the fields (see fig. 10.1). Text fields are enclosed by double quotation marks. Each line in an ASCII file corresponds to one record in a data base file. In a more general sense, an ASCII file is one you can display cleanly with the DOS TYPE command. In the Smart conventions, the delimiters are also specified.

```
"345-98-7593","Ronaldo",52,878.75,"(312) 439-8760","10-01-59"
"498-48-3980","Linden",29,1403.79,"(413) 886-3498","06-20-75"
"239-87-8876","Davis",61,734.56,"(318) 997-6621","05-25-69"
"208-23-0300","Karenski",41,1020.33,"(606) 779-5088","08-20-71"
"887-63-5498","Harris",34,629.23,"(614) 776-3398","07-01-70"
"598-44-5922","Markus",48,887.49,"(303) 797-5939","10-30-65"
"876-33-0989","Lester",55,1516.26,"(617) 873-0979","09-05-75"
"987-65-7653","Marzetti",47,901.45,"(704) 472-0042","10-30-85"
"387-59-8374","Steffans",25,654.34,"(207) 878-4880","10-15-81"
"498-34-5998","Bernstein",30,1004.56,"(916) 475-4228","06-15-75"
"776-39-8763","Adelson",60,956.43,"(203) 739-3095","07-23-45"
"345-54-2287","Aliakbari",35,997.66,"(201) 727-9242","08-15-72"
"198-03-3024","Peters",18,1544.00,"(318) 729-5060","10-01-85"
```

Fig. 10.1. *An example of an ASCII file.*

Fixed Files

Each field in a fixed-format file has the same length in every record (see fig. 10.2). If the data does not entirely fill the field, blank spaces "pad out" the remainder of the field. No delimiters separate the fields, and each line matches one record in a data file. Because there are no delimiters, the lengths of the fields in the external file must match the lengths of corresponding fields in the Smart data file. If the field lengths do *not* match, data will be read incorrectly.

```
345-98-7593Ronaldo        52      878.75(312) 439-876010-01-59
498-48-3980Linden         29     1403.79(413) 886-349806-20-75
239-87-8876Davis          61      734.56(318) 997-662105-25-69
208-23-0300Karenski       41     1020.33(606) 779-508808-20-71
887-63-5498Harris         34      629.23(614) 776-339807-01-70
598-44-5922Markus         48      887.49(303) 797-593910-30-65
876-33-0989Lester         55     1516.26(617) 873-097909-05-75
987-65-7653Marzetti       47      901.45(704) 472-004210-30-85
387-59-8374Steffans       25      654.34(207) 878-488010-15-81
498-34-5998Bernstein      30     1004.56(916) 475-422806-15-75
776-39-8763Adelson        60      956.43(203) 739-309507-23-45
345-54-2287Aliakbari      35      997.66(201) 727-924208-15-72
198-03-3024Peters         18     1544.00(318) 729-506010-01-85
```

Fig. 10.2. *A Fixed-format file.*

Smart Files

Used within the Smart system for transferring files from one module to another, Smart files are similar to ASCII files (see fig. 10.3). Text fields are enclosed in double quotation marks, but fields are delimited by spaces (not commas). Note that the field names are contained on the first line of the file.

```
"SSN" "LAST" "AGE" "WAGE" "PHONE" "EMPDATE"
"345-98-7593" "Ronaldo" 52 878.75 "(312) 439-8760" "10-01-59"
"498-48-3980" "Linden" 29 1403.79 "(413) 886-3498" "06-20-75"
"239-87-8876" "Davis" 61 734.56 "(318) 997-6621" "05-25-69"
"208-23-0300" "Karenski" 41 1020.33 "(606) 779-5088" "08-20-71"
"887-63-5498" "Harris" 34 629.23 "(614) 776-3398" "07-01-70"
"598-44-5922" "Markus" 48 887.49 "(303) 797-5939" "10-30-65"
"876-33-0989" "Lester" 55 1516.26 "(617) 873-0979" "09-05-75"
"987-65-7653" "Marzetti" 47 901.45 "(704) 472-0042" "10-30-85"
"387-59-8374" "Steffans" 25 654.34 "(207) 878-4880" "10-15-81"
"498-34-5998" "Bernstein" 30 1004.56 "(916) 475-4228" "06-15-75"
"776-39-8763" "Adelson" 60 956.43 "(203) 739-3095" "07-23-45"
"345-54-2287" "Aliakbari" 35 997.66 "(201) 727-9242" "08-15-72"
"198-03-3024" "Peters" 18 1544.00 "(318) 729-5060" "10-01-85"
```

Fig. 10.3. *A sample Smart file.*

Using the Read Command (4-Read)

The Read command is found on command list 4 (see fig. 10.4); there is no quick key for this command. When you select the command, the first menu prompts you to identify the external file type (see fig. 10.5).

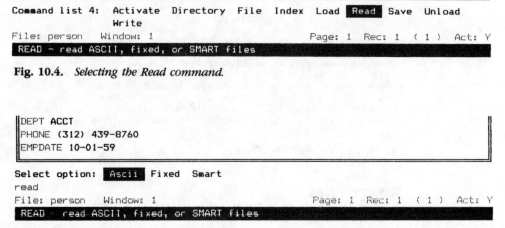

Fig. 10.4. *Selecting the Read command.*

Fig. 10.5. *Selecting which file type to Read.*

After you select a file type, Smart prompts you to enter the name of the external file. Because the Smart system has no convention for extensions of the names of external files, no pop-up menu appears; you must enter the file name and the extension if it has one. If you make a mistake in entering the name, Smart does not recognize the mistake at this point; an error message appears only after you select the fields.

The external file does not have to contain data for all fields in the Smart file; the external file may contain data for only a few fields, or for all of them. A pop-up menu of field names prompts you to select the names of fields that are to be filled from the external file. The field identifiers (numbers or names) refer to the fields in the Smart data file; the order in which you enter the identifiers must match the order in which they appear in the external file. (For more discussion of the use of field names and numbers, see "Identifying Fields" in Chapter 1.)

But what if the external file contains extra data that you do not want read into the Smart file? If the external file is a delimited ASCII or Smart file, you can enter a field number 0, which tells the system to skip that field. With a fixed-format external file, however, you must read all fields; and remember that the field lengths must match those in the Smart file.

After you identify the fields, Smart executes the command. As the file is read, a count of the number of records is displayed on the command line.

If your file contains keys, you should now execute Key Update to make the key files current; the Read command does not update the keys automatically.

Using the Write Command (4-Write)

Just as you can read data *from* an external file, you can write data *to* an external file. The Write command is found on command list 4 (see fig. 10.6); there is no quick key for the command.

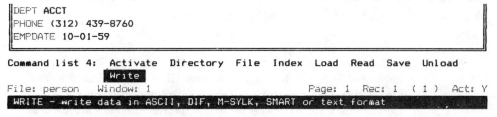

Fig. 10.6. *Selecting the Write command.*

The first option list of the Write command prompts you to specify All or Summarized (see fig. 10.7). Selecting All indicates that each record in the file is to generate one record in the new external DOS file. Selecting Summarized indicates that the values from certain fields will be aggregated in a specified manner. (For example, the total WAGE by DEPT would be a Summarized file. This option is explained later in this chapter.)

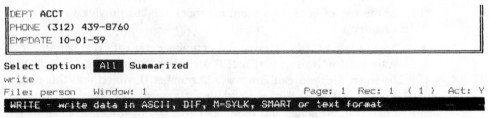

Fig. 10.7. *Choosing a Write option.*

The Write All Option

If you choose Write All, a pop-up menu of fields appears. After selecting fields from this menu, you choose which type of output file is to be generated (see fig. 10.8).

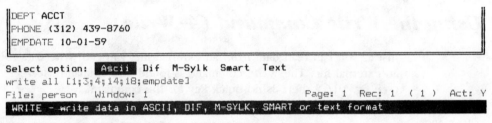

Fig. 10.8. *Choosing a file type for Write command output.*

You know by now that ASCII files are generated in the format illustrated in figure 10.1 and that Smart files are generated in the format shown in figure 10.3. Text files are generated in a fixed format: fields are separated by spaces, and field names are used as headers in the first record of the file.

The DIF and M-SYLK formats are special interface protocols used by certain spreadsheet programs; you may need to write your file in one of these two formats if you are exporting data to a spreadsheet other than the Smart Spreadsheet.

After you select a file format, the program prompts you to enter the name of the output file. Smart does not append an extension; you may supply your own if one is needed.

The Write Summarized Option

Instead of writing a file that contains one record for every record in your data file, you may need to write a summarized file, in which several input records are aggregated for each output record. For example, the sum of the WAGE field for each DEPT field entry would be written to a summarized file; the sum of the WAGE by DEPT for each SEX would also be in a summarized file.

Defining a Summarized Write File

If you choose to write a summarized file, you must select one of three options (see fig. 10.9). The first option to select is Define.

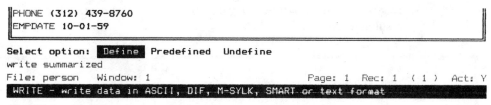

Fig. 10.9. *The Write Summarized options.*

If you are defining a new specification, type a new name in response to the prompt for the definition file name; if you are revising an existing definition, select the name and press Enter. If you are defining a one-dimensional summary (such as the sum of WAGE by DEPT), select Row; if the summary is to be two-dimensional (such as the sum of WAGE by DEPT across SEX), select Column/row (see fig. 10.10).

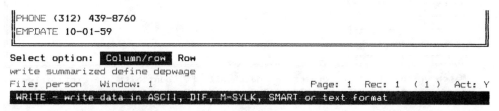

Fig. 10.10. *The Write Summarized dimension options.*

After selecting a dimensions option, you are prompted to select a match option (see fig. 10.11).

```
PHONE (312) 439-8760
EMPDATE 10-01-59

Select option:  Complete  Partial
write summarized define depwage row
File: person   Window: 1                    Page: 1  Rec: 1  ( 1 )  Act: Y
WRITE - write data in ASCII, DIF, M-SYLK, SMART or text format
```

Fig. 10.11. *The Write Summarized match options.*

Selecting the Complete match option indicates that search items must match completely to qualify for summarization. For example, the name of the city *Oak Park* must be spelled out in full to match. If you were to select Partial, then the word *Oak* would constitute a match. (The effect is similar to that of the Partial option in the Find command.)

Defining a Row (Write Summarized Row). The row-definition screen shown in figure 10.12 was completed to summarize wages in each department. Figure 10.13 shows the contents of the resulting text file.

```
┌─ Summary Definition ══════════════════════════════════════════════════
│
│              COL FLD WAGE_____  _____  _____  _____  _____
│    ROW FLD
│  DEPT_____
│
│              PRINT WAGE_____  _____  _____  _____  _____
│
│                            ┌──────────────────────────────────────────────
│  SEARCH      PRINT         │    1
│  UNIQUE____  UNIQUE____    │    1
│  _____  _____    │
│  _____  _____    │
│  _____  _____    │
│  _____  _____    │
│  _____  _____    │
│  _____  _____    │
│  _____  _____    │
│  _____  _____    │
│  _____  _____    │
└────────────────────────────┴──────────────────────────────────────────

F2 Match unique   F3 Match others   F4 Match all   F5 Count hits  F6 List fields
F7 Insert slot    F8 Delete field   F10 Finished     PgUp(left)  Pgdn(right)

WRITE - write data in ASCII, DIF, M-SYLK, SMART or text format
```

Fig. 10.12. *A completed Write Summarized row-definition screen.*

```
DEPT                      WAGE
ACCT                   3365.86
MFGR                   2401.45
SALE                   2626.61
MKTG                   4080.59
DATA                    654.34
```

Fig. 10.13. *A Write Summarized row text file.*

Notice that DEPT was specified as the row field in figure 10.12, indicating that the resulting output file will have one row for each department. The SEARCH field has been designated UNIQUE (by pressing the F2 key); all departments will appear in the output file. If you wanted output only for certain departments, you would enter the department codes on the SEARCH field lines. You also can specify entries on the SEARCH field line if you want the rows to appear in a specific order, or if you want an output line even when there are no detail records in the data file. A maximum of 99 entries can be entered. The PRINT field indicates which label will be printed in the file; this setting can be changed, if needed.

The WAGE field has been designated the COLUMN FIELD (COL FLD), indicating that the first column will be the sum of the wages—the sum for each department, in this example. You can enter several column designations for additional numeric fields, or you can press F5 to specify a count of the number of records within each department.

The only numerical operation available here is summarization; you may not specify averages or maximum or minimum values. If you need to perform other calculations, summarize the original data and send the summary to the Spreadsheet for further calculations. (The Summarize command works with the Send command as well as the Write command.) Only numeric fields should be specified in the body of a Write Summarized definition.

Summarizing Data in Two Directions (Write Summarized Column/Row). In the preceding example, the Row option was used to produce a table summarized in only one dimension (the DEPT field). Although the table could contain several fields, only the WAGE field was used in the example.

By using the Column/row option, you can write a table with data summarized in two directions. Figure 10.14 shows the contents of a file created with the Column/row option. The WAGE field is summarized by DEPT in column 1 and "broken out" in columns 2 and 3 according to the contents of the SEX field. Later in this chapter, you will see how to send this kind of table to the Spreadsheet module.

DEPT	M	F
ACCT	3365.86	0.00
MFGR	0.00	2401.45
SALE	734.56	1892.05
MKTG	2564.33	1516.26
DATA	654.34	0.00

Fig. 10.14. *A text file created with the Write Summary column/row option.*

Figure 10.15 shows the Write Summary definition used to generate the output in figure 10.14. Note that (as in fig. 10.12) the DEPT field is designated as ROW FIELD (ROW FLD), and SEARCH is set to UNIQUE; these specifications cause each row to contain data for an individual department. By designating the SEX field as the COLUMN FIELD (COL FLD), you cause the program to generate one column for each unique value in the SEX field. (Fig. 10.14 shows one column for Male and another for Female.)

```
═ Summary Definition ══════════════════════════════════════════════════

                    COL FLD SEX_____
      ROW FLD
   DEPT_____
                    SEARCH UNIQUE____  _____  _____  _____  _____
                    PRINT  UNIQUE____  _____  _____  _____  _____


   SEARCH        PRINT          ┌──────────────────────────────────────────────
                              1 │
   UNIQUE____  UNIQUE____     1 │
   _____  _____       │
   _____  _____       │
   _____  _____       │
   _____  _____       │        CELL FLD WAGE_____
   _____  _____       │
   _____  _____       │
   _____  _____       │
   _____  _____       │
   _____  _____       │

F2 Match unique  F3 Match others  F4 Match all   F5 Count hits  F6 List fields
F7 Insert slot   F8 Delete field  F10 Finished   PgUp(left)  Pgdn(right)
```

WRITE - write data in ASCII, DIF, M-SYLK, SMART or text format

Fig. 10.15. *A Write Summarized definition screen.*

The WAGE field was designated the CELL FIELD (CELL FLD); this field is the source of the data in the body of the table. With the Column/row option, only one field may make up the body of a table.

Creating an External File (Write Summarized Predefined)

After you create a Write Summarized definition, you can use it to create an external file. First, you select the Write Summarized Predefined command (refer to fig. 10.9). At the prompt, select the name of a definition file.

The system then prompts you to choose a format for the external file that is to be created (refer to fig. 10.8). The final prompt asks for the name of that file. You should answer carefully; Smart will write over any existing file without asking for confirmation.

Erasing Files (Write Summarized Undefine)

Any Summarize definitions you no longer need can be erased from the disk with the Write Summarized Undefine command. The command works *immediately*; no prompt asks whether you really want to erase the file.

Using the Send Command (5-Send, Alt-Z)

As you have learned, the Write command creates an external file in one of five formats; after creating the file, you can continue to work in the Data Base Manager. One of the formats in which you can create a file is the Smart format (refer to fig. 10.3). This format is used for transferring data from one Smart module to another.

If you want to write a file, transfer the data to another module, and read the file just written, the Send command can do the work for you. The Send command is found on command list 5; the quick key is Alt-Z.

Although the Send command options look much like those for Write, there are some differences.

Sending Data to Another Module (Send All)

After selecting Send All, you are prompted for the name of the Smart module to which the data is to be passed (see fig. 10.16). After you select a destination, you must choose the fields from a pop-up menu. If you select either the Communications or the Word Processor option, you see the prompt shown in figure 10.17.

```
WAGE      878.75
STATUS Y
SKILL CKP
DEPT ACCT
PHONE (312) 439-8760
EMPDATE 10-01-59



Select option:  Communications  Spreadsheet  Wordprocessor
send all
File: person   Window: 1                          Page: 1  Rec: 1  ( 1 )  Act: Y
SEND - send information to another application
```

Fig. 10.16. *The destination options for the Send All command.*

```
WAGE       878.75
STATUS Y
SKILL CKP
DEPT ACCT
PHONE (312) 439-8760
EMPDATE 10-01-59
```

Select option: **Data** Text
send all wordprocessor [1;3;4;14;18;19]
File: person   Window: 1   Page: 1 Rec: 1 (1) Act: Y
SEND - send information to another application

Fig. 10.17. *Choosing a Send All command option.*

Select Data if the information being sent will ultimately be used as data—either the source of data in a Word Processor Merge command or as data within the Spreadsheet. If the information is to be included as text in the body of a Word Processor document (either immediately or after transmission), select Text.

The final prompt asks for an optional name of a project file that will be initiated in the new Smart module. This feature is valuable when you develop complex applications that involve several modules. If you do not want to start a project file in the new module, simply press Enter. The data then is sent immediately to the module you have selected, the current module is terminated, all files are closed, and the selected module is automatically initiated. The data you have sent will appear on the screen in the format appropriate to the module.

The Send Summarized Option

The Send Summarized and Write Summarized command options are exactly alike, except that when you choose the Send Summarized Predefined option, you are prompted to indicate the destination module (see fig. 10.16). The Send Define option creates the same type of definition file as does Write Define; in fact, a definition created in one can be used in the other. Send Undefine erases the definition file.

Conclusion

Each module of the Smart system has enough features to stand on its own; if you wanted a complete data manager system and didn't care about word-processing or spreadsheet capabilities, you could select the Smart Data Base Manager. However, the full strength of the integrated Smart system becomes apparent when you use more than one module and share data between them. The Read and Write commands permit you to import and export data in various formats, including the special Smart format. The Send command is used to pass data automatically from one module to another and to transfer control immediately to the destination module. As you will see in the other parts of this book, each module has its own Send command.

Chapter 11

Using the Query Command (1–Query, Alt-Q)

No command in the Smart Data Base Manager is more powerful, yet more misunderstood, than the Query command. You can use Query to create an index that allows you to work with just a portion of your data file. The rules for creating the index may be simple or extremely complex. You can create an index to look only at the records containing "high-end" or "low-end" values (or both) within the file or within a category: "the five top sales representatives in each territory," for example. The Query command can be used to count occurrences: "number of customers by type of trade within each territory." And you can use Query to perform calculations to change values in a field: "each sales representative over quota receives a 5% raise."

This chapter explores the many facets of the Query command and provides examples and suggestions for using it easily and efficiently. The Query command is on command list 1 (see fig. 11.1); the quick key is Alt-Q.

```
PHONE (201) 727-9242
EMPDATE 08-15-72


Command list 1:  Autohelp  Browse  Create  Delete  Enter  Find  Goto  Help
                 Print  Query  Report  Scroll  Update
File: person    Window: 1                 Page: 1  Rec: 12  ( 12 )  Act: Y
QUERY - select records meeting specified criteria
```

Fig. 11.1. *Selecting the Query command.*

The primary function of the Query command is to create an index of the records that meet your search criteria. Suppose, for example, that your current data base task involves only those employees who live in Massachusetts. You first use the Query command to create an index, and then use the Order command to order the file by that index. Remember that this is a two-step process; the Query command by itself will not limit the view of the file.

Search criteria, as the examples in this chapter demonstrate, can be straightforward; they can also be complex, involving multiple fields that contain alphanumeric, numeric, date, and other types of data.

The Query command always operates *within* the existing file view. The file does not return automatically to a sequential order at the time of execution. That aspect of the Query command can be a great advantage when you perform multiple, successive screenings. For instance, if your first combination of Query and Order commands limits records to those of individuals living in Massachusetts, your next Query would begin with that selection. If your next Query limits the view to records of individuals who are married, you end up with only married Massachusetts residents. As you will see, however, you can apply both of these conditions at once instead of using successive queries.

It is also important to note that both the selection of records and the *order* of their presentation are maintained from query to query. Knowing this may save you significant processing time. If you want an alphabetical list of the married Massachusetts residents, for instance, you first order your personnel file by the key field, LASTNAME. Next, you execute the Query command to select the Massachusetts residents, and then use the Order command to limit your file by the index resulting from the query. Finally, you execute Query again to select only married individuals, and (using the Order command) you order the records by this index, as well. The resulting file will still be in alphabetical order by LASTNAME.

Actually, this example involves an extra step. You could eliminate that step by using a compound Query criterion to select STATE and MARITAL STATUS at the same time. In the following examples, I will show how this is done.

As long as you don't change your data file, an index can be used over and over again. For instance, if you have a file of products, you can create indexes of products by category, style, or price. But remember to create new indexes if you add new products.

The second most common use of the Query command does not create an index at all. You can use the Query command to change the contents of your file, using any calculation or function available in the Smart Data Base Manager. You can perform the calculation for all records in the file (or, more exactly, all records in the current order); or, during the query itself, you can specify the conditions under which the calculation is to be performed. But because the results of the calculation go directly into the file, this feature is dangerous as well as powerful. If you are unsure about the outcome of a complex query of this type, you may want to make a backup copy of the file before proceeding.

Finally, the Query command can be used to provide summary statistics about the file, such as the counts of records and high and low values within specified categories.

The Query Main Menu

The Query main menu, shown in figure 11.2, has seven options.

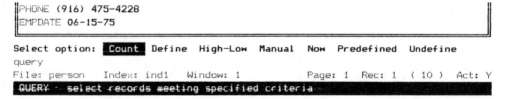

Fig. 11.2. *The main menu of the Query command.*

Defining Query Conditions (Query Define)

Like many other complex commands, the Query command can be used to create a definition and store it in a file for later use with the Predefined option. A stored query definition can also be retrieved and edited. You can provide a definition immediately (see "Creating a Definition and Using It Immediately"), but storing the definition can be invaluable if the criterion is long or complicated, or if the definition is to be used frequently. Even if the criterion changes periodically, you may find it more convenient to store the query definition and then edit it at a later time with the Define option.

When you execute Query Define, a pop-up menu appears, listing any existing definition file names (see fig. 11.3). You can either type a name for a new definition or use the pointer to identify an existing definition for editing.

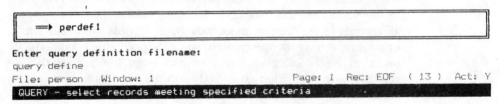

```
   ⟹ perdef1
```
```
Enter query definition filename:
query define
File: person   Window: 1                    Page: 1  Rec: EOF  ( 13 )  Act: Y
QUERY - select records meeting specified criteria
```

Fig. 11.3. *A menu of definition names for Query Define.*

The Query Editor screen is used to enter the search criteria and calculations that are to be stored in the definition file. The cursor-control keys are used in the editor, and you press F10 to save the definition. As you can see in figure 11.4, the editor screen is large enough to accommodate long, complex criteria and calculations. Each line may include a maximum of 255 characters. The editing capabilities available here are available also in the Text-Editor.

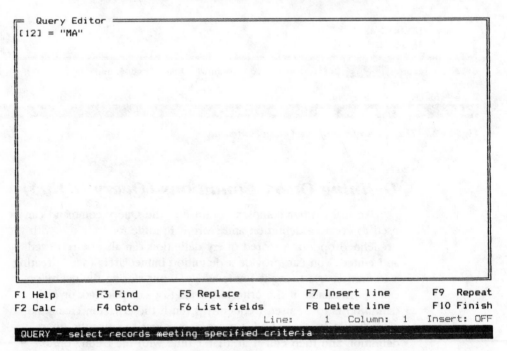

```
╒═ Query Editor ════════════════════════════════════════════════════╕
│[12] = "MA"                                                         │
│                                                                    │
│                                                                    │
│                                                                    │
│                                                                    │
│                                                                    │
│                                                                    │
│                                                                    │
│                                                                    │
│                                                                    │
│                                                                    │
│                                                                    │
│                                                                    │
╘════════════════════════════════════════════════════════════════════╛

F1 Help       F3 Find       F5 Replace       F7 Insert line      F9  Repeat
F2 Calc       F4 Goto       F6 List fields   F8 Delete line      F10 Finish
                                     Line:    1   Column:   1   Insert: OFF
QUERY - select records meeting specified criteria
```

Fig. 11.4. *The Query Editor screen and options.*

In the example in figure 11.4, the search criterion is

[12] = "MA"

This criterion means, "Find records with the string *MA* in field 12 (STATE)." In addition to embedding fixed values (such as *MA*) in a query definition, you can include project variables, such as:

[AGE] > $AGE

Under the control of a project file, a value can be assigned to the variable *$AGE*. That value is substituted for the variable wherever the variable appears in the query definition. Thus you can use one definition repeatedly, under varying conditions, without having to change it.

Functions can also be used within a query definition. The following definition selects records having an employment date (EMPDATE) between 6/20/65 and 6/20/85:

days([EMPDATE]) >= days("6/20/65") and
days([EMPDATE]) <= days("6/20/85")

The *days* function yields the number of days between the specified date and 12/31/1899. (Refer to Chapter 30 for further information.)

Be careful when you finish using the editor and save your work with the F10 key; the system checks only the *syntax* of your definition, not the contents. Thus, you could type a field name in error, but if the construction of the statements is correct, you would not get an error message until you want to use the definition.

Be aware also that you have only saved the definition at this point; you have not used it yet, nor have you changed the order of the file. You do only one step at a time, here.

Conditions in the definition may be as straightforward as a simple search for a matching string such as "MA," or they may be extremely complex. Figures 11.5 and 11.6 provide additional examples of search criteria.

```
 ┌─ Query Editor ═══════════════════════════════════════
╟[12] = "MA" and [MS] = "M"
```

Fig. 11.5. *Search criteria for STATE and MARITAL STATUS.*

```
 ┌─ Query Editor ═══════════════════════════════════════
╟[12] = "MA" or  [MS] = "M"
```

Fig. 11.6. *Search criteria for records of employees who live in Massachusetts or who are married.*

Note the use of the words *and* in figure 11.5 and *or* in figure 11.6. In the first case, *both* conditions must be true; the individuals whose records you want to find must live in Massachusetts *and* must be married. In the second example, you select records of individuals who live in Massachusetts *or* who are married and live in other states. The results are very different.

Figure 11.7 shows a compound selection: you want to find records for individuals who live in Massachusetts *or*, if they live outside the state, are married *and* work in the accounting department. The use of parentheses here is important for proper evaluation of the expression. The employees are selected if they live in "MA" *or* if the expression enclosed in parentheses is true. For the expression in parentheses to be true, the employee must be married *and* must work in the accounting department (*[dept]* = *"ACCT"*).

```
┌─ Query Editor ══════════════════════════════════════════════════
[12] = "MA" or ([MS] = "M" and [dept] = "ACCT")



```

Fig. 11.7. *A compound search criterion.*

A definition may include only a search criterion, as shown in figures 11.5, 11.6, and 11.7, or it may specify the calculation of data in the file. To specify a calculation for records meeting certain conditions, you first enter the criteria, the word *replace*, the name of the destination field, and finally the formula. Figure 11.8 is an example. Notice that all qualified individuals receive a raise in salary equal to the percentage in the PCT field.

```
┌─ Query Editor ══════════════════════════════════════════════════
[12] = "MA" or
([ms] = "M" and [dept] = "ACCT")
replace [wage] = [wage]*(1+[pct]/100)


```

Fig. 11.8. *Using "replace" to specify a calculation.*

You also can specify several destination fields at one time, as shown in figure 11.9. The formula in figure 11.9 not only calculates the new wage, but also replaces the STATUS field with a "Y" for the same records. To make multiple replacements, you enter the word *replace* once, and separate with a comma (,) the replacement expressions.

```
┌─ Query Editor ═══════════════════════════════════
│[12] = "MA" or
│([ms] = "M" and [dept] = "ACCT")
│replace [wage] = [wage]*(1+[pct]/100),
│[status] = "Y"
│
│
```

Fig. 11.9. *Replacing multiple destination fields.*

You must be careful if you *replace* the value in a field that is contained in a key; the system does not automatically update the key for you, nor do you get a message reminding you to do so. If you later order the file by the key, your records will not be in the order you expect. Use the Key Update command to make sure that the keys are maintained. If you don't update the keys, you will find that ordering by a key may yield incorrect results or that you get warning messages as you execute some commands.

You also should be aware that the Query command does not automatically ignore deleted records; you might want to specify this condition (see fig. 11.10) if you plan to use a command that uses deleted records, such as Print.

```
┌─ Query Editor ═══════════════════════════════════
│[wage] > 800 and not (deleted)
│
│
```

Fig. 11.10. *The condition for skipping deleted records.*

The Query command usually proceeds from one record to the next. If your file is not ordered by a key, you have no choice about the sequence. However, if the file *is* ordered by a key field and that field is used in the search, you can use a special *where* clause to perform the Query more efficiently. (This is similar to using the key field in the Find command.)

First, you order your file by the key field. Then you enter the word *where* before the Query search criterion, as shown in figure 11.11. This indicates to Smart that the fast, index-oriented query is to be performed. However, you can use only the "equal" operator (=) with *where;* you cannot use any of the other operators. If necessary, you can combine a *where* specification with a regular search criterion.

```
┌─ Query Editor ═══════════════════════════════════
│where [dept] = "MKTG" REPLACE [WAGE] = [WAGE] * 1.1
│
│
```

Fig. 11.11. *Using the "where" clause.*

Using a Definition in a Search
(Query Predefined)

After defining a query, you execute it by selecting the Query Predefined command sequence. Although the pop-up menu displays the names of query definitions in the current subdirectory, you can type in the name of any other definition, provided that you supply the correct path. The three Query Predefined options are shown in figure 11.12.

```
┌─ Window 1 ═════════════════════════════════════════════════════
║SSN 198-03-3024
║FIRST Howard E.
║LAST Peters
║AGE 18
```

Fig. 11.12. *Selecting a Query Predefined option.*

Specifying Record Conditions and Ordering a File by Index
(Query Predefined Index)

Select Index if you plan to order your file according to the conditions of your query definition. When you select Index, you are prompted for the name of an index file; a pop-up menu displays the names of existing files. You can reuse an index file name (if you are not currently using the index), or you can supply the name for a new index. The numbers of the records that meet your conditions then are placed in the index file. Remember that creating an index does *not* alter the order of the file; use the Order command to change the order.

Calculating with "Replace" or Getting a Record Count
(Query Predefined Neither)

If you are using the *replace* clause simply to perform a calculation, select Neither; you do not need to create an index. The system will proceed through the file, make the necessary changes to your file, and display the count of records affected. No index is created. You should also select Neither if you want only a count of the number of records that meet the search conditions.

Displaying Records That Meet Search Criteria
(Query Predefined Screen)

If you select the Screen option, the system will display on-screen each record that meets the search criteria. You can proceed to the next record by pressing any key, or you can terminate the search by pressing Esc. The Query Predefined Screen command can be used in much the same way as the Find command, except that you can specify more complex conditions with Query. But be careful: the Query command always begins searching with the first record of the file.

Creating a Definition and Using It Immediately (Query Now)

The Query Define command sequence is used to create and store a query definition for later use in Query Predefined. To perform a straightforward query or one that you won't use repeatedly, you can select Query Now, create the definition, and use it immediately. However, you won't be able to save the definition in a file for later use.

Query Now has the same Index, Neither, and Screen options as Query Predefined. After you select an option, enter your query definition and press F10 to begin execution. Although the definition from the Query Now command sequence is not saved permanently, the most recent definition is kept for editing if you need to correct your work. The definition is displayed the next time you execute Query Now.

Selecting Records Manually (Query Manual)

Writing out a query definition to select records you want to include in an index file is sometimes impossible (or not worth the trouble). In such cases, you can use the Query Manual command to select manually the records you want.

Select Query Manual, and then choose an index file from the menu. (The Neither and Screen options are not available here.) As the system "steps through" the records, press *y* or *n* to indicate which records are to be selected. See figure 11.13 for an example of this process.

Identifying Related Records in a Field (Query High-Low)

Up to this point, you have seen the Query command used to select records strictly on the basis of their match to the search conditions. "Does the employee live in Massachusetts?" "Is the employee married?" There has been no statement of relationship between records, however.

```
┌─ Window 1 ════════════════════════════════════════════════════════════╗
║  SSN            FIRST      LAST       AG S M DE DEG CA STREET            CITY     ║
║   345-98-7593 Rosanna    Ronaldo    51 M M 3  BA  2  546 Olive Hill    Oak Park  ║
║   498-48-3980 Debbie     Linden     29 F S 1  MA  2  409 Pleasant St   Amherst   ║
║   239-87-8876 Michael    Davis      61 M M 1  MBA 2  180 Lewis Ave.    Covington ║
║ ═⇒208-23-0300 Julius     Karenski   41 M D 0  PhD 1  18 Olive St.      Louisvill ║
║   887-63-5498 Jeff       Harris     34 M M 4  BA  5  1201 Horton Rd.   Lyndhurst ║
║   598-44-5922 LeAnne     Markus     48 F W 1  MBA 1  14 Crumpet Ave.   Alamosa   ║
║   876-33-0989 Marilyn    Lester     55 F M 4  AB  3  6 Greenville St   Yarmouth  ║
║   987-65-7653 David      Marzetti   47 M D 0      1  20 Grayln Dr.     Wilmingto ║
║   387-59-8374 Charles    Steffans   25 M M 2  BS  2  44 Center Drive   Brunswick ║
║   498-34-5998 Paula      Bernstein  30 F S 3  MA  3  18 Worcester St   Beaumont  ║
║   776-39-8763 Alfred     Adelson    60 M M 0  BA  1  14 Spring St.     Hartford  ║
║   345-54-2287 Ellen      Aliakbari  35 F S 0      1  2171 University   Westfield ║
║   198-03-3024 Howard E.  Peters     18 M S 0      1  10 Dennis Drive   Winnfield ║
║                                                                                  ║
╚══════════════════════════════════════════════════════════════════════════════════╝
```

Select record (y or n)
Record 4 out of 13 - 3 records selected
File: person   Window: 1   Page: 1 Rec: 4 (4) Act: Y
QUERY - select records meeting specified criteria

Fig. 11.13. *Selecting records manually.*

The Query High-Low command sequence is used to select records
based on a record-to-record relationship; it does so by identifying
records that contain either the highest or lowest values for certain
fields. For example, you may want to select records of the five top
sales representatives; you could also select the top five within each
territory. The number does not have to be five; it can be any number
you choose. You can also select the bottom five—if, for instance, you
need to decide who gets the axe—or both the top and bottom.

The High-Low command options are shown in figure 11.14.
Choose the High option to select records with the highest values in a
specified field; choose the Low option to select the records with the
lowest values. By choosing Both, you can select both the highest and
the lowest values.

Select option: Both **High** Low
query high-low
File: person   Window: 1   Page: 1 Rec: 1 (1) Act: Y
QUERY - select records meeting specified criteria

Fig. 11.14. *Query High-Low options.*

Next, as shown in figure 11.15, you indicate whether you want to use the entire file (All), or whether you want the High-Low values broken down by a key field (Category). If you wanted to find the five employees with the highest salaries in the entire company, you would select All. If you wanted to find the five highest salaries in each department, you would select Category. The order of the file does not matter if you select All; however, if you select Category, the file must be ordered by the key field used for the category breakdown. The key order is used to identify the category. Thus, if you want to see the lowest salaries by department, you must order the file by the DEPT field.

```
Select option: All  Category
query high-low high
File: person    Window: 1                    Page: 1  Rec: 1  ( 1 )  Act: Y
QUERY -- select records meeting specified criteria
```

Fig. 11.15. *Selecting the Query High-Low All option.*

The next prompt asks you to indicate how many "members" to keep after the records have been found. If you want to see the top five in each category, type 5. (You must select a number; the value does not default to 1.) Then select from the pop-up menu the field that is to be used for the evaluation. If you are looking for individuals with the top wage, select WAGE. Although you will normally use a numeric or a date field here, you can use any field type.

Select an index file to use, and press Enter. The system then creates the index and displays the number of records you have specified. You can order the file by the index you have just created.

Producing Counts of Records (Query Count)

The Query command can also be used to count records within key-field groupings. Again, you must order your file by a key field; for the count to make any sense, you must also perform the count on this same key field. For instance, if you want a count of individuals by department, you must first order the file by the key field DEPT, and then select Query Count DEPT. The system will progress through the file, from the first logical record to the last, printing a count whenever the value in the count field changes. If you make sure to order your file by the key field for the categories—so that, for example, all records for employees in accounting come first, then all records for employees in sales, and so on—the report will look right. If you forget to order by the key field, or if you select a field other than the key field, no error message will appear, but the report will not be usable.

Unfortunately, you cannot simply perform a Sort to arrange the records in the order you want. If you want a count of the employees by sex, you must add a Key (the SEX field), order the file by the key, and then select Query Count. (The Write and Send commands afford some record-counting capabilities without requiring you to order the file.)

If your key comprises a major key field and one or more minor key fields, you can also designate the minor fields as count fields. For example, if the key of the DEPT file is made up of the DEPT and SEX fields, you can specify both fields as count fields; you will get a count of the individuals in the company by department by sex. Output is always to the printer (see fig. 11.16).

```
QUERY   : Count duplicates
File    : person
Key     : DEPT
Field   : DEPT
Field   : SEX
Date    : 11-22-85
```

ACCT	M	Count : 4
ACCT	Count : 4	
DATA	M	Count : 1
DATA	Count : 1	
MFGR	F	Count : 2
MFGR	Count : 2	
MKTG	F	Count : 1
MKTG	M	Count : 2
MKTG	Count : 3	
SALE	F	Count : 2
SALE	M	Count : 1
SALE	Count : 3	

Fig. 11.16. *The printout of a Query Count by DEPT by SEX.*

Erasing a Query Definition (Query Undefine)

To erase a Query definition you have created with the Query Define command, use the Query Undefine command.

Conclusion

To make the most of your mastery of the Smart Data Base Manager, you should have a solid understanding of the Query command. Its capabilities can be invaluable in selecting the appropriate records for use in reports or transactions. Once a set of records is selected, it can be used repeatedly in multiple commands; you do not need to perform the screening operations over and over again.

The Query command itself does not sort your data; neither does it disturb the existing sort order. If you want your outcome to be in the same sort order as an existing key field, you should probably order the file by that key before proceeding with the query. If you want the final order to be different from the order of any existing key, you may use a key to specify a *where* condition on that field, thus reducing the time needed for the query.

You can specify selection criteria with multiple conditions, if necessary, or you may decide to perform several passes through the data, screening further and further each time you order the file by a new index. Remember that the Query command by itself does not select the records. You must use the Order command to limit the number of records viewed.

The Query command is also used to perform calculations either on the entire file or on selected records. You can designate one or more destination fields, but be careful if one of them is a key field.

Chapter 12

Using the File-Specs and Utilities Commands

Several miscellaneous and utility commands are included in the Smart Data Base Manager to make working with your system easier and to increase flexibility.

Getting File Information (2–File-Specs, Alt-F)

The File-Specs command is found on command list 2 (see fig. 12.1); the quick key is Alt-F. This command is used to display useful information about the current file. Figure 12.2 shows the six options on the main menu of the File-Specs command.

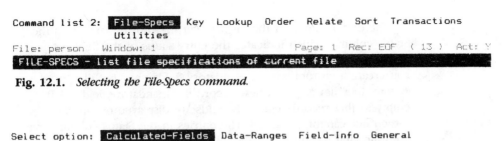

```
Command list 2: File-Specs  Key  Lookup  Order  Relate  Sort  Transactions
                Utilities
File: person   Window: 1                     Page: 1  Rec: EOF  ( 13 )  Act: Y
FILE-SPECS - list file specifications of current file
```

Fig. 12.1. *Selecting the File-Specs command.*

```
Select option: Calculated-Fields  Data-Ranges  Field-Info  General
               Key-Fields  Running-Totals
File: person   Window: 1                     Page: 1  Rec: EOF  ( 13 )  Act: Y
FILE-SPECS - list file specifications of current file
```

Fig. 12.2. *The File-Specs main menu.*

Displaying Information about Fields (Field-Info)

Probably the most useful option on the menu is Field-Info. As shown in figure 12.3, this command displays information about each field in the current screen.

Field No	Field Title	Type	Length	Key	Total	Status
1	SSN	S	11	Y		N
2	FIRST	A	9	N		N
3	LAST	A	10	Y		N
4	AGE	NO	2	N	N	N
5	SEX	A	1	N		N
6	MS	A	1	N		N
7	DEP	I	2	N		N
8	DEG	A	3	N		N
9	CAR	I	2	N		N
10	STREET	A	15	N		N
11	CITY	A	10	N		N
12	ST	A	2	N		N
13	ZIP	A	5	N		N
14	WAGE	N2	10	N	N	N
15	STATUS	A	1	N		N

```
F4  Next screen            F2 Print screen              F10 Exit
file-specs field-info
File: person   Window: 1                    Page: 1  Rec: EOF  ( 13 )  Act: Y
FILE-SPECS - list file specifications of current file
```

Fig. 12.3. *The screen displayed by the File-Specs Field-Info option.*

The only column on the display that may not be familiar is the Status column, which indicates the entry status of the field. Remember that you can make a field mandatory or read-only when you create a custom screen. Mandatory fields must be filled in; the system does not accept a new record if a mandatory field is left empty in that record. Read-only fields are displayed on the data-entry screen but cannot be edited. The entries in the Status column have the following meanings:

N	No special entry status
M	Mandatory entry status
R	Read-only entry status
(blank)	Field not in current screen

Displaying General File Information (General)

The General command is used to display general information about the file in the current window (see fig. 12.4). The information shown is

The last date on which records were added to the file

The last date on which records were updated

The number of records in the file

The record format (fixed or variable field length)

The protection status (password protected or unprotected)

The number to be entered in the count field of the next record, if a count field is defined

The record length in characters

```
Information on file: person

Last date added:       10-31-85
Last date updated:     11-26-85

File length:           13 Records
Record format:         Fixed length

Protect status:        Unprotected

Count field value:     14

Record Length:         118




F4  Next screen          F2 Print screen          F10 Exit
file-specs general
File: person   Window: 1                    Page: 1  Rec: EOF  ( 13 )  Act: Y
FILE-SPECS - list file specifications of current file
```

Fig. 12.4. *The screen displayed by the File-Specs General command sequence.*

Displaying Key Fields (Key-Fields)

Selecting the Key-Fields option displays the screen shown in figure 12.5. This screen shows the names of both major and minor key fields, their numbers within the file, their sorting order, and their length.

```
Key Field Information
        Field number  Title          Asc/Descending  Key length

major        1        SSN                 A              11

major        3        LAST                A              10
minor        2        FIRST               A               9
```

Fig. 12.5. *An example of a File-Specs Key-Fields screen.*

Displaying Field Calculations (Calculated-Fields)

Figure 12.6 shows the screen that displays calculations for any calculated fields in the file. Select File-Specs Calculated-Fields to display this screen.

```
Calculated Field Equations

Field 11 [Offer] =
([Rating]/100+1)*[Wage]
```

Fig. 12.6. *A Calculated Fields screen.*

Displaying Lower and Upper Data-Range Limits (Data-Ranges)

If you have defined a screen for the file and have specified data ranges for certain fields, use the File-Specs Data-Ranges command to display the lower and upper limits of those ranges (see fig. 12.7).

```
Ranges of data that may be entered
Field title          Lower limit       Upper limit

Rating                   1                 10
```

Fig. 12.7. *Displaying the upper and lower limits of data ranges.*

The last option, Running-Totals, displays the value of any fields you defined as running-total fields when you created the file. The Running-Total value also is available through the Project Processing facility (see Chapter 32).

Using the Utilities Command (2-Utilities)

The Utilities command offers a variety of options for maintaining your files and data (see fig. 12.8). The Utilities command is found on command list 2; there is no quick key for this command.

```
PHONE (312) 439-8760
EMPDATE 10-01-59

Command list 2:  File-Specs  Key  Lookup  Order  Relate  Sort  Transactions
                 Utilities
File: person3   Window: 1                    Page: 1  Rec: 1  ( 1 )  Act: Y
UTILITIES - file utilities
```

Fig. 12.8. *Selecting the Utilities command.*

Figure 12.9 shows the nine options, or subcommands, on the main Utilities menu.

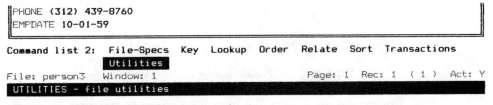

```
PHONE (312) 439-8760
EMPDATE 10-01-59

Select option:  Alter-Count  Concatenate  Duplicates  Erase  File-Fix
                New-Password  Purge  Restructure  Totals-Recalc
File: person3   Window: 1                    Page: 1  Rec: 1  ( 1 )  Act: Y
UTILITIES - file utilities
```

Fig. 12.9. *Main menu options of the Utilities command.*

Renumbering the Count Field (Alter-Count)

The Utilities Alter-Count command sequence is used to renumber the count field for an entire file or to set the value for the next record entered. After you select this option, the system prompts you to enter a value:

Enter the new count:

The system then displays the options shown in figure 12.10. Select Next to assign the value you have entered to the count field of the next record entered; current records are left unchanged. Select Renumber to renumber all records, beginning with the first *physical* record in the file.

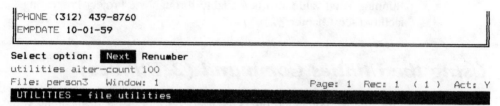

PHONE (312) 439-8760
EMPDATE 10-01-59

```
Select option: [Next] Renumber
utilities alter-count 100
File: person3   Window: 1                    Page: 1   Rec: 1  ( 1 )   Act: Y
UTILITIES - file utilities
```

Fig. 12.10. *The Utilities Alter-Count Next and Renumber options.*

Appending Files (Concatenate)

The Utilities Concatenate command sequence appends the contents of an active file to the file in the current window. Both the source and destination files must be identical in structure, however.

When you execute the command, you are prompted to

Select source filename:

A pop-up menu displays the names of the active files. Use the cursor to point to the source file you want to append to the current file, and press Enter. If you have established key fields, you must execute the Key Update command after you complete the concatenation, in order to make sure that your keys are updated.

Identifying and Deleting Duplicate Records (Duplicates)

Although the Smart Data Base Manager offers no foolproof way to prevent records with duplicate contents in the key fields, you can use the Utilities Duplicates command sequence to identify and delete records with duplicate key entries. Ensuring that there are no duplicates is important in many applications, such as personnel or inventory data bases. A personnel file should contain only one record for each Social Security Number, for example; an inventory file should have only one record for each item number.

Begin by ordering the file by the key that is to be checked for duplicates. (The Utilities Duplicates command checks only the *major* key.)

Figure 12.11 shows a sample file with duplicate records. You can have the system either delete these duplicate records immediately or report their physical record numbers, as in figure 12.12. I highly recommend that you first choose Utilities Duplicates Report, and then visually check the suspect records. The Utilities Duplicates Delete command sequence finds all records having identical values in the key field; for every such group of records, every record but the first is deleted. For example, figure 12.12 shows that records 1 and 7 both have the value *ACCT* in the key field, which is DEPT. If you were to use Utilities Duplicates Delete, record 1 would be retained because it has the first occurrence of *ACCT,* and record 7 would be deleted. Because this may not be the result you want, you may want to use the Report option first.

When you delete duplicate records, they are *marked for deletion*, not physically removed from the file. Use the Utilities Purge command to remove deleted records.

Erasing a File or Custom Screen (Erase)

Use the Utilities Erase command to delete a data base file or a custom screen (see fig. 12.13).

If you select the File option, a pop-up menu shows the names of the data base files in the current subdirectory. Select a file from the menu or type the name and path of a file in another subdirectory. Although the names of all data base files (including active files) are displayed, you cannot erase an active file. You must use Unload first if you want to erase an active file.

```
┌─ Window 1 ═══════════════════════════════════════════════════╗
║   DEPT DEPNAME                                                ║
║ ══▶ACCT Accounting                                           ║
║   ACCT Accounting                                            ║
║   DATA Data Processing                                       ║
║   DATA Data Processing                                       ║
║   MDSE Merchandising                                         ║
║   MDSE Merchandising                                         ║
║   MFGR Manufacturing                                         ║
║   MFGR Manufacturing                                         ║
║   MKTG Marketing                                             ║
║   MKTG Marketing                                             ║
║   SALE Sales                                                 ║
║   SALE Sales                                                 ║
║                                                              ║
║                                                              ║
║                                                              ║
║                                                              ║
║                                                              ║
╚══════════════════════════════════════════════════════════════╝

Command:

File: dept    Key: 1    Window: 1              Page: 1  Rec: 1  ( 1 )  Act: Y
```

Fig. 12.11. *Sample file with duplicate records.*

```
                 UTILITIES : Duplicates Report
                 File : dept   Key : DEPT
                 Date : 12-08-85

                 Data : ACCT
                         Record : 1
                         Record : 7

                 Data : DATA
                         Record : 5
                         Record : 11

                 Data : MDSE
                         Record : 6
                         Record : 12

                 Data : MFGR
                         Record : 2
                         Record : 8

                 Data : MKTG
                         Record : 4
                         Record : 10

                 Data : SALE
                         Record : 3
                         Record : 9
```

Fig. 12.12. *A sample Utilities Duplicates report.*

```
║STATUS A
║SKILL CKP
║DEPT ACCT
║PHONE (312) 439-8760
║EMPDATE 10-01-59
```

```
Select option: █File█ Screen
utilities erase
File: person3   Window: 1                    Page: 1  Rec: 1  ( 1 )  Act: Y
·UTILITIES - file utilities
```

Fig. 12.13.   *Selecting a Utilities Erase option.*

If you select Screen, the pop-up menu shows the names of all screens for the file in the current window. Select the screen to erase, using the cursor keys to move the pointer. Even though the menu shows the standard screen and the current screen, they cannot be erased. The standard screen can never be erased. If you want to erase a custom screen that is active, you must unload it first.

Reconstructing a Damaged .PIX File (File-Fix)

The Utilities File-Fix Data command has two purposes. If you have created a variable-length file, the Data Base Manager maintains a file with the extension *.PIX* that contains the length of each record in the file and other essential information. (No such file is created for fixed-length files.) If for some reason this .PIX file is damaged, you can use the Utilities File-Fix Data command sequence to reconstruct the .PIX file. Smart has no error message to indicate that a .PIX file needs to be fixed; you will notice that the file needs to be fixed only because it will appear to have an incorrect number of records, and operations using keys will not work correctly.

This command has another use if you are using the Smart Data Base Manager on a network. When you update a record on a network, the system automatically locks that record during the updating so that only you can access the record. Under normal circumstances, the system unlocks the record when you finish working with it so that other users can access the record. However, if something goes wrong while you are updating the record—if the system goes down, for example—the record remains locked. The File-Fix Data command can be used to unlock any locked records. This command, which can be used on only an *inactive* file, should be used with care; it probably should be used only by the administrator of the system or data base.

Every data base file, whether variable- or fixed-length, has an associated screen file with the extension *.DBS*. This .DBS file indicates field locations and types, and it is crucial to the use of the data base. If the .DBS file is damaged, you should use the File-Fix Screen command to re-create it. Be careful when you use this command, however; it destroys every custom screen, leaving only the standard screen.

Adding, Changing, or Deleting a Password (New-Password)

The Utilities New-Password command is used to add, change, or delete a password for the current file or screen. If you are deleting or changing the password, you are prompted to enter the current password. If you are adding or changing a password, you are prompted to enter the new password also.

Deleting Records from a File (Purge)

As indicated earlier, the Utilities Purge command sequence is used to remove any deleted records from a file. Remember that a deleted record is only "marked for deletion" but is still physically within the file. For a complete discussion of this command, refer to the section on deleting records in Chapter 8.

Transferring Data from One File to Another (Restructure)

Use the Utilities Restructure command to transfer data from another file into the current file. Refer to Chapter 7, Handling Multiple Files, for a complete discussion of this command.

Recalculating Field Totals (Totals-Recalc)

With this command, you can recalculate the running totals for all fields and any calculated fields.

Conclusion

The File-Specs and Utilities commands can help you manage your files more effectively. Several File-Specs options provide much-needed information about the file. That information can be used to produce system documentation for yourself or other users.

The Utilities commands can be used to move data from one file to another, to purge deleted records, or to erase unneeded files or screens. Using one of the Utilities commands, you can delete duplicate records, recalculate totals, or reconstruct .PIX files.

Part II

Using Smart's Spreadsheet

Chapter 13

Introduction to the Smart Spreadsheet

Around the office, nearly everyone has a chance to work with a pencil-and-paper spreadsheet at one time or another. A spreadsheet is just a piece of paper divided into rows and columns. Numbers and other information are written in the spaces, called "cells," where rows and columns intersect. Some of the entries on the worksheet are entered as input from the keyboard; that is, the values are not derived from any other figures on the sheet. The entries might be numeric values such as numbers of employees, dollars, or percentages. Other input entries on the worksheet might include date and time values or text items such as department names.

Not all of the entries on a worksheet are input items; some are calculated from other entries. A total, for example, might be calculated at the bottom of a column of figures. Sometimes you even have "totals of totals." To prepare such a spreadsheet with pencil and paper, you have to get out the old calculator, perform the calculations, and write in the answers.

Preparing a large manual spreadsheet may not be so bad if you have to do it only once. But the ineffectiveness of the paper spreadsheet becomes readily apparent when someone comes to you and says, "What would the totals look like if you changed these three figures?" and "Can you get me the answers before the meeting in 10 minutes?"

An electronic spreadsheet, such as the Smart Spreadsheet, is really just a computerized form of the pencil-and-paper version. You still have to enter the input values (for example, your judgment is still required to estimate the budget for the Accounting department), but you don't have to perform the calculations. To have the computer perform the calculations, you write formulas in the cells that are to contain the calculated values. Then, when you enter the input values, the calculations are performed automatically.

The results of calculations can also be used as input for other calculations. You can appreciate the beauty of an electronic spreadsheet when you have to change a few figures, because you don't have to go back and perform all the calculations again—the computer does them for you. (This assumes, of course, that you have constructed the formulas correctly!)

Certain features of the Smart Spreadsheet simplify the construction of your worksheet. If you have a set of input and calculation cells in a column for the month of January, for example, you can use the Copy command to create similar columns for the rest of the months and for the yearly totals. If you need more space in the middle of the worksheet, you can use the Insert command to add a row or column. The rest of the worksheet is moved to accommodate the added rows or columns. If you want to rearrange your worksheet to make it more presentable or easier to work with, you can move portions of the sheet to other areas.

Some commands in the Spreadsheet are used to control the formatting and display of spreadsheet data. You can use the Justify command to control the position of text within cells, you can use the Reformat command to change the number of decimal places that are displayed, or you can change the format in which dates are displayed on your worksheet.

The Graphics command is used to create and print graphs from the data in your worksheet. Several different formats are possible, including bar graphs, line graphs, and hi-lo and pie charts. A full range of legend, title, color, pattern, and size options are available. The graphics capabilities of the Spreadsheet are competitive with those of many software packages that have been developed *just* to create graphs.

Rows and Columns

Like a paper spreadsheet, a worksheet in the Smart Spreadsheet module consists of columns and rows. Figure 13.1 shows an empty worksheet screen. Notice that the columns and rows have numbers.

In figure 13.1, you can see columns 1 through 7 and rows 1 through 18. (By changing the width of your columns, you can view a larger or smaller number of columns on the screen.) You can view only a portion of your worksheet at any time; the rest of it is still "out there," however. By moving the cursor, you can view the other sections of the worksheet.

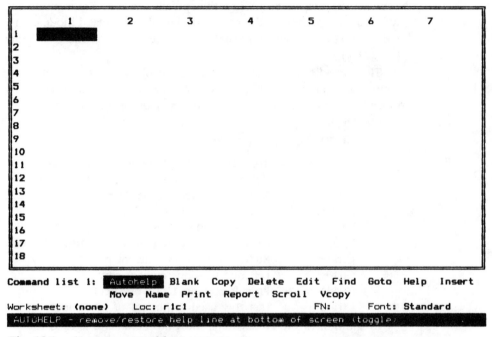

Fig. 13.1. *An empty spreadsheet screen.*

Each cell has an "address" that is made up of the row and column numbers. For example, the cell in row 1, column 1, has the address *r1c1*. The status line shows the cursor's location on the worksheet, along with the name of the worksheet, the font in the current cell, and the font that has been specified for new input items.

Spreadsheet Size

The Smart Spreadsheet has 999 rows and 9999 columns, but you probably will not use all of them in one worksheet. You can produce such a large spreadsheet because the Smart Spreadsheet "ignores" blank cells. If you don't make an entry in a cell, that cell is not stored in the disk file; nor does the cell consume space in RAM when you use the worksheet. Because all spreadsheets have many blank cells, the effective size of the sheet you can create is much larger than it would be if the blank cells consumed memory space.

Like the Smart Word Processor, the Spreadsheet has both an Enter mode and a Command mode. You use the Escape key to toggle between the two modes. When the spreadsheet is in Enter mode, the word *Enter:* appears on the command line. In Command mode, you see a listing of various commands on one of the command lists (refer to fig. 13.1).

The spreadsheet cursor is a highlighted block filling the cell. In figure 13.1, cell r1c1 is highlighted. You can use the cursor keys to move the cursor to another cell. Other cursor-movement keys can also be used:

Keystroke	Moves cursor to
Home	Top cell, current column, current screen
End	Bottom cell, current column, current screen
Tab	Right cell, current row, current screen
Shift-Tab	Left Cell, current row, current screen
PgUp	Up one window (18 rows), current column
PgDn	Down one window (18 rows), current column
Ctrl-→	Right one window, current row
Ctrl-←	Left one window, current row
Ctrl-Home	Row 1, column 1 of worksheet
Ctrl-End	Last row used, column 1 of worksheet

In addition to the cursor keys, the Goto command is used to move the cursor to a specified cell in the current worksheet or to another worksheet in either the same window or a different window. When you use Goto, you specify the cell by the row and column designation or by name.

Entering Data in Enter Mode

To enter a number in Enter mode, just make sure that the cursor is on the right cell and type the number. As soon as you type the first digit of the value, the prompt on the command line changes to

    Enter value:

Any numbers you type appear after this prompt. When you press Enter, the numbers appear in the cell. (The cell can store numbers with a maximum size of 15 significant digits.) After you enter the number in Enter mode, the second line of the command area indicates that the contents of the cell is a value, and the cell value is displayed there.

Sometimes the first digit you type will not be a number; valid initial characters for a numeric value include the minus sign (−) for a negative number and the decimal point (.). If you enter the dollar sign ($) in front of a number, the dollar sign is displayed in front of the value in the cell. The presence of this formatting character does not prevent the use of the cell value in calculations, however.

Not all cells contain values; formulas also are entered in the cells of a spreadsheet. For example, a cell that stores the sum of a column of values is based on a formula. You can enter formulas in two ways. If you type an equal sign (=) after the Enter prompt, the prompt changes to:

Enter Formula:

You can then enter a formula containing up to 240 characters. If your formula is *really* long, press Alt-F instead of pressing the equal sign. This keystroke takes you to the large-formula editor, where you can construct a formula as long as 1,000 characters.

Numeric and Text Operators

Formulas can contain any of the usual arithmetic and algebraic operators, as well as special text operators:

Numeric Operators

+	**Addition**
−	**Subtraction**
*	**Multiplication**
/	**Division**
^	**Exponentiation**

Text Operators

&	Concatenate with a separating space
|	Concatenate without a separating space

In addition to these operators, you can use any of the Smart functions in your formulas. (See Chapter 31, "Using Smart's Mathematical Functions," for more information on Smart functions.)

Perhaps the simplest formula you could write would be

    1+2

This formula would work, of course, even though there would not be much point to entering it. But if the numbers were in separate cells, using a formula might be worth the trouble. For instance, suppose that the 1 is in row 1 column 2 (r1c2) and the 2 is in row 2 column 2 (r2c2), and you want the sum to appear below the numbers. The formula in row 3 column 2 (r3c2) would read

    r1c2+r2c2

The result of the formula will be recalculated if you change the contents of cell r1c2 or r2c2, and then press F5 to recalculate the worksheet.

Later, you will learn how to change from manual to automatic recalculation and why you might want to use one method instead of the other.

What if you want to add the values in 75 rows rather than 2? Do you have to type the individual addresses for each cell in the column? No, you use the SUM function. SUM is one of the most often-used functions in the Spreadsheet. The following formula sums the values in rows 1 through 75 of column 5:

    SUM(r1:75c5)

Notice that the colon (:) is used to designate "through." The colon could also be used to designate consecutive columns. For example, the formula:

    sum(r1:75c5:10)

calculates the sum of a "block" (several rows and columns); the block extends from row 1 through row 75, from column 5 through column 10.

When entering a formula, you can type the column numbers, or you can have Smart enter them for you while you move the cursor. To have Smart enter the formula given previously, perform the following steps:

1. Using the cursor keys, move the cursor to cell r76c5.
2. Press the equal sign (=). The command line displays EnterFormula:.
3. Type *sum(*, and the word appears on the command line.
4. Move the cursor to r1c5 and press F2.

5. Move the cursor to r75c5, and the argument changes to r1:75c5.

6. Type *)*.

7. Press Enter, and the formula is complete.

When you press F2 the first time, you in effect "drop an anchor" to designate the beginning of the cell block (or *range*). Pressing Enter marks the the end of the block. By having the program enter the cell addresses, you can save the step of finding the cells and writing down the addresses before you enter the formula.

How complicated can you get with a formula? You can not only use any of the numeric, date, time, text, business, statistical, or logical functions, but also include IF statements in your formula. Figure 13.2 shows an example of a formula with multiple IF statements.

```
╔══ Formula Editor ══════════════════════════════════════════════════╗
║ if days(r9c2) >= days("1/1/85")                                     ║
║    and days(r9c2) <= days("12/31/85") then .05 else                ║
║                                                                    ║
║ if days(r9c2) >= days("1/1/86")                                    ║
║    and days(r9c2) <= days("12/31/86") then .06 else                ║
║                                                                    ║
║ if days(r9c2) >= days("1/1/87")                                    ║
║    and days(r9c2) <= days("12/31/87") then .07 else .08            ║
║                                                                    ║
║                                                                    ║
║                                                                    ║
║                                                                    ║
║                                                                    ║
║                                                                    ║
║                                                                    ║
║                                                                    ║
╚════════════════════════════════════════════════════════════════════╝
F1 Help       F3 Find      F5 Replace        F7 Insert line      F9  Repeat
F2 Calc       F4 Goto      F6 Define block   F8 Delete line      F10 Finish
                                     Line:    1   Column:  1    Insert: ON
```

Fig. 13.2. *A formula on the editor screen.*

Relative and Absolute Cell References

The cell references in the formula in figure 13.2 are known as *relative addresses*. If you were to copy the formula

r1c1+r2c1

from cell r3c1 to r3c2, the formula in r3c2 would read:

r1c2+r2c2

The capability of copying formulas on a relative basis is one of the wonderful features of a spreadsheet. The formula in this example says, in effect, "Add the value two cells above the current cell to the value one cell above the current cell, and place the answer in the current cell."

If your calculations are the same from column to column, you can often use the Copy command with relative addressing. Sometimes, however, you want to specify that the source data *must* come from a certain row, column, or cell, no matter what cell contains the formula. A copy of the formula still needs to reference the row, column, or cell you originally designated. Referencing cells in this way is called *absolute* addressing. Examples of absolute addresses are

r[11]c[5]   Always row 11; always column 5
r[11]c5   Always row 11; column is relative
r11c[5]   Row is relative; always column 5

Notice that square brackets are used to signify absolute row or column numbers. In formula entry, if you are moving the cursor and the system is entering the cell references, you can use F3 to change from relative addressing, which is the default setting, to absolute addressing.

Entering Dates

Before entering a date in a worksheet cell, you need to decide which date format you want to use. The DATE1 format can display the date as *12-Jan-85,* and the DATE2 format can show the date as *01/12/85;* however, you should refer to the Configure command at the Main Menu for a complete set of options. When you begin to enter a date, first type @ to select DATE1 or # for DATE2. The value that is stored in the cell is actually the number of days since Dec. 31, 1899. The system just displays the cell contents in a more recognizable form.

Entering Text

Text can be entered directly if the initial character is a letter. If the first character is not a letter, you should precede the entry with double quotation marks ("). Text entries can be up to 99 characters in length.

Time values are entered as text. Precede the entry with double quotation marks. Enter the time as HH:MM:SS (hours, minutes, and seconds) or just HH:MM. If you are using the 12-hour convention, add AM or PM after the entry.

Some Precautions

When you are working on your worksheet, it is entirely *RAM resident*; that term means that a complete copy of the worksheet is stored in the computer's memory. This can be both an advantage and a disadvantage.

With your worksheet resident in RAM, you can make changes without affecting the copy on disk. The Spreadsheet is therefore an excellent vehicle for performing "what if" analyses. You can try all kinds of scenarios and never change the original copy on disk. When you save the worksheet, however, the original is overwritten if you save the worksheet under the original name.

On the other hand, if a power outage occurs while you are working, you are at a serious disadvantage. Because there is no record on disk of the work you have done since the last time you saved the worksheet, you will lose any changes you have made. If you make a considerable number of changes, be sure to use the Save command periodically.

Handling Spreadsheet Files

The procedures for identifying, saving, and unloading spreadsheet files are similar to the methods you use in the other modules. You may already be familiar with the commands Load, Activate, Save, and Unload.

When you first enter the Spreadsheet, a blank window is displayed. If you want to load an existing worksheet, you need to move to Command mode. (You can also use the Parameters command to have a worksheet loaded automatically when you enter the Spreadsheet module.) The Smart Spreadsheet defaults to Enter mode, so you must press Escape to change to Command mode.

Loading a Worksheet (4–Load, Alt-L)

The Load command is found on command list 4; the quick key is Alt-L (see fig. 13.3.) When you load a worksheet, it is read from the disk and placed in the current window.

```
16
17
18
```

```
Command list 4:   Activate  Directory  File   Index  Load  Matrix  Password
                   Read  Save  Unload  Write
Worksheet: (none)    Loc: r1c1                        FN:      Font: Standard
 LOAD - load a worksheet into the current window
```

Fig. 13.3. *Selecting the Load Command.*

When you select the Load command, a pop-up menu appears, showing the names of all the worksheet files in the current default subdirectory (see fig. 13.4).

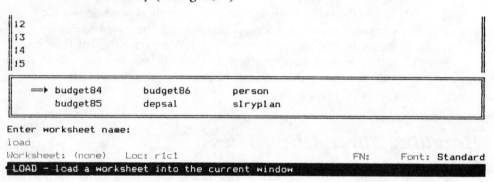

```
12
13
14
15
```

```
  ==▶ budget84      budget86      person
      budget85      depsal        slryplan
```

```
Enter worksheet name:
load
Worksheet: (none)    Loc: r1c1                        FN:      Font: Standard
 LOAD - load a worksheet into the current window
```

Fig. 13.4. *The Load file menu.*

Use the cursor keys to move the arrow to the desired worksheet, and then press Enter. You can also select the worksheet by typing its name. If you need to load a file that is not in the current subdirectory, you must specify the directory path along with the name of the file. You can also display a pop-up menu of files in another directory by typing the directory path and the file specification and then pressing F5. The following example tells Smart to look in the Account directory to find all files with the extension .WS (the worksheet files).

\account*.ws

When the pop-up menu appears, you simply move the cursor to the name of the desired file and press Enter.

If you have attached a password to your worksheet, you are now prompted to enter the password. (For more information on the Password command, see Chapter 17.)

If you enter the name of a worksheet that does not exist, the following prompt is displayed:

```
Create new worksheet (y/n)
```

Answer *y* to create a new worksheet. The current window is cleared, and the previous worksheet remains active.

Activating a Worksheet (4-Activate)

The Activate command, found on command list 4, is used in much the same way as the Load command. The main difference is that when you use the Activate command, the worksheet is not displayed in the current window. You can activate that worksheet later, but the worksheet in the current window is left in place. To move the activated worksheet to the current window, you use the Goto command. The Index command displays a list of all loaded or active worksheets.

If you activate a worksheet without having loaded one into the current window, the activated worksheet is still not displayed. This is in contrast with the Load and Activate commands in the Smart Data Base Manager. You may remember that if, in the Data Base Manager, you activate a file without first loading a different one, the Activate command is treated as a Load, and the file is displayed in the current window.

Saving a Worksheet to a Disk File (4-Save, Alt-S)

The Save command is found on command list 4, and the quick key is Alt-S. Using the Save command causes the current worksheet to be written to a disk file and remain displayed in the window. Because Smart worksheets are RAM resident, using the Save command often is a good habit to acquire. You can protect yourself against losing a substantial amount of work in the event of a power outage or a hardware malfunction.

When you initiate the Save command, you are prompted to

```
Enter worksheet name:
```

If you want to save the file under the current name, just press Enter. If a worksheet file with the same name already exists on the disk, that file is replaced by the file containing the current worksheet. If such a file does not exist, the file is created.

You may want to save the file under a new name, however. If you are examining various scenarios of a budget, for example, you may want to save each scenario under a different name. In such a case, type a new name in response to the prompt and press Enter. If you already have a file on disk with that name, Smart asks whether you want to overwrite it. If you do not, you are prompted to enter another name.

If your worksheet has not yet been named, you must enter a name before you can save the file.

Clearing a Worksheet from Memory (4–Unload, Alt-U)

The Unload command is found on command list 4, and the quick key is Alt-U. You use the Unload command to clear a worksheet from memory in order to make room for other worksheets you want to load.

If only one worksheet is active and it is in the current window, the Unload command does not require any further action. If you have modified but not saved the worksheet, however, you see the following prompt:

    Worksheet has been modified. Save before unloading (y/n)

If you press *n*, the window is cleared. If you type *y*, the worksheet is saved to the disk under the current name and cleared from RAM. If you want to keep both the original disk version and a copy of the one you have modified, you must save the worksheet under a different name.

If more than one worksheet is active when you select Unload, you are prompted to

    Enter worksheet name:

You must type the name of the worksheet you want to unload; no pop-up menu displays the names of the active worksheets. If you have forgotten the names of the worksheets, you can use the Index command to display them. When you supply the name of an active worksheet and press Enter, an unmodified file is removed from RAM immediately. As previously mentioned, if the file has been modified, you are asked whether you want to save it before unloading the worksheet.

When the worksheet in the current window is unloaded, the window is cleared and the name is changed to *none*. You have one other option when you use the Unload command. In response to the prompt for a worksheet name, you can type the word *ALL*. Entering *ALL* instructs Smart to clear all worksheets from memory.

You must be careful when you use Unload All; *you are not prompted to save the files before they are unloaded.* You are cautioned, however, with the prompt

> Are you sure (y/n)

If some of your worksheets have been modified and you have not saved each modified worksheet, the changes are lost when you select Unload All. This option works differently in the Data Base Manager, in which Unload All automatically saves all files.

You leave the Spreadsheet module by pressing F10 and selecting Quit. You will then see the following prompt to save the worksheet:

> Save modified worksheet [name] (y/n)

The name of the worksheet appears in place of *[name]* in the prompt. Answer *y* to save the worksheet or *n* to discard any changes you have made. After you have selected Quit, you cannot press Escape to remain in the Spreadsheet module; you must leave the module.

Conclusion

The Smart Spreadsheet is a powerful tool for the creation, maintenance, and use of electronic spreadsheets. A solid understanding of the basic concepts will lead you to a full appreciation of the power and flexibility of the different commands.

This chapter has explained the four commands used to handle files in the Smart Spreadsheet module: Load, Activate, Save, and Unload. Before you can use a worksheet, it must be loaded or activated. To keep a copy of the worksheet on disk, use the Save command. You use the Unload command to clear a worksheet from RAM in order to make way for other worksheets.

Now that you know how to load your worksheets, what do you do with them? The following chapter on Data Manipulation describes some of the commands you use to construct a worksheet. Also included in this section on the Smart Spreadsheet module are explanations of the commands you need to build, change, and use spreadsheets within the Smart system.

Chapter 14

Formatting Worksheet Cells

Formatting commands in the Smart Spreadsheet module are used to alter the appearance of the worksheet on the screen and in printed reports. These commands control column width, justification of text and values, the display of decimals, selection of fonts, and text attributes such as boldface and underscoring.

Some formatting commands are used to establish the format of text or data to be entered; other commands are used to alter the format of existing text or values. Cells that do not contain entries cannot be formatted, because Smart allocates memory space only to cells that contain text, values, or formulas. To Smart, empty cells "do not exist," in effect, although they appear on screen and can be addressed by formulas. A cell exists only after you make an entry, and only then can the cell be formatted.

The format associated with a cell remains associated with that cell when the worksheet is saved to disk. The same format will be in effect the next day, when you load the worksheet and begin working with it again. As you will learn in Chapter 15, however, some commands erase the formats. For example, the Blank and Delete commands erase any formats associated with cells. When you blank a cell, it "no longer exists," and so the cell cannot have a format. When you delete a range, other rows, columns, or cells, which have their own formats, assume the locations of the deleted areas.

Formatting New Values and Text (3–Value-Format)

The Value-Format command, found on command list 3, is used to set the default format for newly entered values (see fig. 14.1). The formatting options for Value-Format apply to the numbers you enter in cells, as well as to the values resulting from formulas. The Value-Format settings are valid for the duration of your session with the specified worksheet or until you change the settings. Other worksheets that are active at the same time may have different Value-Format settings, no matter whether the worksheets are later displayed in the same window or in other windows.

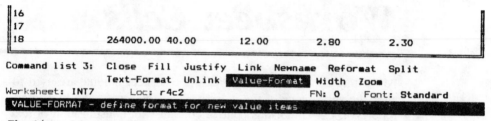

Fig. 14.1. *Selecting the Value-Format command.*

The four Value-Format options are Bar, Date, E-Notation, and Normal (see fig. 14.2). After you choose any of these options, you are prompted to select the justification:

> Left Right Center

These options control the placement of cell contents when their width is less than the width of the cell.

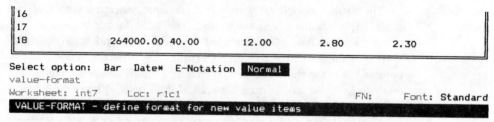

Fig. 14.2. *The Value-Format options.*

Formatting Numeric Values (Value-Format Normal)

The Normal option is the one you will probably use most frequently. After you have selected that command and an option from the justification menu, the following options are displayed:

Currency Numeric Percent

Selecting the Currency option causes Smart to place a dollar sign (or another selected currency symbol) to the left of the value. If you select Numeric, no symbol is displayed. When Percent is chosen, a percent sign (%) appears to the right of the value and the decimal point is displayed in a position indicating fractions of a percent. The value .096, for example, is displayed as 9.6% if one decimal position is selected.

Remember that you can also enter a leading dollar sign in Enter mode by first typing the $, followed by the number you want to enter.

If you select either Currency or Numeric, you are then prompted to select one of the following options:

Commas   Nocommas

The Commas option places a comma after every third digit to the left of the decimal point.

Finally, you see the following prompt:

Enter decimal positions (0-9):

You can choose to display as many as nine decimal positions in cells containing numeric values. The value displayed is automatically rounded to the number of decimal places you have selected. Be aware, however, that regardless of the number of decimal places you choose to have displayed, the Spreadsheet always uses the *real* value in the cell in formulas, as figure 14.3 illustrates.

The numbers in r2c2, r3c2, and r4c2 of figure 14.3 were entered with two decimal places. The correct total of these values is displayed in r6c2. Columns 3 and 4 contain the same numbers as column 1; the only difference is that the cells are formatted to display only one decimal place in column 3 and no decimals in column 4. Notice that both the individual numbers and the totals have been rounded. Column 4 seems to show that 1+3+4 = 7. Some people might be upset by this.

	1	2	3	4	5	6	7
1	████████						
2		1.05	1.1	1			
3		2.65	2.7	3			
4		3.55	3.6	4			
5		------------------------------					
6	Total:	7.25	7.3	7			
7							
8	Total						
9	Rounded						
10	Values:	7.25	7.4	8			
11							
12	Col. 3 formula:		round(r2c3,1)+round(r3c3,1)+round(r4c3,1)				
13							
14							
15							
16							
17							
18							

Enter:

Worksheet: decsam   Loc: r1c1   FN: Font: **Standard**
ENTER - enter a formula, a value or text into the current cell

Fig. 14.3. *Rounding decimal numbers.*

To get around this problem, you can calculate the total as the sum of the rounded numbers, as shown in row 10. The formula used to calculate r10c3 is shown in row 12. The answer is not the correct sum of the real values, but the worksheet looks better now.

Choosing Date Formats (Value-Format Date)

The Date option is used to display new numeric entries in any of three date formats. Each date format has a different layout; you should select a layout for each format in the Configure command of the main menu.

The Date1 format displays the abbreviation of the month between the numeric year and month. Date2 displays the numeric month, day, and year separated by slashes (/) or dashes (−). Date3 shows the month abbreviation followed by the numeric year.

In the Spreadsheet, dates are actually stored as numbers that represent the number of days since the beginning of the 20th century. For example, 12345 represents 10/19/33. Because you will probably not enter this type of a number for a date, you should preface a date entry with the symbol @ for a Date1 display and # for a Date2 display. You can then enter the date in a more natural format, such as 10/19/33.

Using Scientific Notation (E-Notation)

If you want to display large or small numbers in scientific notation, use the E-Notation option. You can select the number of decimal positions.

Creating Simple Bar Graphs (Bar)

An elementary bar graph can be displayed with the Bar format option. A plus sign (+) is displayed for each unit of positive value, and a minus sign (−) is displayed for each unit of negative value (see fig. 14.4). A period (.) represents a zero value. If the value in the cell exceeds the column width in characters, the cell is filled with asterisks (*). (See this chapter's section on the Width command if you need to correct this problem.) If the underlying value contains decimals, the integer part of the value is used to create the bar.

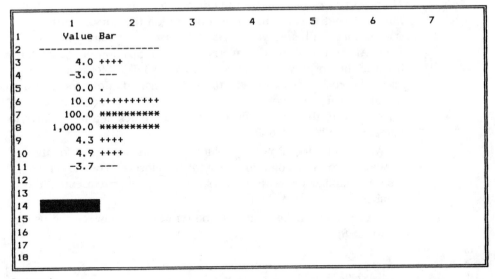

Fig. 14.4. *Effect of the Value-Format Bar option.*

Justifying Text Entries (3-Text Format)

With the Text-Format command, found on command list 3, you have only three options:

Left Center Right

The option you select determines the justification of newly entered text. Existing entries are not affected; you can change the justification of those entries with the Justify command.

Reformatting Existing Values and Text (3-Reformat, Alt-Q)

The Reformat command is found on command list 3, and the quick key is Alt-Q. This command is used to change the format of values that have already been entered into a worksheet. When you select Reformat, the following menu is displayed:

Block Columns Rows All Formula-Display

Although you can still move the cursor after this menu is displayed, this command is easier to use if you position the cursor on the starting location before you select Reformat. (If you are going to select All, you don't have to worry about the position of the cursor because the entire worksheet is reformatted.) The Block option is used to specify a block of cells to be reformatted. Move the cursor to the upper left corner of the block and press F2 to "drop the anchor." Then move to the lower right corner of the block and press Enter to complete the block definition.

When you select Rows or Columns, you are prompted for the number of rows or columns you want to reformat. You can either type the number or move the cursor so that the system enters the number.

After you designate a range to be reformatted, you see the prompt shown in figure 14.5.

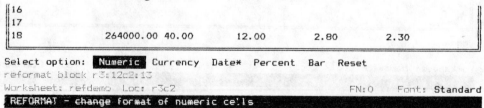

Fig. 14.5. *Options of the Reformat command.*

Changing Value Formats

The Reformat options are similar to the Value-Format options, although they are not grouped in the same way. If you select the Numeric option, you are then prompted to select one of the following:

Normal E-Notation

The Normal option displays numeric values as you are probably used to seeing them; E-Notation is primarily for scientific use. If you select Normal, you are prompted to select one of the following:

Commas Nocommas

Whether you have selected Normal or E-Notation, the final prompt is

Enter decimal positions (0-9):

After you respond to the prompt, the numeric cells in the specified range are reformatted; cells containing text are unaffected. The displayed figures are rounded to the number of decimal places you have specified. Remember, however, that the underlying numbers still are stored in their full form, which is used in all formulas.

Selecting a Currency Format (Reformat Currency)

The prompts for the Currency option are the same as for the Numeric option. The Currency option positions a dollar sign ($) in front of the displayed value. If you plan to have a dollar sign in the cell, set the column width one character wider than you would if you weren't using a dollar sign. (The Width command is discussed later in this chapter.) If a cell contains more characters than can be displayed at the current setting, the cell displays asterisks (*).

Changing the Date Format (Reformat Date)

The Date option is used to change from one date format to another. The prompt is

Enter date type (1-3):

Refer to the section on the Value-Format command in this chapter for a discussion of the three types of date formats.

Using a Percentage Format (Reformat Percent)

The Percent option displays a percent sign (%) to the right of a number and causes the number to be displayed as if it were divided by 100. You are prompted to enter the number of decimal places. Remember, the underlying number in the cell is still in its original form. For example, the number .3345 is displayed as 33.5% if you select Percent and specify one decimal place. But the underlying value still is treated as .3345 in formulas.

Changing a Bar-Graph Display (Reformat Bar)

The Bar option is used to display the types of elementary bar graphs shown earlier in figure 14.4. This option works just like the Bar option of the Value-Format command.

Resetting Cell Formats (Reformat Reset)

The Reformat Reset command is used to reformat a cell or a block of cells that has been changed to a Date or a Bar format. This command restores cells to their previous format. There are no options other than your selection of the range.

In the financial model that is developed in chapter 15, we want to reformat the numbers in rows 3 through 12 so that they are displayed with one decimal place. Some of the assumption variables on row 18 also need to be changed. Figure 14.6 shows the model after the cells have been reformatted.

	1	2	3	4	5	6	7	8	9	10
1										
2										
3		75.9	76.7	77.4	78.2	79.0	79.8	80.6	81.4	82.2
4		30.4	30.7	31.0	31.3	31.6	31.9	32.2	32.6	32.9
5		---								
6		2.8	2.8	2.8	2.8	2.8	2.8	2.8	2.8	2.8
7		27.6	27.9	28.2	28.5	28.8	29.1	29.4	29.8	30.1
8		2.3	2.3	2.3	2.3	2.3	2.3	2.3	2.3	2.3
9		25.3	25.6	25.9	26.2	26.5	26.8	27.1	27.5	27.8
10		---								
11		12.1	12.3	12.4	12.6	12.7	12.9	13.0	13.2	13.3
12		13.1	13.3	13.5	13.6	13.8	13.9	14.1	14.3	14.4
13		---								
14		0.05	0.05	0.05	0.05	0.05	0.05	0.05	0.05	0.05
15										
16										
17										
18		264,000	40		12		2.8		2.3	

Command:

Worksheet: int8   Loc: r1c1   FN: Font: **Standard**

Fig. 14.6. *The reformatted model.*

Viewing Formula Text (Reformat Formula-Display)

The Reformat Formula-Display command is used to alternate between display of the values in calculated cells and the text of the formulas. The formulas can be either numerical calculations or formulas for manipulating text entries. The prompt is

Text Values

Choosing the Text option causes Smart to display the formulas of individual cells rather than the results of the formulas. Choosing Values causes the values to be displayed again. If the columns are too narrow to show the whole formula, you can view the formula in the control area by moving the cursor to the cell and pressing Escape to invoke Enter mode.

Rejustifying Text Entries (3-Justify, Alt-J)

The Justify command is found on command list 3; the quick key is Alt-J. This command is used to change the justification of existing text, values, or formulas within a specified range. (The justification of newly-entered text or values is established with the Value-Format and Text-Format commands.) The first option is

Left Center Right

Selecting Left positions the cell contents at the left edge of the cell. Selecting Right positions the contents at the right. Center causes the contents to be centered in the cell. Examples are shown in figure 14.7.

```
10  <------------->< ------------->< ------------->
11  LEFT               CENTER              RIGHT
12  ----               ------              -----
13  10.33              10.33               10.33
14  02-May-43          02-May-43           02-May-43
15  $19.95             $19.95              $19.95
16  +++++              +++++               +++++
17  33.45%             33.45%              33.45%
18  -44.40             -44.40              -44.40
```

```
Enter:

Worksheet: jusdemo  Loc: r1c1                    FN:     Font: Standard
  ENTER - enter a formula, a value or text into the current cell
```

Fig. 14.7. *Examples of justification.*

In figure 14.8, the development of our financial model takes another step. Month names have been entered in row 2; they are right-justified. Left-justified row names have been entered in column 1. The titles of the assumption variables have been entered in rows 16 and 17; they are left-justified, except for the *Average Shares:* title, which is right-justified.

	1	2	3	4	5	6	7	8	9	10
1				INTERNATIONAL DIVISION						
2		Jan	Feb	Mar	Apr	May	Jun	Jul	Aug	Sep
3	Net Sales.	75.9	76.7	77.4	78.2	79.0	79.8	80.6	81.4	82.2
4	Gross Prof	30.4	30.7	31.0	31.3	31.6	31.9	32.2	32.6	32.9
5										
6	G&A Exp...	2.8	2.8	2.8	2.8	2.8	2.8	2.8	2.8	2.8
7	EBIT......	27.6	27.9	28.2	28.5	28.8	29.1	29.4	29.8	30.1
8	Int Exp...	2.3	2.3	2.3	2.3	2.3	2.3	2.3	2.3	2.3
9	EBT.......	25.3	25.6	25.9	26.2	26.5	26.8	27.1	27.5	27.8
10										
11	Tax.......	12.1	12.3	12.4	12.6	12.7	12.9	13.0	13.2	13.3
12	Net Income	13.1	13.3	13.5	13.6	13.8	13.9	14.1	14.3	14.4
13										
14	EPS.....	0.05	0.05	0.05	0.05	0.05	0.05	0.05	0.05	0.05
15										
16	Average		Gr Prof		Sales		G&A		Intst	
17	Shares:		Rate %		Grow %		Expense:		Expense:	
18	264,000		40		12		2.8		2.3	

Enter:

Worksheet: int9   Loc: r1c1   FN: Font: **Standard**

ENTER - enter a formula, a value or text into the current cell

Fig. 14.8. *The financial model with right-justified and left-justified headings and titles.*

Changing Column Width (3-Width)

The Width command, found on command list 3, is used to change the width of one or more columns on your worksheet. Blank cells cannot be formatted, but you can change the width of blank columns. The width settings are saved with the worksheet. Columns can vary in width from 0 to 80 characters. If you want to hide a column in the middle of your worksheet or display additional columns, set the width to 0. The default column width is established in the Parameters command of the Spreadsheet.

Begin by positioning the cursor on the first column to be changed; then execute the Width command. The prompt is

`Enter width: xx`

(The current width of the column is displayed where the *xx* appears.) Enter a number between 0 and 80. If you enter a number outside this range, you will get an error, but not until after you specify the columns.

You then see the options

`Columns All`

If you select All, every column in the worksheet is set to the width you have entered. If you select Columns, you are prompted to

`Enter number of columns:`

You then enter the number of columns whose width you want to change. You can either type a number or use the cursor to indicate the extent of the group of columns. Press Enter to complete the command. If you press Enter without entering a number, only the current column is changed.

Changing the width of a column does not change the contents of any cell in that column. If the column is not wide enough to show the cell contents, the cell is filled with asterisks (*) to inform you of this condition.

Figure 14.9 shows the results of adjusting column widths in the financial model. First, the width of all columns was changed to 6, and then the width of column 1 was changed to 12.

Selecting Type Fonts (2-Font, F6)

The Font command, found on command list 2, is used to select a font for new entries or change the font of existing entries. The Font Select command sequence sets fonts for new entries; the Font Change sequence sets fonts for existing entries. The quick key for Font Select is F6.

Choosing a Font for New Entries (Font Select)

To select a font for new entries, issue the Font Select command. You are then prompted to enter a font number between 0 and 10

```
            1        2     3     4     5     6     7     8     9    10    11
  1   ▮▮▮▮▮▮▮▮▮       INTERNATIONAL DIVISION
  2              Jan   Feb   Mar   Apr   May   Jun   Jul   Aug   Sep   Oct
  3   Net Sales..  75.9  76.7  77.4  78.2  79.0  79.8  80.6  81.4  82.2  83.0
  4   Gross Prof.  30.4  30.7  31.0  31.3  31.6  31.9  32.2  32.6  32.9  33.2
  5              ---------------------------------------------------------
  6   G&A Exp....   2.8   2.8   2.8   2.8   2.8   2.8   2.8   2.8   2.8   2.8
  7   EBIT.......  27.6  27.9  28.2  28.5  28.8  29.1  29.4  29.8  30.1  30.4
  8   Int Exp....   2.3   2.3   2.3   2.3   2.3   2.3   2.3   2.3   2.3   2.3
  9   EBT........  25.3  25.6  25.9  26.2  26.5  26.8  27.1  27.5  27.8  28.1
 10              ---------------------------------------------------------
 11   Tax........  12.1  12.3  12.4  12.6  12.7  12.9  13.0  13.2  13.3  13.5
 12   Net Income.  13.1  13.3  13.5  13.6  13.8  13.9  14.1  14.3  14.4  14.6
 13              ---------------------------------------------------------
 14   EPS......    0.05  0.05  0.05  0.05  0.05  0.05  0.05  0.05  0.05  0.06
 15              ---------------------------------------------------------
 16      Average       Gr Prof      Sales       G&A        Intst       Tax
 17      Shares:       Rate %       Grow %      Expense:    Expense:    Rate%
 18      264,000        40          12          2.8         2.3         48
```

Command:

Worksheet: int10   Loc: r1c1   FN: Font: Standard

Fig. 14.9. *The financial model with new column widths.*

(see fig. 14.10). Fonts 11 and 12 can also be selected if you have defined them as custom fonts.

Before selecting a font, be sure that your printer supports that font; the special code that invokes the font may not work with all printers. Some printers are fully supported by the Smart system and can print all the fonts; some are only partially supported. When you first install the system, be sure to select the menu option corresponding to your printer.

```
 15   ---------------------------------------------------------
 16      Average       Gr Prof      Sales       G&A        Intst       Tax
 17      Shares:       Rate %       Grow %      Expense:    Expense:    Rate%
 18      264,000        40          12          2.8         2.3         48
```

Enter new font number:
0 Standard   1 Italics   2 Subscript   3 Superscript   4 Strikeout   5 Greek
6 L-graphic   7 B-graphic 8 Gothic   9 Script   10 Small Caps
FONT - select font for new items or change font for existing items

Fig. 14.10. *Selecting fonts.*

When you select a font, the name of the font shown on the status line changes. This is one way to be aware of the fonts used in your document. (The *FN:* indicator on the status line shows the font of the character at the current cursor position.) If you have a color monitor, different fonts appear in different colors.

A monochrome graphics monitor also can display the different fonts. Try changing the Display mode (on command list 5) to Graphics and watch what happens.

In addition to the 12 font numbers, you can also specify boldface and underscores with Font Select. For instance, if you want underscored italic type, enter *1U* at the prompt. The letters *U* and *u* control the underscoring; *B* and *b* control boldface:

Attribute	*On*	*Off*
Underscore	U	u
Bold	B	b

If you want underscored boldface type, you can use the letters together. For example, entering *0UB* results in standard font, bold and underscored.

Two quick keys let you easily control the boldface and underscore attributes. Ctrl-B toggles the bold feature, and Ctrl-U controls the underscore feature. Remember, however, that these quick keys are used to select a font, not change one.

Changing the Font of Existing Entries (Font Change)

To change the font of existing entries, use the Font Change command. You are first prompted for a font number, as in the Font Select command (refer to fig. 14.10). After you enter a font number, you are prompted for a range:

```
Block Columns Rows All
```

If you select Columns or Rows, position your cursor before issuing the command. You are then prompted for the number of rows or columns. Type the number or use your cursor to have the system enter the number of rows or columns.

If you select Block, move the cursor to the top left of the range and press F2 to drop the anchor; then move to the lower right of the range and press Enter.

If you select All, there are no additional prompts.

After you issue the Font Change command, the *selected* font is unaffected. Any new entries are added to the worksheet in the font chosen with the Font Select command.

Altering Row and Column Number Display (Rownumbers and Colnumbers)

Normally, a worksheet displays the row and column numbers in the window. If you want to turn off this display to improve the appearance of the screen or to gain additional row or column space, use the Rownumbers or Colnumbers commands found on command list 2. Because these commands are both "toggles," they are used to turn the display off and back on.

The display (or nondisplay) of row and column numbers applies to a worksheet within a window. The display in another window, even if it is the same worksheet, is unaffected.

Figure 14.11 shows the same worksheet displayed with and without row and column numbers. Note that the window number is not shown when the row or column numbers are hidden.

#1	1	2	3	4	5	6	7	8	9	10	11
1				INTERNATIONAL DIVISION							
2		Jan	Feb	Mar	Apr	May	Jun	Jul	Aug	Sep	Oct
3	Net Sales..	75.9	76.7	77.4	78.2	79.0	79.8	80.6	81.4	82.2	83.0
4	Gross Prof.	30.4	30.7	31.0	31.3	31.6	31.9	32.2	32.6	32.9	33.2
5		————									
6	G&A Exp....	2.8	2.8	2.8	2.8	2.8	2.8	2.8	2.8	2.8	2.8
7	EBIT.......	27.6	27.9	28.2	28.5	28.8	29.1	29.4	29.8	30.1	30.4
8	Int Exp....	2.3	2.3	2.3	2.3	2.3	2.3	2.3	2.3	2.3	2.3
9	EBT........	25.3	25.6	25.9	26.2	26.5	26.8	27.1	27.5	27.8	28.1

	Jan	Feb	Mar	Apr	May	Jun	Jul	Aug	Sep	Oct	Nov
INTERNATIONAL DIVISION											
Net Sales..	75.9	76.7	77.4	78.2	79.0	79.8	80.6	81.4	82.2	83.0	83.8
Gross Prof.	30.4	30.7	31.0	31.3	31.6	31.9	32.2	32.6	32.9	33.2	33.5
	————										
G&A Exp....	2.8	2.8	2.8	2.8	2.8	2.8	2.8	2.8	2.8	2.8
EBIT.......	27.6	27.9	28.2	28.5	28.8	29.1	29.4	29.8	30.1	30.4	30.7

```
Command list 2:  Border  Colnumbers  Font  Graphics  Lock  Paint  Rownumbers
                      Sort  Titles  Unlock
Worksheet: intrnatl Loc: r1c1                              FN:     Font: Standard
COLNUMBERS - remove/restore column numbers (toggle)
```

Fig. 14.11. *Selecting the Colnumbers command.*

Conclusion

Controlling the display of data in your worksheet can greatly enhance its appearance and meaning, whether the worksheet is displayed on paper or on the screen. This chapter has covered the formatting commands you use to specify and alter the appearance of the cells in your worksheet. Formats can be selected either before or after the data is entered into a cell or a group of cells. Whatever format is selected, the "real" value within the cell is unchanged.

Chapter 15

Manipulating Data

If you plan to create your own worksheets, be sure to read this chapter. It discusses the commands you use for copying and moving data, text, and formulas, and the commands for deleting and inserting portions of worksheets. The concepts of relative and absolute addressing are particularly important when you use the Copy and Move commands; these concepts are also discussed in this chapter.

This chapter presents a model that illustrates the use of the data-manipulation commands. One worksheet from this model is shown in figure 15.1; this is the final product. During the course of this chapter, the model will be developed step-by-step, illustrating use of the necessary commands. In this way, you will understand both the use of the commands and the process of developing the model.

The model was designed so that the user can change any of the assumptions at the bottom of the screen and observe the change in the financial figures in the worksheet. The current assumptions are

Average number of shares: 264,000
Gross profit percent: 40
Annual sales growth: 12
G&A expense per year: 2.8 (000)
Interest expense per year: 2.3 (000)
Tax rate: 48%

```
           1     2     3     4     5     6     7     8     9    10    11
1  [       ]              INTERNATIONAL DIVISION
2                 Jan   Feb   Mar   Apr   May   Jun   Jul   Aug   Sep   Oct
3  Net Sales.. 75.9  76.7  77.4  78.2  79.0  79.8  80.6  81.4  82.2  83.0
4  Gross Prof. 30.4  30.7  31.0  31.3  31.6  31.9  32.2  32.6  32.9  33.2
5              ----------------------------------------------------------
6  G&A Exp....  2.8   2.8   2.8   2.8   2.8   2.8   2.8   2.8   2.8   2.8
7  EBIT....... 27.6  27.9  28.2  28.5  28.8  29.1  29.4  29.8  30.1  30.4
8  Int Exp....  2.3   2.3   2.3   2.3   2.3   2.3   2.3   2.3   2.3   2.3
9  EBT........ 25.3  25.6  25.9  26.2  26.5  26.8  27.1  27.5  27.8  28.1
10             ----------------------------------------------------------
11 Tax........ 12.1  12.3  12.4  12.6  12.7  12.9  13.0  13.2  13.3  13.5
12 Net Income. 13.1  13.3  13.5  13.6  13.8  13.9  14.1  14.3  14.4  14.6
13             ----------------------------------------------------------
14 EPS...... 0.05  0.05  0.05  0.05  0.05  0.05  0.05  0.05  0.05  0.06
15             ----------------------------------------------------------
16   Average       Gr Prof      Sales       G&A          Intst       Tax
17   Shares:       Rate %       Grow %      Expense:     Expense:    Rate%
18   264,000       40           12          2.8          2.3         48
```

```
Command list 1:  Autohelp  Blank  [Copy]  Delete  Edit  Find  Goto  Help  Insert
                 Move  Name  Print  Report  Scroll  Vcopy
Worksheet: INTALL    Loc: r1c1                    FN:     Font: Standard
COPY - copy part of the worksheet to another location
```

Fig. 15.1. *The completed spreadsheet model.*

The user of this model can move the cursor to any of the
assumption-value cells on row 18 and change a value, and the entire
worksheet will be recalculated. Let's see how the model was built.

The beginnings of the model are shown in figure 15.2. Column 1
shows the values and the calculations for January; column 2 shows
(for illustrative purposes) the formulas used in the calculated cells in
column 1.

The following list explains the contents of the cells in column 1.

Row   Explanation

1   *Net Sales.* Input. To be calculated from annual growth rate
     (row 15) for February through December.

2   *Gross profit.* Calculated from the net sales * gross profit
     percentage (assumption in row 14 / 100).

4   *G&A expense.* One of the assumption variables (row 16).

5   *Earnings before interest.* Gross profit – G&A expense.

6   *Interest expense.* Assumption variable (row 17).

7   *Earnings before taxes.* EBT – interest expense.

```
          1        2      3     4     5     6     7     8     9    10    11
1      75.90
2      30.36 r1c1*r14c1/100
3    ------------
4       2.80 r16c1
5      27.56 r2c1-r4c1
6       2.30 r17c1
7      25.26 r5c1-r6c1
8    ------------
9      12.12 r7c1*r18c1/100
10     13.14 r7c1-r9c1
11   ------------
12      0.05 r10c1/r13c1*1000
13  264000.00 shares
14     40.00 gp rate
15     12.00 grow rate
16      2.80 G&A exp
17      2.30 int exp
18     48.00 tax rate
```

```
Enter:
Value
Worksheet: int2    Loc: r1c1                        FN:0    Font: Standard
 ENTER - enter a formula, a value or text into the current cell
```

Fig. 15.2. *Values and formulas for the January calculations.*

9   *Tax.* EBT * tax rate percent (row 18 / 100)

10   *Net Income.* EBT - tax.

12   *Earnings per share.* Net income / number of shares (row 13) expressed in thousands.

This model is fine for January. Change any of the assumptions in rows 13 through 18, and the calculations for January change. If you have set Auto-Recalc (found on command list 5) to Automatic, the recalculation takes place automatically. If Auto-Recalc is set to Manual, you have to press F5 to perform the calculation.

The formulas in this simple model are not complex—just ordinary arithmetic. Notice that the rates in the assumptions in rows 13 through 18 are expressed as percentages rather than decimal fractions. When the rates are used in formulas, they must be divided by 100.

Using the Copy Command (1-Copy, Alt-C)

First, you need to copy the formulas for January to fill in the formulas for February through December. There is one problem, however. Normally, when you copy a formula, the system recognizes that the cell addresses are relative, and the appropriate adjustments are made. For instance, when you copy cell r5c1 to cell r5c2, the formula in r5c2 becomes r2c2-r4c2. The references to column 1 have become references to column 2. This is the result you want.

However, the assumptions in columns 13 through 18 are in column 1 only; you don't plan to repeat them in columns 2 through 12. Therefore, any references to the assumptions must be *absolute* rather than *relative* references. For example, if a formula in column 10 needs to use one of the assumptions, the formula should refer to column 1 instead of column 10.

In preparation for use of the Copy command, the formulas in rows 2, 4, 6, 9, and 12 have been changed so that the assumption variables in rows 13 through 18 are referenced by absolute addresses (see fig. 15.3.). The square brackets enclosing the row and column numbers indicate absolute addresses.

```
            1        2      3      4      5     6     7     8     9     10     11
1         75.90
2         30.36  r1c1*r[14]c[1]/100
3       ------------
4          2.80  r[16]c[1]
5         27.56  r2c1-r4c1
6          2.30  r[17]c[1]
7         25.26  r5c1-r6c1
8       ------------
9         12.12  r7c1*r[18]c[1]/100
10        13.14  r7c1-r9c1
11      ------------
12         0.05  r10c1/r[13]c[1]*1000
13    264000.00  shares
14        40.00  gp rate
15        12.00  grow rate
16         2.80  G&A exp
17         2.30  int exp
18        48.00  tax rate
```

```
Enter:
Value
Worksheet: int2     Loc: r1c1                           FN:0    Font: Standard
ENTER - enter a formula, a value or text into the current cell
```

Fig. 15.3. *Absolute addresses.*

The Copy command is found on command list 1, and the quick key is Alt-C. This command is used to copy one or more cells on a worksheet. If you copy cells that contain text or values, the data is copied directly. If you copy formulas that contain addresses, the relative addresses are changed to reflect the position of the new cell; absolute addresses remain unchanged.

The Copy command has three options:

> Down From Right

Copy Down makes a copy of all or part of a row. Copy Right copies all or part of a column, and Copy From copies a block of cells. The Copy Down and Right commands copy to areas adjacent to the source row or column. Use the From option to copy to a nonadjacent area of the worksheet.

Copying Cells in a Row (Copy Down)

Before you execute this command, position the cursor on the leftmost cell of the row you want to copy. The Copy Down command has two options:

> Row Single-Cell

If you specify Row, you are prompted to

> Enter length of row:

The "length of row" refers to the number of columns you want to copy in the current row. Type the number and press Enter. Instead of entering the number, you can move the cursor to the right and have the system enter the number for you. As you move the cursor, the value to the right of the prompt increases. Press Enter when you have reached the desired location. You are then prompted to

> Enter number of copies:

The answer to this prompt determines how many copies will be made. Note that when you use the Copy command, the copied data overlays existing data; additional rows are not inserted. If you need to insert rows to make room for the copied data, use the Insert command (see "Using the Insert Command" later in this chapter).

Using the Copy Down Single-Cell command sequence is equivalent to using the command Copy Down Row and specifying a length of 1. Use this command sequence for copying just one cell.

Copying Cells to the Right (Copy Right)

The Copy Right command is similar to Copy Down. You begin by placing the cursor on the cell at the top of the portion of the column to be copied, and then you execute the command.

When you select Copy Right Column, you are prompted for the length of the column (the number of rows) you want to copy. Either type the number or move the cursor to the last row you want to copy, and press Enter; the system then enters the number of rows for you.

You are then prompted to

```
Enter number of copies:
```

Your answer tells Smart how many new columns to produce. The command Copy Right Single-Cell is equivalent to Copy Right Column with a length of 1, but using Copy Right Single-Cell saves a few keystrokes.

To copy the values and formulas from column 1 (January) to columns 2 through 12 for the example worksheet, use the following steps:

1. Place the cursor on r2c1 and select Copy Right. (We'll come back to r1c1 later.)

2. Select the Column option.

3. In response to the prompt, move the cursor down to row 12 (see fig. 15.4). You don't want to copy the assumption variables.

4. Press Enter.

5. In response to the prompt for the number of copies, enter *11* because you need eleven more months for the model.

The "almost finished" product is shown in figure 15.5. The model is not quite finished, because you still need to contend with row 1 (Sales).

An annual growth rate is supplied as an assumption variable in row 15 of the model (cell r15c1). To apply this assumption to the sales row, you need to enter a formula in r1c2. In figure 15.6, the formula has been entered and the calculation has been performed. You can see the formula on the second command line at the bottom of the screen. (In Enter mode, the formula at the cursor cell is displayed on the command line. If you are developing a worksheet in which you don't want other people to see the formulas, use the Lock Protect command, which is discussed in Chapter 17.)

	1	2	3	4	5	6	7	8	9	10	11
1	75.90										
2	30.36										
3	----------										
4	2.80										
5	27.56										
6	2.30										
7	25.26										
8											
9	12.12										
10	13.14										
11	----------										
12	0.05										
13	264000.00										
14	40.00										
15	12.00										
16	2.80										
17	2.30										
18	48.00										

```
Enter length of column: 11
copy right column length
Worksheet: int4      Loc: r12c1                          FN:O      Font: Standard
COPY - copy an area of the worksheet to another area
```

Fig. 15.4. *Using the Copy Right Column Length command.*

	1	2	3	4	5	6	7	8	9	10	11
1	75.90										
2	30.36	0.00	0.00	0.00	0.00	0.00	0.00	0.00	0.00	0.00	0.00
3	----	----	----	----	----	----	----	----	----	----	----
4	2.80	2.80	2.80	2.80	2.80	2.80	2.80	2.80	2.80	2.80	2.80
5	27.56	-2.80	-2.80	-2.80	-2.80	-2.80	-2.80	-2.80	-2.80	-2.80	-2.80
6	2.30	2.30	2.30	2.30	2.30	2.30	2.30	2.30	2.30	2.30	2.30
7	25.26	-5.10	-5.10	-5.10	-5.10	-5.10	-5.10	-5.10	-5.10	-5.10	-5.10
8											
9	12.12	-2.45	-2.45	-2.45	-2.45	-2.45	-2.45	-2.45	-2.45	-2.45	-2.45
10	13.14	-2.65	-2.65	-2.65	-2.65	-2.65	-2.65	-2.65	-2.65	-2.65	-2.65
11											
12	0.05	-0.01	-0.01	-0.01	-0.01	-0.01	-0.01	-0.01	-0.01	-0.01	-0.01
13	264000.00										
14	40.00										
15	12.00										
16	2.80										
17	2.30										
18	48.00										

```
Command:

Worksheet: int4      Loc: r2c1                           FN:O      Font: Standard
```

Fig. 15.5. *The almost-completed model.*

	1	2	3	4	5	6	7	8	9	10	11
1	75.90	76.66									
2	30.36	30.66	0.00	0.00	0.00	0.00	0.00	0.00	0.00	0.00	0.00
3	-----	-----	-----	-----	-----	-----	-----	-----	-----	-----	-----
4		2.80	2.80	2.80	2.80	2.80	2.80	2.80	2.80	2.80	2.80
5		27.56	27.86	-2.80	-2.80	-2.80	-2.80	-2.80	-2.80	-2.80	-2.80	-2.80
6		2.30	2.30	2.30	2.30	2.30	2.30	2.30	2.30	2.30	2.30
7		25.26	25.56	-5.10	-5.10	-5.10	-5.10	-5.10	-5.10	-5.10	-5.10
8	-----	-----	-----	-----	-----	-----	-----	-----	-----	-----	-----
9		12.12	12.27	-2.45	-2.45	-2.45	-2.45	-2.45	-2.45	-2.45	-2.45
10		13.14	13.29	-2.65	-2.65	-2.65	-2.65	-2.65	-2.65	-2.65	-2.65
11	-----	-----	-----	-----	-----	-----	-----	-----	-----	-----	-----
12		0.05	0.05	-0.01	-0.01	-0.01	-0.01	-0.01	-0.01	-0.01	-0.01
13	264000.00										
14	40.00										
15	12.00										
16	2.80										
17	2.30										
18	48.00										

```
Enter:
Formula: r1c1*(1+r[15]c[1]/12/100)
Worksheet: int4    Loc: r1c2                          FN:0   Font: Standard
ENTER - enter a formula, a value or text into the current cell
```

Fig. 15.6. *Formula entered in row 1, column 2.*

Notice that the formula in r1c2 refers to the value in r1c1, which contains the net sales for January; the formula multiplies that value by the quantity 1 plus the monthly growth rate. The monthly growth rate is calculated from the value in cell r15c1, which contains the yearly growth-rate percentage. The formula in r1c1 refers to the yearly growth-rate assumption through an absolute reference, *r[15]c[1]*. That assumption value is divided by 12 to produce a monthly percentage, and the percentage is divided by 100 to convert it to a decimal.

You need to carry this logic—"look back at the previous cell in this row"—across to the other 10 columns of the model so that you can calculate figures for the next 10 months. To do this, select Copy Right Single-Cell and specify 10 copies (see fig. 15.7).

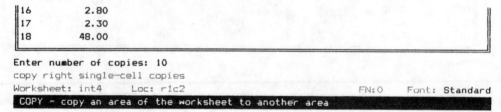

```
| 16    2.80
| 17    2.30
| 18    48.00

Enter number of copies: 10
copy right single-cell copies
Worksheet: int4    Loc: r1c2                          FN:0   Font: Standard
COPY - copy an area of the worksheet to another area
```

Fig. 15.7. *Selecting Copy Right Single-Cell and specifying 10 copies.*

Figure 15.8 shows the completed model after the formula in r1c2 has been copied. Refer to chapter 14 for examples of reformatting using this model.

```
         1      2     3     4     5     6     7     8     9    10    11
 1     75.90 76.66 77.43 78.20 78.98 79.77 80.57 81.38 82.19 83.01 83.84
 2     30.36 30.66 30.97 31.28 31.59 31.91 32.23 32.55 32.88 33.20 33.54
 3     --------------------------------------------------------------------
 4      2.80  2.80  2.80  2.80  2.80  2.80  2.80  2.80  2.80  2.80  2.80
 5     27.56 27.86 28.17 28.48 28.79 29.11 29.43 29.75 30.08 30.40 30.74
 6      2.30  2.30  2.30  2.30  2.30  2.30  2.30  2.30  2.30  2.30  2.30
 7     25.26 25.56 25.87 26.18 26.49 26.81 27.13 27.45 27.78 28.10 28.44
 8     --------------------------------------------------------------------
 9     12.12 12.27 12.42 12.57 12.72 12.87 13.02 13.18 13.33 13.49 13.65
10     13.14 13.29 13.45 13.61 13.78 13.94 14.11 14.27 14.44 14.61 14.79
11     --------------------------------------------------------------------
12      0.05  0.05  0.05  0.05  0.05  0.05  0.05  0.05  0.05  0.06  0.06
13  264000.00
14     40.00
15     12.00
16      2.80
17      2.30
18     48.00
```

```
Enter:
Formula: r1c1*(1+r[15]c[1]/12/100)
Worksheet: int4    Loc: r1c2                    FN:0    Font: Standard
ENTER - enter a formula, a value or text into the current cell
```

Fig. 15.8. *The completed model.*

Copying Cells to Other Areas (Copy From)

The Copy Down and Copy From commands can copy only to areas adjacent to the source row or column. These commands cannot copy both rows and columns at one time, nor can they copy part of a worksheet to other worksheets. To perform these tasks, use the Copy From command.

When using Copy From, you are prompted to

Enter name or block reference:

If you have not already done so, position the cursor on the upper left cell of the block you want to move; press F2 to "drop the anchor." Then move the cursor to the lower right cell of the block and press Enter. These steps define the source block.

Then, the same prompt is displayed again:

Enter name or block reference:

Your answer to this prompt designates the destination block. You can either move the cursor to the upper left cell of the block or type the cell address or name. (You can assign names to cells or groups of cells with the Name command. Refer to Chapter 16 for more information.)

You can copy a range to another active worksheet by prefacing the cell address or name with the name of the destination worksheet. To copy a block to the cell r5c10 in a worksheet named *budget85*, for example, you could enter

budget85.r5c10

If the destination worksheet has a range named *table1*, you could enter

budget85.table1

You can specify a source block from a different worksheet in a similar manner, but if you use cell addresses to designate a range, you must provide the range of rows and columns of the source block rather than just the address of the upper left cell. Use *colons* to indicate the rows and columns:

budget85.r5:10c12:17

There are several good reasons for using range names instead of row and column designations; these reasons are discussed fully in Chapter 16.

If you have a formula that references cells in another worksheet, the Copy command adjusts those relative addresses in the same way it adjusts them in the current worksheet.

Using the Vcopy Command (1-Vcopy)

The Vcopy command, found on command list 1, operates like the Copy command. Instead of copying formulas, however, it copies the results of the formulas and converts the results to values. Use the Vcopy command if you want the destination cells to have values identical to the displayed formula results in the source cells.

The Vcopy command can be useful in retaining the results of various "what if" scenarios. For instance, you run the model and Vcopy the results; then change the assumptions, run the model again, and compare the new results to those of the previous run. Remember that, because the cells copied with the Vcopy command are now *values*, they do not change when you alter the values of the cells used in the original formulas.

Using the Move Command (1-Move, Alt-M)

The Move command is found on command list 1, and the quick key is Alt-M. This command is used to change the location of cell contents within the worksheet. As you are constructing a worksheet, you often need to rearrange the contents to make the worksheet more readable or easier to use.

Moving values or text should certainly be no problem for a computer program; any good text editor or word processor can do that. Smart's Move command is valuable because it goes beyond simply moving data: cell references in formulas are automatically adjusted each time cells are moved. Formulas in cells within the moved range that reference other cells in the range must be adjusted to reflect the new cell locations. Cells *outside* the range that contain formulas referencing cells in the moved range have to be adjusted, as well! Because Smart adjusts cell references, the calculated values of the formulas in the worksheet do not change when Move is used.

When you execute the Move command, the source cells overwrite the cells in the destination range; ideally, you want to overwrite blank cells. But be careful about this command: any formatting options that apply to the source range are also moved. (Refer to Chapter 14 for more information on formatting cells.) After the move is complete, the cells in the source range become blank, and their formatting is removed.

The Move command options are

     Block Columns Rows

These options are explained in the following sections.

Moving Columns (Move Columns)

Before you execute the Move Columns command, first position the cursor on the leftmost column to be moved. When you select the command, the first prompt is

     Enter number of columns:

You can either type the number of columns to be moved (including the current column) or move the cursor to the right edge of the group of columns so that the system enters the number of columns.

Then press Enter. (If you just press Enter in response to the prompt, the default value is 1.)

The next prompt is

`Enter column number of destination:`

At this prompt you enter the number of the column *after which* the designated range of columns is to be moved; or you can use the cursor to enter the number for you. If you want the range to begin with column 26 in the new location, for example, you enter 25. The total number of columns in your worksheet remains unchanged after the move; no blank columns are created, and columns to the right of the destination range are automatically shifted to the right to make room. You are not in danger of overwriting any data. (This is *not* true with the Move Block command, however.)

Moving Rows (Move Rows)

The Move Rows command is similar to the Move Columns command. Position the cursor on the uppermost row you want to move, and select the command. The first prompt is

`Enter number of rows:`

Enter the number or move the cursor to have the system enter the number for you. Then press Enter. (If you just press Enter without a value, the default is 1.)

The next prompts is

`Enter row number of destination:`

You then enter the number of the row *after which* you want to position the designated range or origin rows. You can also move the cursor so that the system enters the destination row for you. Press Enter to complete the command.

No additional rows are created by this command. You do not create any blank rows, nor do you run the risk of overwriting the data in any of the existing rows. The rows after the destination range are shifted downward to accommodate the moved rows, and the source rows are deleted. If you *do* want to create blank rows, use the Insert command.

Moving Blocks (Move Block)

Because the results of the Move Block command can be quite different from those of the other two forms of the Move command, you must be careful. With the Move Block command, you *do* run the risk of overwriting any data or formulas in the destination range (if they exist), and the cells in the source range are left blank at the completion of the command. The total number of rows and columns remains unchanged.

The first prompt of the Move Block command is

`Enter name or block reference:`

If you haven't already done so, move your cursor to the cell in the upper left corner of the source range; press F2 to drop the anchor. Then move the cursor to the lower right cell, and press Enter to complete the source-range definition.

The second prompt is the same as the first:

`Enter name or block reference:`

In answer to this prompt, either type the cell address of the upper left corner of the destination range or move the cursor; then press Enter.

For the construction of the financial model, the assumption variables must be moved from rows 14 through 18 to row 13 (refer to fig. 15.8). You can use the Move Block command to accomplish this.

In the following sequence, r14c1 is moved to r13c2. Figure 15.9 shows the beginning of the execution of the command. The cursor has been placed on r14c1, the command has been executed, and the following prompt is displayed:

`Enter name or block reference:`

If the block contained more than one cell, you would press F2 to drop the anchor, then move the cursor to the bottom right corner of the range and press Enter. Because this block contains only one cell, you can just press Enter to define the source range.

In figure 15.10, the cursor has been moved to r13c2 to establish the destination range. Notice that the address *r13c2* appears on the command line.

Figure 15.11 shows the worksheet on completion of the Move command. The cursor has been placed on r2c1 and Enter mode has been invoked so that the formula appears on the command line. Note that the formula has been automatically adjusted to reference the new position of the gross profit rate of 40 percent, which has just been moved to r13c2. None of the displayed calculation results have changed as a result of the move.

```
          1      2      3      4      5      6      7      8      9     10     11
1      75.90  76.66  77.43  78.20  78.98  79.77  80.57  81.38  82.19  83.01  83.84
2      30.36  30.66  30.97  31.28  31.59  31.91  32.23  32.55  32.88  33.20  33.54
3    ----------------------------------------------------------------------------
4       2.80   2.80   2.80   2.80   2.80   2.80   2.80   2.80   2.80   2.80   2.80
5      27.56  27.86  28.17  28.48  28.79  29.11  29.43  29.75  30.08  30.40  30.74
6       2.30   2.30   2.30   2.30   2.30   2.30   2.30   2.30   2.30   2.30   2.30
7      25.26  25.56  25.87  26.18  26.49  26.81  27.13  27.45  27.78  28.10  28.44
8    ----------------------------------------------------------------------------
9      12.12  12.27  12.42  12.57  12.72  12.87  13.02  13.18  13.33  13.49  13.65
10     13.14  13.29  13.45  13.61  13.78  13.94  14.11  14.27  14.44  14.61  14.79
11   ----------------------------------------------------------------------------
12      0.05   0.05   0.05   0.05   0.05   0.05   0.05   0.05   0.05   0.06   0.06
13  264000.00
14      40.00
15      12.00
16       2.80
17       2.30
18      48.00
```

Enter name or block reference:
move block
Worksheet: int5   Loc: r14c1   FN:0   Font: Standard
MOVE - move rows or columns

Fig. 15.9. *Defining the source range for Move Block.*

```
          1      2      3      4      5      6      7      8      9     10     11
1      75.90  76.66  77.43  78.20  78.98  79.77  80.57  81.38  82.19  83.01  83.84
2      30.36  30.66  30.97  31.28  31.59  31.91  32.23  32.55  32.88  33.20  33.54
3    ----------------------------------------------------------------------------
4       2.80   2.80   2.80   2.80   2.80   2.80   2.80   2.80   2.80   2.80   2.80
5      27.56  27.86  28.17  28.48  28.79  29.11  29.43  29.75  30.08  30.40  30.74
6       2.30   2.30   2.30   2.30   2.30   2.30   2.30   2.30   2.30   2.30   2.30
7      25.26  25.56  25.87  26.18  26.49  26.81  27.13  27.45  27.78  28.10  28.44
8    ----------------------------------------------------------------------------
9      12.12  12.27  12.42  12.57  12.72  12.87  13.02  13.18  13.33  13.49  13.65
10     13.14  13.29  13.45  13.61  13.78  13.94  14.11  14.27  14.44  14.61  14.79
11   ----------------------------------------------------------------------------
12      0.05   0.05   0.05   0.05   0.05   0.05   0.05   0.05   0.05   0.06   0.06
13  264000.00
14      40.00
15      12.00
16       2.80
17       2.30
18      48.00
```

Enter name or block reference: r13c2
F2 Drop anchor   F3 Absolute/Relative
Worksheet: int5   Loc: r13c2   FN: Font: Standard
MOVE - move rows or columns

Fig. 15.10. *Defining the destination range for Move Block.*

	1	2	3	4	5	6	7	8	9	10	11
1	75.90	76.66	77.43	78.20	78.98	79.77	80.57	81.38	82.19	83.01	83.84
2	30.36	30.66	30.97	31.28	31.59	31.91	32.23	32.55	32.88	33.20	33.54
3	---	---	---	---	---	---	---	---	---	---	---
4	2.80	2.80	2.80	2.80	2.80	2.80	2.80	2.80	2.80	2.80	2.80
5	27.56	27.86	28.17	28.48	28.79	29.11	29.43	29.75	30.08	30.40	30.74
6	2.30	2.30	2.30	2.30	2.30	2.30	2.30	2.30	2.30	2.30	2.30
7	25.26	25.56	25.87	26.18	26.49	26.81	27.13	27.45	27.78	28.10	28.44
8	---	---	---	---	---	---	---	---	---	---	---
9	12.12	12.27	12.42	12.57	12.72	12.87	13.02	13.18	13.33	13.49	13.65
10	13.14	13.29	13.45	13.61	13.78	13.94	14.11	14.27	14.44	14.61	14.79
11	---	---	---	---	---	---	---	---	---	---	---
12	0.05	0.05	0.05	0.05	0.05	0.05	0.05	0.05	0.05	0.06	0.06
13	264000.00	40.00									
14											
15	12.00										
16	2.80										
17	2.30										
18	48.00										

```
Enter:
Formula: r1c1*r[13]c[2]/100
Worksheet: int5     Loc: r2c1                          FN:0    Font: Standard
ENTER - enter a formula, a value or text into the current cell
```

Fig. 15.11. *The model after the Move command has been completed.*

The process of moving the rest of the assumption variables to row 13 is similar.

Using the Insert Command (1–Insert, Alt-I)

The Insert command, found on command list 1, is used to add blank rows, columns, or blocks to your worksheet (see fig. 15.12). When you insert new blank ranges, the formulas in the shifted cells are automatically adjusted to reflect the new cell numbers. The quick key for this command is Alt-I.

The Insert command has three options:

Block Columns Rows

In the following sections, you'll become familiar with these options as we finish creating our financial model.

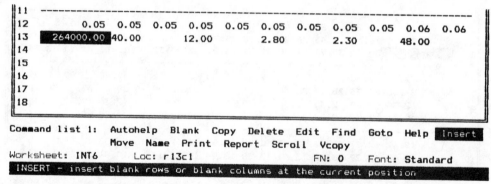

Fig. 15.12. *Selecting the Insert command.*

Inserting Columns (Insert Columns)

If you compare figure 15.11 with figure 15.1, you can see that you need to insert two rows above row 1 to make room for the titles, and one column before column 1 to make room for the line labels.

To insert columns in the worksheet, move your cursor to the column *before which* you want to insert the new columns and execute the command. You are then prompted to

Enter number of columns:

You can respond with a number or move the cursor to the right so that the system enters the number for you. Then press Enter. (If you don't enter a number, the value defaults to 1.)

In response to the command, the columns to the right of the designated column are shifted to the right, and the formulas in the cells are adjusted. The cursor remains on the original column. Any format settings are shifted along with the data and formulas; the new columns revert to the default format settings.

Inserting Rows (Insert Rows)

To insert rows in the worksheet, move the cursor to the row *above which* you want to insert the new rows. When you select the command, the following prompt appears:

Enter number of rows:

Respond by typing the number of rows you want to insert or by moving the cursor so that the system enters the number. Then press Enter. (Again, if you don't enter a number, the value defaults to 1.)

When the command is executed, the rows are shifted down and the formulas in the cells are adjusted. The cursor remains on the original row. Format settings are shifted along with the affected rows.

Figure 15.13 shows the model after the new rows and columns have been inserted. Titles still need to be added, and some formatting remains to be done.

	1	2	3	4	5	6	7	8	9	10
1										
2										
3		75.90	76.66	77.43	78.20	78.98	79.77	80.57	81.38	82.19
4		30.36	30.66	30.97	31.28	31.59	31.91	32.23	32.55	32.88
5										
6		2.80	2.80	2.80	2.80	2.80	2.80	2.80	2.80	2.80
7		27.56	27.86	28.17	28.48	28.79	29.11	29.43	29.75	30.08
8		2.30	2.30	2.30	2.30	2.30	2.30	2.30	2.30	2.30
9		25.26	25.56	25.87	26.18	26.49	26.81	27.13	27.45	27.78
10										
11		12.12	12.27	12.42	12.57	12.72	12.87	13.02	13.18	13.33
12		13.14	13.29	13.45	13.61	13.78	13.94	14.11	14.27	14.44
13										
14		0.05	0.05	0.05	0.05	0.05	0.05	0.05	0.05	0.05
15										
16										
17										
18		264000.00	40.00		12.00		2.80		2.30	

```
Enter:
Formula: r3c2*r[18]c[3]/100
Worksheet: int7    Loc: r4c2                    FN:0    Font: Standard
ENTER - enter a formula, a value or text into the current cell
```

Fig. 15.13. *The model after rows and columns have been inserted.*

Inserting Blocks (Insert Block)

With the Insert Block command, you can define a range to be inserted in the body of a worksheet. You define the range by using the F2 key to drop the anchor at the upper left corner, entering the address or "pointing" with the cursor to the bottom right corner of the range, and pressing Enter.

This command causes data and formulas on the same rows as the specified range to be shifted to the right, opening up a "hole" in your worksheet. Be careful not to insert a block in the middle of a table such as the one in our example model, because the columns will be moved out of alignment. If you accidentally insert a block where you do not want it, use the Delete command to close up the "hole."

Using the Delete Command (1–Delete, Alt-D)

The Delete command is found on command list 1, and the quick key is Alt-D. This command erases columns, rows, or blocks from your worksheet, shifts the remainder of the worksheet to close the gaps, and automatically adjusts formulas to reflect new cell addresses. Be careful: unless you save the worksheet before you begin deleting, there is no way to recover the deleted material.

The Delete command differs in an important way from the Blank command, which is discussed later in this chapter. The Delete command removes the designated range and closes the intervening space; columns are moved to the left, or rows are moved up. The Blank command, on the other hand, clears out the data or text in the range, but the rest of the worksheet does not shift position. In both cases, however, the text and data are gone.

The options for the Delete command are

Block Columns Rows

The sections that follow show how to use these options and explain the differences between Delete and Blank.

Deleting Columns (Delete Columns)

To delete columns, position the cursor on the column you want to delete (or the leftmost column, if you want to delete a range of columns) and issue the command. You are prompted to

Enter number of columns:

You can type a number or move the cursor to the right to have the system enter the number; then you press Enter. (If you don't enter a number, the value defaults to 1, indicating only the current column.)

The designated columns are then deleted. The remaining columns to the right are shifted left, and formulas are automatically readjusted. If any formulas in columns to the right of the deleted range referenced cells in the deleted range, the formulas are readjusted to refer to cells to the left of the deleted range. You may not get an error message, but the formula results may be wrong.

Deleting Rows (Delete Rows)

To delete rows from the worksheet, move the cursor to the first row you want to delete and issue the command. The prompt is

Enter number of rows:

Type the number of rows you want to delete, or move the cursor to have the system enter the number. Press Enter. If you don't enter a number, the value defaults to 1.

The rows you have specified are deleted, and the rows below them are shifted upward. Formulas are automatically readjusted. Take the same care when deleting rows as when deleting columns; you can have the same problems with formula references to cells in deleted areas.

Deleting Blocks (Delete Block)

When you issue the Delete Block command, you are prompted to

Enter name or block reference:

Move the cursor to the upper left cell of the block that is to be deleted and press F2 to drop the anchor. Then move the cursor to the lower right cell of the block and press Enter to complete the range designation. Instead of using the cursor, you can type the range addresses (for example, *r5:12c7:11*); you can also enter the name of a range, if a range name has been assigned to the block you want to delete.

When you have executed the command, the designated range is deleted, and cells on the same rows to the right of the deleted range are shifted to the left to fill the gap.

Figure 15.14 illustrates the effect of deleting a block. The highlighted block in the window on the left is about to be deleted; the corresponding block in the window on the right has already been deleted.

Notice that in rows 6 through 10, the cells to the right of the block have shifted to the left because columns 2 and 3 have been deleted. By examining the cell entries, you can see that the entry originally in r6c4 is now in cell r6c2, the entry originally in r6c5 is now in r6c3, and so on.

#1	1	2	3	4	5
1	r1c1	r1c2	r1c3	r1c4	r1c5
2	r2c1	r2c2	r2c3	r2c4	r2c5
3	r3c1	r3c2	r3c3	r3c4	r3c5
4	r4c1	r4c2	r4c3	r4c4	r4c5
5	r5c1	r5c2	r5c3	r5c4	r5c5
6	r6c1	r6c2	r6c3	r6c4	r6c5
7	r7c1	r7c2	r7c3	r7c4	r7c5
8	r8c1	r8c2	r8c3	r8c4	r8c5
9	r9c1	r9c2	r9c3	r9c4	r9c5
10	r10c1	r10c2	r10c3	r10c4	r10c5
11	r11c1	r11c2	r11c3	r11c4	r11c5
12	r12c1	r12c2	r12c3	r12c4	r12c5
13	r13c1	r13c2	r13c3	r13c4	r13c5
14	r14c1	r14c2	r14c3	r14c4	r14c5
15	r15c1	r15c2	r15c3	r15c4	r15c5
16	r16c1	r16c2	r16c3	r16c4	r16c5
17	r17c1	r17c2	r17c3	r17c4	r17c5
18	r18c1	r18c2	r18c3	r18c4	r18c5

#2	1	2	3	4
1	r1c1	r1c2	r1c3	r1c4
2	r2c1	r2c2	r2c3	r2c4
3	r3c1	r3c2	r3c3	r3c4
4	r4c1	r4c2	r4c3	r4c4
5	r5c1	r5c2	r5c3	r5c4
6	r6c1	r6c4	r6c5	r6c6
7	r7c1	r7c4	r7c5	r7c6
8	r8c1	r8c4	r8c5	r8c6
9	r9c1	r9c4	r9c5	r9c6
10	r10c1	r10c4	r10c5	r10c6
11	r11c1	r11c2	r11c3	r11c4
12	r12c1	r12c2	r12c3	r12c4
13	r13c1	r13c2	r13c3	r13c4
14	r14c1	r14c2	r14c3	r14c4
15	r15c1	r15c2	r15c3	r15c4
16	r16c1	r16c2	r16c3	r16c4
17	r17c1	r17c2	r17c3	r17c4
18	r18c1	r18c2	r18c3	r18c4

```
Enter name or block reference: r6:10c2:3
F2 Drop anchor    F3 Absolute/Relative
Worksheet: del1    Loc: r10c3                      FN:0    Font: Standard
DELETE - delete a block, or any number of rows or columns
```

Fig. 15.14. *The effect of the Delete Block command.*

Using the Blank Command (1–Blank, Alt-B)

The Blank command is found on command list 1, and the quick key is Alt-B. This command is used to erase values, text, and formulas from designated rows or columns or a specified block. In addition, you can use Blank All to erase the entire worksheet in the current window.

Be sure that you understand the difference between Blank and Delete. The Blank command removes the data and formulas from the cells, but the deleted range is still in place; no other cells are shifted. The Delete command, as you have seen, not only erases the data and formulas but also "closes up" the worksheet, removing the deleted block, rows, or columns.

If you have locked cells in the block, rows, or columns you want to blank, the system refuses to execute the command. (See Chapter 17 for information about locking cells.) The following message appears on the command line:

```
Block contains [nr] locked cells. First locked cell at [address]
```

In this message, the number of locked cells in the designated range appears in the place of *[nr]*, and the cell address of the first locked cell appears in the place of *[address]*. If, however, you execute the Blank All command, the locked cells are ignored and if you answer *y* to the prompt, the entire worksheet is blanked.

Using the Blank command is similar to using Delete. The four Blank options are shown in figure 15.15.

	1	2	3	4	5	6	7	8	9	10
1										
2										
3		75.90	76.66	77.43	78.20	78.98	79.77	80.57	81.38	82.19
4		30.36	30.66	30.97	31.28	31.59	31.91	32.23	32.55	32.88
5										
6		2.80	2.80	2.80	2.80	2.80	2.80	2.80	2.80	2.80
7		27.56	27.86	28.17	28.48	28.79	29.11	29.43	29.75	30.08
8		2.30	2.30	2.30	2.30	2.30	2.30	2.30	2.30	2.30
9		25.26	25.56	25.87	26.18	26.49	26.81	27.13	27.45	27.78
10										
11		12.12	12.27	12.42	12.57	12.72	12.87	13.02	13.18	13.33
12		13.14	13.29	13.45	13.61	13.78	13.94	14.11	14.27	14.44
13										
14		0.05	0.05	0.05	0.05	0.05	0.05	0.05	0.05	0.05
15										
16										
17										
18		264000.00	40.00		12.00		2.80		2.30	

```
Select option: Block  Columns  Rows  All
blank
Worksheet: bldemo   Loc: r4c2                    FN:0    Font: Standard
BLANK - blank an area of the worksheet
```

Fig. 15.15. *Selecting the Blank command options.*

Clearing Columns (Blank Columns)

To execute Blank Columns, position your cursor on the first column you want to blank and issue the command. The prompt is

> Enter number of columns:

You can type the number of columns or move the cursor to the right so that the system enters the number for you. Press Enter to complete the command.

The blanked columns are still in place, but they contain no data. Any formatting options applied to the columns are also removed.

Clearing Rows (Blank Rows)

To use the Blank Rows command, position the cursor on the first row to be blanked and issue the command. The prompt is

Enter number of rows:

Type the number of rows or move the cursor downward. Then press Enter to complete the command. The rows are still in place, but the data has been removed.

Clearing Blocks (Blank Block)

When you execute the Blank Block command, you are prompted to

Enter name or block reference:

If you have not already done so, move your cursor to the upper left corner of the block to be blanked; press F2 to drop the anchor. Then move the cursor to the lower right corner of the block and press Enter to complete the block definition. The cells in the defined range now are blanked out, and their contents removed. No cells in the rest of the worksheet are shifted, although formula results may change if the formulas referenced cells in the blanked range. A blank cell is evaluated as a zero if used in a formula.

Clearing the Worksheet (Blank All)

To blank an entire worksheet, use the Blank All command. Be careful when you use this command, however; there is no warning prompt to verify that you really want to blank the worksheet.

Using the Edit Command (1–Edit, Alt-E)

The Edit command is found on command list 1, and the quick key is Alt-E. This command is used to edit existing values, text, or formulas in a cell.

Short formulas (up to 240 characters) are displayed on the command line for editing. If the formula is long, however (maximum 1,000 characters), the full-screen formula editor is invoked automatically.

In the "short" formula editor, the cursor is positioned on the first character of the formula or text. You use the cursor keys to position the cursor within the editing workspace. The Ins key is used to toggle between overlay mode and insert mode, but the status of the Ins key is not shown if the "short" editor is used. If your formula is long enough to require the full-screen formula editor, the status of the Ins key is shown at the right of the status line. You can always invoke the formula editor for any formula by using the quick key Alt-E.

After you have made the necessary changes to your formula, values, or text entries, press Enter to complete the editing process.

Conclusion

Developing a worksheet is usually a step-by-step process. First, you develop the "kernel" of the worksheet that contains the most important elements; then you expand the model to encompass the full range you wish to cover. This chapter has discussed the commands you need to copy and move cells within your worksheet. The Insert and Delete command can be used for increasing or decreasing the size of the worksheet.

Chapter 16

Operating the Spreadsheet

After a spreadsheet is constructed, certain commands are used to make it operate the way you want it to, or to make working with your spreadsheet easier or faster.

The Sort command, introduced in this chapter, is used to rearrange a block of columns or rows, depending on their contents.

This chapter also covers the naming of blocks of cells. In previous chapters, blocks of cells have usually been referenced with "colon notation" to indicate a range. For example, *r1:5c10:17* indicates the block including rows 1 through 5 and columns 10 through 17.

The Name command is used to simplify moving the cursor in the worksheet or moving between worksheets. The Find command can also be used if you are searching for a specific value or text item. The Scroll command provides a practical way of viewing successive portions of your worksheet.

The different methods of initiating calculations are also covered in this chapter.

Establishing Order in Columns and Rows (2-Sort)

The Sort command is found on command list 2; it is used to rearrange cells within a block in ascending or descending order according to the contents of a row or column in that block.

When you select the Sort command, Smart prompts you to

Enter name or block reference:

You can type the block address in row-and-column notation (*r3:7c5:10*, for example). An easier way is to move the cursor to the upper left cell of the block, press F2 to "drop the anchor," and then move the cursor to the lower right corner of the block. The block is highlighted as you go. You can also use a block name, as discussed later in this chapter. Press Enter to complete definition of the block.

The next prompt is

Ascending Descending

After you choose ascending or descending order, you are prompted to choose a sort key in a column or a row:

Column Row

If you select Column, Smart prompts you to

Enter column number of sort key:

By selecting Column, you indicate that the block is to be sorted according to the contents of cells in a particular column of the block; rows within the block are to be rearranged according to that sort key. You can either enter the number of the column or move the cursor so that the system enters the number.

You can specify as many as 15 separate columns as sort keys for the block. Each key can be sorted in ascending or descending order. For instance, if you specify *ascending* order in response to the prompt, you can override this default by typing a *d* after the column. The following example is the response you would enter to sort by column 7 ascending, 10 descending, and 8 ascending:

7 10d 8

If you specify descending order as the default for the sort, you must enter an *a* to override that default for a specific column.

Press Enter when you have entered the values. (If you press Enter without entering a value, the current column is selected as the default.)

If you select Row, you are prompted to

    Enter row number of sort key:

By selecting Row, you indicate that the block is to be sorted according to the contents of cells in a particular row of the block; columns within the block are to be rearranged according to that sort key. As with the column specification, you can designate multiple rows as sort keys.

Press Enter when you have entered the values. (If you press Enter without entering a value, the current row is selected as the default.)

If the sorted cells contain formulas, the formulas are adjusted relative to the new cell locations. Sorting is performed in *collation* sequence; alphabetic characters are grouped together regardless of whether they are in upper- or lowercase. In this sequence, both *ACCT* and *acct* occur before *DATA* in the sort order. In the more usual sort sequence according to ASCII values, *DATA* occurs before *acct*—and, for that matter, before *dATA*—because all uppercase letters have lower ASCII values than do lowercase letters. (*ASCII* is an acronym for American Standard Code for Information Interchange. A complete table of ASCII codes is printed in the appendix to the System Commands section of the *Smart System Manual.*)

Figure 16.1 shows one set of data sorted in two different sequences.

Naming a Block of Cells (1-Name)

The Name command, found on command list 1, is used to give a name to a block of cells. You can use the block name wherever you are prompted for a name or block reference. You also can use a block name with the Goto command to move your cursor from one location to another in the worksheet.

Names are particularly useful if you are consolidating several worksheets into one. Although a formula allows you to reference specific cells in another worksheet, the references are not dynamic. If you move the referenced cells in the source file, the formulas in the destination file do not automatically readjust. But if the reference is

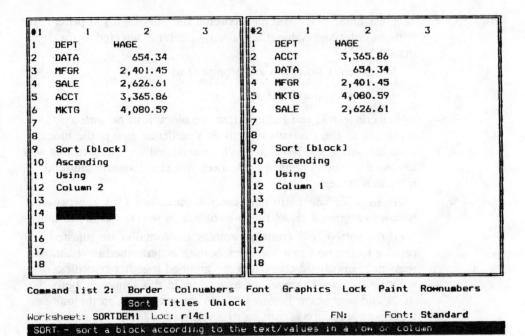

```
#1      1           2        3     #2      1           2        3
1   DEPT    WAGE                   1   DEPT    WAGE
2   DATA        654.34            2   ACCT      3,365.86
3   MFGR      2,401.45            3   DATA        654.34
4   SALE      2,626.61            4   MFGR      2,401.45
5   ACCT      3,365.86            5   MKTG      4,080.59
6   MKTG      4,080.59            6   SALE      2,626.61
7                                 7
8                                 8
9   Sort [block]                  9   Sort [block]
10  Ascending                     10  Ascending
11  Using                         11  Using
12  Column 2                      12  Column 1
13                                13
14  ████████                      14
15                                15
16                                16
17                                17
18                                18
```

```
Command list 2:  Border  Colnumbers  Font  Graphics  Lock  Paint  Rownumbers
                 Sort  Titles  Unlock
Worksheet: SORTDEM1  Loc: r14c1              FN:      Font: Standard
  SORT - sort a block according to the text/values in a row or column
```

Fig. 16.1. *Sorting one set of data two ways.*

```
15  ----------------------------------------------------------------------
16    Average      Gr Prof     Sales      G&A        Intst      Tax
17    Shares:      Rate %      Grow %     Expense:   Expense:   Rate%
18    264,000      40          12         2.8        2.3        48
```

```
Select option:  Define  Edit  Print  Undefine
name
Worksheet: int11     Loc: r1c1              FN:      Font: Standard
  NAME - define, undefine, print or edit user names
```

Fig. 16.2. *Selecting a Name command option.*

to a name in the source file, the system can resolve the formula correctly no matter where the referenced cells are moved.

Figure 16.2 illustrates the menu options for the Name command.

Names are stored as an integral part of the worksheet file. There is no separate command to save names, nor are they saved in a separate file.

Defining a Named Block (Name Define)

To define a block that is to be associated with a name, select Define from the menu. Smart then prompts you to

Enter new name:

The name may be as many as eight characters long and must begin with a letter. Names are not case-sensitive, so it does not matter whether you enter them in upper- or lowercase letters. After you have typed the name, press Enter. Smart then prompts you to

Enter definition for this name:

At this prompt you define the block. You can enter the addresses in row-and-column notation: *r3:7c5:10*. An easier way is to move the cursor to the upper left cell of the block, press F2 to "drop the anchor," and then move the cursor to the lower right corner of the block. The block is highlighted as you go. Press Enter to complete definition of the block.

Printing Block Names (Name Print)

You can use the Name Print command to print a list of block names. Figure 16.3 shows the output of this command. To view a list of block names, use the Name Edit command.

```
User names for worksheet namdemo

apr                 r2:14c5
aug                 r2:14c9
feb                 r2:14c3
jan                 r2:14c2
jul                 r2:14c8
jun                 r2:14c7
mar                 r2:14c4
may                 r2:14c6
```

Fig. 16.3. *An example of the Name Print command's output.*

Editing a Named-Block Definition (Name Edit)

To edit the block definition for a name, use the Name Edit command. A list of names and blocks is displayed, as shown in figure 16.4.

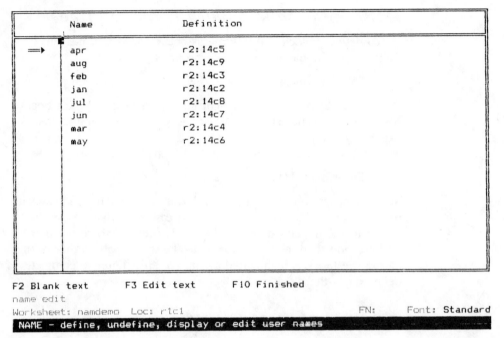

Fig. 16.4. *Displaying a list of names and blocks.*

Use the ↑ or the ↓ key to point to the name of the definition you want to edit. (You are editing the definition, not the name itself.) Press F2 to begin editing. You can use the cursor keys to move back and forth as you edit the definition. Pressing the Insert key toggles between insertion and overwrite modes, but the Insert status is not indicated on-screen.

The Name Edit command can also be used to display a list of the names defined within the worksheet.

Removing a Name (Name Undefine)

To remove a name from the list, select Name Undefine. Smart then prompts you to

    Enter name:

Note that no pop-up menu reminds you of the names. If you need to see a list, use the Name Edit command before using Name Undefine.

Using the Goto Command (1–Goto, F4)

The Goto command is found on command list 1; the quick key is F4. This multipurpose command is used to change windows, bring up a different worksheet in the current window, or move the cursor to a specified physical location, cell, or named block within the current window.

When you select the Goto command, the prompt is

```
Enter worksheet, name, cell reference or window:
```

No pop-up menus appear to aid you with this command. If you want to bring up a different worksheet in the current window, enter the name of an active worksheet in response to the prompt. (Use the Index command to display a list of active worksheets.)

To move the cursor to the upper left corner of a block that has been assigned a name, enter the name of the block in response to the prompt. The possibility for confusion exists if a block in the current worksheet happens to have the same name as a worksheet. Smart will go to the block in the current worksheet instead of displaying the other worksheet.

To go to a specific cell, enter a cell-reference address, such as *r100c50*, at the prompt. You can also combine a worksheet name and either a cell reference or a block name in one of the following formats:

DOMESTIC.r5c6
CANADA.shares

Smart then displays the specified worksheet and moves the cursor to the cell or block indicated to the right of the period. The specified cell (or the upper left cell of the block) appears in the upper left corner of your screen.

To go to another window, type the number of that window in response to the prompt. The cursor then moves to the specified window. The Alt-F7 and Alt-F8 quick keys can be used to move the cursor to the previous or next numbered window. If you are in window 1, for example, Alt-F8 advances you to window 2; press Alt-F8 again, and you advance to window 3.

You can also press a cursor-control key to skip blank cells in your worksheet or to find the last filled cell before a blank cell:

Current Cell	Next Cell	Cursor Stops On
Filled	Filled	Cell before the next blank cell
Filled	Blank	Next filled cell
Blank	Either	Next filled cell

Searching for Errors, Text, and Values (1–Find, F3)

Use the Find command, on command list 1, to look for a cell with specific contents or to hunt down worksheet errors; the quick key is F3. To repeat a previous Find command, you can use the F9 key if you have issued no intervening command; if you have issued other commands since the previous Find command, use the Alt-R key combination.

The Find command looks through your worksheet, starting from the current cursor position and working from left to right and from top to bottom. You cannot search backward through your worksheet. The command menu offers three options:

Error Text Value

If you select Text, the next prompt is

Enter text

Enter a text string that you want to find. Because the search is not case-sensitive, you do not have to worry about upper- or lowercase. The text you search for may be in the middle of a word; you do not have the option to search for "whole word" matches. If the text can be found in the current window without shifting the view of the worksheet, the cursor is moved and the view is unchanged.

If you select Value, you are prompted to

Enter value:

You can find entered values or those that are the results of formulas; be aware, however, that Smart searches for a match with the "underlying" value, not necessarily with the number displayed. You may not be able to find a displayed number that is rounded by a previous use of the Reformat command. (See chapter 14 for more information on Reformat.)

To hunt down errors, select Error; there are no further prompts. Smart searches for error cells and stops at the first one it finds. To display an explanation of the error and to correct it, press Alt-E to edit the cell. The Find command locates only primary errors, not those which result from other errors.

Moving Through the Spreadsheet (1–Scroll, Ctrl-PgUp, Ctrl-PgDn)

Another way to find your way through a spreadsheet is to use the Scroll command, which is found on command list 1; the quick keys are Ctrl-PgUp (to scroll up) and Ctrl-PgDn (to scroll down). The Scroll command is used to scroll the worksheet up or down at different rates of speed.

The Scroll command options are

Down Up

After you select a direction, Smart prompts you to select a scrolling speed:

Enter scroll rate (1 is slowest, 10 is fastest):

You enter a number from 1 to 10, and then press Enter. The number 0 is used to select the fastest speed.

You can change direction while scrolling by pressing the ↑ or ↓ key. To change the rate of scrolling, press a number from 1 to 0 (in this case, the 0 stands for 10). Press any other key to pause; press any key again to resume scrolling. To halt the scrolling altogether, press Escape.

If you use the Ctrl-PgUp or Ctrl-PgDn quick keys, the scrolling rate defaults to 10.

Retaining Title Rows or Columns (2–Titles, Alt-T)

As you move through your worksheet, you may want to keep certain title rows or columns on the screen so that you can more easily determine what you are viewing. If your column headings are in rows 1 through 3, for example, you may want to fix these rows on the screen so that you still know what the columns mean when you scroll down to row 99.

The Titles command is found on command list 2; the quick key is Alt-T. This command is used to fix a number of rows or columns (or both) so that they remain in place as you move through your worksheet. You can fix only the columns at the left of the worksheet and the rows at the top. After you have established title areas, you cannot move the cursor into these areas until you drop the titles. The titles apply to only the version of the worksheet in the current window; if the same worksheet is in another window, you can move the cursor into the areas that are fixed in the other window. Any changes made to the worksheet are not reflected in the first window until titles are dropped, however.

Titles are retained even after you unload a worksheet or go to a different one in the same window.

Before using this command, press Ctrl-Home to position your cursor on row 1, column 1; then select the Titles command. Options on the first menu are

> Drop Fix

If you select Fix, Smart prompts you to choose

> Columns Rows

If you select Columns, you are prompted to

> Enter the number of columns:

You can either type a number or move the cursor so that the system enters the number for you. Press Enter when you finish. (The number defaults to 1 if you just press Enter at the prompt.) The columns you have fixed remain in place as you move right and left to view different portions of your worksheet.

If you select Fix Rows, you are prompted to

> Enter number of rows:

Again, you can either type a number or move the cursor so that the system enters the number for you. Press Enter after you indicate a number. (The number defaults to 1 if you just press Enter at the prompt.) The rows you have fixed remain in place as you move up and down, viewing different portions of your worksheet.

To erase titles settings, choose the Drop option; this command simultaneously removes both column and row titles.

Recalculating the Worksheet (5–Auto-Recalc)

You have the choice of automatically recalculating your worksheet after every change or of recalculating only when you want to. There are good reasons for using either method at different times.

While you are building your worksheet, you probably don't want it to be recalculated automatically; recalculation takes time, and incomplete worksheet sections can cause errors. Even after a worksheet is built, you may want the system to wait until you finish entering several numbers before it recalculates. On the other hand, if you are modeling a worksheet and changing variables as you go (as in the financial model developed in this section), you may want the convenience of automatic recalculation.

The Auto-Recalc command is found on command list 5; it is used to determine whether recalculation is performed automatically or manually. The setting you select remains in effect for the duration of the session or until you change the setting. The default condition is established on line 2 of Parameters.

When you select Auto-Recalc, you are prompted to select one of four options:

Automatic Display Iterate Manual

Usually, you will select Automatic or Manual. To show the current setting, select Display; if the current setting is automatic, for example, the following display appears on the command line:

Recalculation mode: Automatic

If the current setting is Manual, you can press the F5 key to force recalculation. The word *CALC* is displayed on the status line if values have been entered or changed and the worksheet has not been recalculated.

If you select Iterate, calculation of the spreadsheet continues until specified conditions are met; the options are

Count Remove Test

If you select Count, you are prompted for the number of iterations to be performed. You can specify the Count option in either Automatic or Manual mode. To disable the Count option, set the value to zero.

Choosing the Test option causes recalculation to continue until a test value is achieved or a maximum number of calculations is performed. When you select Test, you are prompted to

`Enter name or block reference:`

You respond with the name or block reference of the cell containing the formula being calculated.

Next, you are prompted to

`Enter delta value:`

Recalculation continues until the change in the value of the formula in the test cell gets below the "delta" value.

The next prompt is

`Enter maximum number of iterations:`

If you do not enter a number, the default is 0. Do not set the number too high because you cannot halt processing during iterative recalculation. Note that the recalculation mode and iteration specifications are saved with the worksheet.

Iterative calculation is useful when your spreadsheet contains circular references, which are indicated by the key word *CIRC* on the status line. A circular reference does not necessarily indicate an error; you may find that using a "cut and try" approach is a legitimate modeling technique. The automatic iteration capability of the Auto-Recalc command simplifies that approach.

You use the Remove option to cancel the use of the iteration feature of the Auto-Recalc command.

Using Miscellaneous Spreadsheet Commands

This section explains commands that are unique to the Smart Spreadsheet and deserve special attention. The Fill command is used to generate data values in your worksheet. This command can be useful for developing tables of numbers and can save you the effort of entering them by hand. The Matrix command has many uses, primarily in scientific and statistical work, but some of them can be applied to the business environment.

Using the Fill Command (3-Fill)

The Fill command, on command list 3, is used to generate new data values and enter them in designated cells on a worksheet. Only numeric data can be generated with Fill; you cannot generate text data. The format can be a normal display or a dollar or percent format.

Position the cursor at the starting location before you initiate the Fill command. The primary menu for the Fill command is

Block Columns Rows

If you select Columns or Rows, you should move the cursor to the leftmost column or the uppermost row of the area that you want to fill.

When you select Columns, you are prompted to

Enter number of columns:

Enter the number of columns for the range or move the cursor to the right so that the system enters the number at the prompt on the command line. Press Enter when the number is correct. If you press Enter without typing a number, the value defaults to 1.

When you select Rows, you are prompted to

Enter number of rows:

You then enter the number of rows for the range or move the cursor down so that the system enters the number. Press Enter when the number is correct. If you press Enter without typing a number, the value defaults to 1.

If you select Block, you are prompted to

Enter name or block reference:

You can enter the range by typing the address in row-and-column notation, such as *r3:7c5:10*. An easier method is to move the cursor to the upper left cell of the range and press F2 to drop the anchor. Then move the cursor to the lower right corner of the range; the range is highlighted as you go. Press Enter to complete the definition.

After you have selected the range, the next prompt is

Enter start value:

Your answer should be the value that is to be entered in the first cell of the range—either the leftmost column, the uppermost row, or the upper left corner of the the block. The number can be an integer or a decimal value. To specify a dollar format, precede the entry with a dollar sign (*$5.34*, for example). For a percent format, enter a percent sign after the entry (*25%*).

The next prompt is

Enter increment:

The *increment* is the amount to be added (or subtracted, if the number is negative) from cell to cell. Don't attach a dollar sign or a percent sign to this figure; the formatting is designated by the starting-value entry. The first cell contains the starting value, the next cell is the sum of the starting value and the increment, and so on.

Figure 16.5 illustrates the use of the Fill command. In row 1, the starting value is $5.34 and the increment is 2.5. In cell r3:14c1, the starting value is 25% and the increment is -2. (Enter the increment as a percent rather than a decimal.)

	1	2	3	4	5	6	7
1	$5.34	$7.84	$10.34	$12.84	$15.34	$17.84	
2							
3	25.00%						
4	23.00%		0.27	0.00	-0.27	-0.54	
5	21.00%		0.24	-0.03	-0.30	-0.57	
6	19.00%		0.21	-0.06	-0.33	-0.60	
7	17.00%		0.18	-0.09	-0.36	-0.63	
8	15.00%		0.15	-0.12	-0.39	-0.66	
9	13.00%		0.12	-0.15	-0.42	-0.69	
10	11.00%		0.09	-0.18	-0.45	-0.72	
11	9.00%		0.06	-0.21	-0.48	-0.75	
12	7.00%		0.03	-0.24	-0.51	-0.78	
13	5.00%						
14	3.00%						
15							
16							
17							
18							

Command list 3:   Close Fill Justify Link Newname Reformat Split
                  Text-Format Unlink Value-Format Width Zoom
Worksheet: filldemo Loc: r4c3   FN: 0   Font: Standard
FILL - fill rows, columns or a block with values

Fig. 16.5. *Selecting the Fill Command.*

The block in r4:12c3:6 is filled with values beginning with .27 and incrementing by −.03. Note that the system fills the rows within a column before proceeding to the next column.

The Fill command can also be used to enter numbers that you later reformat in date format. If payroll dates fall every two weeks, for example, you can enter the number of the first date and increment by 14.

Using the Matrix Command (4-Matrix)

The powerful Matrix commands have many uses in scientific and statistical applications, but you may also find them useful in business applications as well. The Matrix command is found on command list 4. The primary menu for the command is shown in figure 16.6. Not all of the commands will be described in this section, but the ones that have the most applicability in the business environment are covered and examples are provided.

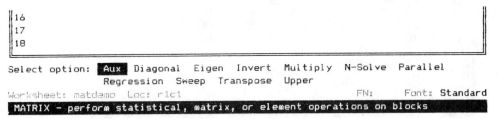

Fig. 16.6. *The Matrix Primary Menu.*

Transposing Columns and Rows (Matrix Transpose)

The Transpose option is used to swap columns for rows and rows for columns. The transposition is performed in place; the transposed matrix replaces the original one. If you want to retain the original matrix, you must use the Copy command first.

Figure 16.7 shows two uses of the Transpose option. (The Fill command was used to generate both of the original blocks on the left.) The upper blocks are both four rows by four columns; notice that the rows have become columns, and vice versa. The lower blocks do not have the same number of rows as columns; there are more rows. Even with a matrix of unequal dimensions, the rows and columns are swapped. In this example, the transposition has created more columns and has reduced the number of rows. The surrounding columns or rows can also be transposed when you transpose a matrix that is rectangular rather than square, so you must be careful.

The Transpose option can be useful if you want to send the contents of your worksheet to the Data Base Manager and you want the worksheet rows to represent fields and the columns to be records. Cell references are not adjusted, however, so you may have to perform a Vcopy first.

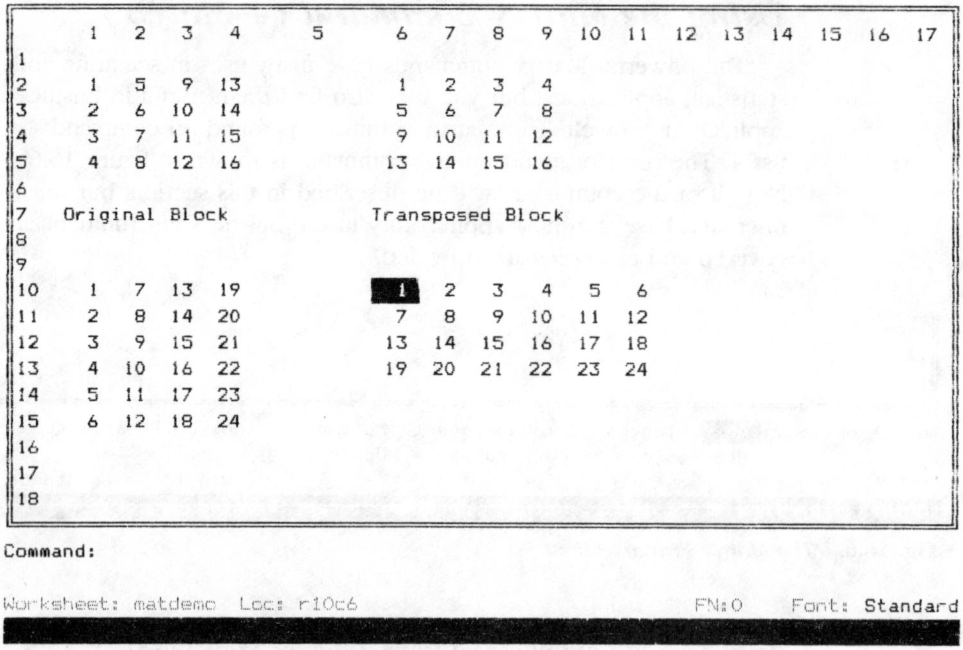

```
         1   2   3   4    5     6   7   8   9  10  11  12  13  14  15  16  17
 1
 2       1   5   9  13          1   2   3   4
 3       2   6  10  14          5   6   7   8
 4       3   7  11  15          9  10  11  12
 5       4   8  12  16         13  14  15  16
 6
 7    Original Block        Transposed Block
 8
 9
10       1   7  13  19          1   2   3   4   5   6
11       2   8  14  20          7   8   9  10  11  12
12       3   9  15  21         13  14  15  16  17  18
13       4  10  16  22         19  20  21  22  23  24
14       5  11  17  23
15       6  12  18  24
16
17
18
```

Command:

Worksheet: matdemo   Loc: r10c6   FN:0   Font: Standard

Fig. 16.7. *Examples of the Transpose option.*

Other Matrix Command Options

The remaining Matrix options are primarily of statistical value. They are listed in table 16.1.

Conclusion

Once you have built your worksheet, you need to know how to use it effectively. This chapter has covered the commands you need to make the best use of the Smart Spreadsheet. The features covered are sorting, block naming, cursor movement, searching, screen viewing, and recalculation.

The following chapter contains additional commands on viewing your worksheet and protecting its contents.

Table 16.1
Matrix Options

Option	Operations
Aux	Calculates determinant, rank, power and normalizes
Diagonal	Calculates sum, product or copy of diagonal.
Eigen	Generates eigenvalues or eigenvectors
Invert	Inverts a matrix
Multiply	Multiplies two matrices
N-Solve	Solves equations in unknowns
Parallel	Performs parallel matrix arithmetic operations
Regression	Multiple linear regression. Results may be stored in a block of cells in your worksheet.
Sweep	Sweeps on a pivot
Upper	Converts to row echelon form.

Chapter 17

Protecting and Viewing Worksheets

Your worksheets can be viewed and changed by anyone unless the worksheets are protected. This chapter focuses on ways to protect your work from inadvertent changes (by you or someone else), and presents the method of saving a file so that formulas are hidden.

This chapter also explores the creation and removal of windows. You can create as many as *50* windows in the Spreadsheet module, and here you'll learn how to use them to your best advantage.

Protecting Worksheets

Blocks of cells can be locked against change; the method you use depends on the *type* of contents in a cell. Entire worksheets also can be protected by a password to prevent unauthorized persons from loading them.

Locking the Worksheet (2–Lock, Ctrl-L)

If you want to prevent cells or blocks of cells from accidental change, use the Lock command, found on command list 2. The quick key is Ctrl-L. The Lock command can be used to protect your worksheet from inadvertent changes; the Unlock command, discussed later in this chapter, can be used to unlock any previously locked cells or ranges. The menu for the Lock command contains eight options:

Blanks Formulas Text Values All Disable Enable Protect

Select the type of cell contents you want to protect. Once a cell is protected, anyone using the worksheet cannot accidentally change or overwrite the contents of that cell.

If you select Blanks or All, there are no further prompts. Selecting Blanks locks all the blank cells in the worksheet. Selecting All locks *all* cells, regardless of type; selecting All makes the worksheet "read only." You might use this option for a lookup table whose contents do not change.

By selecting Formulas, Text, or Values, you indicate that cell contents of that type are to be locked. You select a range at the following prompt:

Block Columns Rows All

If you plan to select Columns or Rows, you should first move the cursor to the leftmost column or the uppermost row of the range that you want to protect.

When you select Columns, you are prompted to

Enter number of columns:

You can type the number of columns to be included in the range, or you can move the cursor to the right so that the system enters the number. Press Enter when the number is correct. If you press Enter without typing a number, the value defaults to 1.

If you select Rows, you are prompted to

Enter number of rows:

Again, you can enter the number of rows to be included in the range or, by moving the cursor down, have the system enter the number. Press Enter when the number is correct. If you press Enter without typing a number, the value defaults to 1.

If you select Block, you are prompted to

Enter name or block reference:

You can type the range in row-and-column notation, such as *r3:7c5:10*. An easier way to indicate the range is to move the cursor to the upper left cell in the range, press F2 to "drop the anchor," and then move the cursor to the lower right corner of the range.

The block range is highlighted as you go. Press Enter to complete definition of the block range.

If you select All, no other input is required.

Temporarily Unlocking Worksheet Cells (Lock Disable)

The Lock Disable command is used to temporarily turn off all cell locks throughout the worksheet. Use the Enable option to reinstate the locks. Even if you unload your file but forget to enable the locks, the lock specifications are retained from session to session.

Preventing Changes and Hiding Formulas (Lock Protect)

If you *really* want to protect the contents of your worksheet against any changes, use the Lock Protect command. Any user is prevented not only from changing but also from *seeing* your formulas. (As an added benefit, a protected worksheet takes less time to load and consumes less memory than does the original worksheet.) To provide complete protection, you should also lock the blanks and the text before you save the worksheet.

To protect a worksheet, you should first save it so that it has not been modified since it was last saved. When you select the Lock Protect command, this prompt appears:

> Are you sure you want to protect this worksheet (y/n)

You should take great care to have a backup copy of your worksheet in its original, unprotected form; give that copy a different name or keep it on a different disk. After you have selected Lock Protect and saved the worksheet to disk, you cannot return the worksheet to its original form.

Unlocking the Worksheet (2-Unlock)

The Unlock command is used to permanently reverse the effects of the Lock command. Unlock is found on command list 2. (Both Lock and Unlock are unavailable at confidence level 2, which provides a minimal obstacle to overt worksheet changes.) Refer to the Introduction for further information about confidence levels.

The command sequence for the Unlock command is exactly like that of Lock. First, you are prompted to select

> Blanks Formulas Text Values All

If you select Blanks or All, there are no further prompts. If you select another type, you are prompted to select a range:

> Block Columns Rows All

You indicate the appropriate range in the same way you select a range for the Lock command. Remember that you cannot reverse the effects of Lock Protect. If you use that command, be *sure* to save a copy of your original worksheet; give the copy a different name or keep it on another disk.

Assigning a Password (4-Password)

Use the Password command, found on command list 4, to protect a worksheet by assigning a password. You can attach as many as three different passwords to a worksheet; passwords must be four characters long and are case sensitive. (*PASS*, for example, is not the same as *pass*.)

The first password you attach always has the ability to save the worksheet; passwords 2 and 3, if you decide to attach them, may or may not have the ability to save.

Attaching a Password to the Worksheet (Password Attach)

The prompt menu of the Password command offers two options:

```
Attach Remove
```

When you select Attach, you are prompted to enter the password. Type a four-character password, and press Enter. Remembering the password is important; the passwords are saved along with the worksheet. In a later session, you will not be able to load the worksheet again without supplying the password.

If you are attaching the second or the third password, the following prompt appears:

```
Save permission for this password (y/n)
```

Your answer (*y* or *n*) depends on whether you want to allow individuals who use this worksheet with this password to save it to disk, thus overwriting the original. If you do not give save permission, the worksheet becomes "read only" for persons using this password; they can use the worksheet and print it, but they cannot save any changes they have made. (Giving the worksheet a new name does not allow the user to save it, either.)

The passwords take effect when you save the worksheet. When you subsequently load the worksheet, this prompt appears:

```
Enter password:
```

Type the password, remembering whether it is in upper- or lowercase, but do not press Enter; the system does that for you because passwords must always be four characters long. If you enter the password incorrectly, you see this error message:

    Incorrect password

Press any key to return to the prompt for the password, and try again.

Removing a Password from the Worksheet (Password Remove)

To remove a password from a worksheet, select the Password Remove command sequence. You are prompted to

    Enter password:

Type the password and press Enter. You can remove any passwords; however, you cannot remove password 1 if the other two do not have save permission; at least one password *must* have save permission.

Using Windows

As in other Smart System application modules, you can split your Spreadsheet screen into several different windows. You can load the spreadsheet windows with different worksheets or simultaneously view different sections of the same worksheet.

Creating a Window (3–Split, Alt-H, Alt-V)

The Split command is used to create another window within the current window. This command, found on command list 3, has two quick keys: Alt-H splits the window horizontally, and Alt-V splits it vertically.

Using the Split command in the Smart Spreadsheet differs in an important way from using the same command in other Smart modules. In the Spreadsheet module, you must position the cursor *prior* to issuing the command. Move the cursor to the row or column *after* the last one you want to leave in the current window, and then issue the command. The prompt menu is

    Horizontal Vertical

You must allow enough space for at least one row and one column per window.

Figure 17.1 shows a screen that has been split into two windows; notice that the upper left corner of the window shows the window number. (If you remove the row or column numbers from the display, the window number is not shown.)

Remember to use the Alt-F8 key combination to move your cursor to the next sequentially numbered window; use Alt-F7 to move to the previous window. If you have only two windows, either key combination toggles between the windows.

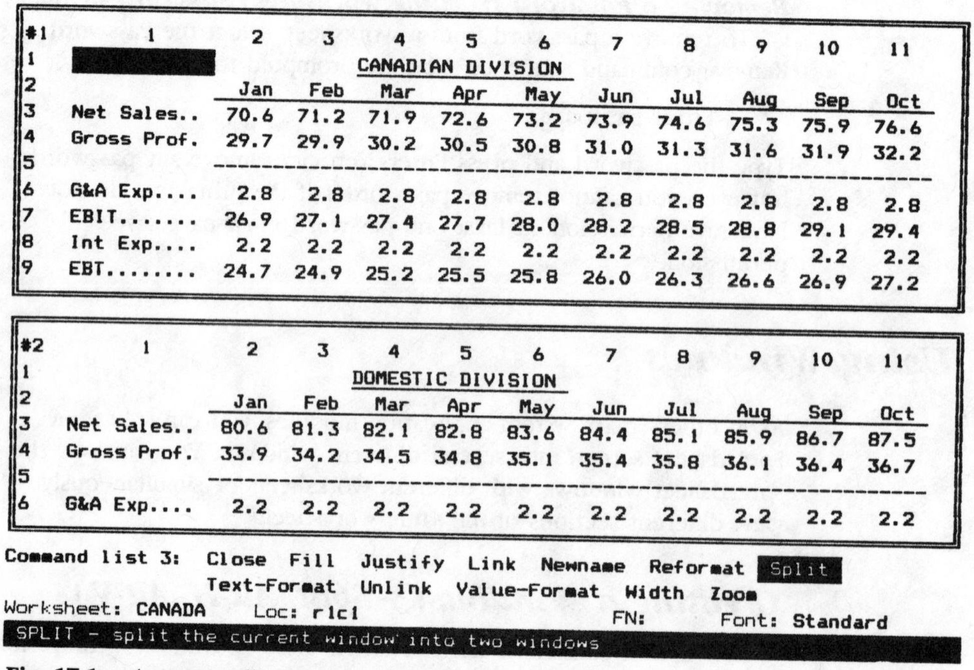

```
#1        1       2     3     4     5     6     7     8     9    10    11
1                        CANADIAN DIVISION
2                 Jan   Feb   Mar   Apr   May   Jun   Jul   Aug   Sep   Oct
3  Net Sales..  70.6  71.2  71.9  72.6  73.2  73.9  74.6  75.3  75.9  76.6
4  Gross Prof.  29.7  29.9  30.2  30.5  30.8  31.0  31.3  31.6  31.9  32.2
5  ------------------------------------------------------------------------
6  G&A Exp....   2.8   2.8   2.8   2.8   2.8   2.8   2.8   2.8   2.8   2.8
7  EBIT.......  26.9  27.1  27.4  27.7  28.0  28.2  28.5  28.8  29.1  29.4
8  Int Exp....   2.2   2.2   2.2   2.2   2.2   2.2   2.2   2.2   2.2   2.2
9  EBT........  24.7  24.9  25.2  25.5  25.8  26.0  26.3  26.6  26.9  27.2

#2        1       2     3     4     5     6     7     8     9    10    11
1                        DOMESTIC DIVISION
2                 Jan   Feb   Mar   Apr   May   Jun   Jul   Aug   Sep   Oct
3  Net Sales..  80.6  81.3  82.1  82.8  83.6  84.4  85.1  85.9  86.7  87.5
4  Gross Prof.  33.9  34.2  34.5  34.8  35.1  35.4  35.8  36.1  36.4  36.7
5  ------------------------------------------------------------------------
6  G&A Exp....   2.2   2.2   2.2   2.2   2.2   2.2   2.2   2.2   2.2   2.2

Command list 3:  Close  Fill   Justify  Link  Newname  Reformat  Split
                 Text-Format  Unlink  Value-Format  Width  Zoom
Worksheet: CANADA     Loc: r1c1                 FN:     Font: Standard
SPLIT - split the current window into two windows
```

Fig. 17.1. *A screen split into two windows.*

Removing a Window (3-Close, Alt-W)

The Close command is used to remove a window from the screen. Close is found on command list 3; the quick key is Alt-W.

When you select the Close command, the current window is removed, and a neighboring window is enlarged to fill the void. Worksheets no longer displayed are still active; they are not automatically unloaded. (However, you cannot close a window that has been enlarged with the Zoom command.)

Making a Window Fill the Screen (3–Zoom, F7)

The Zoom command is used to cause the *current* window to fill the entire screen as if it were the *only* window. Use the Zoom command when you want to view more of a worksheet than you can see in the current window, yet you do not want to close the remaining windows. Zoom is found on command list 3; the quick key is F7. To restore the multiple-window display, use the Zoom command again.

Certain commands used with windows cannot be used when the current window is in Zoom status; they are Goto Window, Split, and Close.

Scrolling Two Windows Simultaneously (3–Link)

The Link command is used to cause the worksheets in two or more windows to scroll simultaneously. As you scroll the view of the worksheet in the current window, the view of the linked window (or windows) also scrolls. Link is found on command list 3.

After you select Link, you are prompted to

    Enter windows to be linked:

Enter the window numbers separated by spaces, as shown in figure 17.2.

The screen shown in figure 17.2 was set up to permit easy comparison of comparable line items on statements for three divisions of the company. (Titles have been fixed at two rows.) As you move the cursor down to the next line in window 1, the displays in the other two windows are advanced automatically to the corresponding lines. Any window in the "network" can be the "driver," causing the other windows to scroll.

You can specify any windows in the Link command; you do not have to include the current window. A window can be established in only one link "network" at a time, but multiple linkages can exist simultaneously.

Link	Effect
1 3 5	Windows 1, 3, and 5 are linked.
1 2	Windows 1 and 2 are linked; windows 3 and 5 remain linked to each other, but not to window 1.

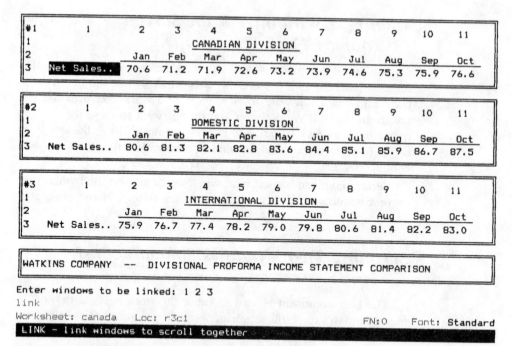

Fig. 17.2. *Entering the numbers of windows to be linked.*

If you use the Zoom command on a window that is linked, any cursor movement while the window is "zoomed" is not reflected in the other windows. In fact, after you restore the window to its original size, the cursor will again be positioned where it was before you issued the Zoom command. The Zoom does not cancel the linkage, however.

Be aware that the linkage and subsequent simultaneous scrolling are based only on relative positions, row for row or column for column. The linkage is not based on the actual contents of any cell. (In the Data Base Manager, a link is established between a data field in one file and a key field in another, based on the field contents.)

Removing Links between Windows (3-Unlink)

The Unlink command is used to remove all links or to remove the link for specific windows. Unlink is found on command list 3.

To remove all links, execute the command and, when you are prompted to enter a window number, simply press Enter. If you want to remove the link for one or more windows, type the numbers of the windows (as you did for the Link command) and then press Enter. Any linked windows that you do not specifically unlink remain linked.

Conclusion

This chapter has covered the methods for protecting your worksheets and for handling windows. You can use the Lock command to protect you worksheets from inadvertent alteration. Blank cells, formulas, text, and values can be locked in any portion of your worksheet. Furthermore, you can completely protect the worksheet by using the Lock Protect command.

You can create as many as 50 windows at one time on your monitor screen. Windows can be linked so that they scroll simultaneously.

Chapter 18

Printing Worksheet Data and Creating Reports

Up to this point, you have been viewing your spreadsheet on only your monitor. Eventually you will want to be able to print all or part of a worksheet on paper so that you can save it for yourself, include it in a report, or show it to someone else. This chapter focuses on the printing of worksheet data.

The Smart Spreadsheet module offers two different "levels" of worksheet printing. The Print command provides a quick and easy way of getting the information on paper. This is the command to use when you simply want the output for yourself, or when you are not particularly interested in a fancy, formal report.

The Report command, on the other hand, is used when you need a formal report. All of the customary options—enhanced printing, headings, page numbers, margins, and indenting—are available with the Report command. Setting up a report may take a little longer but is well worth the time when you need to produce a formal document.

"Quick and Easy" Printing (1–Print, Alt-P)

The Print command is used to produce "quick and easy" printed output of your entire worksheet or of a defined block from the worksheet. The output can be directed to a disk file, if you wish, rather than the printer. In addition to printing the visible display of a worksheet (what you see on the screen), you can also print the underlying formulas to document the worksheet or to help track down problems.

Print is found on command list 1 (see fig. 18.1); the quick key is Alt-P. Bear in mind that formatting options you have selected for the screen display are reflected in the printed output. Column widths, percentages, and numbers in dollar, date, and even "bar" formats are printed exactly as they are formatted in the worksheet. (Enhanced fonts, underscoring, and boldface can be printed if you use the Report command.) On the printed output, columns and rows are aligned as they are on the monitor display.

```
|10      --------------------------------------------------------------
|11  Tax........   14.6  14.7  14.9  15.0  15.2  15.3  15.5  15.6  15.8  16.0
|12  Net Income.  15.8  15.9  16.1  16.3  16.4  16.6  16.8  16.9  17.1  17.3
|13      --------------------------------------------------------------
|14  EPS......    0.04  0.04  0.04  0.04  0.04  0.04  0.04  0.04  0.04  0.04
|15  --------------------------------------------------------------
|16   Average      Gr Prof    Sales      G&A        Intst      Tax
|17   Shares:      Rate %     Grow %     Expense:   Expense:   Rate%
|18   400,000       42         11          2.2        1.3        48

Command list 1:  Autohelp  Blank  Copy  Delete  Edit  Find  Goto  Help  Insert
                 Move  Name  Print  Report  Scroll  Vcopy
Worksheet: DOMESTIC  Loc: r1c1                        FN:      Font: Standard
PRINT - print text or formulas
```

Fig. 18.1. *Selecting the Print command.*

Compare printing a worksheet with printing data in the Smart Data Base Manager. In the Data Base Manager, you can use the Query and Order commands to select certain records or to rearrange the order in which they appear on the printout. You also can specify which fields are to be printed and the sequence in which they appear. But when you print a Smart spreadsheet, "What you see is what you get."

Printing the Worksheet Display (Print Text)

After you select the Print command, the first options are

Formulas Text

Selecting Text causes the system to print the normally visible display of the worksheet, including text entries, values, dates, and the displayed results of formulas. (The name of the option is somewhat misleading. All displayed cell contents are printed—not just those containing "text.") Row and column numbers are not printed.

Smart then prompts you for the range to be printed:

Block Worksheet

If you select Block, you are prompted to

Enter name or block reference:

You can type the range address in row-and-column notation, such as *r3:7c5:10*. An easier way to specify the range is to move the cursor to the upper left cell of the range, press F2 to "drop the anchor," and then move the cursor to the lower right corner of the range. The block range is highlighted as you go. If you have defined a block with a name, you can enter the name. (See Chapter 16 for information on naming blocks.) Press Enter to complete definition of the range.

If you select Worksheet, the entire worksheet is printed; the range is from row 1, column 1, through the last row and column used.

You can select the destination of the output by answering the next prompt:

Disk Printer

If you select Disk, you are prompted for the file name; a file then is created with the name you provide. The system does not automatically provide an extension as it does in the other applications. If you want an extension, you must provide it yourself. If a file with the same name already exists, no prompt asks if you want to overwrite that file. Be careful!

The Configure setting on the main menu controls the number of characters per line in the disk file. Form-feed characters are embedded in the file to create page breaks.

If you decide to send the output directly to the printer, you are prompted to choose the type style:

Compressed Normal

If you are trying to fit the maximum amount of data on a page, select Compressed. This capability is available only if your printer supports compressed printing. Most dot-matrix printers can print in compressed mode, but daisywheel printers cannot. (If you find that your printer offers compressed type but is only printing 80 characters on a line, change the "characters per line" setting in the Configure command of the Main Menu. To cause the new setting to take effect, you must quit and then reenter the Smart system.)

If your worksheet or block is too wide to be printed on one page, the output is sectioned. You can piece the sections together to view your entire worksheet. (Get out the cellophane tape!)

Whether you select Compressed or Normal printing, you are now prompted to

Enter number of copies:

Press Enter if you want only one copy; if you want to print more than one, enter the number to be printed (the maximum is 99) and press Enter.

Note that you cannot use enhanced fonts with the Print command; not even such common features as underscoring and boldface can be printed. The Print command is for "quick and easy" printing; use the Report command for enhanced printing.

Printing the Worksheet Formulas (Print Formulas)

Keeping a printout of formulas that you have defined in a worksheet is good for documentation purposes. A printout of the formulas can often help you pinpoint possible errors, too.

The prompts for the Print Formula command are

Block Worksheet

If you select Block, you are prompted to designate the range. If you select Worksheet, formulas for the entire worksheet are printed. In either case, you are then prompted to select the print style:

Compressed Normal

The same restrictions that apply when printing Text Compressed also apply when printing Formulas Compressed. (However, you cannot print your formulas to a disk file.)

Figure 18.2 shows a printout of certain formulas from a worksheet in our financial model. Note that the formulas are sorted by row and by column.

```
FORMULAS FOR WORKSHEET domestic

ROW    COL      FORMULA

  3      3      r3c2*(1+r18c[5]/12/100)
         4      r3c3*(1+r18c[5]/12/100)
         5      r3c4*(1+r18c[5]/12/100)
         6      r3c5*(1+r18c[5]/12/100)
         7      r3c6*(1+r18c[5]/12/100)
         8      r3c7*(1+r18c[5]/12/100)
         9      r3c8*(1+r18c[5]/12/100)
        10      r3c9*(1+r18c[5]/12/100)
        11      r3c10*(1+r18c[5]/12/100)
        12      r3c11*(1+r18c[5]/12/100)
        13      r3c12*(1+r18c[5]/12/100)
  4      2      r3c2*r18c[3]/100
         3      r3c3*r18c[3]/100
         4      r3c4*r18c[3]/100
         5      r3c5*r18c[3]/100
         6      r3c6*r18c[3]/100
         7      r3c7*r18c[3]/100
         8      r3c8*r18c[3]/100
         9      r3c9*r18c[3]/100
        10      r3c10*r18c[3]/100
        11      r3c11*r18c[3]/100
        12      r3c12*r18c[3]/100
        13      r3c13*r18c[3]/100
  6      2      r18c[7]
```

Fig. 18.2. *A sample printout of formulas.*

Printing Formal Reports (1-Report)

The Report command is used to print formal reports from your worksheet. Reports can be printed in either Normal or Enhanced mode and multiple ranges from a single worksheet can be printed in one report. Headings, footings, page numbers, and dates can also be included as part of the page format. Because reports tend to be used repeatedly and the specifications for the Report command are more complex than those of Print, you first must define the report's characteristics; then you can print the report in either Normal or Enhanced mode.

The Report command is found on command list 1. The initial menu options are shown in figure 18.3.

Defining a Report (Report Define)

Before you can print a report, you must define it. When you select Define, you are prompted to

```
Enter report definition filename:
```

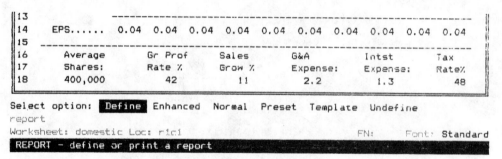

```
||13       --------------------------------------------------------------------------
||14    EPS......   0.04  0.04  0.04  0.04  0.04  0.04  0.04  0.04  0.04  0.04
||15       --------------------------------------------------------------------------
||16    Average        Gr Prof      Sales       G&A          Intst       Tax
||17    Shares:        Rate %       Grow %      Expense:     Expense:    Rate%
||18    400,000        42           11          2.2          1.3         48
```

Select option: **Define** Enhanced Normal Preset Template Undefine
report
Worksheet: domestic Loc: r1c1   FN: Font: Standard
REPORT - define or print a report

Fig. 18.3. *Selecting an option from the Report menu.*

Select a name from the pop-up menu, or type a new name and press Enter. If you select the name of an existing definition, you can then edit or change it. You can establish default settings for the report definition by using the Report Preset command, which is discussed later in this chapter.

The report definition screens in figures 18.4, 18.5, and 18.6 show the definitions for the printed report in figure 18.7.

```
╔═ Report Definition: COMPREP ═══════════════════════════════════
║     Heading
║
║         Justification:   Left  Center
║  ⟹    Line 1:  WATKINS COMPANY DIVISIONAL REPORT
║         Line 2:  Pro-Forma 1987 Income Statements
║         Line 3:
║         Blank lines after heading:   0  1  2  3
║
║
║     Footing
║
║         Line 1:  Confidential. Not for use without proper authorization.
║         Line 2:
║         Line 3:
║         Blank lines before footing:  0  1  2  3
║
║
║     Fixed Horizontal Title Blocks
║         Group 1:  ▌
```

F1 Help   F2 Edit text   F3 Blank text   F10 Finished
report define comprep
Worksheet: domestic Loc: r1c1   FN: Font: **Standard**
REPORT - define or print a report

Fig. 18.4. *Defining a report heading and footing.*

```
╔═ Report Definition: COMPREP ══════════════════════════════════════╗
║                                                                    ║
║                                                                    ║
║        Fixed Horizontal Title Blocks                               ║
║  ══▶     Group 1: ███                                              ║
║          Group 2: ███                                              ║
║          Group 3: ███                                              ║
║                                                                    ║
║        Fixed Vertical Title Blocks                                 ║
║          Group 1: ███                                              ║
║          Group 2: ███                                              ║
║          Group 3: ███                                              ║
║                                                                    ║
║        Report Body Blocks                                          ║
║          Group 1: ██domestic.dom,intrnatl.inl,canada.can██         ║
║          Group 2: ███                                              ║
║          Group 3: ███                                              ║
║                                                                    ║
║                                                                    ║
║        Date in heading:  Alpha-Date  █Numeric-Date█  No-Date       ║
║        Lines to enclose report:  Yes  █No█                         ║
║                                                                    ║
╚════════════════════════════════════════════════════════════════════╝
F1 Help    F2 Edit text    F3 Blank text    F10 Finished
report define comprep
Worksheet: domestic Loc: r1c1                    FN:    Font: Standard
██REPORT - define or print a report██
```

Fig. 18.5. *Defining fixed horizontal and vertical title blocks and body blocks.*

```
╔═ Report Definition: COMPREP ══════════════════════════════════════╗
║          Group 3: ███                                              ║
║                                                                    ║
║        Date in heading:  Alpha-Date  █Numeric-Date█  No-Date       ║
║        Lines to enclose report:  Yes  █No█                         ║
║        Page numbers:  Left  Right  █Center█  Left-Right  Right-Left  No-Numbers ║
║        Start page number:  █1█                                     ║
║        Spacing:  █Single█  Double                                  ║
║                                                                    ║
║        Continuous form printing:  █Yes█  No                        ║
║        Lines per inch in draft mode:  █6█  8                       ║
║        Characters per inch in draft mode:  10  █12█  17            ║
║                                                                    ║
║        Form length (lines):  █66█                                 ║
║        Form width (positions):  █85█                              ║
║                                                                    ║
║        Top margin (lines):  █1█                                   ║
║        Bottom margin (lines):  █3█                                ║
║        Left indent (positions):  █1█                              ║
║  ══▶  Right indent (positions):  █1█                              ║
╚════════════════════════════════════════════════════════════════════╝
F1 Help    F2 Edit text    F3 Blank text    F10 Finished
report define comprep
Worksheet: domestic Loc: r1c1                    FN:    Font: Standard
██REPORT - define or print a report██
```

Fig. 18.6. *Defining a report layout.*

```
                    WATKINS COMPANY DIVISIONAL REPORT
                    Pro-Forma 1987 Income Statements          January 29, 1986

                    DOMESTIC DIVISION
                 Jan   Feb   Mar   Apr   May   Jun   Jul   Aug   Sep   Oct   Nov   Dec
Net Sales..    80.6  81.3  82.1  82.8  83.6  84.4  85.1  85.9  86.7  87.5  88.3  89.1
Gross Prof.    33.9  34.2  34.5  34.8  35.1  35.4  35.8  36.1  36.4  36.7  37.1  37.4

G&A Exp....     2.2   2.2   2.2   2.2   2.2   2.2   2.2   2.2   2.2   2.2   2.2   2.2
EBIT.......    31.7  32.0  32.3  32.6  32.9  33.2  33.6  33.9  34.2  34.5  34.9  35.2
Int Exp....     1.3   1.3   1.3   1.3   1.3   1.3   1.3   1.3   1.3   1.3   1.3   1.3
EBT........    30.4  30.7  31.0  31.3  31.6  31.9  32.3  32.6  32.9  33.2  33.6  33.9

Tax........    14.6  14.7  14.9  15.0  15.2  15.3  15.5  15.6  15.8  16.0  16.1  16.3
Net Income.    15.8  15.9  16.1  16.3  16.4  16.6  16.8  16.9  17.1  17.3  17.5  17.6

EPS......      0.04  0.04  0.04  0.04  0.04  0.04  0.04  0.04  0.04  0.04  0.04  0.04

  Average      Gr Prof     Sales      G&A         Intst      Tax
  Shares:      Rate %      Grow %     Expense:    Expense:   Rate%
  400,000        42          11         2.2         1.3        48

                    INTERNATIONAL DIVISION
                 Jan   Feb   Mar   Apr   May   Jun   Jul   Aug   Sep   Oct   Nov   Dec
Net Sales..    75.9  76.7  77.4  78.2  79.0  79.8  80.6  81.4  82.2  83.0  83.8  84.7
Gross Prof.    30.4  30.7  31.0  31.3  31.6  31.9  32.2  32.6  32.9  33.2  33.5  33.9

G&A Exp....     2.8   2.8   2.8   2.8   2.8   2.8   2.8   2.8   2.8   2.8   2.8   2.8
EBIT.......    27.6  27.9  28.2  28.5  28.8  29.1  29.4  29.8  30.1  30.4  30.7  31.1
Int Exp....     2.3   2.3   2.3   2.3   2.3   2.3   2.3   2.3   2.3   2.3   2.3   2.3
EBT........    25.3  25.6  25.9  26.2  26.5  26.8  27.1  27.5  27.8  28.1  28.4  28.8

Tax........    12.1  12.3  12.4  12.6  12.7  12.9  13.0  13.2  13.3  13.5  13.6  13.8
Net Income.    13.1  13.3  13.5  13.6  13.8  13.9  14.1  14.3  14.4  14.6  14.8  15.0

EPS......      0.05  0.05  0.05  0.05  0.05  0.05  0.05  0.05  0.05  0.06  0.06  0.06

  Average      Gr Prof     Sales      G&A         Intst      Tax
  Shares:      Rate %      Grow %     Expense:    Expense:   Rate%
  264,000        40          12         2.8         2.3        48

                    CANADIAN DIVISION
                 Jan   Feb   Mar   Apr   May   Jun   Jul   Aug   Sep   Oct   Nov   Dec
Net Sales..    70.6  71.2  71.9  72.6  73.2  73.9  74.6  75.3  75.9  76.6  77.3  78.1
Gross Prof.    29.7  29.9  30.2  30.5  30.8  31.0  31.3  31.6  31.9  32.2  32.5  32.8

G&A Exp....     2.8   2.8   2.8   2.8   2.8   2.8   2.8   2.8   2.8   2.8   2.8   2.8
EBIT.......    26.9  27.1  27.4  27.7  28.0  28.2  28.5  28.8  29.1  29.4  29.7  30.0
Int Exp....     2.2   2.2   2.2   2.2   2.2   2.2   2.2   2.2   2.2   2.2   2.2   2.2
EBT........    24.7  24.9  25.2  25.5  25.8  26.0  26.3  26.6  26.9  27.2  27.5  27.8

Tax........    11.8  12.0  12.1  12.2  12.4  12.5  12.6  12.8  12.9  13.1  13.2  13.3
Net Income.    12.8  13.0  13.1  13.2  13.4  13.5  13.7  13.8  14.0  14.1  14.3  14.4

EPS......      0.04  0.04  0.04  0.04  0.04  0.04  0.04  0.04  0.04  0.04  0.04  0.04

  Average      Gr Prof     Sales      G&A         Intst      Tax
  Shares:      Rate %      Grow %     Expense:    Expense:   Rate%
  350,000        42          11         2.8         2.2        48


Confidential. Not for use without proper authorization.

                                        1
```

Fig. 18.7. *A sample report printout.*

If you choose to use headings and footings, they can contain a maximum of three lines of 60 characters each; they appear at the top and bottom of each page. Headings and footings entered by a block reference are limited by the margins of the report. (An example of a block reference is *r1c1:7*.) Headings (but not footings) can be either left-justified or centered relative to the form width (see fig. 18.4). You can specify from 0 to 3 blank lines between the headings or footings and the text of the report itself.

The data for the body of the report is specified in the groups under the heading *Report Body Blocks* (fig. 18.5). You can define as many as three sets of "print groups" in a Spreadsheet report. By definition, a print group starts on a new page; thus you have some direct control over pagination. If you wanted to place each division's data on a separate page, you could define each divisional worksheet as a print group. Print groups can be related to each other or totally unrelated. For example, you could have one print group for each of three divisions of your company or have completely different formats altogether.

Within each print group, you can specify several block references to be printed one after the other. You can specify as many block references as will fit in the 40-character space allotted on the definition screen. Notice that the three blocks specified in figure 18.5 come from three different worksheets (each must be active) and that the block reference is to a named range within each worksheet. Each name references *r1:19c1:13* in the respective worksheet. By using short worksheet names and block names, you can specify more blocks on a 40-character line.

If the block references are separated by commas, as in figure 18.5, the blocks are printed one above the other on the page. If the references are separated by semicolons, the blocks are printed side-by-side. Any portions of blocks that do not fit on the page width are continued on successive pages.

In addition to specifying report body blocks, you can also specify horizontal and vertical title blocks. These appear on each page of the printed report, in much the same way that titles for a worksheet appear in a fixed location on the screen. If, for instance, you have specified r4:500c1:6 as a print group, the column titles might be in r1:3c1:6. You would want to specify this block of cells as the horizontal title block for that the print group. The column titles in r1:3c1:6 would then be printed on every page.

If you specify inclusion of a date in the heading of your report, the current system date is printed on the right side of the last line of the report's heading. If the date is not set automatically when you boot your computer, remember to enter the correct date.

Lines to enclose the report are drawn at the top and bottom of each page, between the body of the report and the heading or footing.

Page numbers are printed at the bottom of the page (refer to fig. 18.7). The starting page number is the number that appears on the first printed page. If you are producing a report to appear within a larger report from another source, you will probably want to keep page numbering consecutive within the larger report; your starting number therefore will not necessarily be 1.

You can select either single or double spacing. This is the one option that permits presentation of the body of the worksheet in a format different from that of the screen display.

If you want the printer to pause between pages, select No for continuous form printing. Vertical lines per inch and horizontal characters per inch can be specified, as shown in figure 18.6, provided that your printer supports these options.

Select a form length from 20 to 120 lines, and a form width from 20 to 255 characters. The heading is centered in relation to the form width you select. The width specified can be greater than the number of characters per line selected in the Main Menu Configure command. This feature can be particularly useful if you want to write an extremely wide report to a disk file. If you have a utility program for printing reports sideways on a dot-matrix printer, your page can be 255 characters "across."

The settings for top and bottom margins specify the number of lines to the physical edge of the paper. If you specify page numbers you must specify a bottom margin of at least 3 lines.

The left and right indent settings control the number of spaces that are left blank between the normal first (or last) print positions and the first (or last) position at which the printer can place a character. A left indent can be useful if you need to allow room for holes to be punched so that the printout can be bound in a notebook.

After you have specified the necessary options, press F10 to return to the command level of the Spreadsheet.

Printing a Plain Report (Report Normal)

When you have created the definition, you are ready to print the report. Use the Report Normal command to begin regular printing. You are prompted to

`Enter report definition filename:`

Move the cursor to the name of the desired definition in the pop-up menu and press Enter. You are then prompted to choose a destination:

`Disk Printer`

If you select Disk, you are prompted for a file name. Enter a name and press Enter. Unlike the Print command, the Report command automatically appends the file extension .PRN to the file name. If a .PRN file with the same name already exists, the system writes over it without a prompt; you must be careful if you have a report on your disk that you want to retain.

If you select Printer, you can either type the number of copies or simply press Enter to signify one copy.

Printing a Report with Different Fonts (Report Enhanced)

To produce reports using the different fonts available in the Smart Spreadsheet, select the Enhanced option. (Refer to Chapter 14 to learn how to select or change fonts in your worksheet.) The prompts are the same as for the Report Normal command sequence. Figure 18.8 shows part of the same report as in figure 18.7 printed with different fonts. Notice that the division title is printed in Gothic, names of months are in italic, and the assumption variable titles are in small caps. Depending on the capabilities of your printer, you may be able to print all or only some of the available fonts.

Although you can write a report to a disk file with the Enhanced option, the special control codes for the different fonts are stripped out.

Establishing Default Options (Report Preset)

The Report Preset command is used to establish default options similar to those in the Report Define command. Actually, when you first install the Spreadsheet module, you should select Preset and enter the default values that you will usually want to have in effect.

```
                WATKINS COMPANY DIVISIONAL REPORT
                 Pro-Forma 1987 Income Statements              01-28-86

                         DOMESTIC DIVISION
              Jan   Feb   Mar   Apr   May   Jun   Jul   Aug   Sep   Oct   Nov
Net Sales.. 80.6  81.3  82.1  82.8  83.6  84.4  85.1  85.9  86.7  87.5  88.3
Gross Prof. 33.9  34.2  34.5  34.8  35.1  35.4  35.8  36.1  36.4  36.7  37.1

G&A Exp....  2.2   2.2   2.2   2.2   2.2   2.2   2.2   2.2   2.2   2.2   2.2
EBIT....... 31.7  32.0  32.3  32.6  32.9  33.2  33.6  33.9  34.2  34.5  34.9
Int Exp....  1.3   1.3   1.3   1.3   1.3   1.3   1.3   1.3   1.3   1.3   1.3
EBT........ 30.4  30.7  31.0  31.3  31.6  31.9  32.3  32.6  32.9  33.2  33.6

Tax........ 14.6  14.7  14.9  15.0  15.2  15.3  15.5  15.6  15.8  16.0  16.1
Net Income. 15.8  15.9  16.1  16.3  16.4  16.6  16.8  16.9  17.1  17.3  17.5

EPS.......  0.04  0.04  0.04  0.04  0.04  0.04  0.04  0.04  0.04  0.04  0.04
```

Average Shares:	Gr Prof Rate %	Sales Grow %	G&A Expense:	Intst Expense:	Tax Rate%
400,000	42	11	2.2	1.3	48

Fig. 18.8. *A sample printout of an enhanced report.*

For instance, if you usually want to have page numbers on your reports, enter that option in the Preset settings. Then the defaults will be as you want them when you define a new report.

Printing a Page-Layout Description (Report Template)

The Report Template command sequence prints a description of the page layout for a specified definition. The layout for the report in figure 18.7 is shown in figure 18.9.

Erasing a Report Definition (Report Undefine)

To erase a report definition from your disk, use the Report Undefine command.

Conclusion

This chapter has covered the methods of creating printed output from your worksheet. The Print command is used to create "quick-and-easy" reports. Use the Report command to produce more formal reports.

```
            WATKINS COMPANY DIVISIONAL REPORT
            Pro-Forma 1987 Income Statements          January 29, 1986
```

```
                              Form length:    66
                              Form width:     85
                              Top margin:      1
                              Bottom margin:   3
                              Text lines:     57
                              Text width:     83
                              Left indent:     1
                              Right indent:    1
                              After header:    1
                              Before footer:   1
                              Date:        ALPHA
                              Enclose text:   NO
                              Page #:      CENTER
```

```
Confidential. Not for use without proper authorization.
                          Page #
```

Fig. 18.9. *A sample printout of a report layout.*

Chapter 19

Integrating the Spreadsheet and Other Modules

At the heart of the Smart System is the ability to integrate each application module with the others. Each module has commands for reading and writing external (DOS) files and for sending text or data to the other modules. This chapter focuses on using these commands and capabilities within the Spreadsheet.

Reading External Files into the Worksheet (4 –Read)

The Read command, which is found on command list 4, is used to read external files into the Spreadsheet. When you read a file into the worksheet, the data is inserted beginning at the current cursor position; be sure to position the cursor before you begin executing the command. Three types of files can be read into the Spreadsheet; they are indicated by the Read menu options:

    Dif Text 123

A Text file is a file in Smart format. The file is either written with the Write command from one of the application modules or created by an external program. Text entries in the file are enclosed in double quotation marks (″); values are *not* enclosed in quotation marks. Each entry on a line is separated from the others by a space, and one line in the file represents one row in the worksheet. The file contains no formulas or formatting codes.

With no additional conversion, a worksheet in Lotus 1-2-3 format can also be read directly into the Smart Spreadsheet. Formulas and most functions are maintained, as are formats, underscoring, and column widths. Specific 1-2-3 data-management functions *not* converted are

> @DAVG
> @DCOUNT
> @DSUM
> @DMAX
> @DMIN
> @DSTD
> @DVAR

Any 1-2-3 macros in the worksheet are read into your worksheet as text.

A DIF file is a file in *Document Interchange Format*, which is common to many spreadsheet programs. Use the DIF option to read files in this format; these files should have the extension .DIF.

Writing Worksheet Data to Different Files (4 – Write)

The Write command, on command list 4, is used to write the contents of a worksheet to a disk file. Files can be written in any of five different formats.

When you select the Write command you can choose one of two options, Block or Worksheet. If you specify Block, Smart prompts you to

    Enter name or block reference:

You can type the range in row-and-column notation, such as *r3:7c5:10*. An easier way to indicate the range is to move the cursor to the upper left cell of the range, press F2 to "drop the anchor," and then move the cursor to the lower right corner of the range. The block range is highlighted as you go. Press Enter to complete definition of the block range.

At the completion of block specification, or if you have chosen to write the whole worksheet, the next prompt is

    Dif Document Smart Text 123

Select the type of disk file you want to create.

You specify Dif format to write a file in the Data Interchange Format, which, as I explained before, is common to many popular spreadsheet programs. The file is written with the extension .DIF.

A Document file has special internal codes to make it compatible with Smart's Word Processor. Fonts and formatting are retained when this kind of file is written. The extension supplied for this type of file is .DOC.

A Smart file has the extension .DAT. This format is used to pass data to the Data Base Manager. Text entries are enclosed in double quotation marks; values are not. Each entry is separated from others by a space, and each line in the file represents a row in the worksheet.

A Text file (with the extension .TXT) is formatted to look almost like the worksheet, except that there are no fonts, underscoring, or boldface attributes. Use this type of file to import the worksheet to a word processor other than the Smart Word Processor.

A 123 file, as the name implies, is formatted to be read directly into the Lotus 1-2-3 spreadsheet program. The file extension is .WKS. Use this format if you need to give your worksheet to someone who has 1-2-3 but does not yet have Smart. Be careful, however, because many functions found in Smart are not supported in 1-2-3.

Passing Worksheet Data to Other Application Modules (5–Send)

The Send command is used to pass data directly from your worksheet to another Smart application module and then to immediately transfer control to that module. Send is found on command list 5.

The primary prompt of the Send command is

```
Communications Data-Manager Wordprocessor
```

These options are explained in the sections that follow.

Sending Data to Communications

If you send data to the Communications module, the resulting file is ready for transmission over your modem to another computer system. The options for Send Communications are

```
Document Graphics Smart Text
```

Use the Document format when the result is to be included in a Smart Word Processor document at the other end of the transmission line. Select Graphics, which sends a graph file that has been created with the Graphics Generate command, if the graph is to be viewed or included within a document.

You should specify Smart format if the recipient of the file wants to read the worksheet data into the Smart Data Base Manager. If you want to send the file in a format that is almost the same as the worksheet, with displayed values instead of formulas, select the Text option.

If, on the other hand, your correspondent wants to use the worksheet within the Smart Spreadsheet module, do not use the Send command at all. Simply enter the Communications module and transmit the worksheet file itself. The file name is the worksheet name; the extension is .WS.

Be aware that worksheets, documents, and graphics contain special control characters, and so you *must* use the Xmodem transmission option. Smart and Text files are pure ASCII files and can be sent with or without Xmodem.

If you select Document, Smart or Test, you are prompted to

Enter name or block reference:

You can type the range in row and column notation, such as *r3:7c5:10*. An easier way to indicate the range is to move the cursor to the upper left cell of the range, press F2 to drop the anchor, and then move the cursor to the lower right corner of the range. The block range is highlighted as you go. Press Enter to complete definition of the block range.

If you select Graphics, the prompt is

Enter graph filename:

A pop-up menu displays the names of graphs in the current subdirectory.

The final prompt, regardless of the type of file sent to the Communications module, is

Enter project file for next application:

If you have already built a project file within the Communications module and you want to initiate that file, enter its name; if no such file exists or if you don't want to initiate a project file, simply press Enter. (All Send command sequences terminate with this project-file prompt.)

Sending Data to the Data Base Manager

If you send data to the Data Base Manager, you are prompted to

Enter name or block reference:

After you do so, you are prompted for the name of a project file to initiate within the Data Base Manager.

When a file is sent to the Data Base Manager, each row from the specified block becomes a record, and each column becomes a field. Default field names of F001, F002, etc. are established. (If you prefer to create one record in the Data Base Manager for each column in the worksheet, use the Matrix Transpose command to swap the rows for columns and the columns for rows before issuing the Send command. Deleting unnecessary rows or columns before sending a file to the Data Base Manager is a good idea.)

Sending Data to the Word Processor

If you choose to send data from the Spreadsheet to Smart's Word Processor, there are three options:

Document Graphics Both

If you choose Document, you are prompted to select first a range and then a project file to initiate within the Word Processor. If you select Graphics, you are asked to enter the name of a graph file. If you select Both, you are prompted for both the graph file name and the range. The final prompt is for the project file.

Within the Word Processor, the data from the worksheet is displayed in a new document with no name assigned. Each row is now a line, the columns are aligned, and the graph is the "default" graph to be identified in the Graphics command.

When you execute the Graphics command in the Word Processor to include a graph in the body of a document, a pop-up menu displays the names of the graph files you have saved. If you send a graph from the Spreadsheet to the Word Processor, that graph file is identified as the default on the pop-up menu.

Conclusion

Within the Smart Spreadsheet, the capability of importing and exporting data greatly adds to the power of the system. By reading data from an external file, you can interface the Spreadsheet with other software packages without having to retype the data. Similarly, the Write command allows you to create a file that you can later import to a different system.

The Send command is used within the Smart Spreadsheet to pass data or graphs to another Smart module and to immediately initiate that module. This feature is the basis of the Smart System's integration.

Chapter 20

Using Graphics

The Graphics command in the Smart Spreadsheet really is more than just a single command; it is a complete subsystem with capabilities to rival those of stand-alone graphics programs. But graphics-only programs do not share Smart's wealth of Spreadsheet commands and functions that help you prepare the data.

The data for Spreadsheet graphics comes from your worksheets; the output can be sent to the screen (if you have a compatible monitor), to a dot-matrix printer with graphics capabilities, or to a plotter. Graphs can be edited: you can draw lines, enter text, or erase elements of the graph. A completed graph can be saved for inclusion in the body of a Word Processor document or for later display on your monitor in a "slideshow" presentation.

The available graph types are

> Bar Charts
> > Vertical Bars
> > Horizontal Bars
> > Stacked Bars
> > Three Dimensional Bars
> > Histograms
>
> Step Charts

Line Graphs
> Normal
> Layers
> X-Y Graphs

Pie Graphs
> Two Dimensional
> Three Dimensional ("Cake")

Hi-Low Graphs

This chapter provides a description of the Graphics command features, examples of their use and construction, and tips on preparing high-quality graphs.

Using the Graphics Command (2–Graphics, Ctrl-G)

The Graphics command is found on command list 2; the quick key, Ctrl-G, can be used to repeat the most recent graphics output command (Generate, Matrix-Print or Plot). Selecting this command causes the primary menu shown in figure 20.1 to be displayed.

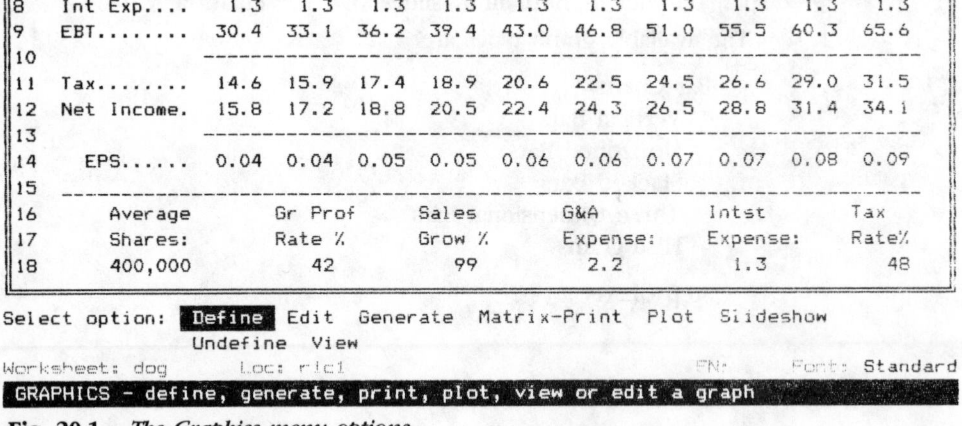

```
            1        2     3     4     5     6     7     8     9    10    11
1  ██████████████          DOMESTIC DIVISION
2                 Jan   Feb   Mar   Apr   May   Jun   Jul   Aug   Sep   Oct
3  Net Sales..  80.6  87.2  94.4 102.2 110.7 119.8 129.7 140.4 152.0 164.5
4  Gross Prof.  33.9  36.6  39.7  42.9  46.5  50.3  54.5  59.0  63.8  69.1
5            ----------------------------------------------------------------
6  G&A Exp....   2.2   2.2   2.2   2.2   2.2   2.2   2.2   2.2   2.2   2.2
7  EBIT......   31.7  34.4  37.5  40.7  44.3  48.1  52.3  56.8  61.6  66.9
8  Int Exp....   1.3   1.3   1.3   1.3   1.3   1.3   1.3   1.3   1.3   1.3
9  EBT........  30.4  33.1  36.2  39.4  43.0  46.8  51.0  55.5  60.3  65.6
10           ----------------------------------------------------------------
11 Tax........  14.6  15.9  17.4  18.9  20.6  22.5  24.5  26.6  29.0  31.5
12 Net Income. 15.8  17.2  18.8  20.5  22.4  24.3  26.5  28.8  31.4  34.1
13           ----------------------------------------------------------------
14 EPS......    0.04  0.04  0.05  0.05  0.06  0.06  0.07  0.07  0.08  0.09
15           ----------------------------------------------------------------
16    Average        Gr Prof      Sales       G&A         Intst       Tax
17    Shares:        Rate %       Grow %      Expense:    Expense:    Rate%
18    400,000        42           99          2.2         1.3         48

Select option: Define  Edit  Generate  Matrix-Print  Plot  Slideshow
               Undefine  View
Worksheet: dog      Loc: r1c1                              FN:    Font: Standard
GRAPHICS - define, generate, print, plot, view or edit a graph
```

Fig. 20.1. *The Graphics menu options.*

Defining a Graph (Graphics Define)

The first step in using Spreadsheet graphics is to define the graph you want to create. As in other modules of the Smart system, you create definitions that are saved to disk for later use. When you execute the Graphics Define command, the first prompt is

Enter graphics definition filename:

Use the cursor keys to point to the name of an existing file in the pop-up menu, or type a new file name. Figures 20.2, 20.3, and 20.4 show the Graphics definition screens. The specifications entered in these screens were used to define the graph shown in figure 20.5. The data for the graph was taken from the financial model that is used throughout this chapter.

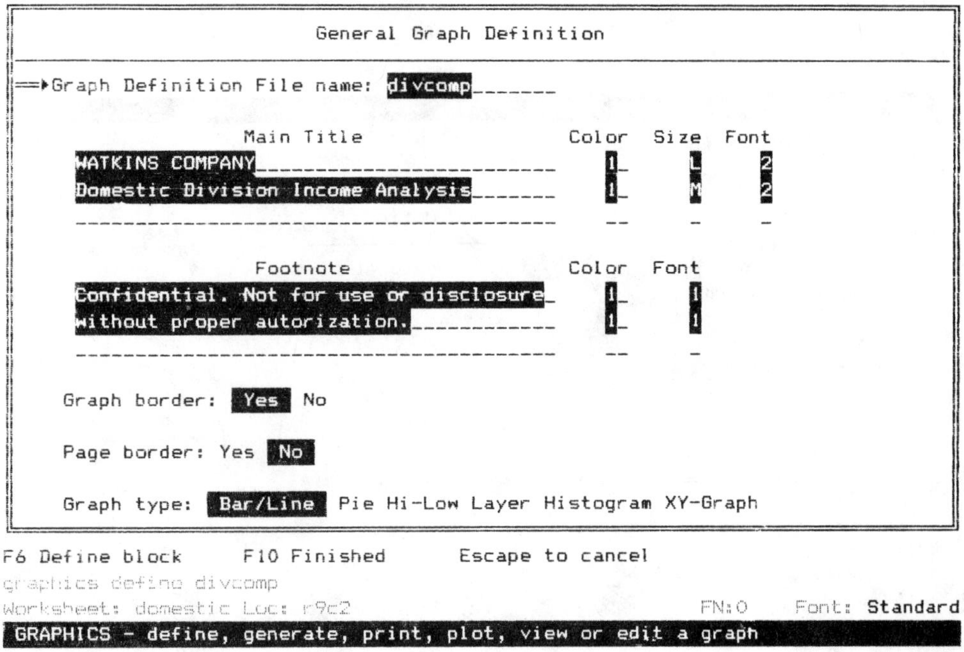

```
                    General Graph Definition

==▶Graph Definition File name: divcomp_____

                Main Title              Color  Size  Font
   WATKINS COMPANY_____   1     1     2
   Domestic Division Income Analysis___   1     M     2
   ----------------------------------     --    -     -

                 Footnote               Color  Font
   Confidential. Not for use or disclosure  1   1
   without proper autorization._____   1   1
   ----------------------------------     --    -

   Graph border:  Yes  No

   Page border:  Yes  No

   Graph type:  Bar/Line  Pie Hi-Low Layer Histogram XY-Graph

F6 Define block      F10 Finished       Escape to cancel
graphics define divcomp
Worksheet: domestic Loc: r9c2                    FN:0   Font: Standard
GRAPHICS - define, generate, print, plot, view or edit a graph
```

Fig. 20.2. *Graphics Bar definition screen 1.*

```
                         Bar-Line Graph Definition

==>        Data block               Legend        Type  Pattern  Color
        r4c2:13 _____    Gross Profit _____  1      2       1
        r11c2:13 _____    Taxes _____  2      6       1
        r8c2:13 _____    Interest _____  2      4       1
        r6c2:13 _____    G & A Expense _____ 2      1       1
        r12c2:13 _____    Net Income _____  3      5       1
        _____    _____  __     __      __


        X-Axis title block:  r2c2:13 _____

                    X-Axis title                  Color  Font
        1987 _____    1     2


                    Y-Axis title                  Color  Font
        DOLLARS _____    1     1

        Options:  No  Yes
```

F6 Define block   F10 Finished   Escape to cancel
graphics define divcomp
Worksheet: domestic Loc: r9c2   FN:0   Font: Standard
GRAPHICS - define, generate, print, plot, view or edit a graph

Fig. 20.3. *Graphics Bar definition screen 2.*

```
                         Bar-Line Graph Options

        Bar dimension:  2-dimensional  3-dimensional  Line
        Bar orientation:  Vertical  Horizontal
        Values on top of bars:  None  Horizontal  Vertical
        Legend position:  None  Bottom  1 2 3 4
        Point type:  Dots  Symbols

==>   Divisions:  Color  Font  Tics/Div.
        X-Axis:    __     _      __
        Y-Axis:    __     _      __


      Grids:      (y/n)  Color   Style
        X-Axis:     _     __       _
        Y-Axis:     _     __       _


      Scaling:    Type   Minimum    Maximum    Increment
        Y-Axis:    _    _____  _____  _____
```

F6 Define block   F10 Finished   Escape to cancel
graphics define divcomp
Worksheet: domestic Loc: r9c2   FN:0   Font: Standard
GRAPHICS - define, generate, print, plot, view or edit a graph

Fig. 20.4. *Graphics Bar definition screen 3.*

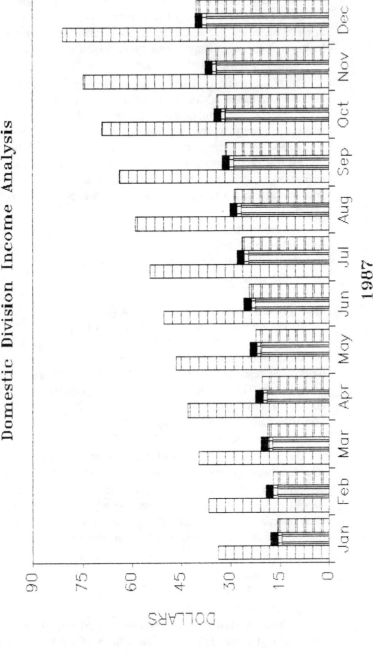

Fig. 20.5. *A sample Bar Graph.*

You move from item to item in the graph definition screens by pressing Enter or by using the cursor keys. You can move back to correct previous items; the PgUp and PgDn keys move the display from page to page. Page 3 can be accessed only if you select *yes* at the options prompt at the bottom of page 2.

The F6 key can be used in some circumstances to select cell contents or range addresses from the current worksheet. When you press F6, you are temporarily returned to the worksheet. You then move the cursor to the beginning of the range you want to select and press F2 to "drop the anchor." Next, you move the cursor to the end of the range and press Enter. You are then returned to the definition screen, and the range address is entered on the screen. (If you are defining a title, the cell contents are entered instead of the cell address.)

The graph definition file name is the file name you specify when you call up the definition screens. If you change the name, you will have both the original definition and the new definition that is stored under the new name.

Specifying a Graph Title (Graph Title)

Three lines of titles are allowed on a graph. You can either type the title on the line, as shown in figure 20.2, or reference a cell on the worksheet. For the latter alternative, press F6 to display the worksheet temporarily; then move the cursor to the desired cell and press Enter. The definition screen is then displayed, and the system enters the contents of the cell (not the cell address) on the line. The title can have as many as 40 characters. Titles are always centered.

The title color you should select depends on the capabilities of your hardware: if you have a monochrome graphics monitor, select 1 or leave the entry blank. If your system has color capability, you should make a trial run to determine what colors are generated. In your manual or in the margins of this book, make note of the colors that appear. Color numbers can range from 0 to 15.

The title size can be one of the following:

L   Large
M   Medium
S   Small

No hard-and-fast rule governs the actual size of the title that is generated; it depends on the capabilities of your printer or plotter. Again, you should run an example for your future reference.

Six different type fonts are available:

1 Stick
2 Roman
3 Script
4 Italic Stick
5 Italic Roman
6 Italic Script

If Smart supports your printer or plotter, each of these fonts is available to you. Graphics font generation does not depend on your hardware's internal fonts.

Adding Footnotes and Borders

Entering footnotes is similar to entering titles. With footnotes, as with titles, you can select both colors and font styles. You cannot select a size, however; the small size is always used. You can enter a maximum of 40 characters. Footnotes are always left-justified and positioned at the bottom of the page.

If you select a graph border, a solid line is drawn around the graph, as shown in figure 20.5. If you select a page border, a line is drawn around the entire page.

Choosing Graph Types

Graph types are selected at the bottom of screen 1. Use the space bar, the minus sign (−) key, or the plus sign (+) key to move the highlighted block to the graph type you want to create; you cannot use the cursor keys here. If you select Bar/Line, use the option at the top of screen 3 to choose a two-dimensional Bar graph, a three-dimensional Bar graph, or a Line graph.

Bar Graph. Screen 2 is used to enter the cell addresses of the data for the graph and the associated titles. This screen differs according to the type of graph being produced. Bar/Line, Layer, and Histogram graphs share the same definition screens, which are shown in figures 20.3 and 20.4.

Notice that a maximum of six data blocks can be defined for the Bar/Line graph type. A data block, in this example, is a row of worksheet data that is represented by a bar on the graph. (Three bars are stacked in figure 20.5.) Columns define the horizontal dimension of the graph (the x-axis). Columns 2 through 13 are used in this case. Use the F6 key to help you define the data block entries.

The legend is printed on the graph to identify the data blocks. In figure 20.5, the legend is printed at the bottom of the graph, but it could be positioned in one of four quadrants. Again, you can use F6 to reference the worksheet, but the actual cell contents instead of the cell addresses are pulled into the definition.

The following options can be entered in the Type column of the definition screen:

B   Bar
L   Line
S   Step
1–6 Stacked Bar

To create a stacked bar graph, assign the same type numbers to the data blocks whose bars are to be stacked. Gross Profit and Net Income are shown as separate bars in figure 20.3. The bars for Taxes, Interest, and G&A Expense are stacked because the data blocks have all been assigned a graph type of 2. The number designations have nothing to do with the order in which the bars appear; you should enter the data blocks in the desired order.

Seven patterns of solids, checks, stripes, etc., can be used for bar graphs, and fourteen patterns are available for pie graphs. Identify the patterns by selecting a number between 0 and 13. Enter colors for each data block as appropriate.

The patterns themselves are shown in the Smart manual. To see how your hardware handles them, you may want to make a test graph.

The range whose address appears on the definition line for the x-axis title block contains the names of the months. The x-axis and y-axis titles can be typed on the appropriate line. Select a color and a font; you don't get to make a choice about the title size.

If you select Yes in answer to the options prompt, you proceed to screen 3 (see fig. 20.4). For the sample graph in figure 20.5, a 2-dimensional graph has been selected. Selecting 3-dimensional causes the bars to be placed one behind another, creating a three-dimensional effect. If you want the bars to appear as thin lines with arrows on top, select the Line graph type.

In the example, the bars are vertical. Select Horizontal to rotate them by 90 degrees.

Values can be placed at the tops of the bars for easier interpretation of the graph. The numbers may be difficult to read, however, if the graph is complex.

Legends can be printed at the bottom of the graph, as in the example, or in one of the four quadrants of the graph. The quadrants are numbered 1 through 4, beginning at the upper right and proceeding counterclockwise.

Axis scaling in a graph is automatic by default; you don't have to worry about the size or placement of the bars. If you want to override the automatic scaling, you can complete the remainder of screen 3.

Histogram. Figures 20.6 and 20.7 show graph definition screens 2 and 3 for the histogram in figure 20.8. (Screen 1 is the same as in the previous example, except for the selection of the graph type.) The histogram always has three dimensions and is a form of 3-dimensional bar graph.

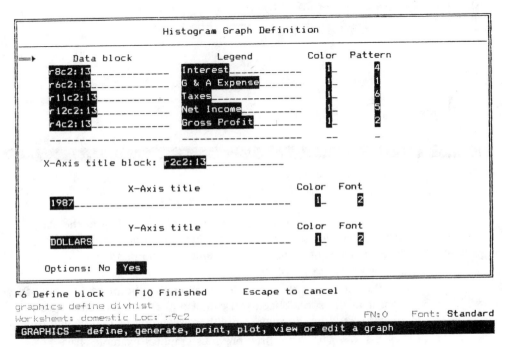

Fig. 20.6. *Histogram definition screen 2.*

Pie Graph. Figures 20.9 and 20.10 show graph definition screens 2 and 3 for the "cake" graph (a 3-dimensional pie graph) shown in figure 20.11. Notice that patterns 0 through 11 were used for the 12 months. The pie slice for December was "exploded" away from the rest of the pie. Only one data block may be specified for a pie graph.

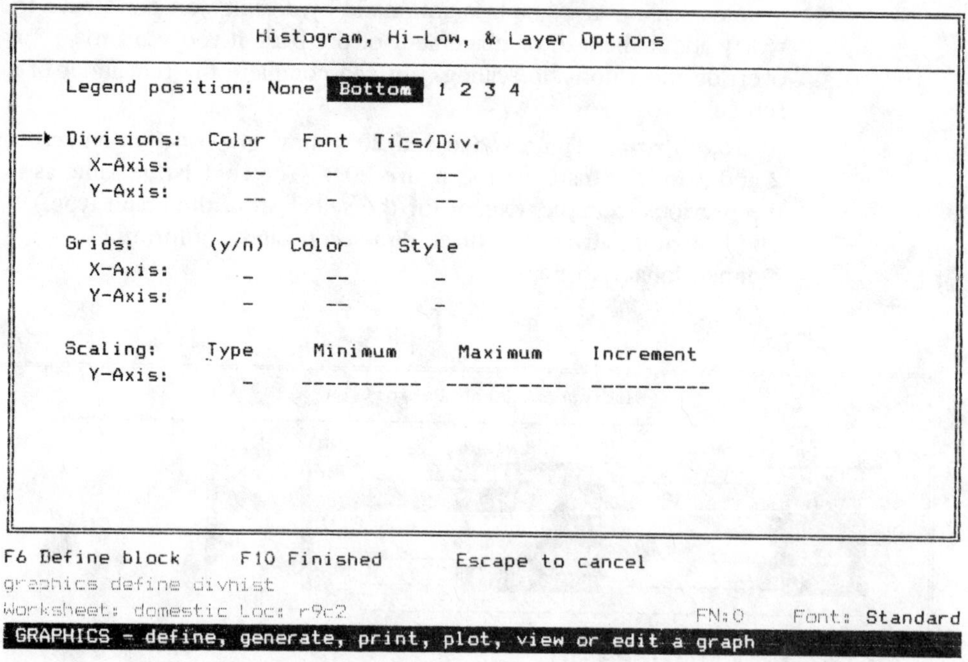

```
┌────────────────────────────────────────────────────────────────────┐
│               Histogram, Hi-Low, & Layer Options                     │
│                                                                      │
│       Legend position: None  Bottom  1 2 3 4                         │
│                                                                      │
│ ══▶ Divisions:   Color    Font   Tics/Div.                           │
│        X-Axis:     --       -       --                               │
│        Y-Axis:     --       -       --                               │
│                                                                      │
│        Grids:    (y/n)   Color     Style                             │
│        X-Axis:     -       --        -                               │
│        Y-Axis:     -       --        -                               │
│                                                                      │
│      Scaling:    Type     Minimum      Maximum      Increment        │
│        Y-Axis:     -     ----------   ----------   ----------        │
│                                                                      │
│                                                                      │
│                                                                      │
│                                                                      │
└────────────────────────────────────────────────────────────────────┘
 F6 Define block     F10 Finished        Escape to cancel
 graphics define divhist
 Worksheet: domestic Loc: r9c2                          FN:0    Font: Standard
 GRAPHICS - define, generate, print, plot, view or edit a graph
```

Fig. 20.7. *Histogram definition screen 3.*

Notice also that you have choices for the labeling of the slices and the legend. You can use the values from the spreadsheet, text labels (names of months, for example) or the percentage that each pie piece makes up of the whole.

The months in the example are shown in the order in which they appear in the spreadsheet; you can also print the pie chart with the pieces sorted by the values, in either ascending or descending order.

X-Y Graph. The three previous graphics examples have illustrated the graphing of continuous numeric values (Income) against discrete text (months). Sometimes, however, you need to plot a series of continuous numeric values against another numeric series in order to show the relationships between the numbers. To do so, select the X-Y graph option.

Figures 20.12 and 20.13 show graph definition screens 2 and 3 for the X-Y graph in figure 20.14. The graph shows the relationship between Net Sales (on the x-axis) and Net Income (on the y-axis).

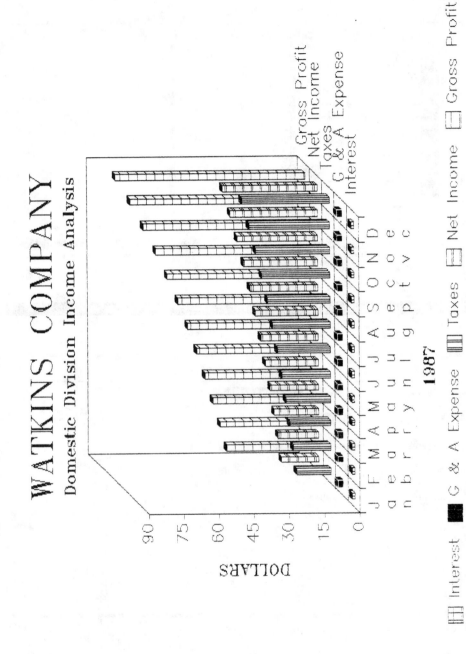

Fig. 20.8. *A sample Histogram.*

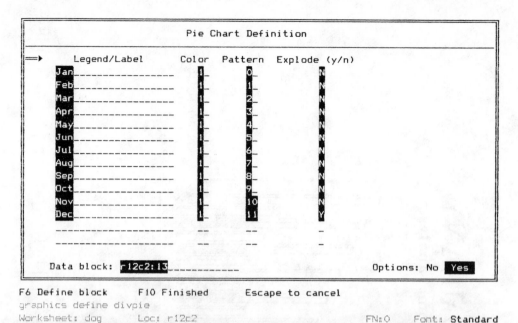

Fig. 20.9. *Pie Graph definition screen 2.*

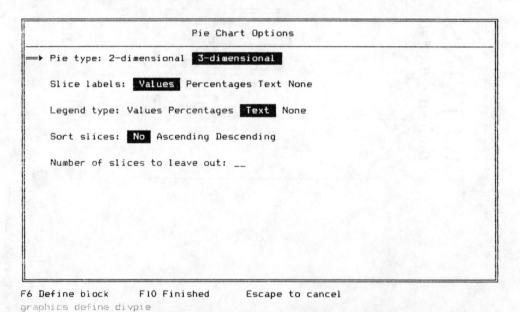

Fig. 20.10. *Pie Chart definition screen 3.*

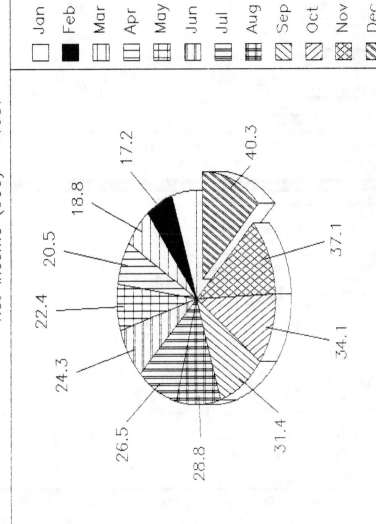

WATKINS COMPANY
Domestic Division Income Analysis
Net Income (OOO) – 1987

Jan
Feb
Mar
Apr
May
Jun
Jul
Aug
Sep
Oct
Nov
Dec

17.2
18.8
20.5
22.4
24.3
26.5
28.8
31.4
34.1
37.1
40.3

Fig. 20.11. *A sample Pie chart.*

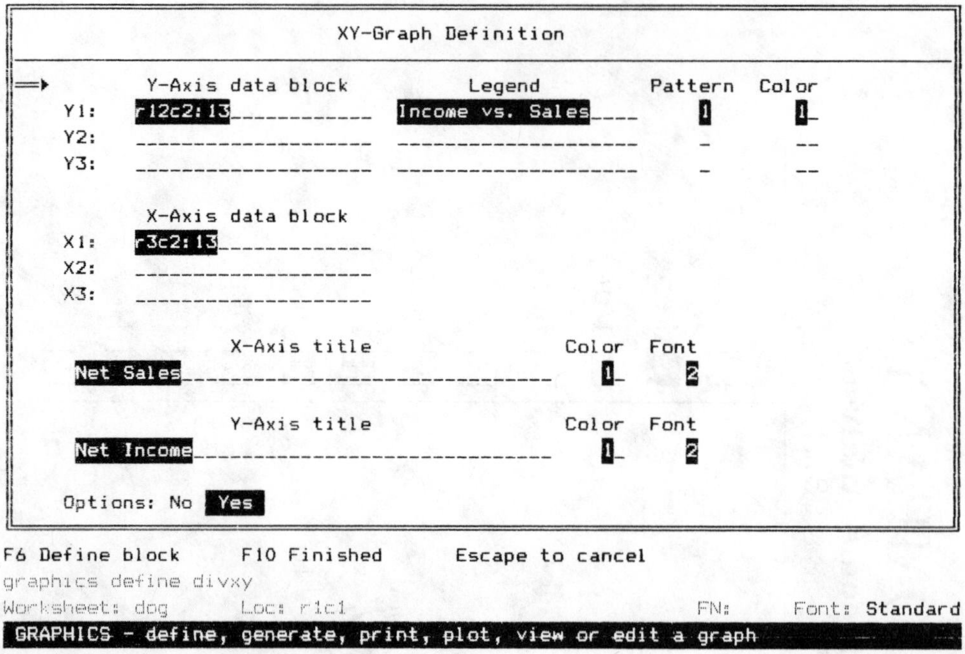

```
                          XY-Graph Definition

==▶        Y-Axis data block          Legend        Pattern  Color
     Y1:  r12c2:13_____   Income vs. Sales____    1       1_
     Y2:  _____   _____    -      --
     Y3:  _____   _____    -      --

           X-Axis data block
     X1:  r3c2:13_____
     X2:  _____
     X3:  _____


                X-Axis title              Color  Font
     Net Sales_____   1_     2

                Y-Axis title              Color  Font
     Net Income_____   1_     2

     Options: No  Yes
```

F6 Define block   F10 Finished   Escape to cancel
graphics define divxy
Worksheet: dog   Loc: r1c1   FN: Font: Standard
GRAPHICS - define, generate, print, plot, view or edit a graph

Fig. 20.12. *X-Y Graph definition screen 2.*

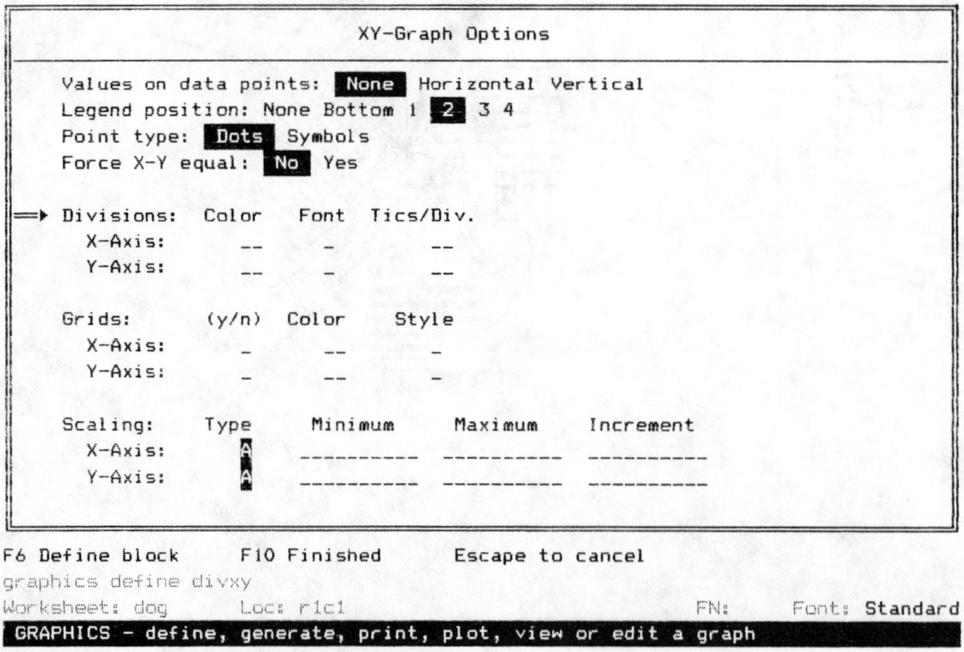

```
                          XY-Graph Options

     Values on data points:  None  Horizontal Vertical
     Legend position: None Bottom 1  2  3 4
     Point type:  Dots  Symbols
     Force X-Y equal:  No  Yes

==▶ Divisions:  Color   Font  Tics/Div.
       X-Axis:    --     -      --
       Y-Axis:    --     -      --


     Grids:     (y/n)  Color  Style
       X-Axis:    _      --     _
       Y-Axis:    _      --     _


     Scaling:   Type   Minimum    Maximum    Increment
       X-Axis:    A    _____ _____ _____
       Y-Axis:    A    _____ _____ _____
```

F6 Define block   F10 Finished   Escape to cancel
graphics define divxy
Worksheet: dog   Loc: r1c1   FN: Font: Standard
GRAPHICS - define, generate, print, plot, view or edit a graph

Fig. 20.13. *X-Y Graph definition screen 3.*

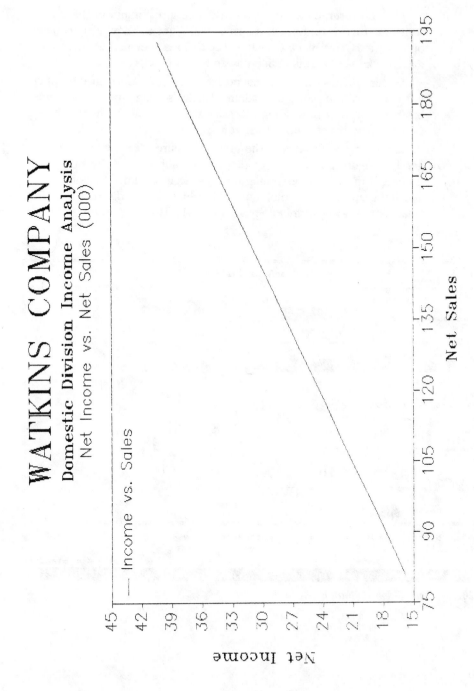

Fig. 20.14. *A sample XY graph.*

Notice on screen 2 that you can define a maximum of three series for this type of graph. Because you want to show Net Income on the y-axis, this block of data (r12c2:13) is specified as the y-axis data block. Net Sales is defined as an x-axis block.

Screen 3 shows that the legend has been positioned in the upper left corner of the plot (in quadrant 2); the scaling type for both axes has been set to *A*, indicating that they will begin at the minimum values in the series, rather than zero.

Line Graph. Compare the graph in figure 20.14 with the line graph in figure 20.17. Both graphs are actually line graphs, but the graph in 20.14 plots numeric values against numeric values, and the graph in 20.17 plots numeric values against discrete text. In Smart Spreadsheet terminology, figure 20.17 is a *Line graph*.

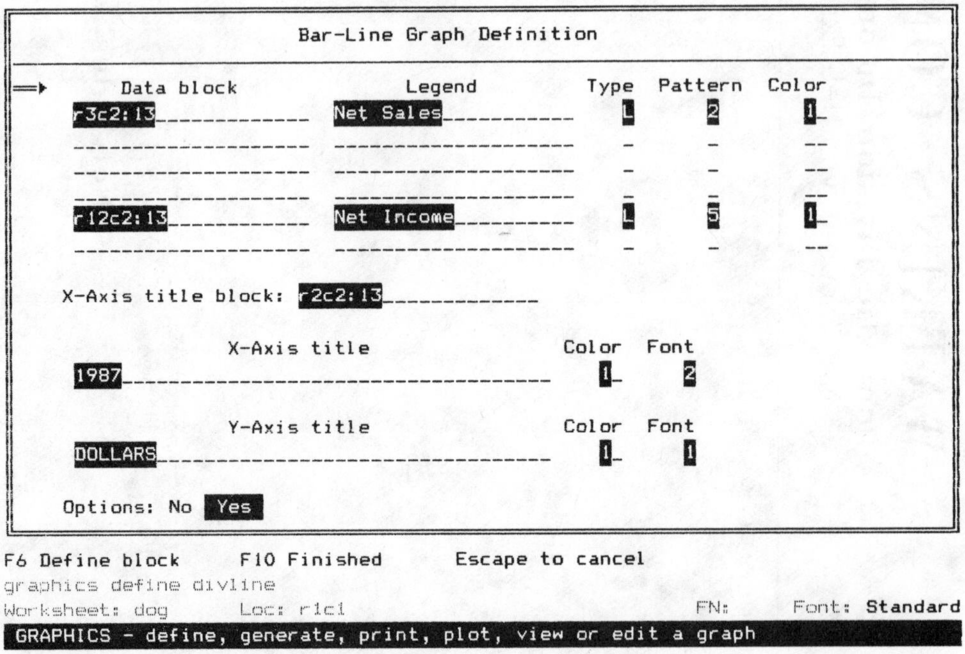

```
                         Bar-Line Graph Definition

═▶         Data block              Legend           Type  Pattern   Color
        r3c2:13_____   Net Sales_____     L      2        1

        _____       _____     -      -        --

        _____       _____     -      -        --

        r12c2:13_____   Net Income_____     L      5        1

        _____       _____     -      -        --


     X-Axis title block:  r2c2:13_____

                     X-Axis title              Color  Font
        1987_____   1      2


                     Y-Axis title              Color  Font
        DOLLARS_____   1      1


     Options: No  Yes
```

```
F6 Define block      F10 Finished       Escape to cancel
graphics define divline
Worksheet: dog      Loc: r1c1                         FN:      Font: Standard
GRAPHICS - define, generate, print, plot, view or edit a graph
```

Fig. 20.15. *Line Graph definition screen 2.*

```
                    Bar-Line Graph Options

    Bar dimension: 2-dimensional 3-dimensional  Line
    Bar orientation:  Vertical  Horizontal
    Values on top of bars:  None  Horizontal Vertical
    Legend position: None Bottom 1  2  3 4
    Point type: Dots  Symbols

==> Divisions:   Color   Font  Tics/Div.
      X-Axis:     --      -      --
      Y-Axis:     --      -      --


    Grids:       (y/n)  Color    Style
      X-Axis:      -      --        -
      Y-Axis:      Y      --        2


    Scaling:     Type   Minimum    Maximum    Increment
      Y-Axis:     -    ---------- ---------- ----------
```

```
F6 Define block     F10 Finished      Escape to cancel
graphics define divline
Worksheet: dog     Loc: r1c1                FN:    Font: Standard
GRAPHICS - define, generate, print, plot, view or edit a graph
```

Fig. 20.16. *Line Graph definition screen 3.*

Figures 20.15 and 20.16 show the definition screens for the graph in figure 20.17. Notice in figure 20.15 that the data blocks do not have to be adjacent. Also notice that the Line graph type has been selected for both blocks. Figure 20.16 shows that the legend has again been placed in quadrant 2. The plot lines have been identified with symbols rather than different line types. You don't have a choice of symbols; the system assigns them.

Grids have been established from the y-axis. The style is 2, which indicates that individual dots, or *pixels*, are used in the grid. The available grids correspond to the line types shown in the manual. Colors can be specified.

Displaying the Graph (Graphics Generate)

After you have defined your graph, use the Graphics Generate command to display the graph on your monitor if it has graphics capability. You don't have to change to graphics mode with the Display command; the system handles the switch for you.

When you select the Generate option, you are prompted to

Enter graphics definition filename:

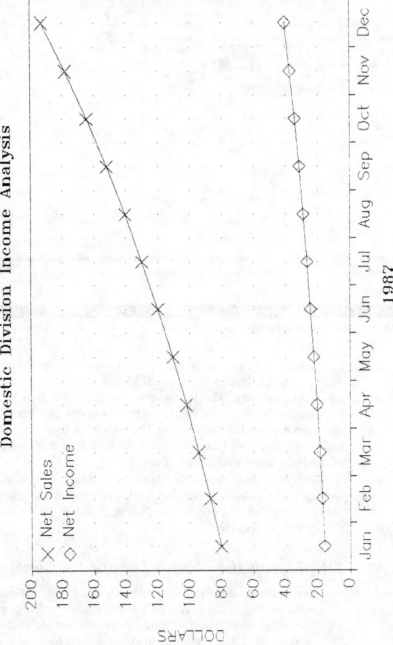

Fig. 20.17. *A sample Line Graph.*

Type the name, or move the cursor to the name in the pop-up menu and press Enter. The next prompt is

> Select option: Black/white Color

You then select the appropriate mode, and you are asked whether you want to save the screen:

> To save screen, enter screen name:

Save the screen if you want to view this graph later by means of the Graphics View or the Slideshow command. If you plan to include the graph in a Word Processor document, you *must* save it. When you save a screen, the file is given an extension .SCN.

Even if you don't have a graphics monitor, you can save the screen at this time. The system saves the screen for you without proceeding to display the graph on the screen. If you do have a graphics monitor and you decide to save the screen, the screen is saved and the graph is displayed for a moment; the system then immediately returns to the command level.

If you want to keep the graph on-screen so you can study it, simply press Enter at the prompt. The graph is displayed on the screen and remains there until you press any key to continue. Then you are prompted again:

> Do you wish to save this screen (y/n)?

If you are pleased with the graph, press *y* to save the screen. Then you are prompted for a name. If you answer *n* at the Save prompt, the system returns you to the command level.

If you are making many changes to a definition and you need to switch back and forth between defining the graph and generating it to examine the effect of the change, use the Ctrl-G quick key to repeat the most recent Graphics Generate command. This key can also be used to repeat the most recent Matrix-Print or Plot command.

Printing the Graph (Graphics Matrix-Print)

When your graph is as you want it, use the Graphics Matrix-Print command to print the graph on a dot-matrix printer. You are prompted to enter the file name; either type the name or use the cursor keys to identify the name in the pop-up menu, and then press Enter. The file names in the pop-up menu are *not* the saved screen files, however; they are the graph definition file names.

Remember: you must save your graph screen only if you want to edit the graph or if you want to include the graph in a Word Processor document or in a Slideshow presentation. If you simply want to print or plot the graph, you do not need to save the screen.

The printer does not start printing your graph right away; the system must first "draw" the graph in memory and then transfer the drawing to paper. Sometimes, the system prints the first part of a graph, then pauses to perform the calculations necessary for printing the second part of the graph.

Remember that you can use Ctrl-G to repeat the most recent Matrix-Print output command.

Plotting the Graph (Graphics Plot)

If you have a plotter, you can plot your graph by using the Graphics Plot command. In addition to being prompted for the name of the file, you are prompted to select

Full-Page Quadrant

If you want your plot to fill the page, select the Full-Page option. If you plan to have as many as four plots on the same page, you can select Quadrant, and the plot will be drawn in the appropriate corner of the page. Remember that the quadrants are numbered from 1 to 4, beginning at the upper right corner and proceeding counterclockwise. These are the same quadrant numbers used for designating the location of legends in graph definitions.

Ctrl-G can also be used with the Graphics Plot command to reexecute the most recent plot.

Viewing the Graph (Graphics View)

To display saved graphs (.SCN files) on your monitor, use the Graphics View command. (This command is similar to the Graphics View File command in the Word Processor.) The result of Graphics View is the same as that of Graphics Generate, except that View offers different display options. You are prompted to select the name of a *saved screen* file from a pop-up menu:

Enter graph filename:

Use the cursor keys to select the file, and press Enter. You are then prompted to select a display option:

Curtain Fade-in Instant

If you select Curtain, the screen looks as though a curtain on a stage is rising to reveal the graph. The Fade-in option sprinkles the screen randomly with pixels, gradually filling in the graph. (You really need to try these!) The Instant option displays the graph all at once.

Press any key to remove the graph and return to the command level. Remember, you can view only saved screen files; this command does not regenerate the graph from the original data. If the data in your spreadsheet has been changed, the saved screen file will not reflect the changes.

Viewing Graphs in Succession (Graphics Slideshow)

If you would like to view several different graphs in succession for a presentation, for example) and you don't want the system to return to the command level and display the worksheet, use the Graphics Slideshow command. This command has its effect only under the control of a project file; issue the command prior to any Graphics View commands in the project file.

Editing Graphs (Graphics Edit)

To spice up a saved-screen graph, you can change it with the Graphics Edit command. In the editor, you can erase portions of the graph, draw lines, insert text, or set color, font, and text-orientation options.

Remember that only a saved graph can be edited. After the graph has been edited, view it on-screen with the Graphics View command. Because the Matrix-Print and Plot options in the Spreadsheet operate from the original definitions, however, you cannot print or plot the edited graph.

So how do you get a printed copy of your edited graph? Include the graph in a Word Processor document and use the enhanced printing. Unfortunately, the quality and resolution are not the same as if the graph had been printed with Spreadsheet Matrix-Print. Figure 20.18 shows an edited version of the graph displayed in figure 20.5.

If you no longer need a graph definition, use the Graphics Undefine command. The pop-up menu displays the names of saved definitions. Using the cursor keys, select the definition you want to "undefine." Then press Enter. The definition is erased immediately.

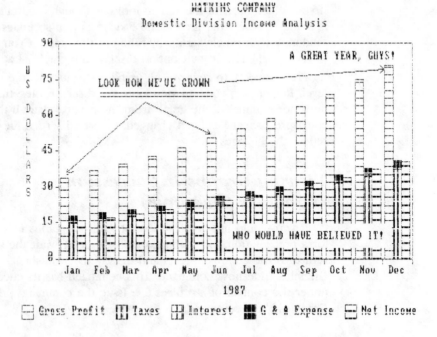

Fig. 20.18. *The edited graph.*

Conclusion

This chapter has described the process of defining and generating graphs from the Smart Spreadsheet module. The graphics module of the Smart system compares favorably with many stand-alone graphics packages. Many examples of graphs have been illustrated in this chapter, along with the definitions for creating them. Compare the output with the definitions to learn how to apply the same techniques in producing your own graphs.

Part III

Using Smart's Word Processor

Chapter 21

Introduction to Smart's Word Processor

If you have never used a word processor, you are in for a treat; if you are converting from another word processor, you will be delighted with the variety of features and ease of use of the Smart Word Processor.

A word processor is used to create and edit documents—letters, articles, books, memos, and manuscripts. You can save the documents for later use, edit them by moving sentences or whole paragraphs within the current document or into other documents, and copy or delete portions of your document. Your document can have features such as italic, boldface printing, and underlining if your printer supports them. And because the Word Processor is integrated within the Smart system, it can share documents, data, and and even graphics with the other applications modules. (Yes, you can print a graph within the body of your document.)

This chapter introduces you to Smart's Word Processor and explains how to create, load, name, and save document files, making them available for further editing.

Working with the Word Processor

The Word Processor has two basic modes of operation. Text Entry mode is used for entering new text and changing existing text. Several special keystrokes for moving the cursor are available in Text

Entry mode. Command mode makes available five lists of commands for moving and formatting text, searching and replacing, printing, and interfacing the Word Processor to other modules of the Smart System.

Entering New Text (Text Entry Mode)

When you begin using the Word Processor, you are in Text Entry mode, as indicated on the autohelp line shown in figure 21.1.

```
O::::L:::::1:::::|::::2::::|::::3::::|::::4::::|::::5:::::|::::6::::|::R::::7::::|::|

F1 Help          F3 Find      F5 Replace       F7 Zoom        F9 Repeat
F2 Next menu     F4 Goto      F6 Font Select   F8 Execute     F10 Quit
Document: (none)    Pg:1   Ln:1    Ps:5    FN:0     Font: Standard        Insert ON
 TEXT-ENTRY - normal text-entry mode
```

Fig. 21.1. *Starting up in Text Entry mode with Insert ON.*

To enter text in this mode, just start typing. Each character appears on the screen as you type. To erase a mistake that you have just entered, use the "destructive backspace" key. If you need to return to a previous part of the line or another part of the document, use one of the cursor-control keys described in the next section. You can then use the Del key to delete individual characters; if Insert mode is on, you can insert new characters between existing ones. If Insert is off, new characters overwrite existing characters. The status of Insert mode is shown at the right end of the status line.

Several helpful markers appear on the screen (see fig. 21.2). The paragraph marker shows where you have entered a "hard" carriage return by pressing Enter. The tab markers show where you have "tabbed over" by pressing the Tab key instead of entering spaces. A page break entered by Smart's Word Processor is shown as a solid single line across the screen; if you force a page break with the Newpage command, the page break appears as a heavy dashed line. The end of the current document is always shown as a diamond.

✳ Use the Visible command to make these markers invisible during the current session. By changing the defaults in the Parameters settings, you can make "markers off" the default condition.

Moving the Cursor

The cursor indicates the current typing position in the document window. If you have pressed the Insert key and Insert mode is on,

```
┌─ Window 1 ═══════════════════════════════════════════════════════════
║     Paragraph Marker: ¶
║     Tab Marker: ▶  ¶
║     Decimal Tab Marker:▼      ¶
║     Page Break by System:¶
║  ────────────────────────────────────────────────────────────────────
║     Page Break by User:¶
║  ----------------------------------------------------------------------
║     End of text: ◆
║
║
```

Fig. 21.2. *Use Smart's visible markers as a guide.*

the cursor appears as a heavy underscore; press Insert again to "toggle off" Insert mode. After you initiate a command, the cursor becomes a full-height block.

Several specialized cursor-control keys are available within Smart's Word Processor to help you move the cursor within the current document. These keys and their functions are listed in table 21.1.

Table 21.1
Cursor-Control Keys

Key	*Function*
Ctrl-G	Move cursor right one word
Ctrl-F	Move cursor left one word
Home	Move cursor to top left corner of current window
End	Move cursor to beginning of last line in current window
Tab	Move cursor right one tab position
Shift-Tab	Move cursor left one tab position
PgUp	Scroll up one page
PgDn	Scroll down one page
Ctrl-←	Move to beginning of current line
Ctrl-→	Move to end of current line
Ctrl-Home	Move to beginning of current document
Ctrl-End	Move to end of current document

Switching to Command Mode

To use the Word Processor's commands, press the Esc key to toggle to Command mode. To go back to Text Entry mode, press Esc again or use the Alt-Y quick key. (The Esc key is also used to cancel a command and return to Command mode.)

As in Smart's other application modules, quick keys can be used to issue commands in the Word Processor. These quick keys are specified as each command is discussed. In the Word Processor, quick keys can be used even in Text Entry mode; this saves you the step of having to exit to Command mode to issue a command.

Concepts

Certain common concepts and phrases recur throughout the Word Processor. One such concept is that of specifying a range over which an action is to take place.

Specifying a Range

If, for instance, you want to delete or move a certain portion of text, you are prompted to define the block to which the command applies. Figure 21.3 shows the range-selection options.

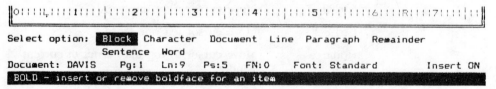

Fig. 21.3. *Specifying a range.*

Throughout the Smart system, a *block* can be specified by moving the cursor to the upper left corner of the block, pressing F2 to "drop the anchor," moving the cursor to the lower right corner of the range, and pressing Enter. The area defined by the block is displayed in reverse video (see fig. 21.4 for an example).

Certain commands that call for a range allow you to specify an individual *character*. Move the cursor to the appropriate position before pressing the *C* for Character.

Select the Document option to specify the entire *document* in the current window.

```
  From the description of your application, it sounds as though
  the  Model 23-B will better suit your needs both now  and  in
  the years to come.   If your growth continues at its   current
  pace, you would exceed the capacity of the 23-A by the summer
  of next year.¶
O::::L::::1::::|::::2::::|::::3::::|::::4::::|::::5::::|::::6::::R::::7::::|::
```

```
Use cursor to mark block
F2  Drop new anchor        F10 or ENTER  End block
Document: DAVIS    Pg:1    Ln:17  Ps:18  FN:0    Font: Standard        Insert ON
DELETE - delete a line, word, sentence, paragraph, block or remainder
```

Fig. 21.4. *Marking a block.*

The Line option will specify only the *line* on which the cursor is positioned; select Paragraph to indicate the currently displayed *paragraph* in which you have your cursor.

Choosing the Remainder option indicates that the range extends from the current cursor position to the end of the document.

Select Sentence to indicate the current *sentence*. The sentence must end with a period; if it ends with another mark of punctuation, such as a question mark, the range will extend to the next period. Selecting Word specifies the current *word* (bounded either by blanks or punctuation).

Effects of Commands

As you will see in the explanations of individual commands, certain commands affect existing text and others affect text that you are about to enter. This distinction can be confusing because, although the end result may be the same and the commands may be similar, the method (and ease) of achieving the result may be different.

For example, you may want a certain sentence underscored within your document. You have two choices. You can enter the sentence and then come back and underscore it with the Underscore Sentence command. Or you can use the Font Select command to underscore all new text entries until you turn off underscoring with the same command.

Document spacing is another example: you can type a document in single-space and then change it to double-space with the Reformat command, or you can start by indicating double-space with the Spacing command. There is no right or wrong way to perform these tasks; use whichever works best for you.

Using the Parameters command, you can set the defaults for your Word-Processor environment. By setting the defaults, you indicate the settings that you want to have in effect when you begin a session. Paragraph justification, for instance, can be set initially at either Normal or Left-Justified in the Parameter specification list. At any time during the session, however, you can change the justification; use the Justify command for new text or the Reformat command for existing text.

Not all defaults for the Word Processor are set in the Parameters settings. Certain all-encompassing settings are established in the Configure command of the main menu. Other document defaults are established with the Print Preset command, which is discussed in Chapter 25.

After you have changed and saved a document, the text and formatting changes will be there when you load the document in a later session. Certain settings, however, apply only to the current session and are not saved with the document. For instance, if you have indicated that new text is to be underscored as you enter it, this condition will not be in effect the next time the document is loaded. The underscore setting, which changes *input conditions* but does not change the *document* until you enter new text, affects the current session only; if you load a new document during the current session, new text will be underscored unless you clear the underscore setting with the Font Select command.

Reserved Memory

For efficiency, Smart uses all of the random-access memory (RAM) you have made available. (You may have reserved a portion of RAM for DOS access when you entered Smart, using the -r entry option.)

Certain Word Processor commands must have a fixed amount of memory available. The mapping of individual bits in the Display Graphics, Draw, and Print Enhanced commands require substantial amounts of memory. If insufficient memory is available for these commands, you receive the following error message:

```
Insufficient Memory
```

To prevent this problem, you should specify on the last line in your Parameters settings the amount of memory to be reserved. The number you enter represents thousands of bytes. The exact number you should specify depends on the type of hardware you have and the amount of memory in your machine. Begin by setting the value to 32 or 48; you want to set it to the lowest value that does not result in the error message.

Because Parameter settings take effect only when you enter the application module, you should press F10 to save the parameters after you have entered the new settings. Then you must exit and reenter the Word Processor so that the new settings can take effect.

Handling Files

This section covers the creation, loading, saving, and naming of document files in the Smart Word Processor. Regardless of whatever else you do in the Word Processor module, you will need this information to know how to save your documents and to make them available for editing.

Loading Files (4 –Load, Alt-L)

The Load command is used to call up a document from a disk file and to make it available for editing in the current window. The Load command is found on command list 4 (see fig. 21.5); the quick key is Alt-L.

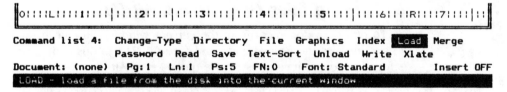

```
|O|:::|L|::::|1|::::|:|:::|2|:::|:|:::|3|:::|:|:::|4|:::|:|:::|5|:::|:|:::|6|:::|R|:::|7|:::|:||

Command list 4:  Change-Type  Directory  File  Graphics  Index  Load  Merge
                 Password  Read  Save  Text-Sort  Unload  Write  Xlate
Document: (none)   Pg:1   Ln:1   Ps:5   FN:0   Font: Standard        Insert OFF
LOAD - load a file from the disk into the current window
```

Fig. 21.5. *Selecting the Load command.*

If your current directory contains Word Processor document files, you see a pop-up menu of their names. Use the cursor-control keys to identify the document you want to edit, and then press Enter. If the document resides in another subdirectory, you must enter the path and file name. If you want to display a pop-up menu of document files that are in another subdirectory, type the name of the directory and the file specification: *invoice**.*doc*, for example. Then press F5 to display the pop-up menu.

If the document is protected by a password, you are prompted to

Enter password:

You are given three attempts at entering the correct password before Smart returns you to the command level. Remember that passwords are "case sensitive"; that is, *PASS* is different from *pass*. (The Password command is discussed later in this chapter.)

Smart Word Processor documents are identified to the system by their file extensions. A .DOC extension indicates that the file is a true *document* file with all the hidden control characters needed for word processing. (If you use the DOS TYPE command to view the contents of one of these files—by entering *type filename.DOC* at the DOS prompt—you would see all kinds of strange symbols on the screen. These symbols represent the control characters.) A .TXT extension means that the file is an ordinary *text* file with no special characters. Based on the extension, the Word Processor automatically changes the way it deals with the file. (Refer to the section on the Change-Type command in Chapter 23 for more details.)

In the Word Processor, only one document can be active in the current window; you cannot have active documents that are not displayed. If you try to load a new document into a window that already contains a document and you have modified the first document, the system asks whether you want to save that document (performing an Unload). Answer by pressing *y* or *n*. If you need two active documents at one time, use the Split command to create a new window for the second document.

Unloading Files (4 –Unload, Alt-U)

To remove a document from the current window without loading a new one, use the Unload command (see fig. 21.6). This command is found on on command list 4; the quick key is Alt-U.

Fig. 21.6. *Selecting the Unload command.*

If you have changed the document, you are asked whether you want to save the modified copy. If you have just created the document and have not given it a name (see the section on the Newname command, later in this chapter), Smart prompts you to enter a name for the document.

Saving Files (4 – Save, Alt-S)

The Smart Word Processor will not let you inadvertently exit the system without giving you a chance to write your modified document to disk. However, you may want to save the document occasionally as you work. Because most (if not all) of your document is kept in RAM as you work on it, you run the risk of losing the changes you have made if the power is interrupted.

Use the Save command to write the document to disk; after a short wait while the command does its work, you can continue working where you left off. The Save command is found on command list 4 (see fig. 21.7); the quick key is Alt-S.

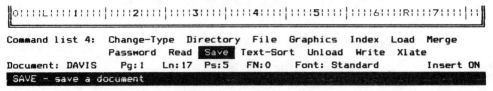

Fig. 21.7. *Selecting the Save command.*

When you select the Save command, you are prompted to enter a file name even if your file already has one. To save the document under its current name, just press Enter. Type a new name if you want to save the document under a different name.

Documents are saved to the current subdirectory unless you provide a path to another subdirectory. If a file with the same name exists in the specified subdirectory, Smart displays a message telling you of this condition and asks you whether you want to overwrite the existing file. Respond by pressing *y* or *n.*

Renaming Files (3–Newname, Alt-N)

You frequently may want to create a new version of an existing document—using a large portion of a previously written letter, for example, in a similar letter to a different customer. To do so, you first load the old document and then give the document in the current window a new name. Then the old document will not be changed when you save or unload the new document.

The Newname command is used to give a new name to the document in the current window. (The name of the file on disk is left unchanged.) Newname is found on command list 3 (see fig. 21.8); the quick key is Alt-N.

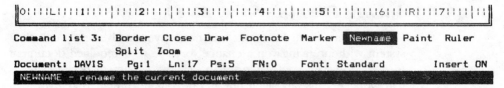

Fig. 21.8. *Selecting the Newname command.*

After you issue the Newname command, you are prompted to enter the new document (or text) file name, which can contain as many as eight letters or numbers. Although the Save command will prompt you to enter a new name, giving your document the new name right after you load the document is safer.

Reading Files (4 –Read)

You know that the Load command brings in a document from the disk and unloads an existing document, if there is one. Sometimes, however, you want to load several documents in succession, so that they appear one right after the other. This technique is useful for documents that contain standard "boiler plate" sections or paragraphs.

The Read command is used for this function (see fig. 21.9). Read is found on command list 4; there is no quick key. To use the Read command, position the cursor at the character *before* which you want to insert the new material, then issue the command. You are prompted with a pop-up menu of file names, just as you are with the Load command. Select the appropriate file and then press Enter. The name of the document in the current window remains unchanged.

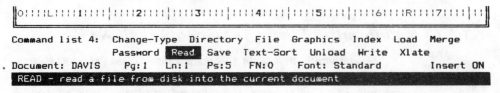

Fig. 21.9. *Selecting the Read command.*

If the document is protected by a password, you are prompted to

Enter password:

You are given three attempts at entering the correct password before you are returned to the command level.

Protecting Your Files (4 – Password)

Word Processor documents can be protected with the Password command, found on command list 4. If a document is protected, you are prompted for the password when you load or read the document or when you print it directly from the disk. The options are

```
Attach Remove
```

If you select Attach, you are prompted to

```
Enter password:
```

Type a four-character password and then press Enter. Smart prompts you to confirm the password:

```
Protect current document with the password "----" (y/n)
```

The password you have entered appears within the quotation marks. Passwords *must* be four characters long and are *case sensitive*; be sure to remember not only the password but also whether it is in upper- or lowercase. If you forget your password, there is no way to recover the file.

The file must be written to disk for the password to be effective. If you quit the Word Processor without saving the document, it will not be protected. Password Attach may also be used to change the password of a document.

To delete a password from a file, issue the Password Remove command. There is no prompt; the document must be loaded in the current window. Remember that for password removal to be permanent, you must save the document to disk.

Converting Files

You can convert files from the WordStar format or from IBM's Document Content Architecture (DCA) format to the Smart Word Processor format.

Converting WordStar Files with W2SMART

If you want to convert a WordStar file, use the W2SMART program from your Smart Graphics Drivers disk. (This program is not automatically copied to your hard disk or working floppy disk during the Install process.) Documentation for using this program is found in Appendix B of the Smart Word Processor manual.

The W2SMART program is executed *outside* of the Smart environment, at the DOS level. The command format for using W2SMART is

    w2smart file1 file2

where *file1* is name of the WordStar file and *file2* is the name of the SMART file that is to be created by W2SMART. To convert a WordStar file called GLENN.WS, for example, you exit the Smart system and enter

    w2smart GLENN.WS GLENN

This example creates a new file called GLENN.DOC. The new file is ready for use with the Smart Word Processor. The original file is left intact. Make sure that you have enough disk space for the new file.

Converting Files to and from DCA Format (4 – Xlate)

The Xlate command (found on command list 4) is used to translate documents to and from IBM Document Content Architecture format, which is sometimes called "Revisable Form Text." If you are translating a file to the Smart Word-Processor Document format, a new .DOC file is created from the original .RFT file. You can also create an .RFT file from a Smart .DOC file. The Xlate command has three options:

    Dca Smart Edit

If you select Dca, Smart prompts you for three file names:

1. Original DCA file (with extension .RFT)
2. Smart file to be created (if you do not enter a name, a file is created with the same name as the DCA file and the extension .DOC)
3. Translation file (default is DCAXLATE.TRN)

The Smart option is used to create a DCA file from a Smart file. The prompts are similar, except that the first prompt is for the input .DOC file and the second, for the output .DCA file.

Use the Edit option to edit font-translation files for use in making a conversion from or to DCA files.

When you use the Xlate command, the original file remains intact and is not destroyed or overwritten. Xlate is executed *within* the Smart Word Processor module.

Conclusion

Armed with the information in this chapter, you are ready to begin exploring the individual commands of the Smart Word Processor. Now that you know how to load, unload, save, rename, and protect your Smart Word Processor files, you are ready to learn how to make changes to the documents.

Chapter 22

Handling and Viewing Word-Processor Text

One of the great powers of a word processor is the ability to move, copy, insert, and delete portions of a document. This chapter covers the ways in which you perform these tasks using the Smart Word Processor, and how to make the best use of the software's capabilities. It covers also ways to keep yourself out of trouble and how to perform "cut-and-paste" operations between documents. Finally, this chapter explains how to create and remove windows, as well as how to make a window fill the entire screen.

Moving Text (1–Move, Alt-M)

If it is true that "great documents are not written, they are rewritten," then the Move command certainly goes a long way toward helping you create those great documents. The Move command, as the name implies, is used to shift certain portions of text to different places within documents. Move is found on command list 1; the quick key is Alt-M (see fig. 22.1).

When you select the Move command, you are prompted to specify a range:

Select option: Block Line Paragraph Remainder Sentence Word

Remember to position your cursor *before* you specify an option. When you select the option, the text within the range is placed in a

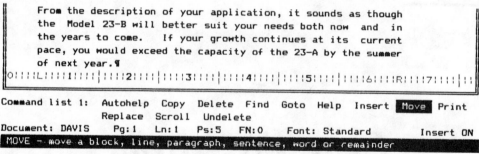

Fig. 22.1. *Selecting the Move command.*

copy buffer; it is not moved automatically. Using Move is a two-step process. First, move the text into the copy buffer; then move the text from the buffer back into the document. (See the next section for information about the Insert command.)

With this cut-and-paste capability, text can be moved within the current document or between documents. The contents of the copy buffer are maintained until you use the Move command again, use the Copy command, deliberately purge the buffer (with the Alt-Minus key combination), or end the session. If you go to a different window or unload the document, the contents of the buffer remain unchanged.

Inserting Text (1–Insert, Alt-I)

The Insert command (see fig. 22.2) is used to insert the contents of the copy buffer into the current document *before* the position of the cursor. Insert is found on command list 1; the quick key is Alt-I.

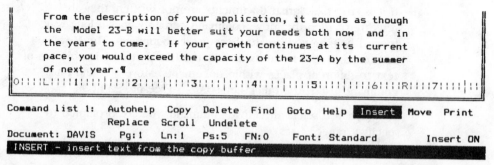

Fig. 22.2. *Selecting the Insert command.*

The Move and Copy commands both work in two stages, together with the Insert command. Move and Copy place the contents of a specified range in the copy buffer; Insert moves text from the buffer to the document. The contents of the buffer are not destroyed by using the Insert command; you can perform successive Insert commands with the same text. The Move and Copy commands both use the same copy buffer.

Do not confuse the Insert command with the insert *condition* of Text Entry mode. With the Insert command, you are moving text from the copy buffer to the document; with the insert *condition* toggled ON, the text you type is inserted into the document. If you press the Ins key and turn the condition OFF, any text you type overwrites the existing text.

Copying Text (1-Copy, Alt-C)

The Copy command is used to make a copy of a range of text (see fig. 22.3). Copy is found on command list 1; the quick key is Alt-C.

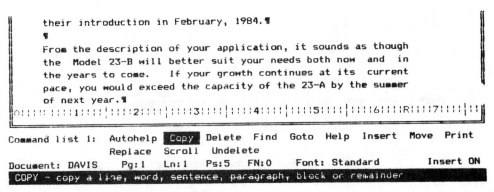

Fig. 22.3. *Selecting the Copy command.*

Like the Move command, Copy places the contents of a specified range in the copy buffer. Unlike Move, however, the Copy command does not remove the text in the range, but leaves it in place. When you have used the Insert command, you will have an additional copy of the text.

When you select the Copy command, you are prompted to specify a range:

Select option: Block Line Paragraph Remainder Sentence Word

Remember to position your cursor *before* you specify an option. After you select the option, the text within the range is placed in the copy buffer; it is not automatically copied. Copy, like Move, is a two-step process. First, copy the text into the copy buffer, then use the Insert command to move the text from the buffer back into the document. (Refer to the previous section about the Insert command.)

Deleting Text (1–Delete, Alt-D)

The Delete command is used to delete portions of text from the current document (see fig. 22.4). Like Move and Copy, the Delete command places the contents of the deleted range into a special buffer, called the *delete buffer*. (This is a different buffer from the one used by the Move and Copy commands.)

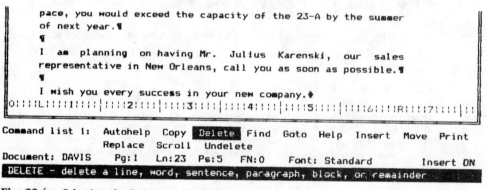

Fig. 22.4. *Selecting the Delete command.*

Delete is found on command list 1; the quick key is Alt-D. Using the quick key only executes the Delete command itself; you still have to select a range from the menu:

Select option: Block Line Paragraph Remainder Sentence Word

Several other specialized Delete quick keys aid in the deletion process:

Key	Function
Ctrl-Y	Delete Line
Ctrl-P	Delete Paragraph
Ctrl-S	Delete Sentence
Ctrl-W	Delete Word

✳ To delete just one character, position the cursor on that character
and press the Delete key.

If you are using the quick keys, be sure to move your cursor to
the desired position *before* pressing the keys. If you are executing
the Delete command by itself, position the cursor before selecting an
option.

Restoring Deleted Text (1-Undelete; Alt-Q)

If you have deleted text that you did not intend to delete, you can
use the Undelete command to restore the text from the delete
buffer. The Undelete command is found on command list 1; the
quick key is Alt-Q (see fig. 22.5).

```
    I  am  planning  on having Mr.  Julius  Karenski,  our  sales
  representative in New Orleans, call you as soon as possible.¶
    ¶
  I wish you every success in your new company.◆
O::::L::::1::::|:::::2::::|::::3::::|::::4::::|::::5::::|::::6:::R::::7::::|::
```

```
Command list 1:  Autohelp  Copy  Delete Find  Goto  Help  Insert  Move  Print
                 Replace  Scroll  Undelete
Document: DAVIS      Pg:1    Ln:23  Ps:50  FN:0     Font: Standard        Insert ON
UNDELETE - undelete the previously deleted text
```

Fig. 22.5. *Selecting the Undelete command.*

To use the Undelete command, position the cursor at the
character *before* which you wish to restore the deleted text material,
and then issue the Undelete command. Undelete does not erase the
contents of the delete buffer; the command can be used repeatedly
to restore the contents of the delete buffer to several positions
within the document, in much the same way that you might use the
Move and Insert commands.

The contents of the delete buffer are changed when you perform
another Delete command or quit the current session. Because Move
and Copy use the copy buffer, those commands do not affect the
contents of the delete buffer.

Creating Windows (3–Split, Alt-H, Alt-V)

Like the other Smart application modules, the Smart Word Processor
"does windows." A window is created with the Split command and

closed with the Close command; use the Zoom command to cause the current window to fill the entire screen.

As many as 50 windows can be defined at any time within the Smart Word Processor, although you will probably never need that many. Why would you want to create windows in the Word Processor? First of all, you would then be able to edit several documents simultaneously, quickly switching back and forth among them.

Windows provide the capability not only to edit multiple documents but also to perform cut-and-paste operations between documents. Using the Copy, Insert, and Move commands, you can insert text from one document into another. (The buffer holds the text to be moved as you "Goto" another window.)

The Split command is used to create additional windows by dividing the current window into two smaller windows. You can create a window also for the display of footnotes. Split is found on command list 3 (see fig. 22.6); the quick keys are Alt-H for creating a horizontal window, and Alt-V for a vertical window.

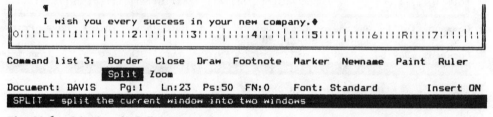

```
¶
    I wish you every success in your new company.♦
O::::L::::1::::|::::2::::|::::3::::|::::4::::|::::5::::|::::6::::R::::7::::|::
```

Command list 3:   Border   Close   Draw   Footnote   Marker   Newname   Paint   Ruler
                  Split Zoom
Document: DAVIS   Pg:1   Ln:23   Ps:50   FN:0   Font: Standard   Insert ON
SPLIT - split the current window into two windows

Fig. 22.6. *Selecting the Split command.*

When you select the Split command, you are prompted to select Horizontal, Vertical, or Footnote. Both the Horizontal and the Footnote options divide the screen into an upper half and a lower half. You are prompted to enter a line number or to move the cursor to the position at which the split is to occur (see fig. 22.7).

```
¶
    I wish you every success in your new company.♦
O::::L::::1::::|::::2::::|::::3::::|::::4::::|::::5::::|::::6::::R::::7::::|::
```

Enter line number, or use Tab or cursor keys to select location:
split horizontal
Document: DAVIS   Pg:1   Ln:23   Ps:50   FN:0   Font: Standard   Insert ON
SPLIT - split the current window into two windows

Fig. 22.7. *Splitting the screen horizontally.*

If you select Split Vertical, you are prompted to enter a column number or to move the cursor to the desired location, and then press Enter. Figure 22.8 shows the screen after it has been split vertically.

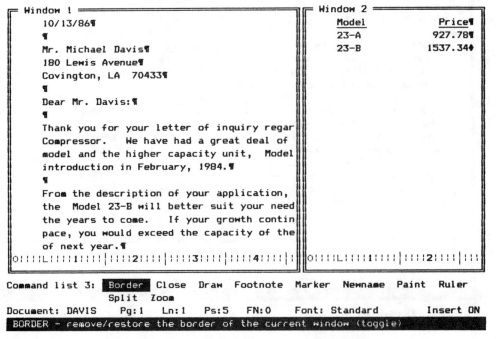

```
╔═ Window 1 ══════════════════════════╗ ╔═ Window 2 ══════════════════╗
║    10/13/86¶                         ║ ║    Model           Price¶    ║
║    ¶                                 ║ ║    23-A           927.78¶    ║
║    Mr. Michael Davis¶                ║ ║    23-B          1537.34◆    ║
║    180 Lewis Avenue¶                 ║ ║                              ║
║    Covington, LA  70433¶             ║ ║                              ║
║    ¶                                 ║ ║                              ║
║    Dear Mr. Davis:¶                  ║ ║                              ║
║    ¶                                 ║ ║                              ║
║    Thank you for your letter of inquiry regar ║                       ║
║    Compressor.  We have had a great deal of   ║                       ║
║    model and the higher capacity unit,  Model ║                       ║
║    introduction in February, 1984.¶  ║ ║                              ║
║    ¶                                 ║ ║                              ║
║    From the description of your application,  ║                        ║
║    the  Model 23-B will better suit your need ║                        ║
║    the years to come.   If your growth contin ║                        ║
║    pace, you would exceed the capacity of the ║                        ║
║    of next year.¶                    ║ ║                              ║
║0::::L::::1::::|::::2::::|::::3::::|::::4::::|  ║0::::L::::1::::|::::2::::|::: ║
╚══════════════════════════════════════╝ ╚══════════════════════════════╝
Command list 3:  Border  Close  Draw  Footnote  Marker  Newname  Paint  Ruler
                 Split  Zoom
Document: DAVIS     Pg:1    Ln:1    Ps:5    FN:0    Font: Standard      Insert ON
 BORDER - remove/restore the border of the current window (toggle)
```

Fig. 22.8. *A screen that has been split vertically.*

Note that a new document has been loaded into window 2. When you split the current window, you are prompted to indicate whether you want to leave the current window empty. An answer of *y* leaves it blank; an answer of *n* places a copy of the current document in the window.

At the bottom of the window, the ruler line is displayed by default. The Ruler command (command list 3) "toggles" display of the ruler line at the bottom of the current window. The command applies individually to each window; you can choose to display the ruler line in one window but not in the other.

Using the Split Footnote command creates a special horizontal footnote-display area at the bottom of the current window. The footnote that is referenced in the body of text in the document window is displayed in this footnote window. As you move the cursor (or scroll) to another part of the document, the footnote window either displays another footnote or (if there is no footnote) remains blank (see fig. 22.9).

```
╔══════════════════════════════════════════════════════════════════════╗
║ ┌─ Window 1 ═══════════════════════════════════════════════════════    ║
║     Covington, LA  70433¶                                              ║
║     ¶                                                                   ║
║     Dear Mr. Davis:¶                                                    ║
║     ¶                                                                   ║
║     Thank you for your letter of inquiry regarding our Model 23-A      ║
║     Compressor.  We have had a great deal of success with  this        ║
║     model and the higher capacity unit1, Model 23-B,  since their      ║
║     introduction in February, 1984.¶                                   ║
║     ¶                                                                   ║
║     From the description of your application, it sounds as though      ║
║     the  Model 23-B will better suit your needs both now  and  in      ║
║     the years to come.   If your growth continues at its  current      ║
║     pace, you would exceed the capacity of the 23-A by the summer      ║
║   0│:::L::::1::::│:::2::::│:::3::::│:::4::::│:::5::::│:::6:::R:::7::::│::║
║    Footnotes ─────────────────────────────────────────────────────    ║
║     1The capacity of the 23-A unit is 900 cfm, whereas the 23-B has a  ║
║     capacity of 1500 cfm.                                              ║
║                                                                        ║
╚══════════════════════════════════════════════════════════════════════╝
```

Select option: Horizontal Vertical ▐Footnote▌ split

Document: DAVIS   Pg:1   Ln:17 Ps:5   FN:0   Font: Standard   Insert ON

▐ SPLIT - split the current window into two windows ▌

Fig. 22.9. *Displaying a footnote.*

Removing Windows (3-Close, Alt-W)

The Close command is used to remove a window; the command is found on command list 3 (refer to fig. 22.8), and its quick key is Alt-W. You can use this command to close either a text window or a footnote window (see fig. 22.10).

If you select Footnote, only the footnote window in the current window is closed; if you close the current window, the entire window disappears, and neighboring windows are enlarged to fill the space on the screen.

If the document in the window has not been changed, the Close command proceeds with no further prompts. If you have changed the document, you are prompted to indicate whether you want to

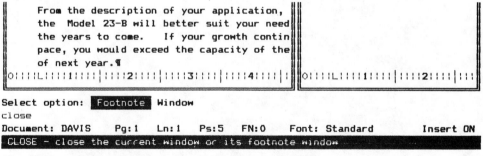

Fig. 22.10. *Selecting the Close command's Footnote option.*

abandon the modified document. If you answer *N*, the document is saved before the window is closed.

Causing a Window to Fill the Entire Screen (3-Zoom, F7)

If you want the current window to fill the entire screen, use the Zoom command. Zoom is found on command list 3; the quick key is F7. Zoom is a toggle command; the first time you select it, the current window fills the screen. Select Zoom again to restore the window to its original size.

Conclusion

If you never need to change what you have written, you don't need to read this chapter. But if you need to move or copy text, delete material (or restore it), or insert new text, this chapter is a must.

Also covered in this chapter are the commands used to split your screen to create windows or to close them. The Zoom command is used to cause one window to fill the entire screen.

Chapter 23

Formatting New and Existing Text

When you have created your document and have moved, copied, inserted, and deleted paragraphs and lines, you need to select the format and type style of your document. Formatting changes can affect margin settings, line spacing, and page breaks; the Smart Word Processor even lets you sort lines of text according to the contents of specified columns. Available type styles include underscored, boldface, and italicized text, superscripts and subscripts, and even Greek characters, depending on the capabilities of your printer.

The Smart Word Processor has several complementary sets of commands you can use in changing formats and type styles. If you want to underscore a certain passage of text, for example, you can select a command that causes new text to be underscored as it is entered. On the other hand, you can enter your text in the normal manner and return to it later and specify that it is to be underscored.

The actual changes made to a document are stored when the document is saved to disk. Therefore, if you reformat your document in double-space and then save it, the document will still be in double-space when you call it again.

Some settings are not saved with the document, however. The command to cause new text to be in double-space, for example, applies to the *session*, not to the document. Any text entered while this command is in effect is saved as double-spaced text, but the double-space option is not in effect when you call up the document the next day.

Any settings that affect the session apply to all documents you edit or create during that session and in that window. If you decide to enter lines in double-space, all the documents you create during that session will be double spaced—unless, of course, you decide to change back to single-space.

In addition to the formatting and typeface settings stored with the document, some print options also are stored. For more information on these print options, see Chapter 25, "Printing and Merging Text."

Formatting New Text

We'll begin with the commands that affect newly entered text. In most cases, the settings apply only to the session and to the current window. A different window might have a totally different setting. To take effect, commands that change the format of new text must be executed before a paragraph is begun.

Justifying Text (2-Justify, Alt-J)

The Justify command is used to select one of four justification modes for new text. Justify is found on command list 2, and the quick key is Alt-J (see fig. 23.1).

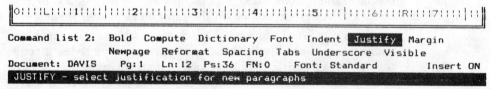

Fig. 23.1. *Selecting the Justify command.*

The justification options are shown in figure 23.2. Normal justification means that both the right and left margins are aligned; there are no ragged edges. Left-Justified leaves a ragged right margin; for example, a business letter prepared on a typewriter is left-justified. The Right-Justified option aligns the right margin, but leaves the left margin ragged. The Centered option causes all text on the line to be evenly spaced between the right and left margins.

Figure 23.3 shows the use of different justification modes. The first paragraph was created with the Left-Justified option in effect; the second paragraph is Normal. The last paragraph uses the Centered option.

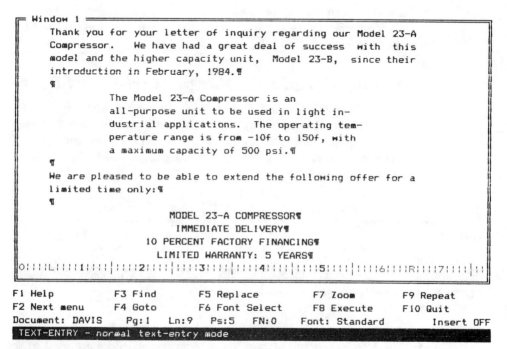

Fig. 23.2.   *The Justification options.*

Fig. 23.3.   *Examples of the justification modes.*

In the second half of this chapter, you will learn how to change the justification of existing text by using the Reformat command.

✳ *Spacing Lines (2-Spacing, Ctrl-V)*

The Spacing command, found on command list 2, is used to establish the line spacing for newly entered text. The quick key for the Spacing command is Ctrl-V (see fig. 23.4).

The default spacing of the Word Processor is controlled within the Parameters settings on command list 5. A setting of 1 indicates single spacing. The maximum spacing is 8; that setting leaves 7 blank

```
|0::::L::::1::::|::::2::::|::::3::::|::::4::::|::::5::::|::::6:::R::::7::::|::|
```

```
Command list 2:   Bold  Compute  Dictionary  Font  Indent  Justify  Margin
                  Newpage  Reformat  Spacing  Tabs  Underscore  Visible
Document: DAVIS      Pg:1    Ln:9    Ps:5    FN:0     Font: Standard          Insert OFF
   SPACING - set spacing for new paragraphs
```

Fig. 23.4. *Selecting the Spacing command.*

lines between lines of text. Each window on the screen can have different spacing. As you will see, the Reformat command is used to alter the spacing of existing text.

Setting Margins (2–Margin, Ctrl-L, Crtl-R)

The Margin command is used to set the left and right margins for new text and to temporarily release the left margin for the first line of a paragraph. The Margin command is found on command list 2, and the quick keys are Ctrl-L for the left margin and Ctrl-R for the right margin (see fig. 23.5).

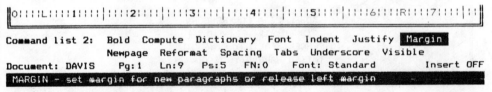

```
|0:::L::::1::::|::::2::::|::::3::::|::::4::::|::::5::::|::::6:::R::::7::::|::|
```

```
Command list 2:   Bold  Compute  Dictionary  Font  Indent  Justify  Margin
                  Newpage  Reformat  Spacing  Tabs  Underscore  Visible
Document: DAVIS      Pg:1    Ln:9    Ps:5    FN:0     Font: Standard          Insert OFF
   MARGIN - set margin for new paragraphs or release left margin
```

Fig. 23.5. *Selecting the Margin command.*

The Margin command has three options, as shown in figure 23.6. The Margin Left and Margin Right command seqences are used to set new left or right margins. When you issue either of these commands, you can set the new margins either by entering the column number of the new margin position or by moving the cursor to that position, and then pressing Enter (see fig. 23.7). Each window on the screen can have different margin settings.

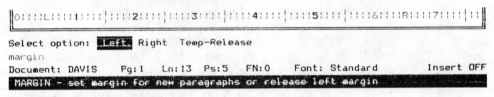

```
|0:::L::::1::::|::::2::::|::::3::::|::::4::::|::::5::::|::::6:::R::::7::::|::|
```

```
Select option:   Left  Right  Temp-Release
margin
Document: DAVIS      Pg:1    Ln:13    Ps:5    FN:0     Font: Standard          Insert OFF
   MARGIN - set margin for new paragraphs or release left margin
```

Fig. 23.6. *The Margin options.*

```
|0::::L::::1::::|::::2::::|::::3::::|::::4::::|::::5::::|::::6::::R::::7::::|::|
```
```
Enter new left margin, or use Tab or cursor keys to move to column:
margin left
Document: DAVIS    Pg:1  Ln:13  Ps:5  FN:0    Font: Standard         Insert OFF
 MARGIN - set margin for new paragraphs or release left margin
```

Fig. 23.7. *Entering the Left Margin specification.*

> After the new margins have been specified, the ruler line at the bottom of the screen changes when you go to a new line in Text Entry mode; the ruler line shows that the left margin (indicated by *L*) and the right margin (*R*) have been moved.

```
From the description of your application, it sounds as though
the Model 23-B will better suit your needs both now  and  in
the years to come.  If your growth continues at its  current
pace, you would exceed the capacity of the 23-A by the summer
of next year.¶
¶
I  am  planning  on having Mr.  Julius  Karenski,  our  sales
representative in New Orleans, call you as soon as possible.¶
¶
I wish you every success in your new company.◆
|0::::L::::1::::|::::2::::|::::3::::|::::4::::|::::5::::|::::6::::R::::7::::|::|
```
```
Use -> and <- keys to move margin.  F10 Finished
margin temp-release
Document: DAVIS    Pg:1  Ln:6  Ps:5  FN:0    Font: Standard          Insert OFF
 MARGIN - set margin for new paragraphs or release left margin
```

Fig. 23.8. *The Margin Temp-Release prompt.*

✳ If you want to release the left margin of the first line of a paragraph temporarily, use the Margin Temp-Release command. The prompt appears as in figure 23.8.

✳ Use the cursor keys to move left by the number of spaces you want to move the margin, and then press F10 or Enter. Then return to Text Entry mode and resume typing. Even if you reformat the paragraph later to change the margins, the number of spaces you released are still maintained outside the left margin, but the remainder of the paragraph is aligned within the margins. (If you later decide to change the margin-release setting, position the cursor on the first character of the paragraph, issue the Margin Temp-Release command, and use the cursor keys to move either farther to the left or back to the right.)

Indenting Text (2–Indent, Ctrl-N)

To establish automatic indentation as you enter new text, use the Indent command, found on command list 2 (see fig. 23.9). The quick key for Indent is Ctrl-N. Each window on the screen can have its own indentation setting. By establishing an automatic indent, you ensure that the first line of each new paragraph will be indented automatically by the number of characters specified. Subsequent lines of the paragraph conform to the established margin settings.

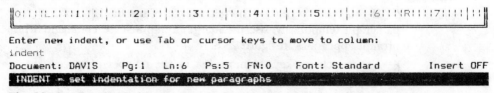

```
||0:::L::::1::::|::::2::::|::::3::::|::::4::::|::::5::::|::::6:::R:::7::::|::||

Command list 2:    Bold  Compute  Dictionary  Font  ▊Indent▊  Justify  Margin
                    Newpage  Reformat  Spacing  Tabs  Underscore  Visible
Document: DAVIS     Pg:1    Ln:6    Ps:5    FN:0    Font: Standard        Insert OFF
 INDENT - set indentation for new paragraphs
```

Fig. 23.9. *Selecting the Indent command.*

To specify the number of spaces to indent, either enter a number in response to the prompt (see fig. 23.10) or use the cursor-control keys to have the system supply the value. The number of spaces to indent is always relative to the current left margin. Entering a 5, for example, indents five spaces to the right of the current margin setting; entering –2 "outdents" the text two spaces to the left of the margin. "Outdenting" the first line of a paragraph can be useful if you like to number your paragraphs and display the numbers outside the left margin.

```
||0:::L::::1::::|::::2::::|::::3::::|::::4::::|::::5::::|::::6:::R:::7::::|::||

Enter new indent, or use Tab or cursor keys to move to column:
indent
Document: DAVIS     Pg:1    Ln:6    Ps:5    FN:0    Font: Standard        Insert OFF
 INDENT - set indentation for new paragraphs
```

Fig. 23.10. *Entering Indent spacing.*

If the margins are changed later, the indentation spacing is maintained in relation to the new margins. For more on changing margin settings, refer to the section on the Reformat command later in this chapter.

Selecting a Font (2-Font Select, F6)

The Font command, found on command list 2, can be used to select a font for new text or to change the font of existing text (see fig. 23.11). The quick key for Font Select is F6.

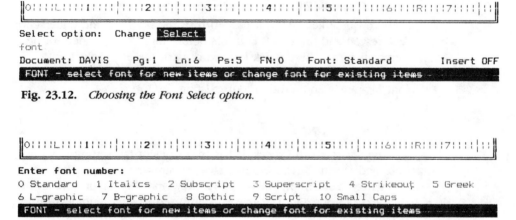

```
O::::L::::1::::|::::2::::|::::3::::|::::4::::|::::5::::|::::6::::R::::7::::|::|

Command list 2:  Bold  Compute  Dictionary  Font  Indent  Justify  Margin
                 Newpage  Reformat  Spacing  Tabs  Underscore  Visible
Document: DAVIS    Pg:1   Ln:6   Ps:5   FN:0    Font: Standard      Insert OFF
FONT - select font for new items or change font for existing items
```

Fig. 23.11. *Selecting the Font command.*

To select a font for new text, issue the Font Select command (see fig. 23.12). You are then prompted to enter a font number from 0 to 10 (see fig. 23.13). Actually, you can enter also the numbers for custom fonts 11 and 12 if you have defined them.

```
O::::L::::1::::|::::2::::|::::3::::|::::4::::|::::5::::|::::6::::R::::7::::|::|

Select option:  Change  Select
font
Document: DAVIS    Pg:1   Ln:6   Ps:5   FN:0    Font: Standard      Insert OFF
FONT - select font for new items or change font for existing items
```

Fig. 23.12. *Choosing the Font Select option.*

```
O::::L::::1::::|::::2::::|::::3::::|::::4::::|::::5::::|::::6::::R::::7::::|::|

Enter font number:
0 Standard   1 Italics   2 Subscript   3 Superscript   4 Strikeout   5 Greek
6 L-graphic  7 B-graphic  8 Gothic   9 Script   10 Small Caps
FONT - select font for new items or change font for existing items
```

Fig. 23.13. *Selecting a font number.*

When you select a font, make sure that your printer supports that font. When a new font is selected, Smart inserts in the file a code that switches your printer to the corresponding font mode. The Smart System fully supports some printers, and they can print all available fonts; some printers are only partially supported. When you first install your Smart system, be sure to select the code that corresponds to your printer.

Notice that the font name shown on the status line changes after you select a font. This is one way to be aware of the fonts in your document. (The *FN:* indicator on the status line shows the font of the character at the current cursor position.) If you have a color monitor, different fonts appear in different colors. Even if you don't have a color monitor, a monochrome graphics monitor can display the different fonts. Try changing the Display mode (command list 5) to Graphics and watch what happens.

In addition to the 12 font numbers, you can also designate boldfacing and underscoring. For example, if you want the text to appear italicized and underscored, enter *1U* at the prompt. The letters *U* and *u* control the underscoring; *B* and *b* control boldface:

Attribute	On	Off
Underscore	U	u
Bold	B	b

If you want your text both underscored and in boldface, you can use the letters together. For example, entering *0UB* selects the standard font, boldfaced and underscored.

Two quick keys make it easy to turn the boldface and underscore features on and off. Ctrl-B controls boldfacing; Ctrl-U, underscoring. Remember that these quick keys work with the Font Select command, not Font Change. The Font Select command selects the font for newly entered text, not existing text.

Setting Tabs (2–Tabs, Alt-T)

The Smart Word Processor has two types of tab settings: Normal Tabs and Decimal Tabs. Normal tabs are similar to those found on a typewriter. You simply press the Tab key, and the cursor advances to the next tab position. Decimal tabs are used to align numbers on the decimal point.

The Tabs command is found on command list 2, and the quick key is Alt-T (see fig. 23.14). If you select Tabs Normal (see fig. 23.15), the screen in figure 23.16 appears.

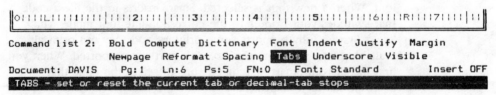

Fig. 23.14. *Selecting the Tabs command.*

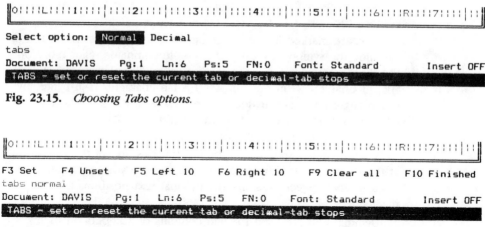

Fig. 23.15. *Choosing Tabs options.*

Fig. 23.16. *The Tabs Setting screen.*

The function keys shown on the command line are used to alter the tab settings. Current tab settings are indicated by the highlighted characters on the ruler line at the bottom of the screen. Figure 23.16 shows the tabs set at positions 10, 20, 30, 40, and 50. (The default tab settings are established in the Word Processor parameters.) When you assign tab settings, the function keys perform the operations listed in table 23.1.

Table 23.1
Function Keys for Setting Tabs

Key	Function
F3	Sets new tab position
F4	Clears specific tab position
F5	Moves cursor 10 positions to left on ruler line
F6	Moves cursor 10 positions to right on ruler line
F9	Clears all current tab settings
F10	Saves all changes and returns to command level

To set a new tab position, you move the cursor to the desired location and press F3. To clear a tab, you move the cursor to that tab position and press F4. Press F10 when all changes have been made.

When entering text, press the Tab key on your keyboard to advance the cursor to the next tab setting.

Tabs are marked in the document by a triangle symbol (▶). You can hide the symbols by using the Visible command. (For more on the Visible command, see the section called "Displaying and Hiding Special Characters" in this chapter.) A tab character is just like any other single character; it does not represent a series of blank characters. Consequently a tab symbol can be deleted, causing the text to the right of the tab character to move left.

A tab character references the column position of the tab setting at the time of entry. This is important, because you may change your tab settings between sessions; the original text positions are maintained.

Decimal tabs are used to align columns of numbers on their decimal points. The procedures for setting and changing decimal tabs are similar to the procedure for setting normal tabs (see fig. 23.16). On the ruler line, a decimal tab appears as a period. An example of the use of decimal tabs is shown in figure 23.17; notice that the visible symbol for the decimal tab is a triangle pointing down (▼). When entering text, press Ctrl-D to advance the cursor to the next decimal tab setting.

Both types of tabs can be set independently in each window.

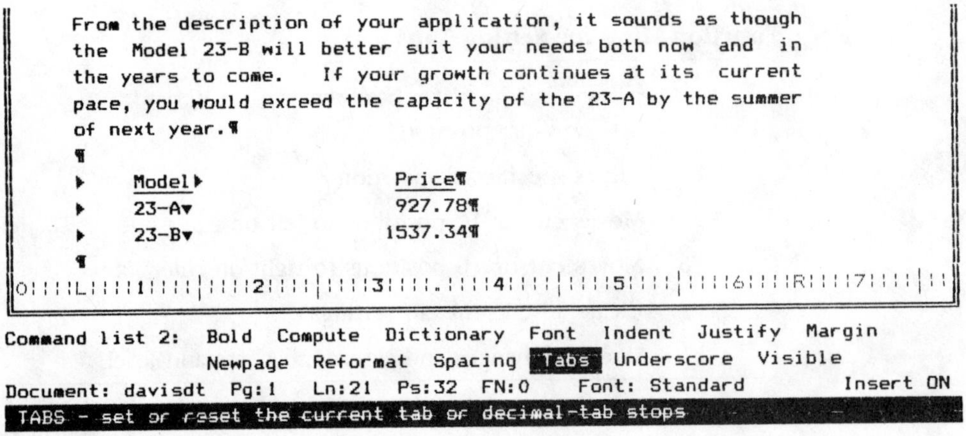

```
From the description of your application, it sounds as though
the  Model 23-B will better suit your needs both now  and  in
the years to come.   If your growth continues at its  current
pace, you would exceed the capacity of the 23-A by the summer
of next year.¶
¶
▶    Model▶             Price¶
▶    23-A▼              927.78¶
▶    23-B▼              1537.34¶
¶
0!!!!L!!!!1!!!!|!!!!2!!!!|!!!!3!!!!.!!!!4!!!!|!!!!5!!!!|!!!!6!!!!R!!!!7!!!!|!!
```

Command list 2: Bold Compute Dictionary Font Indent Justify Margin
                 Newpage Reformat Spacing `Tabs` Underscore Visible
Document: davisdt Pg:1   Ln:21 Ps:32 FN:0   Font: Standard   Insert ON
TABS - set or reset the current tab or decimal-tab stops

Fig. 23.17. *An example of decimal tabs.*

Creating and Using Footnotes
(3–Footnote, Alt-F)

If you have ever typed a document that has several footnotes and have suffered the agony of trying to allocate space for them at the bottom of the page, you'll appreciate the easy footnoting capability of the Smart Word Processor. Each footnote can have as many as three lines, and those lines can be edited. Each footnote is automatically tied to the text so that the footnote is *automatically renumbered* if the referenced text changes positions within the document because you have moved or reformatted the text.

The Footnote command is found on command list 3, and the quick key is Alt-F (see fig. 23.18).

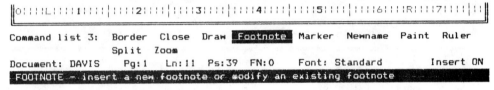

Fig. 23.18. *Selecting the Footnote command.*

The two options of the Footnote command are

    Insert Modify

To insert a footnote, place the cursor on the character before which you want the footnote number to appear, then select the Footnote Insert command. The Footnote input area then appears in the area below the window (see fig. 23.19).

Note that the number *1* appears in the third line of the first paragraph in the body of the letter. The Smart Word Processor generates this number automatically; if you have chosen to have the footnotes appear at the bottom of each page (see Chapter 25 on Print Options), numbering resumes with *1* on each new page. If the footnotes are to appear at the end of the document, the numbering continues sequentially through the document.

If you insert an additional footnote between two existing footnotes, the numbering is automatically adjusted; you never have to enter the footnote number. If you move or copy text that has a footnote, the footnote is carried along with the text, and the renumbering is done for you.

The maximum amount of text that can be entered into a footnote is three lines of 70 characters each. There is no word wrap at the

```
┌─ Window 1 ═══════════════════════════════════════════════
║    10/13/86¶
║    ¶
║    Mr. Michael Davis¶
║    180 Lewis Avenue¶
║    Covington, LA  70433¶
║    ¶
║    Dear Mr. Davis:¶
║    ¶
║    Thank you for your letter of inquiry regarding our Model 23-A
║    Compressor.  We have had a great deal of success with  this
║    model and the higher capacity unit1, Model 23-B,  since their
║    introduction in February, 1984.¶
║    ¶
║    From the description of your application, it sounds as though
║    the  Model 23-B will better suit your needs both now  and  in
║    the years to come.   If your growth continues at its  current
║    pace, you would exceed the capacity of the 23-A by the summer
║    of next year.¶
║Q::::L::::1::::|:::2::::|::::3::::|::::4::::|::::5::::|::::6:::R:::7::::|::
└─────────────────────────────────────────────────────────
```

```
Enter text for footnote 1.  F10 finished                      Insert ON
Line 1: The capacity of the 23-A unit is 900 cfm, whereas the 23-B has a
Line 2: capacity of 1500 cfm.
Line 3:
```

Fig. 23.19. *Entering the Footnote text.*

end of a line; you must manage this task yourself. Be sure to check
the spelling in your footnotes; the Dictionary command does not
check footnotes for spelling errors.

✳ The Word Processor has no explicit Footnote Delete command.
To get rid of a footnote, simply delete the footnote number from the
body of the text, just as you would delete any other character. The
footnote is deleted, and subsequent footnotes are automatically
renumbered.

Footnotes can be changed with the Footnote Modify command.
Use the F10 key to terminate the modification. The Ins key can be
toggled on or off while you modify a footnote, but you must be
careful if you insert new words, because there is no word wrap. If
you exceed the 70-character limit, the system will beep, but any
characters squeezed off the right end of the line are lost.

Drawing Boxes and Lines
(3-Draw box/line, F4)

The Draw command, found on command list 3, is used to create boxes and lines that can be included in the body of your text. Figure 23.20 shows the screen in which you "draw" the boxes or lines that are to be inserted into the document. The function keys take on the functions listed in table 23.2.

Table 23.2
Function Keys for Drawing Boxes and Lines

Key	Function
F2	Loads a previously saved drawing
F3	Saves a current drawing to a file. The automatic file extension is .DRW.
F4	Begins the drawing of the box or the line. You can specify a single, double, heavy, or block box or line. (If you select Double, you are prompted to select either Square or Round corners.)
	Do your column positioning within the Draw editor. If you want the box to begin in column 15 in your document, draw it in column 15 in the editor.
F5	Clears the entire screen
F6	Selects the font of any text within the box. It is probably easiest to type your text, and then to 'surround it with a box.
F10	Exits Draw mode and inserts the drawing on the line before the cursor in your document. (Be sure you position the cursor before you execute the Draw command.)

In figure 23.21, the drawing from figure 23.20 has been inserted in the document. Notice that the graphics characters are represented by symbols on the screen. If you set your screen in graphics mode, you see the box or line. Because these are graphics symbols, you must use the Enhanced option to print the document.

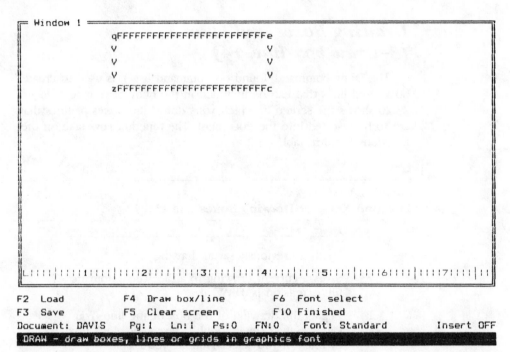

```
╒═ Window !
│         qFFFFFFFFFFFFFFFFFFFFFFFFFFFe
│         V                           V
│         V                           V
│         V                           V
│         zFFFFFFFFFFFFFFFFFFFFFFFFFFFc
│
│
│
│
│
│
│
│
│
│L::::|::::1::::|::::2::::|::::3::::|::::4::::|::::5::::|::::6::::|::::7::::|::
```

F2 Load   F4 Draw box/line   F6 Font select
F3 Save   F5 Clear screen   F10 Finished
Document: DAVIS   Pg:1   Ln:1   Ps:0   FN:0   Font: Standard   Insert OFF
DRAW - draw boxes, lines or grids in graphics font

Fig. 23.20. *The screen used for "drawing" boxes and lines.*

```
╒═ Window !
│    Thank you for your letter of inquiry regarding our Model 23-A
│    Compressor.   We have had a great deal of success  with  this
│    model and the higher capacity unit,  Model 23-B,  since their
│    introduction in February, 1984.¶
│    ¶
│    From the description of your application, it sounds as though
│    the  Model 23-B will better suit your needs both now  and  in
│    the years to come.   If your growth continues at its  current
│    pace, you would exceed the capacity of the 23-A by the summer
│    of next year.¶
│    ¶
│             qFFFFFFFFFFFFFFFFFFFFFFFFFFFe¶
│             V Model        Price       V¶
│             V 23-A         927.78      V¶
│             V 23-B        1537.34      V¶
│             zFFFFFFFFFFFFFFFFFFFFFFFFFFFc¶
│    ¶
│    I am planning on having Mr. Julius Karenski, our sales repre-
│0:::L::::1::::|::::2::::|::::3::::|::::4::::|::::5::::|::::6:::R::::7::::|::
```

F1 Help   F3 Find   F5 Replace   F7 Zoom   F9 Repeat
F2 Next menu   F4 Goto   F6 Font Select   F8 Execute   F10 Quit
Document: davisbx Pg:1 Ln:9 Ps:5 FN:0   Font: Standard   Insert ON
TEXT-ENTRY - normal text-entry mode

Fig. 23.21. *Document after drawing has been inserted.*

Changing between Document and Text Modes (4 – Change-Type)

Normally, when you create a document with the Smart Word Processor, the document is created as a *document* file. All the word-processing capabilities can be used to format the text, and special control codes are built into the document. Sometimes, however, you may want to use the Word Processor to create a pure *text* file such as you might create with a text editor. Text files contain no control codes or formatting characters. Such files are sometimes called *ASCII files*.

The Change-Type command, found on command list 4, is used to change between *document* mode and *text* mode (see fig. 23.22).

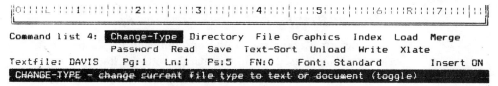

Fig. 23.22. *Selecting the Change-Type command.*

The status line in figure 23.22 shows that the file is a *Textfile* rather than a *Document*, as shown in figure 23.21. A file saved as a text file has the extension .TXT, and a document file has the extension .DOC. When you execute the Load command, .TXT files are not shown in the pop-up menu of file names; you must type the name of the text file (without the extension) to load it. If your text file has an extension other than .TXT, you must supply both the name and the extension.

Unlike lines in Word Processor document files, text-file lines must end in a carriage return and a line feed. Paragraphs and lines cannot be reformatted, and formatting and print options cannot be saved or printed. Tabs can be used when text is being entered, but the tabs are converted to spaces when the document is saved.

If you use the Change-Type command to change a document file to a text file when a document file is loaded, you won't see any immediate differences. When the file is saved as a text file, however, the "soft" carriage returns are converted to hard carriage returns, formatting and printer control codes are removed, and embedded graphics characters are stripped out. Once these changes have been made and the file saved, they are not reversed if the file is changed back to document mode when you later load it.

In addition to using the text-editing capabilities of the text mode of the Word Processor, you can also use the Text-Editor command, found on command list 5.

Formatting Existing Text

Most of the commands discussed thus far in the chapter have affected newly entered text, but other formatting and type-style commands can be used to change text that has already been entered. The results may be the same, but you may find it easier to go back and change existing text instead of changing the text as you enter it. The choice is yours.

Reformatting Text (2–Reformat)

The Reformat command, found on command list 2, initiates a series of prompts used to change margin settings, line spacing (single, double, etc.), and justification of existing text (see fig. 23.23.)

```
O:::L:::1:::|:::2:::|:::3:::|:::4:::|:::5:::|:::6:::R:::7:::|::
```

```
Command list 2:   Bold  Compute  Dictionary  Font  Indent  Justify  Margin
                  Newpage  Reformat  Spacing  Tabs  Underscore  Visible
Document: DAVIS     Pg:1    Ln:1    Ps:5    FN:0     Font: Standard        Insert ON
   REFORMAT - reformat the document, paragraph or remainder of the document.
```

Fig. 23.22. *Selecting the Reformat command.*

When you use the Reformat command, you can choose to change the formatting of the Document, the Paragraph, or the Remainder of the document (see fig. 23.24).

```
O:::L:::1:::|:::2:::|:::3:::|:::4:::|:::5:::|:::6:::R:::7:::|::
```

```
Select option:  Document  Paragraph  Remainder
reformat
Document: DAVIS     Pg:1    Ln:1    Ps:5    FN:0     Font: Standard        Insert ON
   REFORMAT - reformat the document, paragraph or remainder of the document.
```

Fig. 23.24. *Choosing a Reformat range.*

After selecting the range, you are prompted to select the justification type (see fig. 23.25). (The justification types were explained previously in this chapter.) If you have selected Document or Remainder and don't want to change the justification of any paragraphs, select the Same option.

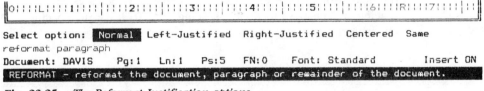

Fig. 23.25. *The Reformat Justification options.*

After selecting the justification, you are prompted to enter new left and right margins (see fig. 23.26). If you don't want to change the margins, just press Enter at each prompt. To change the margins, either enter a value by typing a number or move the cursor to have the system enter the cursor position on the command line. The cursor-position marker does not appear until you have used one of the arrow keys to move the cursor. Press Enter after you have selected the new margin position.

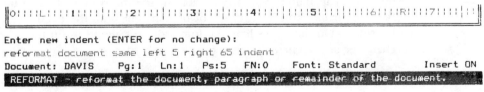

Fig. 23.26. *Margin selection.*

The same specifications apply to the selection of the right margin. Press Enter if you do not want to change the right margin.

The indent prompt appears next (see fig. 23.27). Either type a value or move the cursor so that the system enters the number of spaces for indentation. Indentation is relative to the left margin.

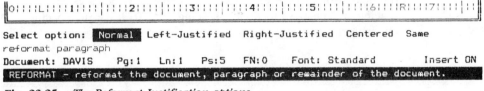

Fig. 23.27. *Selecting a value for Reformat Indent.*

When reformatting the entire document, be careful about changing the Indent specification, because any change will affect the first line of each paragraph. This change applies even to single-line paragraphs, such as the salutation in a letter.

To change the spacing, enter a value from 1 to 8 in response to the next prompt (see fig. 23.28). An entry of 1 indicates single-spacing, a 2 changes to double-spacing, etc. To leave the spacing unchanged, just press Enter.

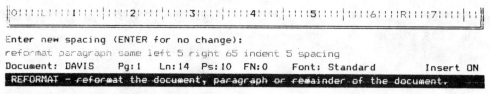

Fig. 23.28. *Specifying Reformat spacing.*

Selecting Boldface (2–Bold)

The Bold command, found on command list 2, is a specialized form of the Font Change command, which is discussed in the next section. There is no quick key for this command (see fig. 23.29).

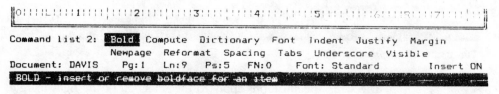

Fig. 23.29. *Selecting the Bold command.*

Using the Bold command, you can insert or delete boldfacing from a range of text (see figs. 23.30 and 23.31). Depending on your monitor's capabilities, you may be able to see the results of using the Bold command; boldfacing may not be apparent until the document is printed. On the status line, the font indicator shows a *B* if the character at the current cursor position is bold.

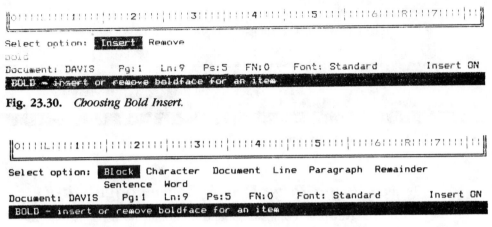

Fig. 23.30. *Choosing Bold Insert.*

Fig. 23.31. *The Bold range options.*

Changing Fonts (Font Change)

To change the font of existing text, use the Font Change command (refer to figures 23.11 and 23.12). You are then prompted for a font number, just as you are when you choose Font Select (refer to fig. 23.13).

After you enter a font number, you are prompted to select a range. The options are the familiar Block . . . Word series mentioned previously. Move the cursor to select a range within the document, and then indicate the range selection on the menu. For instance, if you want to indicate a certain paragraph, move your cursor to that paragraph and then press *P*, or press the space bar to move the highlight block on the command line to indicate the Paragraph option and then press Enter.

The Font Change command does not alter the font setting established by the Font Select command. Any new text is entered in the same font as before.

Underlining Text (Underscore)

Like the Bold command, the Underscore command is used to insert or delete the underscore attribute (see fig. 23.32). The prompts for the Underscore command are similar to those of the Bold command, which are shown in figures 23.30 and 23.31. More monitors can display underscoring than can display boldfacing, but the actual display depends on how your monitor handles underscoring. A *U* in the font indicator on the status line indicates underscoring of the character at the current cursor position.

```
║0::::L::::1::::|::::2::::|::::3::::|::::4::::|::::5::::|::::6::::R::::7::::|::║
```

Command list 2:   Bold Compute Dictionary Font   Indent Justify Margin
                  Newpage Reformat Spacing Tabs Underscore Visible
Document: DAVIS   Pg:1   Ln:9   Ps:5   FN:0   Font: Standard   Insert ON
UNDERSCORE - underscore or remove underscoring on an item

Fig. 23.32. *Selecting the Underscore command.*

Forcing a Page Break (2–Newpage, Alt-E)

The Newpage command, found on command list 2, is used to force a page break in your document (see fig. 23.33). The quick key is Alt-E.

```
║0::::L::::1::::|::::2::::|::::3::::|::::4::::|::::5::::|::::6::::R::::7::::|::║
```

Command list 2:   Bold Compute Dictionary Font   Indent Justify Margin
                  Newpage Reformat Spacing Tabs Underscore Visible
Document: DAVIS   Pg:1   Ln:7   Ps:5   FN:0   Font: Standard   Insert ON
NEWPAGE - insert forced page break before current line

Fig. 23.33. *Choosing the Newpage command.*

To use the Newpage command, move the cursor to the line you want to appear at the top of the new page, and select the command. The options are

Insert Remove

If you want to remove a page break, position the cursor at the top line of the page after the break, and select Remove. Figure 23.34 shows a document with an inserted page break. Notice that the Newpage indicator on the screen is a heavy dashed line.

```
║ ------------------------------------------------------------------------ ║

    I  am  planning  on  having  Mr.  Julius  Karenski,  our  sales
    representative in New Orleans, call you as soon as possible.¶
    ¶
    I wish you every success in your new company.◆
║0::::L::::1::::|::::2::::|::::3::::|::::4::::|::::5::::|::::6::::R::::7::::|::║
```

Command list 2:   Bold Compute Dictionary Font   Indent Justify Margin
                  Newpage Reformat Spacing Tabs Underscore Visible
Document: DAVIS   Pg:2   Ln:1   Ps:5   FN:0   Font: Standard   Insert ON
NEWPAGE - insert forced page break before current line

Fig. 23.34. *The results of the Newpage command.*

Displaying and Hiding Special Characters (2-Visible)

With the Visible command, you can control the display of special text characters that indicate page breaks, paragraph markers, and normal or decimal tabs. The Visible command is found on command list 2; its options are shown in figure 23.35. (To see how these characters appear on-screen, refer to fig. 21.2.)

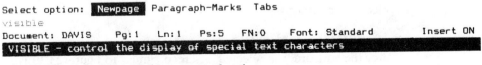

```
Select option:  Newpage  Paragraph-Marks  Tabs
visible
Document: DAVIS    Pg:1   Ln:1   Ps:5   FN:0   Font: Standard        Insert ON
VISIBLE - control the display of special text characters
```

Fig. 23.35. *Selecting a Visible command option.*

Each of the options is a "toggle": each time the option is selected, the display status of the marker is turned on or off. You can change the default settings for marker visibility in the Parameters command of the Word Processor (see fig. 23.36). By changing the settings in Parameters, you will not have to use the Visible command to change those settings during your Word Processor session.

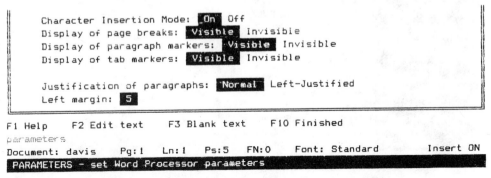

```
Character Insertion Mode:  On  Off
Display of page breaks:  Visible  Invisible
Display of paragraph markers:  Visible  Invisible
Display of tab markers:  Visible  Invisible

Justification of paragraphs:  Normal  Left-Justified
Left margin:  5
```

```
F1 Help    F2 Edit text    F3 Blank text    F10 Finished
parameters
Document: davis    Pg:1   Ln:1   Ps:5   FN:0   Font: Standard        Insert ON
PARAMETERS - set Word Processor parameters
```

Fig. 23.36. *Changing defaults for the Visible command on the Parameters screen.*

Rearranging Lines of Text (4-Text-Sort)

The Text-Sort command, found on command list 4, is used to rearrange lines of text according to values in specified column ranges (see fig. 23.37). The sorting order can be either Ascending or Descending. Collation sorting ensures that upper- and lowercase words are sorted together, instead of sorting first the uppercase entries and then the lowercase entries.

```
|L::::|::::|::::1::::|::::2::::|::::3::::|::::4::::|::::5::::|::::6::::|::::7::::|::|
```

```
Command list 4:   Change-Type  Directory  File  Graphics  Index  Load  Merge
                   Password  Read  Save  [Text-Sort]  Unload  Write  Xlate
Textfile: sortsam  Pg:1   Ln:2   Ps:36  FN:0    Font: Standard          Insert ON
TEXT-SORT - sort a block of text within the current document
```

Fig. 23.37. *Selecting the Text-Sort command.*

After you select the Text-Sort command, you are prompted to
select a sort order:

Ascending Descending

After the sort order is selected, a screen similar to figure 23.38 is
displayed. In this figure, the range used to determine the sorting
order is highlighted. The F2 key is used to drop the anchor, and F10
(or Enter) is used to end the block and begin the sort. Figure 23.39
shows the results of the sort.

```
= Window 1 =
|DEPT  LAST          FIRST          WAGE
|----  ----------    ----------   ---------
|ACCT  Ronaldo       Rosanna        878.75
|MFGR  Linden        Debbie        1403.79
|SALE  Davis         Michael        734.56
|MKTG  Karenski      Julius        1020.33
|ACCT  Harris        Jeff           629.23
|SALE  Markus        LeAnne         887.49
|MKTG  Lester        Marilyn       1516.26
|ACCT  Marzetti      David          901.45
|DATA  Steffans      Charles        654.34
|SALE  Bernstein     Paula         1004.56
|ACCT  Adelson       Alfred         956.43
|MFGR  Aliakbari     Ellen          997.66
|MKTG  Peters        Howard E.     1544.00


|L::::|::::1::::|::::2::::|::::3::::|::::4::::|::::5::::|::::6::::|::::7::::|::|
```

```
<cursor keys>   F2 Drop new anchor    F3 Inspect     F10 or ENTER End block
text-sort ascending
Textfile: sortsam  Pg:1   Ln:15  Ps:15  FN:0    Font: Standard        Insert ON
TEXT-SORT - sort a block of text within the current document
```

Fig. 23.38. *Determining the Sort range.*

```
┌─ Window 1 ════════════════════════════════════════════════════════════════┐
│DEPT LAST         FIRST         WAGE                                         │
│──── ──────────   ──────────    ────────                                    │
│ACCT Adelson      Alfred        956.43                                      │
│ACCT Harris       Jeff          629.23                                      │
│ACCT Marzetti     David         901.45                                      │
│ACCT Ronaldo      Rosanna       878.75                                      │
│DATA Steffans     Charles       654.34                                      │
│MFGR Aliakbari    Ellen         997.66                                      │
│MFGR Linden       Debbie       1403.79                                      │
│MKTG Karenski     Julius       1020.33                                      │
│MKTG Lester       Marilyn      1516.26                                      │
│MKTG Peters       Howard E.    1544.00                                      │
│SALE Bernstein    Paula        1004.56                                      │
│SALE Davis        Michael       734.56                                      │
│SALE Markus       LeAnne        887.49                                      │
│                                                                            │
│                                                                            │
│L!!!!│!!!!!1!!!!!│!!!!2!!!!│!!!!3!!!!│!!!!4!!!!│!!!!5!!!!│!!!!6!!!!│!!!!7!!!!│!!│
└────────────────────────────────────────────────────────────────────────────┘
Command list 4:   Change-Type  Directory  File  Graphics  Index  Load  Merge
                  Password  Read  Save  [Text-Sort]  Unload  Write  Xlate
Textfile: sortsam  Pg:1   Ln:3   Ps:0   FN:0     Font: Standard         Insert ON
TEXT-SORT - sort a block of text within the current document
```

Fig. 23.39.   *The results of the Sort process.*

Be aware that because only one range can be defined, complex sorting rules cannot be applied. Furthermore, only 150 lines of text can be sorted. If you have a complex set of sort rules with multiple ranges, or if you need to sort more than 150 lines of text, you should use the Smart Data Base Manager or the Spreadsheet to perform the sort, and then send the text to the Word Processor.

Conclusion

Both the content and appearance of your documents are important. The formatting commands covered in this chapter can be used to improve the appearance of your Word Processor output.

You have the choice of setting formatting characteristics before or after you enter the text. If you have a great number of changes to make, you may find that making all formatting changes at one time, after you have entered the text, is easier.

Chapter 24

Searching, Replacing, and Moving within Text

If your document is small, you may be able easily to find your way around in it; it may even fit entirely on one screen. But if you are writing a proposal of 100 pages, finding certain sections (or words) by inspection alone is bound to be difficult.

This chapter explains the commands in the Smart Word Processor that simplify getting around in your document and allow you to find and replace text in it.

Searching for Text (1–Find, F3)

The Find command is used to locate designated words or groups of words in your document. Find is on command list 1, and the quick key is F3 (see fig. 24.1).

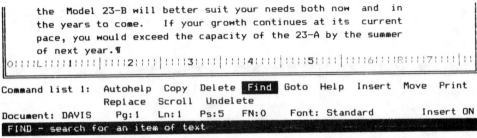

```
    the  Model 23-B will better suit your needs both now  and  in
    the years to come.    If your growth continues at its  current
    pace, you would exceed the capacity of the 23-A by the summer
    of next year.¶
O!!!!L!!!!1!!!!|!!!!2!!!!|!!!!3!!!!|!!!!4!!!!|!!!!5!!!!|!!!!6!!!R!!!!7!!!!|!
```

```
Command list 1:   Autohelp  Copy  Delete  Find  Goto  Help  Insert  Move  Print
                  Replace  Scroll  Undelete
Document: DAVIS      Pg:1    Ln:1    Ps:5    FN:0     Font: Standard          Insert ON
FIND - search for an item of text
```

Fig. 24.1. *Selecting the Find command.*

After selecting the Find command, you are prompted to enter the text to find. (The Find command in the Word Processor is similar to the Find command in the Data Base Manager and the Spreadsheet.) When Find is selected, the last search string issued is displayed in answer to the prompt. If you are searching again for the same string, you can press Enter instead of retyping the string. In figure 24.2, I have instructed Smart to search for the string *23-B*.

```
From the description of your application, it sounds as though
the  Model 23-B will better suit your needs both  now  and  in
the years to come.   If your growth continues at its  current
pace, you would exceed the capacity of the 23-A by the summer
of next year.¶
0!!!!L!!!!1!!!!|!!!!2!!!!|!!!!3!!!!|!!!!4!!!!|!!!!5!!!!|!!!!6!!!!R!!!7!!!!|!!
```

```
Enter search text: 23-B
find
ENTER finished
FIND - search for an item of text
```

Fig. 24.2. *Finding a string.*

After the search string is entered, you have several options (see fig. 24.3). Three directional options are available with the Find command. The *F* option causes the search to proceed forward from the current cursor position to the end of the file. The *B* option causes the search to proceed backward to the beginning of the file. The *G* option starts the search at the beginning of the file and proceeds forward. This is equivalent to positioning the cursor at the beginning of the file and choosing the *F* option.

```
From the description of your application, it sounds as though
the  Model 23-B will better suit your needs both now  and  in
the years to come.   If your growth continues at its  current
pace, you would exceed the capacity of the 23-A by the summer
of next year.¶
0!!!!L!!!!1!!!!|!!!!2!!!!|!!!!3!!!!|!!!!4!!!!|!!!!5!!!!|!!!!6!!!!R!!!7!!!!|!!
```

```
Enter search options ["F"]:
find "23-B"
F Forward    B Backward    G Global    I Ignore case    W Whole word
FIND - search for an item of text
```

Fig. 24.3. *The Find options.*

Two other options allow you further to customize your searches. When the *I* option is chosen, the case of the search string is ignored during the search. The search string will be located whether the characters appear in the text in upper- or lowercase. The *W* option searches for whole words only (strings bounded by blanks.) This option does not ignore punctuation, however.

A directional option and the I or W option can be used at the same time. In addition, a number can be entered to indicate a nonsequential search pattern. For example, entering *4* causes the system to display the fourth occurrence of the string. The options can be entered in either upper- or lowercase.

Both the search string and the options you have entered are maintained in buffers to simplify repeated use of the Find command. The current contents of the text buffer are displayed at the *Enter search text:* prompt; if that string is acceptable, press Enter to proceed. (This same test buffer is used by the Replace command, which is discussed later in this chapter. You will see how useful this buffer is in repeated Find and Replace commands.)

A *wildcard* character can also be used in the search criterion. The search string *198?* will locate both 1984 and 1985 in the document.

The system automatically inserts double quotation marks (") around the search string; you should not type them. If you need to search for a string that has a leading or trailing space, just type the space; the system then leaves an appropriate space in the search string. Be careful, however, not to interpret the spacing caused by normal justification as a true space. The screen may look as though there is more than one space between two words because of the justification, but actually there may be only one space.

To repeat the Find command, press the F9 key, as you would to repeat any other command previously entered. If you have executed another intervening command, use the Alt-R quick key to repeat the most recent Find or Replace command.

Replacing Text (1–Replace, F5)

The Replace command searches the document for a string and then replaces it with another string. Replace is on command list 1, and the quick key is F5 (see fig. 24.4).

The search string is entered in the same way as for the Find command; the two commands even store the search string in the same buffer. The remaining text in the buffer from the last Find or

```
  From the description of your application, it sounds as though
  the  Model 23-B will better suit your needs both now  and  in
  the years to come.   If your growth continues at its  current
  pace, you would exceed the capacity of the 23-A by the summer
  of next year.¶
O:::::L:::::1::::|::::2::::|::::3::::|::::4::::|::::5::::|::::6::::R:::7::::|::
```

Command list 1:   Autohelp Copy Delete Find Goto Help Insert Move Print
                   Replace Scroll Undelete
Document: DAVIS   Pg:1   Ln:1   Ps:5   FN:0   Font: Standard   Insert ON
REPLACE - replace text

Fig. 24.4.   *Selecting the Replace command.*

Replace command is used as a default search string.

The first prompt in the Replace command asks for the search text; the second prompt (see fig. 24.5) asks for the replacement text. The rules for entering the text are the same as for the Find command; you can even use the question mark (?) wild card in the search text. Do *not* use the ? in the replacement text in order to leave the corresponding character unchanged, however, or you will actually substitute the ? for whatever character is in the document.

```
  From the description of your application, it sounds as though
  the  Model 23-B will better suit your needs both now  and  in
  the years to come.   If your growth continues at its  current
  pace, you would exceed the capacity of the 23-A by the summer
  of next year.¶
O:::::L:::::1::::|::::2::::|::::3::::|::::4::::|::::5::::|::::6::::R:::7::::|::
```

Enter replacement text: 255-
replace "23-" with ""
ENTER finished
REPLACE - replace text

Fig. 24.5.   *Replacing text strings.*

Most of the Replace options are similar to the options in the Find command; they can be entered in either upper- or lowercase (see fig. 24.6). Like the Find command, the Replace command has directional options and options for ignoring case and replacing whole words. A new option has been added to the Replace command, however: The Conditional option causes the system to pause and ask whether you want to perform the replacement. Respond by pressing Enter to perform the replacement, pressing the space bar to leave the text unchanged, or pressing F10 to quit.

```
From the description of your application, it sounds as though
the Model 23-B will better suit your needs both now and in
the years to come.   If your growth continues at its current
pace, you would exceed the capacity of the 23-A by the summer
of next year.¶
O!!!!L!!!!1!!!!|!!!!2!!!!|!!!!3!!!!|!!!!4!!!!|!!!!5!!!!|!!!!6!!!R!!!!7!!!!|!!
```

```
Enter replace options: g
replace "23-" with "255-"
F Forward  B Backward  G Global  C Conditional  I Ignore case  W Whole word
REPLACE - replace text
```

Fig. 24.6. *The Replace options.*

If the lengths of the replacement text and the search text are different, the Word Processor automatically reformats the paragraphs for you.

In addition to the options shown in figure 24.6, a number can be entered. This is also similar to the Find command, but there is one important difference. In the Find command, the number 5, for instance, means "find the fifth occurrence" of the string. In the Replace command, a 5 means "change the first five occurrences" that match the search text—*not* "change the fifth occurrence."

The Alt-R quick key can be used to repeat the last Replace command, even if you have used other commands since using Replace. F9 can be used if there have been no intervening commands.

Moving within the Document (1-Goto, F4)

One way to move within your document is by using the cursor keys, of course. The PgUp and PgDn keys change the screen display by 17 lines at a time. This method may be satisfactory if the document is short, but it is tedious if you have a long document.

The Goto command quickly moves the cursor to a location either within the current document or in a document in another window. The locations can be specified by page number, line number, column positions, or "marker." (Markers are discussed later in this chapter.) Windows are referred to by window numbers. The locations may be specified individually or in combination with other window locations.

Goto is found on command list 1, and the quick key is F4 (see fig. 24.7).

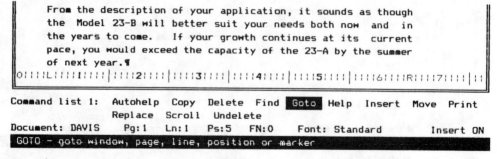

Fig. 24.7. *Selecting the Goto command.*

When you execute the Goto command, the following prompt is displayed:

Enter window, page, line, column or marker:

To go to a specific page in your document, type the letter *P* and then enter the page number. For example, entering *P3* moves the cursor to the beginning of line 1 of the third page of the document. (The page indicator can be an uppercase or a lowercase *P.*) If you request a page beyond the length of your document, no error message is displayed; the cursor moves to line 1 of the last page of the document. Remember that the "page" you specify is the actual document page, not the screen display of 17 lines.

The cursor can also be moved by a number of pages relative to the current page. For example, if you enter *P+2*, the cursor moves to line 1 two pages ahead. If you enter *P-3*, the cursor moves back three pages.

Use an *L* to move the cursor to a different line on the same page of the document. For example, a response of *L5* moves the cursor to the left margin of the fifth line of the current document page. You can combine the use of the page and line locations by separating them with a period. You do not use the *L* for line in this case, however. For instance, *p5.10* positions the cursor at page 5, line 10. If you forget and enter an *L*, no error message is displayed; the cursor moves to line 1 of the requested page.

To move to a specific column on the current line, type a *C* followed by a number. For example, *c10* moves the cursor to column 10. The cursor keys are probably easier to use in this case, however. The column designator can also be used with page and line designators. For example, the entry *P15.20.25* moves the cursor to page 15, line 20, column 25.

You can also move the cursor to a marker you have set. (The Marker command is discussed in the following section.) To move to a marker, supply the name of the marker in response to the prompt. If you have a document with multiple tables, for instance, you might mark the tables as TB1, TB2, etc., to be able quickly to go to them. The search for markers is sequential from the beginning of the file, however; with a large file, a marker near the end may take a minute to find.

Using Markers (3-Marker)

The Marker command is used to set markers within your document for the identification of certain sections. The markers are used with the Goto command. Marker is found on command list 3; there is no quick key (see fig. 24.8).

```
          MFGR Aliakbari   Ellen        997.66¶
          MKTG Peters      Howard E.   1544.00¶
          ◆
|0||||  ||||||1||||L|||2||||  ||||3||||  ||||4||||  ||||5||||  |||||6|||||R|||7||||  ||
```

```
Command list 3:  Border   Close   Draw   Footnote   Marker   Newname   Paint   Ruler
                 Split   Zoom
Document: davis      Pg:2   Ln:1   Ps:15   FN:0      Font: Standard        Insert ON
    MARKER - directory, set, unset, or view user markers
```

Fig. 24.8. *Selecting the Marker command.*

The Marker command has four options (see fig. 24.9).

```
          MFGR Aliakbari   Ellen        997.66¶
          MKTG Peters      Howard E.   1544.00¶
          ◆
|0||||  ||||||1||||L|||2||||  ||||3||||  ||||4||||  ||||5||||  |||||6|||||R|||7||||  ||
```

```
Select option:  Directory   Set   Unset   View
marker
Document: davis      Pg:2   Ln:1   Ps:15   FN:0      Font: Standard        Insert ON
    MARKER - directory, set, unset, or view user markers
```

Fig. 24.9. *The Marker options.*

Setting Markers (Marker Set)

The Marker Set command prompts you for the name of a marker to be set at the current cursor position. Be sure to position the cursor before you execute this command. Although a marker name can be as long as 60 characters, only the first three characters are used and displayed; short and unique names therefore are the best. Marker names are not case sensitive; they are saved with the document and do not appear in the body of the text.

Marker names must begin with a letter but can contain numbers. If you are going to use numbers in the names of the markers, don't use a *P*, *L*, or *C* as the initial letter. Those letters might be interpreted as page, line, or column specifications.

Removing Markers (Marker Unset)

Use the Marker Unset command to remove a marker from the document. The cursor does not have to be on the marker before you issue the command. The prompt asks for the name of the marker to be removed, but no pop-up menu of marker names is displayed. To get a list of the existing markers, use the Marker Directory command.

Displaying a List of Markers (Marker Directory)

The Marker Directory command displays a list of all the markers that have been set in the document. You can go to a marker by using the cursor key to point to its name and pressing Enter.

Finding a Marker (Marker View)

You can also find a marker by using the Marker View command. This command causes the system to proceed through the document, stopping at each marker. The name of the marker is displayed on the command line (see fig. 24.10). Press Enter to proceed to the next marker, or press Esc to end the command and leave the cursor positioned at the current marker.

```
    MFGR Aliakbari  Ellen        997.66¶
    MKTG Peters     Howard E.   1544.00¶
    ◆

0¦¦¦¦¦¦¦¦¦¦1¦¦¦¦L¦¦¦2¦¦¦¦¦¦¦¦3¦¦¦¦¦¦¦¦4¦¦¦¦¦¦¦¦5¦¦¦¦¦¦¦¦6¦¦¦R¦¦¦7¦¦¦¦¦¦

Marker is "tab"
ENTER to go to next marker
Document: markeg   Pg:2   Ln:1   Ps:15   FN:0   Font: Standard          Insert ON
MARKER - directory, set, unset, or view user markers
```

Fig. 24.10. *Using the Marker View command.*

Scrolling Text (1–Scroll, Ctrl-PgDn, Ctrl-PgUp)

The Scroll command is used to scroll the document up or down at different rates of speed ranging from 1 (slowest) to 10 (fastest). (Enter a 0 to represent 10.) Scroll is found on command list 1. The quick keys are Ctrl-PgDn to scroll down and Ctrl-PgUp to scroll up (see fig. 24.11).

```
   From the description of your application, it sounds as though
   the  Model 23-B will better suit your needs both now  and  in
   the years to come.   If your growth continues at its  current
   pace, you would exceed the capacity of the 23-A by the summer
   of next year.¶
0!!!!L!!!!1!!!!|!!!!2!!!!|!!!!3!!!!|!!!!4!!!!|!!!!5!!!!|!!!!6!!!!R!!!!7!!!!|!!

Command list 1:   Autohelp  Copy  Delete  Find   Goto  Help   Insert  Move  Print
                  Replace  Scroll  Undelete
Document: DAVIS      Pg:1    Ln:1    Ps:5    FN:0     Font: Standard          Insert ON
   SCROLL - scroll through a document
```

Fig. 24.11.   *Selecting the Scroll command.*

The two options of the Scroll command are shown in figure 24.12. Scroll Down moves the cursor down through the document; Scroll Up moves the cursor up. After you have selected a direction, you are prompted to select a rate of scrolling speed (see fig. 24.13). Enter a number from 1 to 10 and press Enter.

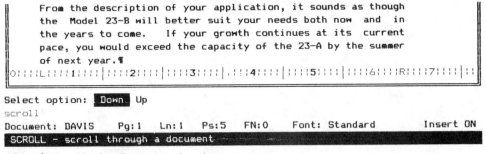

```
   From the description of your application, it sounds as though
   the  Model 23-B will better suit your needs both now  and  in
   the years to come.   If your growth continues at its  current
   pace, you would exceed the capacity of the 23-A by the summer
   of next year.¶
0!!!!L!!!!1!!!!|!!!!2!!!!|!!!!3!!!!|,!!!4!!!!|!!!!5!!!!|!!!!6!!!R!!!!7!!!!|!!

Select option:   Down  Up
scroll
Document: DAVIS      Pg:1    Ln:1    Ps:5    FN:0     Font: Standard          Insert ON
   SCROLL - scroll through a document
```

Fig. 24.12.   *The Scroll command options.*

```
  From the description of your application, it sounds as though
  the  Model 23-B will better suit your needs both now  and  in
  the years to come.   If your growth continues at its  current
  pace, you would exceed the capacity of the 23-A by the summer
  of next year.¶
O::::L::::1::::|::::2::::|::::3::::|::::4::::|::::5::::|::::6:::R::::7::::|::
```

```
Enter scroll rate (1 is slowest, 10 is fastest):
scroll down
Document: DAVIS    Pg:1  Ln:1  Ps:5  FN:0   Font: Standard        Insert ON
SCROLL - scroll through a document
```

Fig. 24.13. *Selecting the scroll rate.*

While scrolling, you can change directions by pressing either the ↑ or ↓ cursor keys. To change the scrolling rate, press a number from 1 to 0. To make the scrolling pause, press any other key; press a key again to resume. To halt the scrolling altogether, press Esc.

If you use the quick keys Ctrl-PgUp or Ctrl-PgDn, the scrolling rate defaults to 10.

Conclusion

The larger your document, the more important it is to be able to move quickly from section to section and to find your way around in the document. The commands discussed in this chapter can be used to locate sections of your document, view different portions, and make changes to selected words or phrases.

Chapter 25

Printing and Merging Text

In the Smart Word Processor, printing consists in sending a document from the current window or from a disk file to the printer (or to another disk file for later printing). Documents can be printed in either of two modes: Normal or Enhanced. Normal mode uses the built-in type fonts and other capabilities of your printer. Enhanced mode allows you to include graphs in your documents; in that mode, printers with the necessary graphics capabilities draw special fonts and graphs dot-by-dot.

Printing Text (1–Print, Alt-P)

The Print command is found on command list 1, and the quick key is Alt-P (see fig. 25.1). Print has five options; the option menu is shown in figure 25.2.

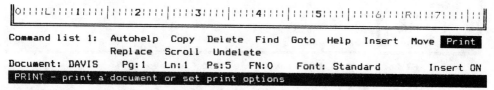

Fig. 25.1. *Selecting the Print command.*

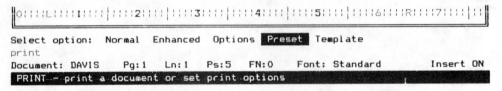

Fig. 25.2. *The Print option menu.*

Before proceeding with Normal or Enhanced printing, you may want to set the Preset defaults. The Print Preset command is used to establish default settings that apply to *all* documents you create in the Word Processor unless you override the defaults for a single document. The default settings of Print Preset are shown in figures 25.3, 25.4, and 25.5.

You should probably establish your settings in Print Preset when you first use the Word Processor, so that the settings reflect the way you want to see your documents printed. After the settings are established, you can use the Print Options command to override the Preset defaults if you want.

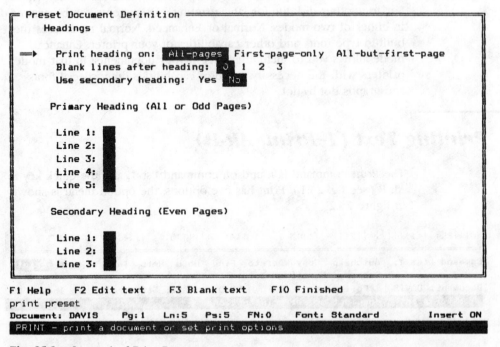

Fig. 25.3. *Screen 1 of Print Preset.*

```
╔═ Preset Document Definition ═══════════════════════════════════╗
║ ═▶    Line 4: █                                                 ║
║       Line 5: █                                                 ║
║                                                                 ║
║    Footings                                                     ║
║                                                                 ║
║       Print footing on: █All-pages█ First-page-only  All-but-first-page ║
║       Blank lines before footing: █0█ 1  2  3                   ║
║       Use secondary footing:  Yes  █No█                         ║
║                                                                 ║
║     Primary Footing (All or Odd Pages)                          ║
║                                                                 ║
║       Line 1: █                                                 ║
║       Line 2: █                                                 ║
║       Line 3: █                                                 ║
║       Line 4: █                                                 ║
║       Line 5: █                                                 ║
║                                                                 ║
║       Secondary Footing (Even Pages)                            ║
║                                                                 ║
╚═════════════════════════════════════════════════════════════════╝
```

F1 Help   F2 Edit text   F3 Blank text   F10 Finished
print preset
Document: DAVIS   Pg:1   Ln:5   Ps:5   FN:0   Font: Standard   Insert ON
PRINT - print a document or set print options

Fig. 25.4. *Screen 2 of Print Preset.*

```
╔═ Preset Document Definition ═══════════════════════════════════╗
║                                                                 ║
║    Date style: █Short-alpha█ Long-alpha  Numeric                ║
║    Page number style: █Arabic█ Roman-Small  Roman-Caps          ║
║    Lines to enclose document:  Yes  █No█                        ║
║    Start page number: █1█                                       ║
║    Footnote text to appear at: █End-of-page█ End-of-document     ║
║                                                                 ║
║    Lines per inch in draft mode: █6█ 8                           ║
║    Characters per inch in draft mode: █10█ 12   17              ║
║                                                                 ║
║    Form length (lines): █66█                                    ║
║    Form width (positions): █80█                                 ║
║                                                                 ║
║    Top margin (lines): █4█                                      ║
║    Bottom margin (lines): █6█                                   ║
║    Left indent (positions): █4█                                 ║
║    Right indent (positions): █8█                                ║
║                                                                 ║
║ ═▶ Single sheet printing:  Yes  █No█                            ║
╚═════════════════════════════════════════════════════════════════╝
```

F1 Help   F2 Edit text   F3 Blank text   F10 Finished
print preset
Document: DAVIS   Pg:1   Ln:5   Ps:5   FN:0   Font: Standard   Insert ON
PRINT - print a document or set print options

Fig. 25.5. *Screen 3 of Print Preset.*

Print Options

Use the Print Options command to change the settings established in the Print Preset command. Both the screens and the options are the same as for the Print Preset command (refer to figs. 25.3, 25.4, and 25.5). The options are stored on disk with the document, so you must save the document in order to retain the options. They remain active from session to session. Most of the options are clearly explained in the Word Processor manual, but a few of them need some additional comment.

Print Control Codes

The following control codes can be inserted in the heading or footing lines to control their format or contents:

Format Control

%L	Left-Justify
%C	Center
%R	Right-Justify

Line Contents

%P	Page Number
%D	Date
%T	Time
%F	Name of file being printed
%n	Parameter n (n = 0 to 9)

You can enter a parameter (such as %1 or %5) if you want the contents of a project-file parameter inserted into the heading or footing of your document. If you are printing your document under the control of a project file, use of this parameter feature can provide additional report-customization capabilities. (For more information about project files and parameters, see Chapter 32.)

Print control codes must be entered in uppercase letters; the codes can be used in combination with other control codes on the same line or with text literals. Separating the control codes with blank space is not necessary unless you want to print a blank character.

Headings and Footings

As many as five lines of primary and secondary headings and footings can be printed on each page. If secondary headings or footings are selected, they are printed on even-numbered pages; otherwise, the primary headings and footings are printed on all pages.

A maximum of 150 characters can be entered on one heading or footing line, but only 132 characters can be printed. The remainder can be control codes.

If you choose to include a date in the heading or footing of your document, make sure that you set the system date when you first turn on your computer; that date is used in the heading or footing. (Setting the date and time is always a good habit anyway.) Dates are specified by placing the control code *%D* in the heading or footing line.

If you choose *Yes* at the *Lines to enclose document:* prompt, a line is drawn at the top and bottom of every page.

Pagination

To include a page number, use the %P control code. For example, the following line prints and centers the text literal *Page:* followed by a space and the page number:

%CPage: %P

The starting page number is the number that appears on the first page of the document when it is printed—*not* the first page to be printed. For example, if you change the starting page number to 3, the first page is numbered 3. (If you need to begin printing from a point other than the beginning of your document, select the first page to be printed when you issue the Print Normal or Enhanced command.)

Page numbers can be printed in Arabic numerals (such as 4), lowercase Roman numerals (iv), or uppercase Roman numerals (IV).

Footnotes

Footnotes can be printed either at the bottom of the page containing the text to which they are attached or at the end of the document. If the footnotes are printed on the same page as the text, they are numbered sequentially on the page; if they are printed at the end, they are numbered sequentially throughout the document.

Page Format

The selection of the number of vertical lines per inch and horizontal characters per inch may be affected by the characteristics of your printer. You may not be able to change these attributes if your printer does not support changes in line spacing and character width. These settings control printing in Normal mode only.

The *Form length (lines):* and *Form width (positions):* prompts refer to the physical size of the paper. For example, if your paper is

11 inches long and you are printing 6 lines per inch, the form length is 66 lines.

The top and bottom margin settings control the number of blank lines that appear between the edge of the paper and the text (or the heading or footing if they have been specified).

The left indentation setting specifies the number of spaces between the left edge of the paper and the left edge of the printing area. The number of spaces is added to the number specified in the margin settings within the document. For example, if you specify a left indentation of 10 on this screen and a left margin of 6 within your document, then 16 spaces separate the edge of the paper from the first character of the printed line. The heading and footing are indented with the text. Right indentation indicates the offset from the right side of the paper.

If you don't have an automatic paper-feed mechanism on your printer or if you want to use cut sheets rather than continuous-form paper, specify single-sheet printing. The system then pauses after printing each page, and you are prompted to insert a new sheet.

Printing the Options (Print Template)

To make a printout of the options you have selected for either the current document (Print Options) or preset (Print Preset), use the Print Template command. A sample of the output is shown in figure 25.6.

```
Print heading on:            ALL-PAGES
Use secondary headings:            NO
Print footing on:            ALL-PAGES
Use secondary footings:            NO


        Form length:      66
        Form width:       80
        Top margin:        3
        Bottom margin:     3
        Text lines:       50
        Text width:       80
        Left indent:       0
        Right indent:      0
        After header:      1
        Before footer:     1
        Date:         NUMERIC
        Enclose text:     NO
        Page #:       ARABIC
```

Fig. 25.6. *Result of selecting Print Template Current-Document.*

Printing in Normal Mode (Print Normal)

Once you have chosen the Print Preset settings and the Print Options and have created your document, you are ready to fire up the printer and create some hard copy.

The Print Normal command uses your printer's built-in fonts and print attributes. All printers can print normal text. Most printers also have the built-in capability of underscoring text and printing in boldface. More and more dot-matrix and laser printers have a number of built-in fonts. If your printer is one of those that are fully supported by the Smart system, several of its fonts may be available (for more information on the Font command, see Chapter 23). If your printer is not one of the supported printers, you may still have several built-in fonts, but you may have to tailor the printer-control codes (at the main menu) for your printer.

For example, you may have to substitute the specific control-character sequence for subscripting. Refer to your printer's technical manual for a listing of the required codes and compare them with the code sequences in Smart.

Whenever possible, use Normal mode and take advantage of the printer's built-in fonts instead of printing in Enhanced mode, because printing in Normal mode is faster. When you use special fonts or include a graph in a document, however, Enhanced mode is required.

When you select Print Normal or Print Enhanced, a pop-up menu of file names is displayed. Use the cursor to select a file to be printed. If you want to print the document in the current window, select *default* (see fig. 25.7); otherwise, select a file from the disk by moving the arrow within the pop-up menu. Remember that you can have two versions of the same file: one in memory (in the current window), and the other on disk. If you have made changes to the document but haven't saved it, the two versions are different.

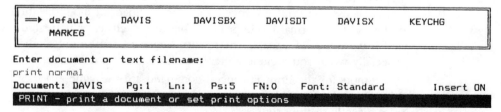

```
 ══▶ default      DAVIS       DAVISBX      DAVISDT      DAVISX      KEYCHG
     MARKEG

Enter document or text filename:
print normal
Document: DAVIS    Pg:1   Ln:1   Ps:5   FN:0    Font: Standard        Insert ON
 PRINT - print a document or set print options
```

Fig 25.7. *Selecting the file in the current window (default).*

You can print the file either to the printer or to the disk. If you want to produce your hard-copy printout at a later time or to transmit the output to another computer, you may want to write the document to a disk file. Enter a file name (with a maximum of eight characters) and press Enter. A file is created with the name you have supplied and the extension .PRN. If a disk file with that name already exists, the Word Processor writes over the file without prompting you to confirm that you want to overwrite the existing file; no other prompts are displayed when you write to a disk file.

If you print directly to the printer, you are prompted to enter the number of copies desired. Press Enter if you want only one copy.

The final prompts ask you for the starting and ending page numbers. If, for example, you have been printing this document and your printer ran out of paper, you could use this option to start the printing over, beginning at the appropriate page. For these prompts, pressing Enter is equivalent to the default of 1 for the starting page, and "end of document" for the ending page.

Two function keys are of special importance. The F2 key cancels the printing and returns you to the command level. F3 cancels the printing, advances the paper to top of form, and prompts you to press any key to begin printing again. The F3 key is equivalent to canceling the print, manually advancing to top of form, and pressing F9 to repeat the Print command. Using the F3 key is faster, however, because the Print command remains active.

If you are printing a file from disk (not the default), you are prompted for a password if the file is protected.

Printing in Enhanced Mode (Print Enhanced)

If you are printing special fonts that are not built into your graphics printer or if you are including a graph in your document, you must use the Print Enhanced command. Enhanced mode printing is slower than Normal mode printing, because each letter is treated as if it were part of a graph; the results, however, can be outstanding, especially when you include a graph in the body of a document.

Prompts for the Print Enhanced command are the same as for Print Normal, except that you can't print to a disk file. You must print directly to the printer.

Merging Text (4-Merge)

To produce multiple copies of a letter with embedded text taken from a data file, use the Merge command, found on command list 4 (see fig. 25.8). Mass mailings and personalized form letters can easily be produced with this command. Instead of using a data file, you can also enter the data from the keyboard. The Merge command works well with data files created in Smart format by the Data Base Manager.

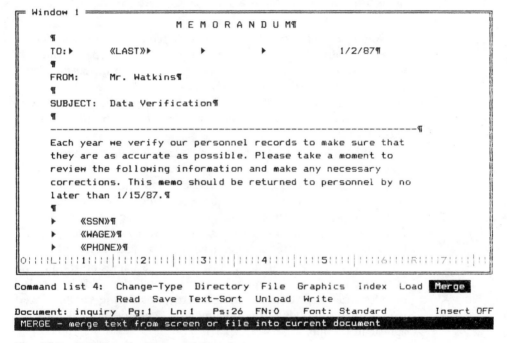

```
┌─ Window 1 ═══════════════════════════════════════════════════════════
│                         M E M O R A N D U M¶
│      ¶
│      TO:▶      «LAST»▶        ▶          ▶          1/2/87¶
│      ¶
│      FROM:     Mr. Watkins¶
│      ¶
│      SUBJECT:  Data Verification¶
│      ¶
│      -----------------------------------------------------------¶
│      Each year we verify our personnel records to make sure that
│      they are as accurate as possible. Please take a moment to
│      review the following information and make any necessary
│      corrections. This memo should be returned to personnel by no
│      later than 1/15/87.¶
│      ¶
│      ▶      «SSN»¶
│      ▶      «WAGE»¶
│      ▶      «PHONE»¶
│0¦¦¦¦L¦¦¦¦1¦¦¦¦¦¦¦¦¦2¦¦¦¦¦¦¦¦¦3¦¦¦¦¦¦¦¦¦4¦¦¦¦¦¦¦¦¦5¦¦¦¦¦¦¦¦¦6¦¦¦¦R¦¦¦7¦¦¦¦¦¦
```

Command list 4: Change-Type Directory File Graphics Index Load **Merge**
                 Read Save Text-Sort Unload Write
Document: inquiry Pg:1 Ln:1 Ps:26 FN:0   Font: Standard   Insert OFF
MERGE - merge text from screen or file into current document

Fig. 25.8. *Selecting the Merge command.*

Merging Data from a File (Merge File)

Before you use the Merge command, make sure that your data file is properly prepared. If the data file is coming from one of the other Smart application modules, you should send it as a text file. Figure 25.9 shows a sample data file exactly as it came from the Data Base Manager. That file is ready for use as input for the Merge command.

```
"SSN"  "LAST"  "AGE"  "WAGE"  "PHONE"  "EMPDATE"
"345-98-7593"  "Ronaldo"  52 878.75 "(312) 439-8760" "10-01-59"
"498-48-3980"  "Linden"  29 1403.79 "(413) 886-3498" "06-20-75"
"239-87-8876"  "Davis"  61 734.56 "(318) 997-6621" "05-25-69"
"208-23-0300"  "Karenski"  41 1020.33 "(606) 779-5088" "08-20-71"
"887-63-5498"  "Harris"  34 629.23 "(614) 776-3398" "07-01-70"
"598-44-5922"  "Markus"  48 887.49 "(303) 797-5939" "10-30-65"
"876-33-0989"  "Lester"  55 1516.26 "(617) 873-0979" "09-05-75"
"987-65-7653"  "Marzetti"  47 901.45 "(704) 472-0042" "10-30-85"
"387-59-8374"  "Steffans"  25 654.34 "(207) 878-4880" "10-15-81"
"498-34-5998"  "Bernstein"  30 1004.56 "(916) 475-4228" "06-15-75"
"776-39-8763"  "Adelson"  60 956.43 "(203) 739-3095" "07-23-45"
"345-54-2287"  "Aliakbari"  35 997.66 "(201) 727-9242" "08-15-72"
"198-03-3024"  "Peters"  18 1544.00 "(318) 729-5060" "10-01-85"
```

Fig. 25.9. *A Smart text file with data for the Merge command.*

Notice that all text literals in the data file are enclosed in double quotation marks and that each record appears on a separate line. The first line of the file contains the field names, which match the variables in the text of the document. You can have as many as 20 different fields in each record; a field can be up to 1,000 characters in length, but the total of all the characters in the record cannot exceed 1,024.

In the body of the text shown in figure 25.8, the substituted variables are enclosed in double angle brackets. Ctrl-J is used to enter the marker on the left of a variable, and the marker on the right is entered with Ctrl-K. On the screen the angle brackets actually appear about half the height of the characters shown in figure 25.8. You must use Ctrl-J and Ctrl-K to enter the double brackets; do not use the angle-bracket keys on your keyboard.

The names of the variables must match the names on the first line of the data file. The document need not use all the fields in the data file (for example, AGE was omitted here); nor do the variables need to appear in the body of the document in the order in which they appear in the file.

If a certain field in the data file is blank in some records of the file, you can insert a plus sign (+) in front of the field name to prevent the printing of a blank line where that variable ordinarily would appear. Blank fields such as these are common in addresses: some of the records in your data file might not have an entry for the name of the company, for example. If you find that a blank line appears in your printout even when you enter the plus sign, then there is a blank or a nonprinting control character either in the data file field or in the document field specifier. To rectify the problem, delete the extra character from your document or update your data file to delete the character there.

When you issue the Merge command, one complete document is printed for each record in the data file. If the variables are of varying lengths, the document is reformatted for each printing so that the proper justification is maintained. You may end up with a different number of pages for each data record. Remember that the Merge command will not work if your working document is a Text file, rather than a Document.

Figure 25.10 shows a memo printed with the Merge command; the text is shown in figure 25.8, and the data file is the one shown in figure 25.9.

```
                    M E M O R A N D U M

TO:        Karenski                            1/2/87

FROM:      Mr. Watkins

SUBJECT:   Data Verification


----------------------------------------------------------------
Each year we verify our personnel records to make sure that
they are as accurate as possible. Please take a moment to
review the following information and make any necessary
corrections. This memo should be returned to personnel by no
later than 1/15/87.

     208-23-0300
     1020.33
     (606) 779-5088
     08-20-71
```

Fig. 25.10. *The results of a Merge printing.*

Merging Data from the Screen (Merge Screen)

If you have a standard letter you send frequently but you have no data file, you can issue the Merge Screen command and enter the data from the keyboard. With this command, you are prompted to enter the variable values on the Merge-text input screen shown in figure 25.11. Press F2 to print the document and F10 to return to command level.

Both Merge File and Merge Screen files can be printed in Normal or Enhanced mode; in this way, the Merge and Print commands are similar. Use the Print Options command to establish options to apply to Merge output. You cannot direct output from Merge to a disk file, however.

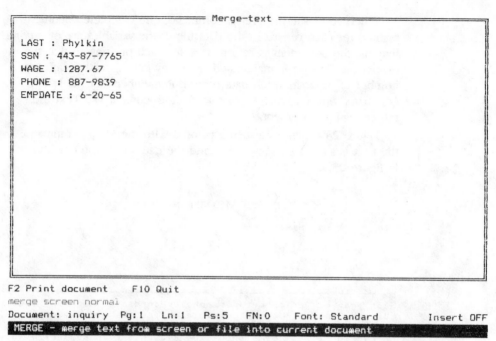

Fig. 25.11. *The Merge-text input screen.*

Conclusion

All of your work in the Smart Word Processor would be fruitless if you could not print high-quality output. This chapter explains how to use the Print command for printing your documents in Normal mode, taking advantage of your printer's built-in fonts, or in Enhanced mode, using your printer's graphics capabilities.

Using the Merge command, you can incorporate data from the Smart Data Manager into the body of your document. You can also supply data directly from the keyboard in the Merge command.

Chapter 26

Integrating the Word Processor with Other Modules

Part of the beauty of the Smart system lies in its integration of the applications modules. You know, for example, that you can produce customized letters by using the Word Processor's Merge command and a file sent from the Data Base Manager. Text files can also be read into the Smart Word Processor when you want to include data from the Data Base Manager or portions of worksheets. If you have the right kind of printer, you can use Smart's unique Graphics command to include in your document a graph produced in the Spreadsheet.

Files read into the Word Processor do not necessarily have to come from other applications modules; you may have created them with the Word Processor itself. This feature gives you the capability of assembling a document from separate smaller "boilerplate" document files.

Text from the Word Processor can be sent (with the Send command) or written (with the Write command) to the other applications modules. If you have created a document that contains a table, for instance, you may want to send that table to the Spreadsheet module for further analysis.

Reading Files into Text (4 –Read)

The Read command is found on command list 4 (see fig. 26.1). Read is used to insert a document file or text file in the document in the current window. The file is read into the current document at the position immediately preceding the cursor's location.

Fig. 26.1. *Selecting the Read command.*

The file that is read in can be either a Word Processor document file, which can be reformatted after it is read into the current document, or a text file with "hard" carriage returns and line feeds at the end of each line. If you tend to insert standard phrases or paragraphs in many documents, this "boilerplate" feature will appeal to you. (Remember that you are prompted for a password if the boilerplate file is protected.)

Unlike some other popular word-processing programs, the Smart Word Processor does not have the capability of "calling" different boilerplate documents in your main document. (A document that is "called" is printed directly from disk; it is not actually stored with the main document in the computer's memory.) To save disk space, you may decide after you finish printing to save the main document without the files you have read into it.

When you select the Read command, a pop-up menu displays the names of document files in the current subdirectory. Move the cursor and press Enter to select a document. If the file you want to read is not a .DOC file or is not in the current subdirectory, you must type the name of the file, preceded by the path if it is different from the current subdirectory. If you want to display a pop-up menu from another directory, type the path and file specification and then press F5. If you are reading in a text file with the extension .TXT, you do not have to type the extension; you must supply any other extension.

Writing Text to a File (4 - Write)

The Write command writes all or part of your document to a disk file. Write is found on command list 4 (see fig. 26.2). As shown in figure 26.3, you select Write options to specify a range to be written to disk.

```
    345-98-7593 Ronaldo    52¶
    876-33-0989 Lester     55¶
    776-39-8763 Adelson    60¶
    239-87-8876 Davis      61¶
    ¶
    These    employees    are  to  be  commended    for    their
outstanding contributions to the company this year, and it is ♦
L::::|::::1::::|::::2::::|::::3::::|::::4::::|::::5::::|::::6::::|::::7::::|::
```

```
Command list 4:  Change-Type  Directory  File  Graphics  Index  Load  Merge
                 Password  Read  Save  Text-Sort  Unload  Write  Xlate
Document: GOODEMPS Pg:1   Ln:1   Ps:10  FN:0    Font: Standard          Insert ON
WRITE - write a portion of the current document to disk
```

Fig. 26.2. *Selecting the Write command.*

```
        These    employees    are  to  be  commended    for    their
    outstanding contributions to the company this year, and it is
L::::|::::1::::|::::2::::|::::3::::|::::4::::|::::5::::|::::6::::|::::7::::|::
```

```
Select option:  Block  Document  Paragraph  Remainder
write
Document: (none)   Pg:1   Ln:1   Ps:10  FN:0    Font: Standard          Insert ON
WRITE - write a portion of the current document to disk
```

Fig. 26.3. *Using the Write command options to specify a range.*

Selecting Remainder causes Smart to write the contents of the current document, starting at the cursor position and continuing to the end of the document. Selecting Document writes the entire document, regardless of the cursor position. Choose Paragraph to write only the paragraph in which the cursor is positioned.

The Block option is used to write a block marked with the F2 key. Remember, however, that in the Word Processor, a block includes every character between the beginning and the end of the block. You cannot mark only certain columns. Thus, an attempt to specify a block consisting only of the names and ages of employees over the age of 40 results in the block specification shown in figure 26.4.

```
┌─ Window 1 ══════════════════════════════════════════════════
│        SSN         NAME       AGE
│      ───────────  ─────────  ───
│      198-03-3024  Peters      18
│      387-59-8374  Steffans    25
│      498-48-3980  Linden      29
│      498-34-5998  Bernstein   30
│      887-63-5498  Harris      34
│      345-54-2287  Aliakbari   35
│      208-23-0300  Karenski    41
│      987-65-7653  Marzetti    47
│      598-44-5922  Markus      48
│      345-98-7593  Ronaldo     52
│      876-33-0989  Lester      55
│      776-39-8763  Adelson     60
│      239-87-8876  Davis       61
│
│       These    employees   are  to  be  commended  for  their
│   outstanding contributions to the company this year, and it is
│ ···|···1···|···2···|···3···|···4···|···5···|···6···|···7···|···
└──────────────────────────────────────────────────────────────

Use cursor to mark block
F2  Drop new anchor          F10 or ENTER  End block
Document: goodemps Pg:1   Ln:15  Ps:34  FN:0    Font: Standard        Insert ON
WRITE - write a portion of the current document to disk
```

Fig. 26.4. *Specifying a block.*

After you specify the range, Smart prompts you to enter a name for the file to be written. The file is written as either a text file or a document file, depending on which type of file is in the current window. (If a file already exists with the name you supply, you are asked whether you want to overwrite it. Answer *y* or *n.*)

Sending Text to Other Applications Modules (5-Send)

To move the contents of a document to another application module, you could, of course, write the data to a file, quit the Word Processor, enter the other module, and finally read the newly created file into that module. Using the Send command is much simpler; Send will transfer the data automatically and start the new module for you. (A similar Send capability is found in each Smart module.)

Send is found on command list 5 (see fig. 26.5). You can send the contents of a document to any of the other three applications modules (see fig. 26.6).

```
"876-33-0989","Lester",55,1516.26,"(617) 873-0979","09-05-75"¶
"987-65-7653","Marzetti",47,901.45,"(704) 472-0042","10-30-85"¶
"387-59-8374","Steffans",25,654.34,"(207) 878-4880","10-15-81"¶
"498-34-5998","Bernstein",30,1004.56,"(916) 475-4228","06-15-75"¶
"776-39-8763","Adelson",60,956.43,"(203) 739-3095","07-23-45"¶
"345-54-2287","Aliakbari",35,997.66,"(201) 727-9242","08-15-72"¶
"198-03-3024","Peters",18,1544.00,"(318) 729-5060","10-01-85"◆
L::::|::::1::::|::::2::::|::::3::::|::::4::::|::::5::::|::::6::::|::::7::::|::
```

```
Command list 5:  Beep  Confidence  Display  Execute  F-Calculator
                 Input-Screen  Macro  Parameters  Remember  Send  Text-Editor
Document: (none)   Pg:1   Ln:6   Ps:0   FN:0   Font: Standard        Insert ON
SEND - send text to another application
```

Fig. 26.5. *Selecting the Send command.*

```
"776-39-8763","Adelson",60,956.43,"(203) 739-3095","07-23-45"¶
"345-54-2287","Aliakbari",35,997.66,"(201) 727-9242","08-15-72"¶
"198-03-3024","Peters",18,1544.00,"(318) 729-5060","10-01-85"◆
L::::|::::1::::|::::2::::|::::3::::|::::4::::|::::5::::|::::6::::|::::7::::|::
```

```
Select option:  Communications  Data-Manager  Spreadsheet
send
Document: (none)   Pg:1   Ln:6   Ps:0   FN:0   Font: Standard        Insert ON
SEND - send text to another application
```

Fig. 26.6. *Send command options.*

The Send command, unlike the Write command, applies to the entire document or text file; you cannot specify a range. If you send data from the Word Processor to either the Smart Data Base Manager or the Spreadsheet, the data must be in ASCII format; text fields must be enclosed in double quotation marks, and spaces or commas must separate all fields. (For information on creating ASCII files, see "Changing between Document and Text Modes" in Chapter 23.) Each record must be on a line by itself. Figures 26.5 and 26.6 are examples of ASCII files.

Sending Data to the Data Base Manager

When sending a file to the Data Base Manager, you are prompted to enter the name of the document to be sent (press Enter for the default document in the current window) and the name of the project file (if any) to be initiated within the Data Base Manager. Just press Enter if you don't want to initiate a project file.

If an existing data file has the same name as the Word Processor document, the system "assumes" that the formats are compatible, and the records from the Word Processor are appended to the Data Base Manager file. If no data file has a matching name, a Data Base Manager file is created. (If you send a document with no name, the system creates a data file called *noname.*)

The system uses the first line of the Word Processor file to determine the structure of the Data Base Manager file that is created. Numeric fields are created for fields in the Word Processor file that contain only numbers; alphanumeric fields are created for other kinds of data, including Social Security numbers, dates, and phone numbers. To send a document to the Data Base Manager, you *must* position your cursor on the first character of the document before sending it. Otherwise, the correct record structure will not be created.

The Data Base Manager assigns these fields the names *F001, F002,* etc. To create more meaningful field names and to correct data types, you may want to create a new file and then use the Utilities Restructure command to move the data into the new file. Although you can't change field names after a file is created, you could change field types from numeric to alphanumeric when you create your new file.

Sending Data to the Spreadsheet

Data also must be in ASCII format when you send data to the Spreadsheet. (You can use only spaces, not commas, as delimiters.) Each *record* in the document becomes a *row,* and each *field,* a *cell.* Fields that contain only numbers become values, and other fields become text. The column widths are adjusted automatically to accommodate the width of the data.

Sending Data to the Communications Module

If you want to use your modem to transmit a file to another computer, you first use the Send Communications command to send your file to the Communications module. The file can be sent to the Communications module either as a document (with all the embedded control codes) or as a pure text (ASCII) file.

If you intend to transmit to another Smart user, use the Document option so that the other user can change the document, add to it, or print it in Enhanced mode. (To send the embedded codes, you must transmit using the Xmodem option.) If you are sending your file to a computer that supports Xmodem, you can use this option to transmit your file. Otherwise, you can use the Text-File option. If the user receiving your file does not have Smart, send your document as a text file.

If you want to transmit a document that is already in a file, you do not have to enter the Word Processor; you can select that file for transmission after you enter the Smart Communications module.

No matter whether you send your document to the Data Base Manager, the Spreadsheet, or the Communications module, you are prompted to save a document that you have modified after loading it. If the document has no name, you are prompted to supply a name.

Importing Graphics into Text (4 –Graphics, Alt-G)

The Graphics command is used to insert in your document a graph that you previously have saved in the Smart Spreadsheet module. (Graph files have the extension .SCN.) The Graphics command is found on command list 4 (see fig. 26.7); the quick key is Alt-G.

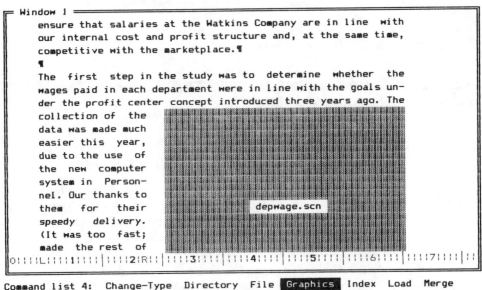

Fig. 26.7. *Selecting the Graphics command.*

You can insert a graph in one of three sizes, and the graph can be either right- or left-justified. The actual graph, positioned within the document, is not displayed on the screen (refer to fig. 26.7). By selecting the View option, however, you can view the graph itself while you are working in the Word Processor.

The three Graphics command options are shown in figure 26.8.

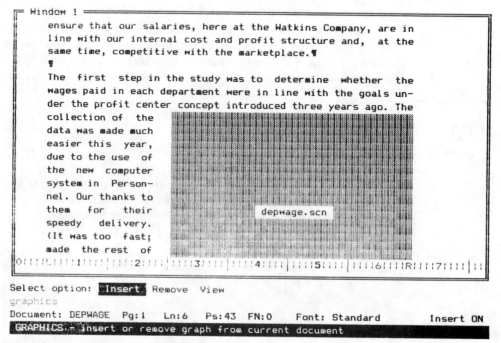

```
┌ Window 1 ════════════════════════════════════════════════════
║  ensure that our salaries, here at the Watkins Company, are in
║  line with our internal cost and profit structure and, at the
║  same time, competitive with the marketplace.¶
║  ¶
║  The first step in the study was to determine whether the
║  wages paid in each department were in line with the goals un-
║  der the profit center concept introduced three years ago. The
║  collection of the
║  data was made much
║  easier this year,
║  due to the use of
║  the new computer
║  system in Person-
║  nel. Our thanks to
║  them for their          depwage.scn
║  speedy delivery.
║  (It was too fast;
║  made the rest of
║O!!!!L!!!!1!!!!|!!!!2!!!!|!!!!3!!!!|!!!!4!!!!|!!!!5!!!!|!!!!6!!!R!!!7!!!!|!!

Select option: Insert  Remove  View
graphics

Document: DEPWAGE  Pg:1  Ln:6  Ps:43  FN:0  Font: Standard      Insert ON
GRAPHICS - insert or remove graph from current document
```

Fig. 26.8. *Graphics command options.*

Inserting a Graph (Graphics Insert)

To insert a graph, you first position the cursor on the line where the graph is to begin, and then select the Graphics Insert command sequence. From a pop-up menu of graph files, you select the name of the graph to be inserted. (The "default" choice selects the graph sent most recently from the Spreadsheet.)

Next, you are prompted to select a graph size. *Large* extends from margin to margin, *Medium* goes halfway across the page, and *Small* goes one-third of the way across the page. The graph can be right-justified or left-justified against the margin. (If you select Large, there is no prompt for justification.)

A shaded area, which represents the position of the graph, is then inserted in the body of the document; the surrounding text is reformatted automatically to compensate for the graph. Figure 26.8 illustrates what the graph looks like on the screen; see figure 26.9 for a printout (made in Enhanced mode) of the same document. This graph is the result of choosing the Medium and Right-Justified options.

```
                    WATKINS COMPANY
                 Personnel Department
                 Annual Salary Study                      05/07/86
```

The annual wage and salary study was conducted this year under the supervision of our auditors, Parkenfarquer, Muckenfuss, and Plattsblatt. The purpose of the study is to ensure that salaries at the Watkins Company are in line with our internal cost and profit structure and, at the same time, competitive with the marketplace.

The first step in the study was to determine whether the wages paid in each department were in line with the goals under the profit center concept introduced three years ago. The

collection of the data was made much easier this year, due to the use of the new computer system in Personnel. Our thanks to them for their speedy delivery. (It was too fast; made the rest of us look slow.)

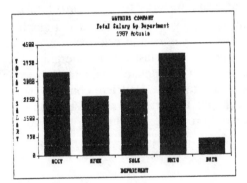

The total wages are shown in figure 1, by department. As you can see, the marketing department again leads the company in total salaries paid. The fact that the accounting department is second is certainly a surprise, but this figure must be compared to the cost and profit ratio table on page 2.

Fig. 26.9. *A graph in a printed document.*

Displaying a Graph (Graphics View)

Although you cannot view the contents of a graph while it is positioned within the document on the screen, you can use the Graphics View command to display any graph in a file or one you have already inserted within the document.

Use the Graphics View File command sequence to view a graph in a disk file. A pop-up menu displays the names of files in the current subdirectory. Use the cursor to select a file name, and then press Enter. The document on your screen is replaced by the graph, which appears exactly as it did when you created it in the Spreadsheet. You cannot change the graph at this time, however. Press any key to return to your document.

The Graphics View Document command sequence is used to display a graph you have already inserted into your document. Position the cursor on any line on which the graph occurs, and then select Graphics View Document to display the graph. Press any key to display the document again.

Removing a Graph from Your Document (Graphics Remove)

To remove a graph from your document, position the cursor on a line adjacent to the graph and select the Graphics Remove command. The text area is automatically restored to its original format.

Certain restrictions apply if you have embedded a graph within your document. For instance, you cannot reformat a paragraph that contains an embedded graph; you must remove the graph before you can reformat the paragraph. If you delete a paragraph that contains a graph, the graph also is deleted. The Undelete command restores only the text, not the graph. The graph is also lost if you use the Move command to reposition the text containing the graph.

Conclusion

The true power of the Smart system becomes evident when you realize how easily the different applications modules can share data, text, and graphics. Each module has the capability to read and write external files; the Send command passes data to another module and immediately transfers control to that module. In the Smart Word Processor, the Graphics command provides the capability to embed graphs from the Spreadsheet in the body of a document.

Chapter 27

Using the Smart Spellchecker

If you are doing a great deal of word processing and it is imperative that each word in your document be spelled correctly, you may want to purchase an additional product—the Smart Spellchecker—to use with your Smart Word Processor. Because not every user needs the spell-checking capability and because the hardware requirements go beyond those needed to operate the rest of the Smart system, Innovative Software has chosen to market this product separately.

If you plan to use the Smart Spellchecker, you will definitely need at least 320K of RAM; furthermore, you must have purchased the Smart Word Processor module as part of the Smart System or as a separate item. Although a hard disk is not mandatory, you will most likely want to have one if you want to use the Spellchecker. The 80,000-word Spellchecker dictionary, which is based on *Webster's Ninth New Collegiate Dictionary*, is contained in a file of 266K bytes. In a floppy-based system the dictionary would fit only on the data disk, leaving little room for your document files.

A hard disk not only expands disk space but also speeds up operation of the Smart Spellchecker; reading from a hard disk is at least 10 times as fast as reading from a floppy. You will be much happier with the operation of the Smart Spellchecker if you have a hard disk.

The Smart Spellchecker

Although the Smart Word Processor can make writing and rewriting easier and improve the appearance of your letters and documents, a document that is sprinkled with misspellings is going to lose some of its impact. Despite all the spelling drills in grade school, let's face it—some of us still can't remember whether *independent* is spelled with an *e* or an *a*.

Because the Smart Spellchecker is integral to the Word Processor, it checks your spelling as you go along; you don't have to save your document and then run a separate program. This feature will speed the processing of your documents and may prevent additional misspellings in later parts of the same document.

In addition to the extensive 80,000-word standard dictionary, you can create your own custom dictionaries and "attach" as many as five of them to any document.

Operating the Smart Spellchecker (2–Dictionary)

When the Smart Spellchecker has been installed, a new command (*Dictionary*, which calls up the Smart Spellchecker) appears on command list 2 (see fig. 27.1). After selecting Dictionary from this command list, you will want to select Spell-check (see fig. 27.2) to begin checking the document in the current window.

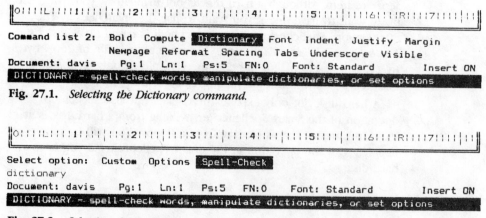

Fig. 27.1. *Selecting the Dictionary command.*

Fig. 27.2. *Selecting the Spell-Check option.*

Selecting a Range

You select the range over which spelling is to be checked by choosing one of the options shown in figure 27.3. You would select Remainder, for example, to check from the cursor position to the end of the document. Generally, you use this option to check spelling periodically as you work on your document.

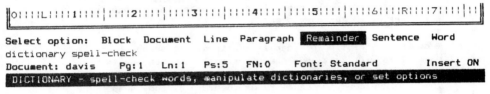

Fig. 27.3. *Spellchecker range specifications.*

If you use the Remainder option, be sure to position the cursor at the beginning of a word. Smart's Spellchecker checks from the cursor position to the end of the word; if the cursor is in the middle of a word, the Spellchecker will probably flag the remaining characters of the word as a misspelling.

Correcting Misspellings

The Smart Spellchecker reads each word in the selected range, checking it against the words in the standard dictionary. Any custom dictionaries attached to the document are also checked. If the Spellchecker finds a word in your document that is not in any available dictionary, that word is highlighted (see fig. 27.4).

You then select a course of action by pressing the appropriate function key:

Replace All (F2)

Every occurrence of the highlighted word is replaced with a word you supply. You use this option if you have misspelled the same word several times in your document. This is a useful option if your misspellings are consistent. If you use this option, the Smart Spellchecker will not pause for corrections of the same misspelling later in the document.

```
┌─ Window 1 ══════════════════════════════════════════════════════════╗
║    ¶                                                                   ║
║    Mr. Michael Davis¶                                                  ║
║    180 Lewis Avenue¶                                                   ║
║    Covington, LA  70433¶                                               ║
║    ¶                                                                   ║
║    Dear Mr. Davis:¶                                                    ║
║    ¶                                                                   ║
║    Thank you for your letter of inquiry regarding our Model 23-A      ║
║    Compressor.  We  have had a great deal of █sucess█ with  this      ║
║    model,  and the higher capacity unit,  Model 23-B since their      ║
║    introduction in February, 1984.¶                                   ║
║    ¶                                                                   ║
║    From the description of your application,  it sounds like the      ║
║    Model 23-B will suit your needs better,  both now and in  the      ║
║    years to come.  if your growth continues at its current pace,      ║
║    you  would exceed the capacity of the 23-A by the  summer  of      ║
║    next year.¶                                                         ║
║    ¶                                                                   ║
║ O¦¦¦¦L¦¦¦¦¦1¦¦¦¦¦¦¦¦¦¦2¦¦¦¦¦¦¦¦¦3¦¦¦¦¦¦¦¦¦4¦¦¦¦¦¦¦¦¦5¦¦¦¦¦¦¦¦¦6¦¦¦R¦¦¦7¦¦¦¦¦¦¦¦
╚═══════════════════════════════════════════════════════════════════════╝
Enter replacement text:
Word misspelled
F2 Replace all  F3 Ignore  F4 Ignore all  F5 Custom  F6 Delete  F7 Corrections
Words: 34      Corrections:   0
```

Fig. 27.4. *Highlighting a misspelled word.*

Ignore (F3)

Use F3 to ignore the current highlighted word and proceed to the next one. You select this option for a special word that you would not expect to find in the dictionary, such as the name of a person or a product. In this example, pressing F3 causes the Spellchecker to ignore the highlighted names of the individual and the product. Any word that is ignored because you press F3 will be highlighted again the next time you check this portion of your document.

Ignore All (F4)

The effect of this key is similar to that of F3, except that *all* occurrences of the highlighted word are ignored. You use F4 if the same word appears throughout the document and you don't want the Spellchecker to stop at every occurrence. After you have pressed F4, the Spellchecker will skip over this word (and other identical spellings of the same word) during the current session. If you unload your document and then load it again, the Smart Spellchecker will again highlight any words it cannot find in a dictionary, including this word.

Custom (F5)

Use this option to add a frequently used word to one of your custom dictionaries. If no custom dictionary exists, the Smart Spellchecker will create one for you and attach it to your document. (More later about custom dictionaries.)

Delete (F6)

This option, which is equivalent to the Delete Word command sequence, deletes the highlighted word from the document.

Corrections (F7)

If the Smart Spellchecker locates words in the standard dictionary in any of the attached custom dictionaries that are similar to the misspelled word, you can press F7 to view as many as 16 suggested corrected spellings in a pop-up menu (see fig. 27.5). You can select a correction by moving the cursor and then pressing Enter; the word you select is substituted for the misspelled word. If you want to. do a global substitution, use the Replace Key F2.

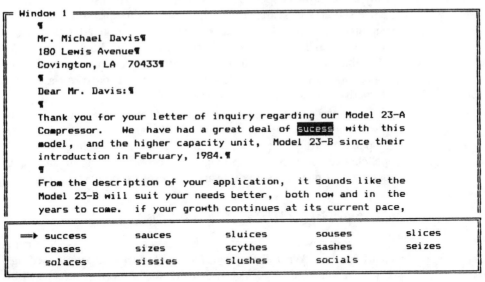

```
= Window 1 =
    ¶
    Mr. Michael Davis¶
    180 Lewis Avenue¶
    Covington, LA  70433¶
    ¶
    Dear Mr. Davis:¶
    ¶
    Thank you for your letter of inquiry regarding our Model 23-A
    Compressor.  We  have had a great deal of sucess  with  this
    model,  and the higher capacity unit,  Model 23-B since their
    introduction in February, 1984.¶
    ¶
    From the description of your application,  it sounds like the
    Model 23-B will suit your needs better,  both now and in  the
    years to come.  if your growth continues at its current pace,
```

⟹ success	sauces	sluices	souses	slices
ceases	sizes	scythes	sashes	seizes
solaces	sissies	slushes	socials	

```
Enter replacement text:
Word misspelled
F2 Replace all  F3 Ignore  F4 Ignore all  F5 Custom  F6 Delete
Words: 0        Corrections:   0
```

Fig. 27.5. *Suggested spelling corrections.*

Note that the word most likely to match the misspelled word is listed first in the menu. If that's the word you want, press Enter. If you want another word in the menu, simply use the cursor-control keys to move the arrow to that word, and then press Enter. However, if the word you really want is not on the menu, you must look it up in your own dictionary (the one on your desk) and type in the correctly spelled word as the replacement. With any luck, you may never have to type any corrections.

Setting Spellchecker Parameters

Pressing the F7 key brings forth the pop-up menu of suggested spelling corrections. However, if you want the menu to appear automatically each time the Smart Spellchecker highlights a misspelled word, you can set *Correction Information: Yes* in the Parameter table on command list 5.

You may not want the correction information to appear automatically. For instance, you may have mistyped a word that you really know how to spell. The Smart Spellchecker usually takes four or five seconds to search the dictionaries and display the menu of suggested corrections, whereas the first step—notification that the word is misspelled—takes only about one second. You also know for a fact that you will not find some words, such as some proper nouns or product names, in your dictionary. You would not want a menu of alternative spellings for these words.

The Smart Spellchecker does a fine job of dealing with phonetic spellings as well as actual misspellings. If you really don't know how to spell a word, you can take a stab at a phonetic spelling; the Spellchecker probably will provide the correct spelling in the pop-up menu. (You may get some unusual suggestions, however!)

Correcting Other Errors

If the first word in a sentence begins with a lowercase letter, the Smart Spellchecker will flag it as having *Bad capitalization* (see fig. 27.6). In this case, the suggested words in the pop-up menu will be capitalized to save you the effort of making the change yourself.

The Spellchecker also will find many errors in capitalization of proper nouns and punctuation of abbreviations. The standard dictionary contains the names and abbreviations of the 50 states, the months, and the days of the week, for example.

```
┌─ Window 1 ═══════════════════════════════════════════════════════
│    ¶
│    Thank you for your letter of inquiry regarding our Model 23-A
│    Compressor.  We have had a great deal of success  with  this
│    model and the higher capacity unit,  Model 23-B,  since their
│    introduction in February, 1984.¶
│    ¶
│    From the description of your application, it sounds as though
│    the  Model 23-B will better suit your needs both now  and  in
│    the years to come.  ▐If▌ your growth continues at its  current
│    pace, you would exceed the capacity of the 23-A by the summer
│    of next year.¶
│    ¶
│    I am planning on having Mr. Julius Karenski, our sales repre-
│    sentative in New Orleans, call you as as soon as possible.¶
│    ¶
│    I wish you every success in your new company.◆
│
├──────────────────────────────────────────────────────────────────
│  ═▶ If
└──────────────────────────────────────────────────────────────────
```

Enter replacement text:
Bad capitalization
F2 Replace all F3 Ignore F4 Ignore all F5 Custom F6 Delete
Words: 77   Corrections: 1

Fig. 27.6. *Bad Capitalization is flagged.*

Words that are repeated next to each other are also flagged. As illustrated in figure 27.7, you will see the message *Word is repeated;* the second occurrence of the word will be highlighted.

```
│    I am planning on having Mr. Julius Karenski, our sales repre-
│    sentative in New Orleans, call you as ▐as▌ soon as possible.¶
│    ¶
│    I wish you every success in your new company.◆
│
│
│
│
│
│
│
│
│
│ 0::::L::::1::::|::::2::::|::::3::::|::::4::::|::::5::::|::::6:::R::::7::::|::
```

Enter replacement text:
Word is repeated
F2 Replace all F3 Ignore F4 Ignore all F5 Custom F6 Delete F7 Corrections
Words: 116   Corrections: 2

Fig. 27.7. *Repeated words are flagged.*

Creating Dictionary Files

Instead of having the misspellings highlighted on the screen, you can have them written to a file; specify File in response to the last prompt in Spell-Check. If you specify a file name, any words not found in either the standard dictionary or any attached custom dictionaries are written to the file, together with the page, line number, and column number where the misspelling occurs. You can then use this file to create a custom dictionary with the Dictionary Custom Create command sequence. The page, line, and column designations in the file will be ignored.

Observing Counts

The Smart Spellchecker always displays at the bottom of the screen a count of the number of words read and the number of corrections made. At the conclusion of Spellchecking, a pop-up menu displays a summary indicating the total number of words read, corrections made, and words added to any custom dictionaries (see fig. 27.8).

```
┌─ Window 1 ═══════════════════════════════════════════════════════════
│    ¶
│    From the description of your application, it sounds as though
│    the  Model 23-B will better suit your needs both now  and  in
│    the years to come.   If your growth continues at its  current
│    pace, you would exceed the capacity of the 23-A by the summer
│    of next year.¶
│    ¶
│    I am planning on having Mr. Julius Karenski, our sales repre-
│    sentative in New Orleans, call you as soon as possible.¶
│    ¶
│    I wish you every success in your new company.◆
│
│  ┌─────────────────────────────────────────────────────────────────┐
│  │                    SPELL CHECK SUMMARY                          │
│  ├─────────────────────────────────────────────────────────────────┤
│  │  Number of words checked:                      128              │
│  │  Number of corrections made:                     3              │
│  │  Number of words added to Custom Dictionaries:   0              │
│  └─────────────────────────────────────────────────────────────────┘
```

Enter any key to continue

Document: DAVIS   Pg:1   Ln:23 Ps:50 FN:0   Font: Standard   Insert ON

Fig. 27.8. *The Spell-Check summary.*

Using Quick Keys

Five quick keys support the Smart Spellchecker:

Key	Command Equivalent
Alt-F2	Dictionary
Alt-F3	Dictionary Spell-Check Word Screen
Alt-F4	Dictionary Spell-Check Paragraph Screen
Alt-F5	Dictionary Spell-Check Remainder Screen
Alt-F6	Dictionary Spell-Check Document Screen

Creating Custom Dictionaries

In addition to the standard dictionary that comes with the Smart Spellchecker, you can create custom dictionaries and attach them to your document so that they are consulted along with the main dictionary. A custom dictionary can be used to store legal terms for a law office, medical words for a doctor's office, or any terms specific to your company or industry. (Innovative Software sells both legal and medical dictionaries separately. However, because they replace the standard American dictionary and are not available as custom dictionaries, they cannot be used simultaneously.)

If you have a readily available source of terms, you can use the Dictionary Custom Create command to read an ASCII file into Smart's internal dictionary-file format. The ASCII file should have one word per line; the words themselves need not be in alphabetical order, however. Because the custom dictionaries are case-sensitive, words that should always be capitalized in common usage should be capitalized in your ASCII file. Insert commas between syllables to indicate allowable hyphenation points.

When you set up the file, you are prompted to specify whether the dictionary is American, English, or French. You will want to specify the same language that you specified as the default language in the Parameters section.

With the Dictionary Custom Update command, you can update your custom dictionary by entering words from the keyboard. If one or more letters of a word are capitalized, you are asked whether you want to retain the capitalization so that capitalization of proper names can be verified. This Dictionary Custom Update command does not check for duplicate entries, however, and correcting entries in the custom dictionary is difficult.

If have created a custom dictionary—for a special project, for example—and you no longer need it, you can erase the custom dictionary with the Dictionary Custom Erase command sequence. Unlike many other Smart system commands that prompt you to select files, the Smart Spellchecker commands do not display menus of existing custom dictionaries; you must know in advance the name of the dictionary to be erased.

Because all custom dictionaries in the Smart Spellchecker have the file extension .CLM, you can use the Directory command to get a listing of the names. (Throughout the Smart Spellchecker, the names of custom dictionaries are not displayed; therefore, you should know the name of your dictionary whenever you need to specify one.) When you enter the name of a dictionary, use only the file name without the extension.

You use the Dictionary Custom List command to write the contents of a custom dictionary to a file for viewing, editing, and subsequent reloading.

Using Dictionary Options

Use the Dictionary Options command sequence to attach as many as five custom dictionaries to a document so that they are consulted automatically along with the main dictionary. You also can change to an English or French standard dictionary instead of the American; note, however, that the language of the custom dictionaries must match the language of the standard dictionary.

Within this menu, you can also specify the number of consecutive hyphenated lines for individual documents.

Be careful when you enter the name of a custom dictionary; the name is not checked when you enter it in the Options selection or when you run the Spellchecker. If you misspell the name of the custom dictionary, it is not attached to the document; you may end up with some misspelled words that are not caught by the custom dictionary.

One final word of caution about custom dictionaries: Be extremely careful when you enter words to a custom dictionary; there is no provision for deleting individual words. To delete words from your custom dictionary, follow these steps:

1. List the Custom Dictionary to a file.
2. Edit the file to delete unnecessary words.
3. Erase the original Custom Dictionary.
4. Re-create the Custom Dictionary from the edited file.

Hyphenating

Use the Dictionary Hyphenate command to hyphenate all or
portions of your document if hyphens were not inserted initially. The
options are

    Document Paragraph Remainder

Once inserted, a hyphen can be removed only by deleting the word.
Remember that Auto-Hyphenation can be controlled only through the
Parameters settings; you cannot establish a setting for an individual
document. If Auto-Hyphenation is on and you retype a word, hyphens
are inserted automatically. For direct control over hyphenation, turn
off Auto-Hyphenation and use the Dictionary Hyphenate command as
needed.

Using Special Parameters

Several special Parameter settings apply to the Dictionary command
(see fig. 27.9).

1. Spellingchecker enabled: Yes.
    Set to *Yes*.
2. Default language: American English French
    Set to match the version you have purchased.
3. Correction information: Yes No
    If you want the pop-up menu of suggested correct
    spellings to appear every time the Smart Spellchecker
    finds a misspelled word, select *Yes*. If you select *No*,
    you still can use the F7 function key to display the
    menu.
4. Custom dictionary hyphenation prompting:
    Set *On* to be prompted for hyphenation points when
    adding words to a custom dictionary during spell-
    checking.

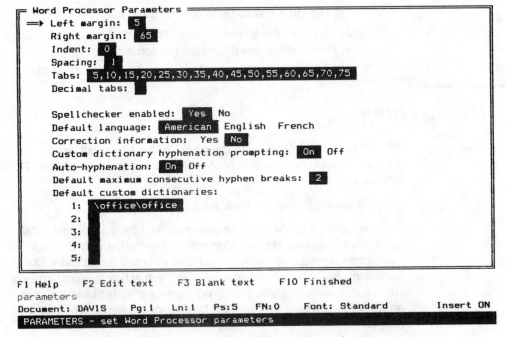

Fig. 27.9. *The Dictionary command's special Parameters settings.*

5. Auto-hyphenation:
   Set *On* to cause words to be hyphenated
   automatically at the end of a line if they do not fit.

6. Default maximum consecutive hyphen breaks:
   Enter the number of lines you would permit to be
   consecutively hyphenated. This is only a default; you
   can change the setting for an individual document by
   using Dictionary Options.

7. Default custom dictionaries:
   If you plan to use certain custom dictionaries (such
   as a legal dictionary in a law office) all the time, you
   probably will want them automatically attached to
   each document. You can enter the names of as many
   as five custom dictionaries.

   Changes in parameter settings do not take effect immediately; the
system initializes the Smart Word Processor to those settings when
you enter the module. If you want a change to take effect
immediately, you must quit the session and begin again.

Conclusion

The Smart Spellchecker is a useful addition to the Smart System. The Spellchecker is as easy to use as the rest of the Word Processor; the Spellchecker operates quickly, especially if the pop-up menu of suggested spelling corrections is not invoked automatically.

The capability of searching custom dictionaries as well as the standard dictionary is a desirable feature. Although adding entries to a custom dictionary is easy, you must be careful; the entries must be correct, because correcting them later is awkward.

If you have been operating your Smart System on a computer with two floppy drives and you want to get the most out of the Smart Spellchecker, you may want to think about getting a hard disk. You also may need to purchase a memory-expansion card to meet the 320K minimum RAM requirement.

Part IV

Using Smart's Communications and Time Manager

Chapter 28

Using Smart's Communications Commands

The Communications module, added to the Smart system in Version 2.0, enables you to connect your computer to your company's mainframe computer, one of the on-line services such as Dow Jones News/Retrieval or The Source, or to another microcomputer also running Smart.

In the simplest form of communication, you type a command that is sent to the remote computer; you then receive the response on your screen. If you are making a simple inquiry and the answer is short, this form of communication is probably adequate. But if the answer is long, you may want to save the output, sending it to your printer, a disk file, the Communications module buffer, or all three. The following quick keys toggle the capture modes:

Key	*Capture Mode*
F5	Buffer
F6	Printer
F7	File

Being able to capture received data in a file is certainly an advantage. Sometimes, however, you may want to transmit files that are already on disk. Smart's Communications commands enable you to send and receive both text and data files.

A text file within the Smart system contains only numbers and letters, and no control characters. To create a text file containing data from one of the applications modules, you use the Write Text command sequence. Files other than text files, however, have structures specific to the Smart system; they contain special control characters that are used by the programs of the application module. These files include .DOC files in the Word Processor and .WS files in the Spreadsheet. Internal files can be sent in the form in which the applications modules create them.

The Communications module can transmit and receive both text and internal files, but the two types of files must be treated differently. You *must* use the Xmodem protocol to transmit internal files because of the special characters they contain. The Xmodem protocol provides additional error checking. Data in the file is broken into blocks, and a number called a *checksum* is transmitted along with the data block. By comparing the data block and the checksum, the receiving computer can tell whether the data block was received without errors. Transmission with the Xmodem protocol usually takes longer than with other protocols. Both the sending and receiving computers must use Xmodem if you plan to use that protocol.

If you are transmitting a text file, you need not use the Xmodem protocol. In fact, you have no choice but to use another protocol if the other computer cannot handle Xmodem. If there is noise on the phone line during the transmission, however, you may find some errors in the received file.

Like the Spreadsheet and Word Processor modules, the Communications module has two modes of operation. Command mode is used to control your computer; Terminal mode sends characters you type to the computer at the other end of the phone line.

Understanding the Status Screen

When you first enter the Communications module, you are presented with the status screen (see fig. 28.1). This screen shows the status of various communications settings. From this screen, you can issue any of the Communications commands found on the five command lists.

To display the terminal screen (fig. 28.2), press F3. This screen displays all the information you type for transmission to the other computer and the information sent back to you. To return to the status screen at any time, press F3 again. You can invoke Command mode from the terminal screen by pressing Escape.

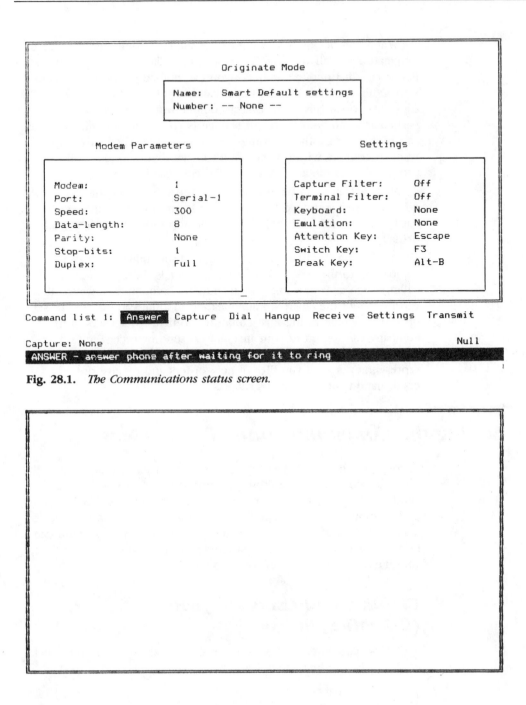

```
                        Originate Mode

                Name:    Smart Default settings
                Number:  -- None --


        Modem Parameters                         Settings


  Modem:            1            Capture Filter:    Off
  Port:             Serial-1     Terminal Filter:   Off
  Speed:            300          Keyboard:          None
  Data-length:      8            Emulation:         None
  Parity:           None         Attention Key:     Escape
  Stop-bits:        1            Switch Key:        F3
  Duplex:           Full         Break Key:         Alt-B



Command list 1:  Answer  Capture  Dial  Hangup  Receive  Settings  Transmit

Capture: None                                              Null
  ANSWER - answer phone after waiting for it to ring
```

Fig. 28.1. *The Communications status screen.*

```
Capture: None                                              Null
```

Fig. 28.2. *The terminal screen.*

When you decide to place a call to another computer, you are in Originate mode. If your modem is an "auto dial" modem—meaning that it can dial phone numbers—you can embed phone numbers in settings files and use the Dial command to initiate the calls. The capability to establish the correct communications settings for the particular remote computer or service is equally important; so is the capability to store these settings in the same file. Then, when you want to connect with one computer or another, you just load the proper settings file and issue the Dial command.

Many settings can be established in those files, but the most common ones you need to change are Baud rate (bits per second), parity, data length (in bits), number of stop bits, and duplex (full or half).

Originating a call and transmitting a file is sometimes called "uploading to the host." The *host* computer is the computer you are calling, such as your company's mainframe computer. However, the capabilities of the Smart Communication module can be used to set up your machine as the host computer so that other users in the company can log on to your machine to send or receive files. For example, a typical application might be one in which sales representatives send you files of new orders and receive order confirmations or stock-status reports.

Setting the Communications Parameters

Settings are the parameters needed for correct communications with the other computer. The Profile command is used to define and "undefine" files containing *profiles,* which are groups of settings for each computer you call. The Settings command can then be used to load a profile for a particular service. The Parameters command can be used also to specify that a particular profile be loaded each time you initiate the Communications module.

Creating and Using Profiles (2–Profile, Alt-P)

The Profile command is found on command list 2, and the quick key is Alt-P. The first prompt is

    Define Undefine

A pop-up menu displays the names of any profiles previously defined. Figures 28.3, 28.4, 28.5, and 28.6 show the input screens used to establish the settings in a profile.

```
┌─ Communication Profile ══════════════════════════════════════════

  ══▶ Name or Prompt:  Fido Bulletin Board
      Mode:  Originate  Answer
      Add Linefeeds:  Yes  No
      Select Emulation Type:  1·
          1) Dumb Terminal
          2) Ansi Terminal
      Keyboard definition file:  ▮
      Mask incoming data to seven bits:   Yes  No
      Enable xon/xoff:  Yes  No
      Tab spacing  8
      Terminal-Filter on:  Yes  No
      Capture-Filter on:  Yes  No
      Dead time limit (seconds):  360


          Originate Settings


      Number:  ▮
      Originate Password:  ▮

F1 Help     F2 Edit text     F3 Blank text     F10 Finished
profile define fido
Capture: None                                              Null
  PROFILE - define/edit or undefine a communications profile
```

Fig. 28.3. *Communications Profile Screen 1.*

The four screens of the communications profile are identical to those of the Settings command. The five major groups of settings are general settings, originate settings, answer settings, modem settings, and text-file transmission settings.

General Settings

In the Smart Communications module, the general settings are used in both Answer and Originate modes.

Name or Prompt. Serves as an identifier in originate mode or as a sign-on message in answer mode.

Mode. If you initiate the call, select Originate. If you answer the call, select Answer.

Add Linefeeds. Some systems require the local computer to add linefeeds at the end of each line of text.

```
┌═ Communication Profile ═══════════════════════════════════════════════┐
│  ═══▶ Dial Prefix:  AT DT                                               │
│       Dial Suffix:  !                                                   │
│       Seconds to wait between re-dials:  60                            │
│       Maximum Number of re-dial attempts:  3                          │
│       Seconds to wait for carrier:  45                                 │
│                                                                        │
│          Answer Settings                                               │
│                                                                        │
│       Receive/Transmit Password: █                                     │
│       Receive Password: █                                              │
│       Transmit Password: █                                             │
│       Connect-Only Password: █                                         │
│       Number of rings:  3                                              │
│       Connection time limit (minutes):  60                            │
│                                                                        │
│          Modem Settings                                                │
│                                                                        │
│       Select Modem Type:  4                                           │
│          1) Null Modem                                                 │
│                                                                        │
└────────────────────────────────────────────────────────────────────────┘
```

F1 Help   F2 Edit text   F3 Blank text   F10 Finished
profile define fido
Capture: None   Null
PROFILE - define/edit or undefine a communications profile

Fig. 28.4. *Communications Profile Screen 2.*

```
┌═ Communication Profile ═══════════════════════════════════════════════┐
│  ═══▶ Select Modem Type:  4                                            │
│          1) Null Modem                                                 │
│          2) Hayes 300                                                  │
│          3) Hayes Smartmodem 1200                                      │
│          4) Hayes Smartmodem 1200B                                     │
│          5) Hayes Smartmodem 2400                                      │
│          6) Popcom C100                                                │
│          7) Popcom X100                                                │
│          8) U.S. Robotics Courier 2400                                 │
│       Modem port:  Serial-1  Serial-2                                  │
│       Baud rate:  110  300  600  1200  2400  4800  9600               │
│       Word length:  5  6  7  8                                        │
│       Parity:  Odd  Even  None  Mark  Space                           │
│       Stop bits:  1.5  1  2                                           │
│       Duplex:  Full  Half                                             │
│                                                                        │
│          Text File Transmission                                        │
│                                                                        │
│       Expand tabs:  Yes  No                                           │
│                                                                        │
└────────────────────────────────────────────────────────────────────────┘
```

F1 Help   F2 Edit text   F3 Blank text   F10 Finished
profile define fido
Capture: None   Null
PROFILE - define/edit or undefine a communications profile

Fig. 28.5. *Communications Profile Screen 3.*

```
┌─ Communication Profile ═════════════════════════════════════════════┐
│    Select Character Delay:  0                                        │
│       0) No Delay                                                    │
│       1) Wait for Echo                                               │
│       #) Delay Time in 1/10 seconds                                  │
│    Select Line Delay:  0                                            │
│       0) No Delay                                                    │
│       1) Wait for CR                                                 │
│       2) Wait for User                                               │
│       3) Wait for Prompt                                             │
│       #) Delay Time in 1/10 seconds                                  │
│       Prompt to wait for:                                            │
│    End of File delay time (seconds):  360                            │
│                                                                     │
│       Advanced User Settings                                        │
│                                                                     │
│    Debug mode:  Off  Decimal  Hex  Character                        │
│    Forced local echo:  Off  On                                      │
│    Maximum number of xmodem retries  9                              │
│ ═▶ Break signal length (in 1/100 seconds)  0                        │
└─────────────────────────────────────────────────────────────────────┘
F1 Help    F2 Edit text    F3 Blank text    F10 Finished
profile define fido
Capture: None                                                  Null
▓PROFILE - define/edit or undefine a communications profile
```

Fig. 28.6. *Communications Profile Screen 4.*

Select Emulation Type. If special ANSI characters are to be received and interpreted to emulate an ANSI terminal, select *2*; otherwise, select *1*.

Keyboard definition file. Used to indicate a file established to redefine the keyboard. Refer to the Keyboard command.

Mask incoming data to seven bits. You should set this to *No*.

Enable xon/xoff. This depends on the protocol used by the other computer.

Tab spacing. Converts tab characters to spaces.

Terminal-Filter on. Select *Yes* if you are using terminal filters (for more information, see the Filter command in this chapter).

Capture-Filter on. Select *Yes* if you are using capture filters.

Dead time limit (seconds). Determines the maximum number of seconds of inactivity before terminating the connection.

Originate Settings

The Originate Settings are used when you call another computer.

Phone Number. The phone number may be entered with or without hyphens.

Originate Password. Enter the password if the remote computer will request one.

Dial prefix and *Dial suffix.* These settings depend on the auto-dial features of your modem. (Some modems, for example, require that modem commands be preceded by the letters *AT.*)

Seconds to wait between re-dials. Enter number of seconds.

Maximum number of re-dial attempts. Enter a number.

Seconds to wait for carrier. Enter a number of seconds.

Answer Settings

In the answer settings, four different levels of password protection can be established to guard against unauthorized access. The originator of the call can issue the appropriate remote commands, depending on the level of access. The four password types are Receive/Transmit, Receive, Transmit, and Connect-Only.

The answer settings are as follows:

Number of rings. Enter the number of telephone rings before answering.

Connection time limit (minutes). Enter the maximum number of *minutes* you want to allow any caller to use your computer.

Modem Settings

The modem settings depend on the characteristics of your modem, the other computer's modem, and the communications port of your computer. To find the correct settings, check your modem manual and the instructions of the communications service you are using. The modem types are Null (connects two computers directly), Hayes, Popcom, and Generic (all other modems).

The modem settings are as follows:

Modem port. Either Serial-1 or Serial-2.

Baud rate (bits per second). The most common settings are 300, 1200, and 2400.

Word length (data bits or data length). Most common are 7 and 8. You must use 8 if you are transmitting with the Xmodem protocol.

Parity. Used for error checking. Select *none* if the data bits setting is 8.

Stop bits. Most common is 1.

Duplex. Select *Full* if you originate the call; *Half* if you answer the call.

Text File Transmission Settings
Change these settings only if you plan to transmit text files.

Expand tabs. Select *yes* if you want to transmit blanks instead of tab characters.

Pad blank lines. Some receiving computers require that blank lines be "padded out" with spaces.

Filter linefeeds. Select *yes* to send only carriage returns, instead of carriage-return, line-feed combinations.

Character delays. Some systems need these changed.

End of File delay time. Number of seconds to wait for a character before closing the received file.

Advanced User Settings
If you want to display received characters as decimal or hexadecimal numbers or if you want to display characters as they are received, bypassing the terminal filter and the high-bit (7 bit) mask, select the appropriate option. Select *off* for normal operation.

If you want to force what you transmit to be displayed on your screen no matter what the duplex setting is, set *Forced local echo* On.

If you have a particularly noisy telephone line and are using the Xmodem protocol, your transmission is terminated after 10 attempts at retransmission. If you want to keep trying to transmit the data, enter the number of Xmodem retries (the maximum allowed is 99). Often, you can get a less noisy line if you hang up the phone and redial.

Some systems require a break signal longer than one frame; you can specify the length of the break signal in hundredths of seconds by entering a value for Break Signal Length.

Changing the Current Settings
(1–Settings, Alt-S)

The Settings command is found on command list 1, and the quick key Alt-S is used to edit the current settings. The three primary options are

        Edit Load Save

The Edit option is used to change the current settings. If you make any changes, they take effect immediately and are in effect only for the duration of the session. This option is the same as the Profile Define command, previously discussed in this chapter.

Use the Save option to save any changes you have made. A pop-up menu displays the names of the existing profiles on the disk. You can select an existing name to overwrite an existing profile, or enter a new name to create a new profile.

The Load option is used to load a profile from an existing disk file. (The Parameters command can be used to select a profile for automatic loading when the Communications module is initiated.)

Changing Duplex Settings (2–Duplex, Alt-U)

The Duplex command is used to change from half duplex to full, or from full to half. The Duplex command is found on command list 2, and the quick key is Alt-U. Changing this setting has the same effect as changing the Duplex setting by means of the Settings Edit command.

In full-duplex mode, the characters you see on your screen are actually echoed back to your machine by the receiving computer. The characters do not appear on-screen until they have been received by the remote computer and transmitted back to you. You should probably use this setting in Originate mode. You can force local echo by selecting the appropriate advanced user setting. When Forced Local Echo is on, characters appear as soon as they are transmitted to the remote computer.

If duplex is set to Half, the characters you type appear on-screen as soon as they are transmitted, instead of being echoed back from the other computer. Use this setting for Answer mode.

Filtering Characters (3–Filters, Alt-L)

If you don't want certain characters to go to the printer, file, screen, or capture buffer, use the Filters command to specify those characters. The command is on command list 3, and the quick key is Alt-L. The two options are

Terminal Capture

Select *Terminal* if you want to filter out characters going to the screen, or *Capture* for characters destined for the buffer, printer, or disk file. In either case, a screen similar to figure 28.7 is displayed.

Terminal Filter Table

[0]	1	2	3	4	5	6	7	8	9	10	11	12	13	14	15
16	17	18	19	20	21	22	23	24	25	26	27	28	29	30	31
32	33	34	35	36	37	38	39	40	41	42	43	44	45	46	47
48	49	50	51	52	53	54	55	56	57	58	59	60	61	62	63
64	65	66	67	68	69	70	71	72	73	74	75	76	77	78	79
80	81	82	83	84	85	86	87	88	89	90	91	92	93	94	95
96	97	98	99	100	101	102	103	104	105	106	107	108	109	110	111
112	113	114	115	116	117	118	119	120	121	122	123	124	125	126	127
128	129	130	131	132	133	134	135	136	137	138	139	140	141	142	143
144	145	146	147	148	149	150	151	152	153	154	155	156	157	158	159
160	161	162	163	164	165	166	167	168	169	170	171	172	173	174	175
176	177	178	179	180	181	182	183	184	185	186	187	188	189	190	191
192	193	194	195	196	197	198	199	200	201	202	203	204	205	206	207
208	209	210	211	212	213	214	215	216	217	218	219	220	221	222	223
224	225	226	227	228	229	230	231	232	233	234	235	236	237	238	239
240	241	242	243	244	245	246	247	248	249	250	251	252	253	254	255

Filtered   Non-Filtered

F2 Toggle Filter Mark   F3 Toggle Display Type   ESC Abort   F10 Finished

Fig. 28.7. *Terminal Filter Table - Decimal.*

Use the cursor-control keys to move the cursor indicator—the square brackets ([]) enclosing the 0 in the upper left corner of figure 28.7—to the character you want to filter out. The F2 key is used to turn filtering on or off for a specific character.

In figure 28.7, the characters are identified by their decimal representations. Use the F3 key to change between hexadecimal mode and character-display mode. (Switch to this display mode to help identify all those "funny little characters.") The characters whose numbers are highlighted in figure 28.7 are the control characters that are not allowed in text files.

Use the F10 key to save changes to the filter settings. Because the filters are stored with the profiles, you should be sure to execute the

Settings Save command if you want to use the new settings in a later session.

Assigning Macros (2–Keyboard, Alt-J)

The Keyboard command, found on command list 2, is used to establish keyboard macros within the Communication module or to redefine the system keys (Attention, Break, and Switch). The quick key for the Keyboard command is Alt-J.

Because regular macros (see the Macro command section in Chapter 33) will not operate in terminal mode, you must use the Keyboard command to set up any macros you want to have in this module. After you select the Keyboard command, a menu of available keys is displayed (see fig. 28.8). Enclose literals in double quotation marks, precede hexadecimal representations with the letter *H*, and enter decimal representations as decimal numbers.

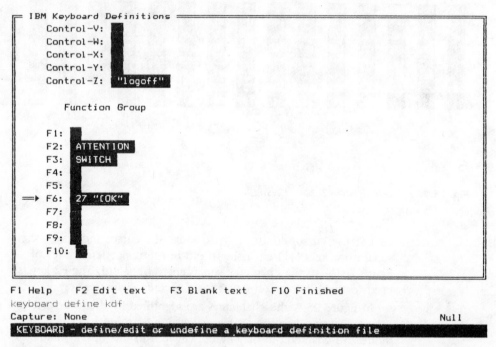

Fig. 28.8. *Using the Keyboard command.*

To reassign the system keys, type the words *attention*, *break*, or *switch* after the keys you want to use. (Do not enclose these words in quotation marks.) Use the F3 key to delete the entry from the original key.

Press F10 to save the keyboard settings. The method in which these settings are tied to a profile differs from the way that filters are attached to a profile. The Keyboard command creates a separate file, which can be used with one or more profiles. Enter the name of the keyboard file in the profile; when the setting is loaded, the keyboard file is loaded also. To use the keyboard settings in the current session, you must edit the settings, save them, then load them again.

Creating a Format Description (2–Format, Alt-E)

The Format command is used to establish the format description of a data file that is received in the Communications module and sent to either the Data Base Manager or the Spreadsheet. This command is found on command list 2, and the quick key is Alt-E.

The Format command defines field types as either Text or Value, splits one input line into several output lines, and combines input lines into one output line. The following information can be entered for as many as 25 fields:

Field start column
Field end column
Field type: Ignored Text Value
Read next input line: Yes No
Start new output line: Yes No

An example of a definition is shown in figure 28.9.

The input for the Format command must be in a fixed format. As output, text fields are surrounded by double quotation marks.

Starting and Stopping Communications

Once you have established the appropriate Communications settings, you are ready to begin a communications session.

Dialing Automatically (1–Dial, Alt-D)

The Dial command is used to dial automatically the telephone attached to the modem. You can either enter a phone number from the keyboard or use a number in the settings list. Dial is found on

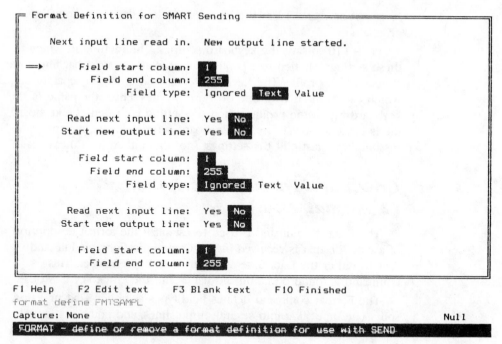

Fig. 28.9. *Using the Format command.*

command list 1, and the quick key is Alt-D. The options for the Dial command are

Carrier Voice

Select Voice if you expect to talk to a person before establishing data transmission. Otherwise, select Carrier.

The second prompt is

Enter number:

Type the phone number to be dialed or press Enter to use the number in the settings. If your modem does not support auto-dial, just bring up the terminal screen and manually dial your phone. When you hear the carrier (the high-pitched "modem tone"), press the button on your modem and begin your communications session.

The number of seconds to wait for a carrier, the number of redials, and the time between redials are established in the settings.

If you have selected Voice, use the Goto command to establish carrier connection after you have completed your conversation. That command is discussed later in this chapter.

Answering Incoming Calls (1–Answer, Alt-A)

The Answer command is used to answer incoming calls. Answer is found on command list 1; the quick key is Alt-A.

If you expect a call from another workstation, you should issue this command prior to the call. If you wait for the phone to ring, you may not have enough time to finish what you are doing and execute the command before the caller "times out."

Severing Communications (1–Hangup, Alt-H)

The Hangup command is used to hang up the phone and sever the communication. Hangup is found on command list 1, and the quick key is Alt-H.

Changing between Voice and Data Communications (2–Goto, F4)

The Goto command is used to switch between voice and data communications. Goto is found on command list 2; the quick key is F4. The prompts are

```
Carrier Voice
```

If you select Voice, the system notifies the other computer of your request. The timing is critical, however: the other person has three seconds to pick up the phone for voice communications.

Transferring Data

The primary purpose of using the Communications module is to transfer data to and from other computers. When you receive data, it can be "captured" on your computer in any of three primary modes.

Capturing Incoming Data (1–Capture, Alt-V, F5, F6, F7)

The Capture command, found on command list 1, is used to direct received characters to the buffer, a file, or your printer. If you have logged on to a system that prints a report to your screen, use the Capture command to print the report as you receive it, to place it in the buffer, or to write it to a file. (The Capture command is *not* used for file transfer; use the Receive command for that purpose. Capture is used only to capture text.)

The quick key Alt-V is used to display contents of the buffer. The following quick keys are also used:

Key	Function
F5	Toggle Buffer Capture
F6	Toggle Printer Capture
F7	Toggle File Capture

When you issue the Capture command, the primary prompt is

Select option: Buffer File Printer

Received data can be captured to multiple destinations simultaneously.

Sending Data to a Buffer (Capture Buffer)

If you select the Buffer option, you are presented with a further set of options:

Begin Clear End Save View

The buffer is an area of memory that can store received characters. By choosing the appropriate option, you can view the contents of the buffer or save the contents of the buffer to a permanent disk file. Selecting Begin starts the capturing of received characters to the buffer; selecting End stops the capturing. If you select Begin again, new characters are appended to the existing contents of the buffer. Use the Clear option to erase the contents of the buffer; you then have an opportunity to write the buffer to a file prior to clearing, if you choose. To avoid losing data because you've run out of buffer space, you should periodically write the buffer to a file or capture to both a file and the buffer simultaneously (or just to the file).

To write the buffer contents to a disk file, use the Save option. After selecting Save, you are prompted for a file name. If a file with the name you enter already exists, you can either append the buffer contents to the file or overwrite the file.

Capturing Data in a File (Capture File)

If you want the received characters to go directly to a file, select the File option. The following prompt is displayed:

Begin End

By selecting either Begin or End, you can control what is written to the file. If you select Begin, you are prompted for a file name. No extension is supplied, however; if you want a file extension, you must supply one.

If the file with the name you enter already exists, you have the option of overwriting the existing file or appending the data to it.

Sending Data to a Printer (Capture Printer)

To send output directly to the printer, select the Printer option. Again, the options are

```
Begin End
```

When you select Begin, the current date and time are automatically printed.

Storing Received Data
(1–Receive, Alt-R)

In contrast to the Capture command, which writes characters appearing on your terminal screen to a file, the Receive command is used to store received data files on your disk. The data is not echoed to the screen as the file is received. The Receive command is found on command list 1; the quick key is Alt-R.

The Receive command has two options

```
Text-File Xmodem
```

If the data file contains special control characters, such as those found in Smart Word Processor document files (.DOC) and Spreadsheet files (.WS), you *must* use the Xmodem protocol. Remember, however, that Xmodem can be used only if the other computer is also using Xmodem to transmit the file.

Receiving Data in Xmodem Protocol

Select Xmodem to use this special error-correcting protocol. Any type of file—not just a data file—can be sent with Xmodem. The advantage of using Xmodem lies in its error-correcting capabilities: the receiving computer double-checks each block of 128 bytes for errors. If any errors are detected, the sending computer is requested to transmit the data block again. This process may take longer than Text-File transmission, but greater accuracy is guaranteed.

After selecting Xmodem, you are prompted to enter a name for the received file. As the file is being received, the system displays a count of the number of blocks received and errors corrected. If you see that the number of errors is high, your file transmission will take longer. If you want, you can terminate the connection and try for a cleaner phone line with less noise.

Because of the special "handshaking" that takes place between the two computers, the receiving computer (which, in this case, is your computer) waits until the sending computer begins to transmit. Your computer will wait for up to two minutes for the file transmission to begin.

Receiving Text-File Data

Using the Text-File option is similar to using the Xmodem option, except that with Text-File, you cannot receive a file containing special control characters. Only "pure" (ASCII) text files can be sent or received with this option. No error checking is performed, apart from the regular parity checking of your system, so transmission errors may occur. With text files, however, such errors are generally not so troublesome as they are with other kinds of files.

Because no special "handshaking" is performed between the sending and the receiving computers when the Text-File option is used, starting the transmission at just the right time may be a little tricky. You don't want your file to end up with extra characters you would have to edit out later.

In addition to supplying a name for the received file, you can also enter an optional expression to be sent to the computer that initiates the transmission. This expression is used to try to eliminate "noise" characters that might produce "garbage" in the file. Your computer won't actually begin recording until the expression is echoed from the other system. Receipt of a Ctrl-Z character terminates the reception of the file and causes the system to close it.

Sending a File (1–Transmit, Alt-T)

If you are sending a file to another computer, use the Transmit command. Like the Receive command, the Transmit command has two options:

    Text-File Xmodem

The Transmit command is found on command list 1, and the quick key is Alt-T.

Remember that the receiving computer must use the same communications protocol that your computer is using. You cannot transmit with Xmodem and receive with Text-File, for example. If

your file contains special control characters, you cannot use the
Text-File option.

Whichever protocol you select, you are then prompted for the
name of the file to be sent. If a file was sent to the Communications
module from one of the other applications modules, choose the
default option on the pop-up menu.

If you are transmitting with Xmodem, the following information is
displayed on your screen:

> Estimated transmission time in minutes
> Total number of blocks to be transmitted
> Current block being transmitted
> Percent of completion

If the phone line is particularly noisy, a great deal of error correction
may be necessary. If a block cannot be sent in 10 attempts, the
transmission is aborted. You may want to end the communications
session and try to obtain a less noisy phone line.

Because Xmodem requires an extra bit to transmit special control
characters, the system automatically switches to a data length of eight
bits, regardless of the settings you have defined. Your settings are
automatically restored after the transmission. They are also changed
when you use the Receive command and, again, are restored
afterward.

Integrating Communications with Other Smart Modules (5 –Send)

Just as in the other Smart modules, the Send command is used to
integrate the Communications module with the others. Use Send to
transfer data from the buffer or a file to another module and to pass
control to that module. Send is found on command list 5.

At the first prompt, you select the receiving application module:

> Data-Manager Spreadsheet Wordprocessor

Data can be sent from one of two sources, as indicated by the next
prompt:

> Buffer File

If you have captured screen output to the buffer, you can send the
buffer contents without first writing the data to a file. Buffer contents
are gathered only by means of the Capture command. A file, on the

other hand, can be created with either the Capture or Receive command. If you select File, you are prompted to enter the name of the file.

The next prompt is

Data Formatted

Your selection determines whether the information in the file is to be sent exactly as it was received (Data) or modified in accordance with a format definition (Format). Refer to the Format command for an explanation of the formatting capabilities (see Chapter 14). If you select Formatted, you are prompted for a format-definition file name.

You are then prompted to enter the name of a project file for the next application. If you want to initiate a project file automatically, enter the name of the file; otherwise, just press Enter. The Communications session then is terminated, and the new module is initiated.

Using Utility Commands

Certain commands in the Communications module are useful in performing specialized tasks or providing helpful information.

The Get Command (3–Get, Alt-G)

The Get command, found on command list 3, is used to insert a received character or line into a variable or a parameter. The quick key for the Get command is Alt-G. This command is most useful within a project file when decisions need to be made based on the line or character retrieved.

The first prompt is

Select option: Character Line

If you select Character, only the next character is inserted into the variable or parameter; selecting Line causes the entire line to be retrieved. The destination of the received character or line is determined by your response to the following prompt:

Variable Text1 Text2 Parameter

If you select Variable, you are then prompted for the name of the variable. (The names of the user-defined variables begin with a dollar sign ($). Enter the name, including the $.) If you select Parameter, you are prompted for the number of the parameter. The parameter may be *%1*, but you enter *only* the number (not the percent sign). There are no subsequent prompts for Text1 or Text2.

The Match Command
(3–Match, Alt-M)

The Match command is used to halt the execution of a project file until certain characters are found. The matched characters can be literals, which must be enclosed in double quotation marks, or decimal or hexadecimal representations of ASCII characters. The character types can be used in combination. Match is found on command list 3, and the quick key is Alt-M.

When you issue the Match command, you are prompted to

Enter character(s):

Note that any filtering you have specified takes place before the system matches the string. If the filter removes the characters you are looking for, the system will never find them. Any high-bit masking also precedes the matching.

Even though processing has been suspended, capturing to the buffer, the printer, or a file can continue, allowing you to diagnose any problems with your Match condition.

The Output Command
(3–Output, Alt-C)

The Output command is used to send a literal string or the contents of a variable to the receiving computer. This command is useful in project processing and can be used to initiate commands on the other computer or to send a "logon" sequence.

Output is found on command list 3, and the quick key is Alt-C. The prompt is

Enter expression(s):

You can enter the expression as a literal enclosed in double quotation marks, or you can enter a variable name. Multiple variables can be used together as output; their names must be separated by semicolons (;). A carriage-return, line-feed combination always follows the expression, unless the final character is a semicolon.

Estimating the Transfer Time (4 – Transfer-Time, Alt-Q)

The Transfer-Time command is used to estimate the number of minutes needed to transmit a given file at the current data-transmission speed. Transfer-Time is found on command list 4; the quick key is Alt-Q.

After selecting this command, you are prompted to enter a file name. The transmission times are approximate; the formula used is

$$\frac{\text{number of characters in the file}}{((\text{bits per second} / 10) * 60)}$$

Be aware, however, that these calculations reflect Text-File transmission times and do not take into account the additional time required for Xmodem error checking or for retransmission of incorrect data blocks.

Conclusion

The commands in the Communication module offer you the ability to link your computer to other computers or on-line services. If the receiving computers are operating under the Smart system, you can easily share internal files, such as Smart Word Processor document files or Spreadsheet worksheets, by transmitting them with the error-correcting Xmodem protocol. Even if the other computer is not running Smart, you can *upload* text files or *download* files from the other system and integrate those files with your applications.

Communications commands can be issued interactively from the keyboard, or you can embed the commands in project files for unattended operation.

Chapter 29

Using Smart's Time Manager

The Smart Time Manager is a convenient electronic calendar and notepad that can help you keep track of your daily, weekly, and monthly appointments. Just as you can make entries on your desk calendar, you can enter meetings and tasks on the Time Manager calendar. By Smart's definition, a *meeting* takes place at a specific time, and a *task* needs to be done sometime during the day, but not at any specific time. A short description can be entered for both meetings and tasks, and, if necessary, you can create a long description (up to 225 characters) to be displayed at the bottom of the daily screen.

If you are the sole user of your system, the default Time Manager file named STD.DTM is adequate for your needs. If several people use the system, each user can keep a separate record of meetings and tasks.

Using Day, Week, and Month Screens

Figure 29.1 shows the day screen and the main menu of the Time Manager. This module has only one command list. Notice the three primary areas on the day screen. The *meetings* area, in the upper left corner of the screen, shows the time and short descriptions of any meetings. The *tasks* area, in the upper right corner, shows task priorities and gives a short description of each task. The *notes* area, in the bottom window, shows an optional long description of the highlighted meeting or task.

```
C:SMSYTM.WS  PAGE 1 LINE 54 COL 16          INSERT ON

date, and the file in use.                                        <
  8:00am Joe - Funding         │ 1: Call SyCon re new program
  9:45am Staff Meeting - Budget│ 2: Review Mary's Job
 11:30am Jane - Lunch - Andre's│ 3: Write Arnold on trip
  3:00pm Alpha - Contract      │
                               │
                               │
                               │
                               │
                               │
                               │
 I talked to Joe about this program, and he feels that SyCon would be the
 right vendor, if their price is in line with the others.  Try to get
 a committment from Larry about the cost and especially the time.

  Meeting Parameters:
 Date: 11-07-85
 Time: 16:30
 Short Description: Call Calif Office

F10 when finished or ESC to cancel
```

Fig. 29.1. *The day screen.*

Using the Time Manager Commands

The command list shows the 13 commands available in the Time Manager. The status line displays the current system time and date and the name of the file in use.

The week screen shows the week's schedule at a glance (see fig. 29.2); a diamond symbol on a time line indicates a meeting. A diamond symbol on the last line (labeled *tasks*) indicates that a task is scheduled for that day.

The month screen (fig. 29.3) shows the month at a glance. Symbols marks days on which meetings are scheduled.

Week of 11-03-85

time	sun 3	mon 4	tue 5	wed 6	thu 7	fri 8	sat 9
-7 am	-	-	-	-	-	-	-
8 am	-	-	-	-	◊	◊	-
9 am	-	-	-	-	◊	-	-
10 am	-	◊	◊	-	-	-	-
11 am	-	-	-	-	◊	-	-
12 pm	-	-	-	-	-	-	-
1 pm	-	-	-	-	-	-	-
2 pm	-	-	-	◊	-	◊	-
3 pm	-	◊	-	-	◊	-	-
4 pm	-	-	-	-	-	-	-
5 pm	-	-	-	-	-	-	-
6 pm	-	-	-	-	-	-	-
+7 pm	-	-	-	-	-	-	-
tasks	-	◊	-	-	◊	◊	-

Today: 12-09-85   File: stm.dtm   Time: 08:53:01AM

Fig. 29.2. *The week screen.*

November 1985

Sunday	Monday	Tuesday	Wednesday	Thursday	Friday	Saturday
					1	2
3	4 ◊	5 ◊	6 ◊	7 ◊	8 ◊	9
10	11 ◊	12	13 ◊	14	15 ◊	16
17	18	19 ◊	20	21 ◊	22 ◊	23
24	25	26	27	28	29	30

Today: 12-09-85   File: stm.dtm   Time: 09:10:22AM

Fig. 29.3. *The month screen.*

Making Entries on the Day Screen (Insert Command)

The Insert command is used to enter a meeting or a task on a day screen. When you select this command, you are prompted to

Select option: Meeting Task

If you select Meeting, the meeting data-entry menu appears (see fig. 29.4).

```
 I talked to Joe about this program, and he feels that SyCon would be the
 right vendor, if their price is in line with the others.  Try to get
 a committment from Larry about the cost and especially the time.
```

```
Command list 1:  Autohelp  Beep  Display  Edit  Find  Goto  Help  Insert  Load
                 Output  Purge  Remove  Use
Today: 12-09-85                 File: stm.dtm                 Time: 08:47:21AM
GOTO - goto a specified date or move a specified number of days +/-
```

Fig. 29.4. *The meeting data-entry screen.*

The date defaults to the date of the day screen, but you can change the date if you want to insert a meeting on a different date. Press Enter to proceed to the line for entry of the time.

The time can be entered in 12- or 24-hour format. For example, the time for a meeting at 3:30 in the afternoon could be entered as *3:30p* or as *15:30*. If the meeting is on the hour, you do not have to enter *:00* after the hour.

The short description, which can be a maximum of 25 characters, will appear in the meetings window of the day screen. To terminate the entry, press F10. Select Edit to change the entry.

If you want to enter a long description (up to 225 characters) for the meeting entry, do *not* press F10 yet. Instead, press Enter to display the description entry window. The description you enter can be a maximum of three lines with 75 characters per line. You must press Enter at the end of each line; Smart provides no word wrap here.

Press F10 to terminate the meeting entry. Your new entry now appears in the meetings window in proper order among the existing entries.

To enter a task, select Task at the prompt. Entering a task is similar to entering a meeting, except that instead of entering a time, you enter a priority number between 1 (highest priority) and 99 (lowest priority). Duplicate priority numbers can be used, but a warning message is supplied. The higher-priority tasks appear at the top of the list.

As with the Insert Meetings command, you can enter a long description of the task. Press Enter after typing in the short description to proceed to the long-description entry window. Press F10 to terminate the procedure.

Erasing One Entry (Remove Command)

The Remove command erases the entry (either a meeting or a task) that is indicated by the highlight block. Make sure that you are pointing to the right entry; the system does not prompt you to confirm the deletion.

Removing All Entries (Purge Command)

If you want to erase all the entries for a given day, week, or month, use the Purge command instead of repeatedly issuing the Remove command. Again, make sure that you have highlighted the right time period; there is no double-check.

Changing an Entry (Edit Command)

The Edit command is used to make changes to an existing meeting or task entry. If you have meetings or tasks that sometimes need to be rescheduled (and who doesn't?), the Edit command is particularly useful. When you change the date or the time, the entry is automatically moved to the correct location on the calendar.

Move the highlighted block to the appropriate entry and issue the command. The editing screen is similar to the Insert screen, but the entries on this screen are already filled in. The Insert key toggles between Overlay and Insert modes, but the mode is not indicated on the screen. Press F10 to save the changed item.

Copying an Entry (Use Command)

The Use command allows you to make a copied variation of an entry instead of changing an existing entry with the Edit command. For instance, if a meeting is held regularly each week, you can use this command to copy the entry to other dates. The Use command permits you to change any of the items if the topic changes from week to week; in this way the Use command is similar to the Edit command.

Displaying the Week Screen (Display Command)

The Display command is used to display the week screen (see fig. 29.2) or the month screen (see fig. 29.3). You are prompted for the display type (either Week or Month). Press Escape or Enter to return to the day screen. Quick keys are Alt-W (Display Week) and Alt-M (Display month.)

Locating a Day Screen (Find Command)

The Find command is used to search for another day screen with a scheduled meeting or task. You have the options of searching for the first day in your calendar with a scheduled item, the last day, the next day, or the previous day.

Displaying Specific Day Screens (Goto Command)

If you want to see the calendar for a specific day, use the Goto command. Enter a specific date, and the calendar for that day is displayed. If you enter an invalid date, you will get the message incorrect command syntax.

Dates are normally entered in the format MM/DD/YY, but if you are working within the the current year, you can enter the date in the format MM/DD.

If you want to skip ahead a certain number of days, just enter the number. Enter a negative number to jump backward.

Loading Time Manager Files (Load Command)

When you first enter the Time Manager, the default file STM.DTM is automatically loaded for you. If you are the only user of this module, this file is sufficient. If several users keep their calendars on the system, however, they can name their own files and use the Load command to call up the files.

The Load command prompts you for a file name, which can be any legal DOS file name and extension. Instead of supplying both a file name and extension, let the system supply the default extension of .STM. When you initiate the Load command, all files with the .STM extension will be displayed in a pop-up menu. Files with other extensions will not be displayed.

Printing Time Manager Reports (Output Command)

Use the Output command to generate a printed report that shows all scheduled tasks and meetings (see fig. 29.5). You are then prompted to select

Short Long

The short output is shown in figure 29.5; if you select Long, the long descriptions are shown under each item.

```
                    NOVEMBER  7, 1985 THURSDAY
                    --------------------------


Priority: 1 ....... Call SyCon re new program

Priority: 2 ....... Review Mary's Job

Priority: 3 ....... Write Arnold on trip

Time: 9:45 Am ..... Staff Meeting - Budget

Time: 11:30 Am .... Jane - Lunch - Andre's

Time: 3:00 Pm ..... Alpha - Contract

Time: 4:30 Pm ..... Call Calif Office
```

Fig. 29.5. *The day report.*

You can request output for the Day, the Week, or the Month; one page per day is generated in each case. If nothing is scheduled on a given day, no output is generated when you request the Week or the Month report.

Conclusion

With today's busy schedules, any aid to time management is welcome. The Smart Time-Manager provides capabilities to help you manage your time, meetings, and tasks in an organized manner.

Part V

Using Smart's Other System Features

Chapter 30

Using Smart's Date, Time, and Text Functions

Throughout the Smart system, you may need to use formulas and functions to perform calculations, table lookups, evaluations for branching, or string concatenations. The Smart system provides several types of operators and a whole library of functions.

The Smart Operators

Operators fall into different categories, reflecting the types of data they deal with and the results they return.

Numeric Operators

The most common operators are numeric—the familiar operators for addition, subtraction, etc. The numeric operators are

Operator	Function
+	Addition
–	Subtraction
*	Multiplication
/	Division
^	Exponentiation

You use these operators when you work with only numbers and expect the answer to be a number. Remember the order of precedence when you use these operators:

1. Parentheses
2. Exponentiation
3. Multiplication and Division
4. Addition and Subtraction
5. Left to right

You may want to use parentheses to clarify the meaning of a formula, even when the standard order of precedence does not make the parentheses necessary. Extra parentheses, inserted for readability, do not affect the calculation.

Text Operators

The text operators, which are used to concatenate text items, are

Operator	Function
&	Concatenate *with* a space separator
|	Concatenate *without* a space

An example of the use of these operators is

$city|","&$state&$zip

This formula concatenates the contents of the variables named *$city*, *$state*, and *$zip*. The comma, entered as a text literal enclosed in double quotation marks, is concatenated with the contents of *$city*; no space separates the two items. The contents of the other variables are concatenated with spaces.

Relational Operators

Both numeric and text operators return a value or a result that can be either printed or inserted in a cell or field. Relational operators, on the other hand, are used to evaluate expressions; these operators return a value of *true* or *false*, which is used to "make a decision"—in a data base query or a spreadsheet formula, for instance. The relational operators are

Operator	Function
=	Equal to
>	Greater than
<	Less than
>=	Greater than or equal to
<=	Less than or equal to
< >	Unequal

In the Data Base Manager, for example, if you want to query for records of individuals earning more than $750.00, the statement is

[wage] > 750

These relational operators can be used for text as well as for numeric data. (If you are comparing values in alphanumeric text fields, you do not have to specify trailing blanks.) Three additional operators can be used *only* with text data:

Operator	Function
!	Contains
!!	Does not contain
==	Compare, ignoring case

A reverse operator (NOT) can be used, if needed, *only* with numeric expressions:

NOT (<numeric expression>)

Logical Operators

Logical operators are used to specify multiple logical conditions at the same time. The operators are

Operator	Function
AND	Both expressions must be true
OR	One expression must be true

For example:

[state] = "MA" and [wage] > 750

Be careful when you use AND and OR; we sometimes say *AND* when, in computer terms, we really mean *OR*. For example, to find all employees in Massachusetts and Connecticut, you might be tempted to write:

[state] = "MA" AND [state] = "CT"

This query would retrieve no records, because one individual cannot reside in both states. The correct form is

[state] = "MA" OR [state] = "CT"

Sometimes you do want to use the AND operator on a single field. Consider the following example:

[zip] >= 63000 AND [zip] <= 63999

Both conditions must be met for the record to be selected; only those ZIP codes greater than or equal to *63000* and less than or equal to *63999* are selected. If you use *OR*, all records are selected because all ZIP codes meet one of those conditions.

Functions

Functions can be used in any expression in the Smart System. Functions can save you time by enabling you to do in one step what would otherwise take several; in fact, functions can provide capabilities that otherwise might not be possible at all. Most functions operate throughout the Smart system, but some are limited to a particular module.

The remainder of this chapter is devoted to an explanation of date, time, and text functions and their uses. Examples are provided where appropriate.

Date Functions

Smart System *date* functions are used to manipulate dates and times. Dates are actually stored as the number of days since December 31, 1899. Time values are stored as alphanumeric values in a special format. The use of date functions can save you many hours of work.

Name:	ADATE
Description:	Alpha Date
Module(s):	All
Format:	adate(d1) d1 = original date

Explanation:	Converts a date in the date 2 format to an alpha date.
Example:	adate(r14c2)
Result:	August 20, 1971
Date:	08-20-71

Name:	ADDDAYS
Description:	Add Days
Module(s):	All
Format:	adddays(d1,n1) d1 = original date n1 = number of days to add or subtract
Explanation:	Returns a date as the original date plus or minus the number of days added or subtracted.
Example:	adddays(r14c2,90)
Original:	08-20-71
Result:	11-18-71

Name:	ADDMONTHS
Description:	Add Months
Module(s):	All
Format:	addmonths(d1,n1) d1 = original date n1 = number of months to add or subtract
Explanation:	Returns a date as the original date plus or minus the number of months added or subtracted.
Example:	addmonths(r14c2,23)
Original:	08-20-71
Result:	07-20-73

Name:	ADDYEARS
Description:	Add Years
Module(s):	All

Format:	addyears(d1,n1) d1 = original date n1 = number of years to add or subtract
Explanation:	Returns a date as the original date plus or minus the number of years added or subtracted.
Example:	addyears(r14c2,16)
Original:	08-20-71
Result:	08-20-87
Name:	DATE1
Description:	Date 1 Format
Module(s):	All
Format:	date1(d1) d1 = date in text format
Explanation:	Converts a date to date 1 format.
Example:	date1(r14c2)
Original:	08-20-71
Result:	20-Aug-71
Notes:	The format of date1 is determined in the Configure command at the main menu.
Name:	DATE2
Description:	Date 2 Format
Module(s):	All
Format:	date2(d1) d1 = date in text format
Explanation:	Converts a date to date 2 format.
Example:	date2(r14c2)
Original:	20-Aug-71
Result:	08-20-71
Notes:	The format of date2 is determined in the Configure command at the main menu.

Name:	DATE3
Description:	Date 3 Format
Module(s):	All
Format:	date3(d1) d1 = date in text format
Explanation:	Converts a date to date 3 format.
Example:	date3(r14c2)
Original:	20-Aug-71
Result:	Aug 71

Name:	DAY (or @DAY)
Description:	Day of the Month
Module(s):	All
Format:	day(d1) d1 = original date
Explanation:	Returns a value representing the day of the month of the given date.
Example:	day(r14c2)
Original:	20-Aug-71
Result:	20.00
Notes:	The value returned is numeric.

Name:	DAYNAME
Description:	Name of the Day of the Week
Module(s):	All
Format:	dayname(d1) d1 = original date
Explanation:	Returns a text string with the name of the day of the week of the given date.
Example:	dayname(r14c2)
Original:	20-Aug-71
Result:	Friday
Notes:	The result is a text string.

Name:	DAYS
Description:	Number of Days since 12/31/1899
Module(s):	All
Format:	days(d1) d1 = original date
Explanation:	Returns the number of days since 12/31/1899.
Example:	days(r14c2)
Original:	25-May-69
Result:	25,347.00
Notes:	Especially useful for checking date ranges: days([empdate]) >= days("1/1/50") and days([empdate]) <= days("12/31/59") The days2 function provides a similar result: days2(n1,n2,n3) n1 = year, n2 = month, n3 = day

Name:	MONTH
Description:	Number of the Month
Module(s):	All
Format:	month(d1) d1 = original date
Explanation:	Returns the numeric number of the month.
Example:	month(r14c2)
Original:	27-Jun-43
Result:	6.00

Name:	MONTHNAME
Description:	Name of the Month
Module(s):	All
Format:	monthname(d1) d1 = original date

Explanation:	Returns the name of the month as a text string.
Example:	monthname(r14c2)
Original:	27-Jun-43
Result:	June

Name:	TODAY (or @TODAY)
Description:	Today's Date
Module(s):	All
Format:	today
Explanation:	Returns today's date in the date2 format.
Example:	today
Result:	02-10-86

Name:	YEAR
Description:	Number of the Year
Module(s):	All
Format:	year(d1) d1 = original date
Explanation:	Returns the number of the year as a number.
Example:	year(r14c2) @year(r14c2)
Original:	05-May-40
Result:	1,940.00 40.00
Notes:	The @year function returns only the last two digits of the year.

Time Functions

The time functions are used to add, subtract, and otherwise manipulate time fields and cells. In the Data Base Manager, time fields are a special data type; in the Spreadsheet, cells containing times are alpha fields in a special format.

Name:	ADDHOURS
Description:	Add Hours
Module(s):	All
Format:	addhours(t1,n1) t1 = a date or a time expression n1 = number of hours (integer)
Explanation:	Adds the number of hours (n1) to the date or time represented by t1. If t1 is a date, the result is a date; if t1 is time, the result is time.

Example:	addhours(r14c2,36)	addhours(r14c5,4)
Original:	11-22-63	11:30am
Result:	11-23-63	15:30:00

Notes:	Only integer hours can be added. Time value "wraps around" only if the 24-hour clock is used.

Name:	ADDMINUTES
Description:	Add Minutes
Module(s):	All
Format:	addminutes(t1,n1) t1 = a date or time expression n1 = number of minutes
Explanation:	Adds a number of minutes to the time or date in the argument t1.

Example:	addminutes(r14c2,22)	addminutes(r14c5,95)
Original:	3:45:37	23:57:32
Result:	04:07:37	01:32:32

Notes:	To "wrap around" midnight, use the 24-hour clock.

Name:	ADDSECONDS
Description:	Add Seconds
Module(s):	All
Format:	addseconds(t1,n1) t1 = time or date expression n1 = number of seconds

Explanation: Adds the number of seconds in n1 to the date or time in t1.

Example: addseconds(r14c2,5280)

Original: 7:37:22

Result: 09:05:22

Name: ATIME

Description: Elapsed Time in AM/PM Format

Module(s):   All

Format: atime(n1)
n1 = number of minutes

Explanation: Result of the expression is the number of minutes elapsed from the beginning of the day (00:00:00). The result is in AM/PM format.

Example: atime(r14c2)   atime(r14c4)

Original: 500   1300

Result: 08:20:00A   09:40:00P

Notes: Function wraps around to PM or to the next day.

Name: ATIME24

Description: Elapsed Time in 24-hour Format

Module(s):   All

Format: atime24(n1)
n1 = number of minutes

Explanation: Result of the expression is the number of minutes elapsed from the beginning of the day (00:00:00). Result is in 24-hour format.

Example: atime24(r14c2)   atime24(r14c4)

Original: 500   1520

Result: 08:20:00   01:20:00

Notes: Function wraps around to the next day.

Name:	HOURS
Description:	Number of Hours Elapsed
Module(s):	All
Format:	hours(t1, [t2]) t1 = date or time t2 = time

Explanation: If t1 is time, function returns the number of hours since the beginning of the day. If t1 is a date, function yields the number of hours since the beginning of the century. Optional time t2 can be added to the elapsed time.

Example:	hours(r14c2)	hours(r14c4)	hours(r14c4,r14c6)
Original:	10:45	01-01-33	14:40
Result:	10.0	289296.0	289310.0

Notes: Result is an integer.

Name:	MINUTES
Description:	Number of Minutes Elapsed
Module(s):	All
Format:	minutes(t1, [t2]) t1 = date or time t2 = time

Explanation: If t1 is time, the function returns the number of minutes since the beginning of the day. If t1 is a date, function yields the number of minutes since the beginning of the century. Optional time t2 can be added to the elapsed time.

Example:	minutes(r14c2)	minutes(r14c4)	minutes(r14c4,r14c6)
Original:	10:45:33	01-Jan-09	14:40:17
Result:	645.0	4734720.0	4735600.0

Notes: Result is an integer value.

Name:	SECONDS
Description:	Number of Seconds Elapsed
Module(s):	All
Format:	seconds(t1, [t2]) t1 = date or time t2 = time
Explanation:	If t1 is time, function returns the number of seconds since the beginning of the day. If t1 is a date, function yields the number of seconds since the beginning of the century. Optional time t2 can be added to the elapsed time.

Example:	minutes(r14c2)	minutes(r14c4)	minutes(r14c4,r14c6)
Original:	10:45:33	01-Feb-01	14:40:17
Result:	38733.0	34300800.0	34353617.0

Name:	TIME and TIME24
Description:	System Time
Module(s):	All
Format:	time time24
Explanation:	Returns the current system time in your chosen configuration. (See the Configure command at the main menu.)

Example:	time	time24
Result:	05:30:58P	17:30:58

Text Functions

Name:	ASC
Description:	ASCII Value
Module(s):	All
Format:	asc(t1) t1 = text field or cell
Explanation:	Returns the ASCII value in decimal form of the first character of the text t1.

Example:	asc(r14c2)	asc(r14c3)	asc(r14c6)
Original:	A	a	ABC
Result:	65	97	65

Name:	CHR
Description:	Character
Module(s):	All
Format:	chr(n1)
	n1 = decimal ASCII representation of a character
Explanation:	Returns a text character corresponding to the numerical argument n1.

Example:	chr(r14c2)	chr(r14c4)
Original:	65.00	353.00
Result:	A	a

Notes:	Original value is interpreted as mod 256; thus chr(353) returns 97.

Name:	CURRENCY
Description:	Currency Conversion
Module(s):	All
Format:	currency(n1)
	n1 = numeric expression
Explanation:	Function returns text expression in currency format.
Example:	currency(r14c2)
Original:	19.95
Result:	$19.95

Name:	FIXED
Description:	Number-to-Text Conversion
Module(s):	All
Format:	fixed(n1,n2)
	n1 = original number
	n2 = number of decimal places

Explanation:	Converts a number to a text string. The number of decimal places is determined by the second argument, n2.
Example:	fixed(r14c2,2) fixed(r14c2,0) fixed(r14c2,3)
Original:	19.956
Result:	19.96 20 19.956
Notes:	Result is rounded to the specified number of decimal places.

Name:	VAL
Description:	Value from Text
Module(s):	All
Format:	val(t1) t1 = text string containing digits
Explanation:	Converts a text string to a value. Conversion is from left to right, and is halted at the first nonnumeric character.
Example:	val(r14c2) val(r14c4) val(r14c6) val(r14c8)
Original:	19.95 25% 23 Skidoo –55
Result:	19.95 25.00 23.00 –55.00
Notes:	The characters "%" and "$" are not considered part of the numeric set, and halt the conversion. The minus sign is interpreted as part of the number.

Name:	STR
Description:	Numeric-to-String Conversion
Modules:	All
Format:	str(n1 , [n2]) n1 = numeric expression n2 = optional number of significant digits
Explanation:	Converts a number to text. If n2 is omitted, the entire number is converted, regardless of the numeric display. If n2 is entered, it specifies the number of significant digits. Rounding may take place.

Example:	str(r14c2,2)	str(r14c2)	str(r14c2,6)
Original:	5280.345		
Result:	5300	5280.345	5280.35

Notes: Compare to the FIXED function, in which you specify the number of decimal places. STR can be used to specify the number of significant digits. Rounding takes place.

Name: LEFT

Description: Left Portion of String

Module(s): All

Format: left(t1,n1)
t1 = text string
n1 = number of characters to extract

Explanation: Extracts the leftmost portion of a string of text. The argument n1 specifies the number of characters to be extracted.

Example: left(r14c2,4)

Original: Dogs and Cats

Result: Dogs

Name: RIGHT

Description: Right Portion of a String

Module(s): All

Format: right(t1,n1)
t1 = text string
n1 = number of characters to extract

Explanation: Extracts the right portion of a string of text. The argument n1 specifies the number of characters to be extracted.

Example: right(r14c2,4)

Original: Dogs and Cats

Result: Cats

Name:	MID
Description:	Middle Portion of String
Module(s):	All
Format:	mid(t1 , n1 [, n2]) t1 = text string n1 = starting position n2 = optional length of returned string
Explanation:	Extracts the middle portion of a string of text. N1 specifies the beginning position within the string. The optional second numeric argument n2 specifies the length of the returned string. If n2 is omitted, the entire portion of the string to the right of n1 is returned.
Example:	mid(r14c2,6,3) mid(r14c2,6)
Original:	Dogs and Cats
Result:	and and Cats
Notes:	If argument n2 is omitted, MID functions like RIGHT, except that you specify the starting position instead of the length of the string.

Name:	LEN
Description:	Length of String
Module(s):	All
Format:	len(t1) t1 = text expression
Explanation:	Returns the length of the text as an integer number.
Example:	len(r14c2) len(" 2345 ")
Original:	Dogs and Cats
Result:	13.00 6.00

Name:	MATCH
Description:	Matches a String
Module(s):	All
Format:	match(t1,t2 [,n1]) t1 = text string to search in t2 = text string to search for n1 = optional starting position in t1

Explanation:	Function returns a number, which is the starting location of t2 in t1; n1 indicates the point in t1 at which the search begins. If n1 is omitted, n1 defaults to 1. If the string t2 is not found, the function returns a zero.

Example:	match(r14c2,".")	match(r14c5,"am",6)
Original:	Debbie A. Linden	Name: James Taylor
Result:	9.00	8.00

Name:	TRIM
Description:	Trims Leading and Trailing Spaces
Module(s):	All
Format:	trim(t1) t1 = text string
Explanation:	Removes all leading and trailing spaces from a text string. Returns a text string.
Example:	trim("St. Louis ")|","&trim("Missouri")&"63132"
Result:	St. Louis, Missouri 63132
Notes:	This function is useful when concatenating strings.

Name:	LOWER
Description:	Lowercase Conversion
Module(s):	All
Format:	lower(t1) t1 = text string
Explanation:	Converts text to lowercase. Returns text.
Example:	lower(r14c2)
Original:	WATKINS
Result:	watkins
Notes:	Only alphabetic characters are affected. Numbers in the text string are unaffected.

Name:	UPPER
Description:	Uppercase Conversion
Module(s):	All
Format:	upper(t1) t1 = text string
Explanation:	Function converts text to uppercase. Returns text.
Example:	upper(r14c2)
Original:	watkins
Result:	WATKINS
Notes:	Only alphabetic characters are affected. Numbers in the text string are unaffected.

Name:	PROPER
Description:	Proper-Name Conversion
Module(s):	All
Format:	proper(t1) t1 = text string
Explanation:	Converts the text string so that the first letter of each word is uppercase and the rest are lowercase.
Example:	proper(r14c2)
Original:	horton a. watkins
Result:	Horton A. Watkins
Notes:	Be careful; if a Roman numeral follows the name, *III* becomes *Iii*.

Name:	CELLTEXT
Description:	Cell-Contents Display Format
Module(s):	Spreadsheet
Format:	celltext(t1) t1 = text expression representing cell address
Explanation:	Function returns a text expression that is an exact representation of what is displayed in the cell, including blanks and format characters. Individual cells or blocks of cells can be addressed.

Example:	celltext("r15c2")	celltext("r15c5:7")
Original:	$2.33	01/01/86 34.56% 10:16pm
Result:	$2.33	01/01/86 34.56% 10:16pm

Notes: Celltext can be used with Length to calculate the width of a column.

Example: len(celltext("r15c2"))

Result: 10.00

Name: MAKECELL

Description: String Cell-Reference

Module(s):   Spreadsheet

Format: makecell(n1,n2)
n1 = row number expression
n2 = column number expression

Explanation: Creates a cell-reference text string in the form *r1c2*.

Example:	makecell(row,column)	makecell(r14c5,r14c6)
Original:		5.00 18.00
Result:	r14c2	r5c18

Name: MAKEBLOCK

Description: Block-Reference String

Module(s):   Spreadsheet

Format: makeblock(n1,n2,n3,n4)
n1 = starting row number, n2 = ending row number
n3 = starting column, n4 = ending column

Explanation: Creates a block-reference text string in the form *r1:2c5:18*.

Example: makeblock(r14c2,r14c3,r14c4,r14c5)

Original: 1.00 2.00 5.00 18.00

Result: r1:2c5:18

Name:	REPEAT
Description:	Repeats a Text String
Module(s):	All
Format:	repeat(t1,n1) t1 = text string n1 = number of occurrences
Explanation:	Repeats a text string a number of times, as determined by the value of n1.
Example:	repeat(r14c2,r14c3)
Original:	=∗ 5.00
Result:	=∗=∗=∗=∗=∗

Name:	REINVERT
Description:	Converts Inverted Name to Noninverted Name
Module(s):	Data Base Manager
Format:	reinvert(t1) t1 = text string
Explanation:	Converts an inverted name to the original uninverted format.
Example:	reinvert("Watkins Horton")
Result:	Horton Watkins

Chapter 31

Using Smart's Mathematical Functions

This chapter presents Smart's business and mathematical functions. The relational operators that are usable with the date, time, and text functions covered in Chapter 30 can be used also with these functions.

Business Functions

Following are examples of the business functions available within the Smart System. When you use these functions, make sure that the interest rate and the term are expressed in the same units of time: If the term is expressed in years, the interest should be expressed as an annual rate. If the term is expressed in months, the interest rate should be the annual rate divided by 12.

Name:	FV
Description:	Future Value
Module(s):	All
Format:	fv(n1, n2, n3) n1 = payment amount, n2 = term, n3 = interest rate
Explanation:	Calculates the future value of a current one-time payment at a specified interest rate over a term expressed in years.

Example:	fv(159.66, 3, .5)
Result:	538.85
Notes:	This is not the same function as @FV or FVA, which follow. Compare this function to PV, which calculates present rather than future value.

Name:	FVA (or @FV)
Description:	Future Value Annuity
Module(s):	All
Format:	fva(n1, n2, n3) n1 = equal payment amount, n2 = term years n3 = interest rate
Explanation:	Calculates the future value of a series of equal payments, given the term in years and the annual interest rate.
Example:	fva(100, 5.5, .1)
Result:	689.12
Notes:	If you use @FV, n2 = interest and n3 = term.

Name:	INTEREST
Description:	Interest Rate
Module(s):	All
Format:	interest(n1, n2, n3) n1 = principal, n2 = payment, n3 = term years
Explanation:	Calculates interest rate from principal, payment, and term.
Example:	interest(12462.21, 1000, 20)
Result:	0.05
Notes:	Payment is annual.

Name:	IRR (or @IRR)
Description:	Internal Rate of Return
Module(s):	All
Format:	irr(n1, block) n1 = first approximation block = income stream

Explanation:	Calculates the internal rate of return for a stream of positive and negative payments. The calculation is iterated 20 times.
Example:	irr(.10, r14c2:7)
Result:	0.08
Stream:	−100 50.00 25.00 10.00 15.00 20.00
Name:	NPV
Description:	Net Present Value
Module(s):	All
Format:	npv(n1, block) n1 = interest rate, block = cash flow stream
Explanation:	Calculates the net present value of a stream of cash flows, assuming a constant interest rate.
Example:	npv(.07, r14c2:6)
Result:	303.28
Stream:	25 50 25 70 200
Notes:	Slightly different from the @NPV formula.
Name:	PMT (or @PMT)
Description:	Payments
Module(s):	All
Format:	pmt(n1, n2, n3) n1 = principal, n2 = term, n3 = interest rate
Explanation:	Calculates the equal payments required to pay back the principal at the specified rate over the term.
Example:	pmt(12462.21, 20, .05)
Result:	1,000.00
Notes:	See PRINCIPAL, INTEREST, and TERM.
Name:	PRINCIPAL
Description:	Principal
Module(s):	All

Format:	principal(n1, n2, n3) n1 = payment amount, n2 = term, n3 = interest rate
Explanation:	Calculates the beginning principal amount needed to produce the payment over the term at the interest rate.
Example:	principal(1000, 20, .05)
Result:	12,462.21
Notes:	See PMT, INTEREST, and TERM.
Name:	PV
Description:	Present Value
Module(s):	All
Format:	pv(n1, n2, n3) n1 = future lump-sum payment, n2 = term n3 = interest rate
Explanation:	Calculates the value today of a lump-sum payment in the future, given the term and the interest rate.
Example:	pv(538.85, 3, .5)
Result:	159.66
Notes:	Compare to FV, which calculates the future value of a lump sum payment.
Name:	PVA (or @PV)
Description:	Present Value Annuity
Module(s):	All
Format:	pva(n1, n2, n3) n1 = payment amount, n2 = term, n3 = interest rate
Explanation:	Calculates today's value of a set of equal annuity payments over a specified term at a given rate.
Example:	pva(1000, 20, .05)
Result:	12,462.21
Notes:	Same as @PV and PRINCIPAL functions

Name:	TERM
Description:	Calculates Term
Module(s):	All
Format:	term(n1, n2, n3) n1 = principal, n2 = payment, n3 = interest rate
Explanation:	Calculates the term, given the principal, the payment amount, and the interest rate.
Example:	term(12462.21, 1000, .05)
Result:	20.00
Notes:	See PRINCIPAL, PMT, and INTEREST.

Name:	SLN
Description:	Straight-Line Depreciation
Module(s):	All
Format:	sln(n1, n2, n3) n1 = original cost basis, n2 = salvage value n3 = useful life of asset, in years
Explanation:	Returns the straight-line annual depreciation of an asset over its useful life.
Example:	sln(r14c2, r14c3, r14c4)
Original:	12,000 5,000 3
Result:	2,333.33
Notes:	Result is the same as (n1−n2)/n3.

Numeric Functions

Numeric functions operate on numeric values only. These functions can be used in a variety of applications.

Name:	ABS (or @ABS)
Description:	Absolute Value
Module(s):	All
Format:	abs(n1) n1 = numeric value

Explanation:	Returns the absolute value of a numeric value in a field, cell, or expression.		
Example:	abs(r14c2)	abs(r14c4)	abs(r14c2*r14c4)
Original:	–5.00	5.00	
Result:	5.00	5.00	25.00

Name:	INT
Description:	Integer Value
Module(s):	All
Format:	int(n1) n1 = numeric field, cell or expression
Explanation:	Returns the integer value that is less than or equal to n1.

Example:	int(r14c2)	int(r14c4)	@int(r14c6)
Original:	23.40	–3.50	–3.50
Result:	23.00	–4.00	–3.00
Notes:	Function @int returns a different value for negative numbers.		

Name:	MOD
Description:	Modulus
Module(s):	All
Format:	mod(n1, n2) n1 = first numeric value n2 = second numeric value
Explanation:	Returns the remainder when n1 is divided by n2.
Example:	mod(r14c2, r14c3)
Original:	9.00 7.00
Result:	2.00

Name:	PI
Description:	Pi
Module(s):	All
Format:	pi

Explanation:	Function returns value of pi.
Example:	pi
Result:	3.141592654
Name:	ROUND (or @ROUND)
Description:	Rounds a Numeric Expression
Module(s):	All
Format:	round(n1) n1 = numeric field, cell, or expression n2 = number of decimal places
Explanation:	Returns a numeric value rounded to the specified number of decimal places.

Example:	round(r14c2, 2)	round(r14c2, 1)
Original:	5.245	
Result:	5.250	5.200

Notes:	Remember that the decimal precision feature in the Spreadsheet displays a value as though it were rounded, although it is not really rounded. This function actually rounds the value.

Random Functions

Random functions return random values that fall within a specified range according to one of several distribution patterns. These functions are used most often in modeling and simulation applications.

Name:	EXPONENTIAL
Description:	Random Number from an Exponential Curve
Module(s):	All
Format:	exponential(n1) n1 = numeric mean of curve
Explanation:	Returns a number randomly selected from an exponential distribution.

Example:	exponential(5)
Result:	0.74
Notes:	The value changes every time you recalculate the worksheet.

Name:	NORMAL
Description:	Random Number from a Normal Distribution
Module(s):	All
Format:	normal(n1) n1 = standard deviation
Explanation:	Returns a number randomly selected from a normal distribution.
Example:	normal(8.3)
Result:	–9.16
Notes:	The value changes every time you recalculate the worksheet.

Name:	RAND (or @RAND)
Description:	Random Number between 0 and 1
Module(s):	All
Format:	rand
Explanation:	Returns a random number in the range 0 to 1.
Example:	rand
Result:	0.32
Notes:	Same as the UNIFORM function with an argument of 1.

Name:	UNIFORM
Description:	Random Number
Module(s):	All
Format:	uniform(n1) n1 = top end of uniform range
Explanation:	Returns a number at random in the range 0 to n1.
Example:	uniform(100)
Result:	66.95
Notes:	Value changes every time you recalculate the worksheet.

Statistical Functions

These statistical functions are available in all modules of the Smart System.

Name:	AVERAGE (or @AVG)
Description:	Average
Module(s):	All
Format:	average(n1, n2, n3 . . . nn) n1 = numeric
Explanation:	Returns the arithmetic mean. Empty fields or cells are not averaged; zero values are averaged.
Example:	average(r14c2:6)
Original:	5.00 10.00 15.00 20.00 25.00
Result:	15.00
Notes:	Same as SUM/COUNT.

Name:	COUNT (or @COUNT)
Description:	Counts Items in List
Module(s):	All
Format:	count(n1, n2, n3 . . . nn) n1 = numeric
Explanation:	Returns a count of items in a list. Empty fields or cells are not counted; zero values are counted.
Example:	count(r14c2:6)
Original:	5.00 15.00 0.00 25.00
Result:	4.00

Name:	FACTORIAL
Description:	Factorial Calculation
Module(s):	All
Format:	factorial(n1) n1 = positive number

Explanation:	Calculates the product of the integer numbers between 1 and n1.
Example:	factorial(4) 1 * 2 * 3 * 4
Result:	24.00 24.00

Name:	MAX (or @MAX)
Description:	Maximum Value in a List
Module(s):	All
Format:	max(n1, n2 ... [, nn]) n1 = numeric
Explanation:	Returns the maximum value in a list of values.
Example:	max(r14c2:6)
Original:	1.00 5.00 3.00 7.00 8.00
Result:	8.00
Notes:	Nonnumeric entries are ignored.

Name:	MIN (or @MIN)
Description:	Minimum Value in a List
Module(s):	All
Format:	min(n1, n2 ... [, nn]) n1 = numeric
Explanation:	Returns the minimum value from a list of values.
Example:	min(r14c2:6)
Original:	1.00 5.00 3.00 7.00 8.00
Result:	1.00
Notes:	Nonnumeric entries are ignored.

Name:	STD (or @STD)
Description:	Standard Deviation in a Population
Module(s):	All
Format:	std(n1, n1 ... [, nn]) n1 = numeric

Explanation:	Returns the standard deviation of the population in a list.
Example:	std(r14c2:6)
Original:	12.34 32.50 9.78 45.99 21.44
Result:	13.41
Notes:	Nonnumeric values are ignored. The list must have a minimum of two entries. Returns the square root of the value returned by @VAR.

Name:	STDEV
Description:	Standard Deviation of a Sample
Module(s):	All
Format:	stdev(n1, n1 . . . [, nn]) n1 = numeric
Explanation:	Returns the standard deviation of the sample for a list of items.
Example:	stdev(r14c2:6)
Original:	12.34 32.50 9.78 45.99 21.44
Result:	15.00
Notes:	Nonnumeric values are ignored. The list must have a minimum of two entries. Returns the square root of the value returned by the VAR function.

Name:	VAR
Description:	Sample Variance
Module(s):	All
Format:	var(n1, n1 . . . [, nn]) n1 = numeric
Explanation:	Returns the variance of a sample for the list of items.
Example:	var(r14c2:6)
Original:	12.34 32.50 9.78 45.99 21.44
Result:	224.92
Notes:	Nonnumeric values are ignored. The list must have a minimum of two entries. Use @VAR for variance of the population.

Name:	SUM (or @SUM)
Description:	Sum of Numeric Values
Module(s):	All
Format:	sum(n1, n1 . . . [, nn])
	n1 = numeric
Explanation:	Returns the arithmetic sum of the values in a list.
Example:	sum(r14c2:6)
Original:	12.34 32.50 9.78 45.99 21.44
Result:	122.05
Notes:	Nonnumeric values are ignored.

Name:	SUMSQ
Description:	Sum of Squares
Module(s):	All
Format:	sumsq(n1, n1 . . . [, nn])
	n1 = numeric
Explanation:	Returns the sum of the squares of items in a list.
Example:	sumsq(r14c2:6)
Original:	12.34 32.50 –9.78 45.99 21.44
Result:	3,878.93
Notes:	Nonnumeric values are ignored.

Logical Functions

Logical functions provide varying forms of abbreviated table-lookup facilities, If . . . Then . . . Else capabilities, and True/False evaluations.

Name:	CASE
Description:	Case Match
Module(s):	All

Format:	case v1 (s1, r1) (s2, r2) . . . (sn, rn) else v2
	v1 = original value
	s1 = search match 1, r1 = return value 1
	v2 = default value
Explanation:	Case works like a "short" table-lookup function. The function matches the original value v1 against s1, s2, etc. If a match is found, the corresponding *r* value is returned. If no match is found, the default v2 is returned.
Example:	case r14c2 (1,2390) (2,3540) (3,1770) (4,2390) else 999
Original:	2.00
Result:	3,540.00
Notes:	There must be an exact match between the original value and a search value. Either numeric values or text items are acceptable. For range matches, use HLOOKUP or VLOOKUP. Search items do not have to be in order.

Name:	SELECT
Description:	Selection
Module(s):	All
Format:	select(e1, r1) (e2, r2) . . . (en, rn) else v1
	e1 = logical expression
	v1 = default value
Explanation:	Each logical expression is evaluated in turn. For the first one found to be true, the corresponding *r* value is returned. If no expression is true, the default value v1 is returned.
Example:	select(r14c2>2, 100) (r14c3<5, 20) (r14c4=10, 55) else 999
Original:	2.00 4.00 10.00
Result:	20.00
Notes:	Logical expressions do not have to refer to the same set of fields or cells. Numeric and text values may be mixed.

Name:	IF
Description:	If . . . Then . . . Else
Module(s):	All

Format:	if (e1) then v1 else v2
	e1 = logical expression
	v1, v2 = result expressions

Explanation: The logical expression e1 is evaluated. If it is true, v1 is returned; if it is false, v2 is returned. Expressions may be nested; the first true expression terminates the function. Values or expressions can be returned.

Example: see figure 31.1

Original: 2.00   4.00   10.00

Result: 20.00

Notes: The If . . . Then . . . Else expression corresponds to the example for the SELECT function.

```
┌─ Formula Editor ═══════════════════════════════════════════════════════════
│if r14c2 > 2   then 100 else
│if r14c3 < 5   then 20  else
│if r14c4 = 10 then 55  else 999
│
│
```

Fig. 31.1. *An If . . . Then . . . Else test.*

Name:	CHOOSE (or @CHOOSE)
Description:	Ordinal Match
Module(s):	All
Format:	choose (v1, i1, i2, i3 . . . in)
	v1 = original value
	i1 = item one

Explanation: Similar to the case function, except that the item returned is determined by the value of v1. If v1 evaluates to 2, the third item in the list is returned.

Example: choose(r14c2, "north", "south", "east", "west")

Original: 2.00

Result: east

Notes: If the original value is zero, blank, or text, the first item in the list is returned. There is no Else condition, as there is with the CASE function.

Name:	FALSE (or @FALSE)
Description:	False Condition
Module(s):	All
Format:	false
Explanation:	Returns the false indicator (0) for use with logical expressions.
Example:	if r14c2 < 10 then false else true
Original:	5.00
Result:	0.00

Name:	TRUE (or @TRUE)
Description:	True Condition
Module(s):	All
Format:	true
Explanation:	Returns the true indicator (1) for use with logical expressions.
Example:	if r14c2 < 10 then false else true
Original:	55.00
Result:	1.00

Name:	LOGICAL
Description:	Logical Evaluation
Module(s):	All
Format:	logical(e1) e1 = expression containing logical operator(s) and operands
Explanation:	Returns true (1) if the expression is true, or false (0) if the expression is false.
Example:	logical(r14c2 > 0)
Original:	5.72
Result:	1.00

Name:	NOT	
Description:	Tests for Opposite	
Module(s):	All	
Format:	not(e1) e1 = logical expression	
Explanation:	Returns false (0) if the expression is true, or true (1) if the expression is false.	
Example:	not(r14c2 = "ACCT")	not(r14c2 <> "ACCT")
Original:	ACCT	
Result:	0.00	1.00

Name:	ISNUMBER		
Description:	Tests for Numeric Value		
Module(s):	All		
Format:	isnumber(v1) v1 = value		
Explanation:	Returns true (1) if the value v1 is a number, or false (0) if the value is not a number.		
Example:	isnumber(r14c2)	isnumber(r14c4)	isnumber(r14c7)
Original:	ACCT	55.00	01-01-86
Result:	0	1	1

Name:	ISSTRING
Description:	Tests for String Value
Module(s):	All
Format:	isstring(v1) v1 = value

Explanation:	Returns true (1) if the value v1 is a string, or false (0) if the value is not a string.
Example:	isstring(r14c2) isstring(r14c4) isstring(r14c7)
Original:	ACCT 55.00 01-01-86
Result:	1 0 0
Notes:	A date in Spreadsheet is evaluated as a number; in the Data Base Manager, a date is evaluated as a string.

Name:	COLLATE
Description:	Compares Text Expressions
Module(s):	All
Format:	collate(t1, t2) t1 = first text expression t2 = second text expression
Explanation:	The two text expressions are compared, ignoring case. If t1 $<$ t2, result is –1; if t1 = t2, result is 0; if t1 $>$ t2, result is 1.
Example:	collate(r14c2, r14c3) collate(r14c3, r14c6)
Original:	McAliffe MCALIFFE McCarthy
Result:	0.00 –1.00
Notes:	All punctuation characters are evaluated as being equal.

Transcendental Functions

The following *transcendental* functions, used primarily in scientific and mathematic applications, are available in the Smart system:

Function	Description
COSH	Hyperbolic cosine
EXP	Value of the natural logarithm *e*
LN	Natural logarithm base e
LOG10	Logarithm base 10
POWER	Raise to a power

SINH	Hyperbolic sine
SQRT	Square root

Trigonometric Functions

The following *trigonometric* functions are available in the Smart system:

Function	Description
ACOS	Arccosine calculation
ASIN	Arcsine calculation
ATAN	Arctangent calculation
ATAN2	Tangent with quadrant identification by the angle
COS	Cosine
SIN	Sine
TAN	Tangent

Input Functions

The following functions are used for input within the Smart system:

Name:	ASK
Description:	Asks for Input
Module(s):	All
Format:	ask(t1) t1 = text for prompt
Explanation:	Causes the text to be displayed on the command line and the value of the response to be entered into the cell or field.
Example:	ask(r14c2)
Original:	Enter the number of employees:
Result:	20.00

Name:	INCHAR
Description:	Input Character
Module(s):	All
Format:	inchar
Explanation:	Returns ASCII value of next key pressed.
Example:	inchar
Result:	114.00
Notes:	Particularly useful in project files for rapid execution

Name:	NEXTKEY
Description:	Next Key Pressed
Module(s):	All
Format:	nextkey
Explanation:	Returns the ASCII value of the next key waiting in the keyboard buffer. Program execution does not pause.
Example:	nextkey
Notes:	Useful for project files.

Miscellaneous Functions

The following miscellaneous functions are available within the Smart system:

Name:	CERROR
Description:	Command Error
Module(s):	Project files
Format:	if cerror = n1 then . . . n1 = error number
Explanation:	Returns any error number resulting from the preceding command in a project file. The error numbers are found in Appendix A of the Formula Reference section in the Smart System Manual.

Name:	COLUMN
Description:	Column Number
Module(s):	Spreadsheet
Format:	column
Explanation:	Returns the column number of the spreadsheet cell.
Example:	column
Result:	2.00.

Name:	ROW
Description:	Row Number
Module(s):	Spreadsheet
Format:	row
Explanation:	Returns the row number of the spreadsheet cell.
Example:	row
Result:	14.00

Name:	DELETED
Description:	Row Deleted
Module(s):	Data Base Manager
Format:	deleted
Explanation:	Useful in Data Base Manager Query command or in project files to determine whether the current record is deleted.
Example:	[dept] = "ACCT" and not (deleted)

Name:	ERROR
Description:	User-Defined Error
Module(s):	All
Format:	if e1 then v1 else error e1 = logical condition v1 = value

Explanation:	Used to create a user-defined error condition, based on the specifications of the logical condition. The error is displayed as *error 35*.
Example:	if r14c2 < 10 then .1 else error
Original:	25.00
Result:	Error 35

Name:	FILE
Description:	Tests for Existence of File
Module(s):	All
Format:	file(f1) f1 = filename and extension
Explanation:	Used to test for the existence of a file on disk. You must supply both the file name and the extension; a path is required if the file is not in the current subdirectory. The result is 1 if the file exists, or 0 if it does not exist.
Example:	file(r14c2) file(r14c4)
Original:	account.ws canada.ws
Result:	0.00 1.00
Notes:	Can be used in project files to make them more "foolproof."

Name:	HLOOKUP (or @HLOOKUP)
Description:	Horizontal Lookup
Module(s):	Spreadsheet
Format:	hlookup(s1, b1 [, o1]) s1 = item to search for b1 = block to search in o1 = offset from top row of block (optional)
Explanation:	The function searches the top row of the block for a value less than or equal to the search item. If no offset is provided, the function returns the value from the corresponding column on the last row of the block. If the offset is provided, it represents the number of rows from the top of the table.
Original:	5.20 4.47

Example:	hlookup(3, r16:19c2:6)	@hlookup(6.2, r16:19c2:6, 2)

Table:	0.50	3.00	5.00	7.00	9.00
	0.71	1.73	2.24	2.65	3.00
	1.41	3.46	4.47	5.29	6.00
	2.12	5.20	6.71	7.94	9.00

Notes: If you expect to find an exact match, the items in the top row need not be in order. The HLOOKUP function cannot handle a nonmatching element whose value lies between items in the top row of the table.

If you expect that the value of a search item might lie between the values in the top row, you must use @HLOOKUP and make sure that the values in the top row are in order. If no match is found, the column with the value less than s1 is used. In the example, the column for value 5 is used because the value 6.2 lies between 5 and 7.

Both HLOOKUP and @HLOOKUP can operate on values or text items.

Name: VLOOKUP (or @VLOOKUP)

Description: Vertical Lookup

Module(s): Spreadsheet

Format: vlookup(s1, b1 [, o1])
s1 = item to search for
b1 = block to search in
o1 = offset from top row of block (optional)

Explanation: The function searches the left column of the block for a matching value that is less than or equal to s1. If no offset is provided, the value from the row containing the matching item is returned. If an offset is provided, the offset value indicates the number of columns to the right of the left column; the value in that column is returned.

Original:	5.20	4.47

Example:	vlookup(3, r16:19c2:5)	@vlookup(6.2, r16:19c2:5, 2)

Table:	0.50	0.71	1.41	2.12
	3.00	1.73	3.46	5.20
	5.00	2.24	4.47	6.71
	7.00	2.65	5.29	7.94

Notes:	The VLOOKUP function must find an exact match, or an error occurs. With @VLOOKUP, however, a range is permissible: the value is retrieved from the row whose value matches or is less than the search item. In the example shown, 5.00 is the last item in the column that is less than or equal to the search value 6.2.
	Both VLOOKUP and @VLOOKUP work with text values as well as numeric values.

Name:	INDEX
Description:	Offset Cell Contents
Module(s):	Spreadsheet
Format:	index(b1, r1, c1) b1 = block r1 = offset rows c1 = offset columns
Explanation:	Returns the contents of a cell in the designated block, offset from the upper left corner of the block by r1 rows and c1 columns.
Example:	index(r15:17c2:4, 1, 2)
Result:	8.00

Table: 1.00 4.00 7.00
2.00 5.00 8.00
3.00 6.00 9.00

Notes:	The offset values indicate the number of rows down or columns over, but do not indicate the number of the row or column in the block. A row offset of 0 returns a value from the first row.

Name:	ISERR
Description:	Tests for Error
Module(s):	Spreadsheet
Format:	iserr(r1) r1 = cell reference
Explanation:	Returns true (1) if the cell contains an error, or false (0) if the cell does not contain an error.
Example:	iserr(r14c2)
Original:	Error 29
Result:	1.00

Name:	ISCALC
Description:	Tests for Spreadsheet Calculation
Module(s):	Worksheet
Format:	iscalc
Explanation:	Returns true (1) if the worksheet needs to be recalculated, or false (0) if it does not.
Example:	iscalc
Result:	1.00

Name:	ISNA
Description:	Tests for N/A
Module(s):	Spreadsheet
Format:	isna(r1) r1 = cell reference
Explanation:	Returns true (1) if the cell contains *N/A*, or false (0) if not. A cell contains *N/A* if the cell refers to a block name that has been undefined or to a worksheet that has been unloaded.
Example:	isna(r14c2)
Original:	N/A
Result:	1.00

Name:	NA
Description:	Not Available
Module(s):	Spreadsheet
Format:	if e1 then na else v1 e1 = logical expression v1 = value
Explanation:	Returns *N/A* if e1 is true, or v1 if it is not.
Example:	if r14c2 < 1000 then na else r14c2
Original:	100.00
Result:	N/A

Name:	ISBLANK
Description:	Tests for Blank Cell
Module(s):	Spreadsheet
Format:	isblank(r1) r1 = cell reference
Explanation:	Returns true (1) if the cell is blank, or false (0) if it is not blank.
Example:	isblank(r14c2)
Result:	1.00

Name:	NULL
Description:	Empty or Default String
Module(s):	All
Format:	null
Explanation:	Returns a string equal to the default value (see Notes) or an empty string, or tests a string for this condition.
Example:	[phone] = null and not(deleted)
Original:	(000) 000-0000
Notes:	Data Base Manager date field default: "00/00/00" Phone field default: (000) 000-0000 An empty cell in the Spreadsheet is not null; use the ISBLANK function to test for an empty cell.

Name:	NOCHANGE
Description:	No Change
Module(s):	Data Base Manager
Format:	nochange
Explanation:	Used to prevent the change of a field in the Data Base Manager.
Example:	if [quote] = null then [price]*[quant] else nochange
Notes:	The example prevents the change of the original contents of the quote field, even if price or quantity change.

The following two functions apply only to the Data Base Manager:

Name:	Record Numbers
Module:	Data Base Manager

Returns a physical or logical record number as indicated.

Physical record numbers are returned relative to the entire file in sequential order:

PRECORD   Physical record number

PRECORDS   Total number of records in file

Logical record numbers are returned relative to the current order of the file (index or key):

RECORD   Logical record number

RECORDS   Total number of logical records in file

Name:	TOTALS
Description:	Running Total of Field
Module(s):	Data Base Manager
Format:	totals(f1)

f1 = name or number of field for which totals are maintained

Explanation:	Primarily for use in project files; the total may be used in an expression.
Example:	lprint totals([tax])

Chapter 32

Using Smart's Project Processing

Although the ability to issue Smart commands one at a time from the keyboard provides ultimate flexibility for the knowledgeable user, that way of using the Smart System has its disadvantages. Some repetitive processes call for several steps to be performed in succession every time. These processes may be simple utilities that help with your work, or they may be complete applications.

Not everyone who uses the Smart System has the same level of expertise. As the system designer, you may want to develop an application for use by people who don't know anything about Smart. Not only do you want to ensure that all the steps are executed in the right order, but you also want the application to perform as much error checking as possible.

The Project Processing feature of the Smart System provides the capability of developing and executing sequences of commands contained within a disk file. Some of the commands in this chapter can be issued from the command level of a Smart application module; other commands are available only in the Project Processing environment or in particular modules. Each of the Project Processing commands is discussed in this chapter.

Project Processing files must contain commands specific to one module only; you cannot have both Data Base Manager and Word Processor commands in one file, for example. The execution of a project file can be transferred to another module, however, by a direct statement or by using the Send command.

Project File Operations

Project Processing commands are found on command list 5 of the application modules and on command list 3 of the main menu (see fig. 32.1.) The two commands associated with Project Processing are the Remember and Execute commands. The Remember command and its options are used to create and edit project files; the Execute command is used to begin the execution of a project file.

```
Command list 5:  Beep  Confidence  Display  Execute  F-Calculator
                 Input-Screen  Macro  Parameters  Remember  Send  Text-Editor
File: person    Window: 1                          Page: 1  Rec: 1  ( 1 )  Act: Y
 REMEMBER - create a new project file or modify an existing file
```

Fig. 32.1. *Command List 5.*

Creating and Editing a Project File (Remember)

Project Processing files can be created in several ways. The Smart Text-Editor (or another editor outside of Smart) can be used to create a file. You can also use the Remember Edit environment, which is similar to the Text-Editor. But the easiest way to create a project file is by using the Remember Start command (see fig. 32.2).

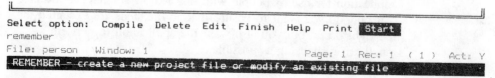

```
Select option:  Compile  Delete  Edit  Finish  Help  Print  Start
remember
File: person    Window: 1                          Page: 1  Rec: 1  ( 1 )  Act: Y
 REMEMBER - create a new project file or modify an existing file
```

Fig. 32.2. *Selecting the Remember Start command.*

After you select the Remember Start command and supply a project-file name, all commands you issue interactively are automatically recorded in the file. Instead of looking up the format of each command and writing the commands into a file, you simply issue the commands you need, and the system writes them to the file for you. Even if you make a mistake, you don't need to exit Remember mode; just enter the correct command and continue. Later, you can use the Remember Edit command to edit the file and remove or correct the errors.

Not every keystroke is entered in the project file, however. The commands for initiating the Smart data-entry screens are entered in the project file, for example, but the cursor movements and the data entered are not recorded. When you enter data in a spreadsheet, you are asked whether the data is to be entered on the sheet every time or whether the values are variables that should be changed each time the project file is run.

After you have finished entering the commands you want to record in the project file, select Remember Finish. This command stops the recording and compiles the commands so that the files are executed more efficiently. If you use the Remember Start or Remember Edit commands, the compilation is automatic. If you have created the project file in another editor or if you are upgrading to Smart 3.0 from previous versions, you must first select Compile before executing your project file.

If you have to compile a project file, you may do so either with or without line numbers. When you use the Remember Finish or Remember Edit commands, the system uses line numbers by default. A file without line numbers is a bit smaller, but if you want to be able to execute a file with Singlestep On or Quiet Off, you must use line numbers. (The Singlestep and Quiet options are discussed later in this chapter.)

When the file has been created with Remember Start and Remember Finish commands, use the Remember Edit command if you need to change the contents of the file or to add commands that are particular to project files. The Project File Editor screen, in figure 32.3, shows a short program for accumulating the values in a field.

The cursor keys used in the Text-Editor are available also in the Project File Editor. In addition to the function keys displayed at the bottom of the screen, the following keys can be used:

Keystrokes	Functions
Alt-F3	Reads in a disk file at cursor position
Ctrl-Y	Deletes a line (does not place line in delete buffer)
Alt-F2	Clears entire project editor
Esc	Exits project editor without saving

If you need to duplicate a line, first delete it by pressing F8. This keystroke moves the line to the Delete buffer; by pressing F7, you can then insert the line from the buffer as many times as you like.

```
┌─ Project File Editor ═══════════════════════════════════════════
│ comment  ********  ACCUMULATE FIELDS THROUGHOUT A FILE  *********
│ QUIET ON
│ %9 Enter field name:
│ let %9 = UPPER("%9")
│ let %3 = 0
│ goto record rec-number 1
│ label nexrec
│ let %3 = %3 + [%9]
│ if record = records then jump done
│ goto record next
│ jump nexrec
│ comment  *********  all done ... write last record  *********
│ label done
│ menu clear 7 0
│ beep 2
│ MENU PRINT 10 5 7 0 Total of %9 is: %3
│ MESSAGE Press <SPACE> to continue ...
│ REPAINT
│
└
```

```
F1 Help        F3 Find        F5 Replace              F7 Insert line        F9  Repeat
F2 Calc        F4 Goto        F6 List fields          F8 Delete line        F10 Finish
                                            Line:      1    Column:   1    Insert: ON
REMEMBER - create a new project file or modify an existing file
```

Fig. 32.3. *The Project File Editor.*

If you need more room than is available on one line, use the backslash (\ ) at the end to indicate that the project-file line continues on the next screen line.

Running a Project File (Execute)

To run the project file, issue the Execute command (refer to fig. 32.1). You are then prompted for the name of the project file to be run; execution begins immediately. The settings in your Parameters file determine some of the characteristics of execution (see fig. 32.4). If Singlestep is set to *Yes*, execution pauses after each line. If Quiet execution is set to *No*, each command is displayed on the command line as it is executed. Using these settings can be valuable for "debugging" a project file; the settings can be controlled from within the file, as well as by the Parameters settings.

To halt execution of a project file at any time, press Ctrl-Z. You are prompted to

Cancel or suspend execution (c/s)

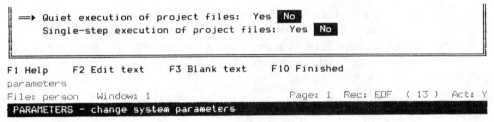

Fig. 32.4. *Setting project file parameters.*

Press *C* to cancel or *S* to suspend execution. If you suspend execution, you can perform Smart commands; before you can resume execution, however, you must restore all conditions (windows, records, etc.) to the state they were in when you suspended execution.

To resume execution, issue the Execute command again. Execution begins from the point at which it was suspended.

Project File Commands

The following section presents each of the project file commands. Note that although the case (upper or lower) of project-file contents is usually immaterial, LABELS and SCREEN NAMES are case sensitive and must be consistent.

Display Commands

Display commands are used to provide instructions or information to the operator of a project file.

The Beep Command

The Beep command is used to produce a tone or bell and to display an optional message in the control area.

Format: Beep n m
              n = number from 1 to 5, m = message
              (optional)

Example: Beep 3 End of Job

The maximum number of characters in the message is 78. The Beep command does not cause execution to pause as the message is displayed. To alert a user and allow time for the message to be read, use a Beep command followed by the Message or Wait command.

The Beep command defaults to one tone if the command is entered by itself. If you want to issue a message with one tone, enter the number *1*. Don't confuse this command with the Beep command in the application modules, which is used to turn on and off the audible error signal.

The Message Command

To issue a message in the control area without sounding a tone, use the Message command. Execution is suspended until you press any key. The maximum visible size of the message is 78 characters.

Format: Message m
                m = message

Example: Message Insert invoice form in printer.

The Wait Command

The Wait command suspends execution for a specified number of seconds and displays an optional message. If you press any key before the time is up, execution continues.

Format: Wait s m
                s = number of seconds to wait, m = message
                (optional)

Example: Wait 10 Phase 1 completed.

Because the Beep command does not pause to allow you to read the message, and because the Wait command does not beep, you may want to use the Beep command followed by the Wait command.

Control Commands

Control commands are used to control termination of a project file and execution of subsequent project files.

The Execute Command

If you want to execute another project file from within the current project file, and then continue with the original project file, use the Execute command. This is similar to the Execute command on command list 5 of the applications modules.

Format: Execute f
                f = project file name
                Execute f In-Memory

Example: Execute INVOICE

If the subordinate project file is small enough (less than 64K) and enough RAM is available, you can specify In-Memory for faster execution.

The Transfer Command

If you want to execute another project file from within the current one, but you do *not* want the current file to continue after execution of the subordinate file, use the Transfer command.

Format:	Transfer f
	f = project file name
	Transfer f In-Memory
Example:	Transfer ENDMONTH

The End Command

The End command halts execution of the current project. If the last line of the project file normally is executed, you do not need to enter an End statement as the final command. The End command is needed only when a certain condition causes termination.

Format:	End
Example:	if file("press.db") A = 0 then End

Note that the file name is enclosed in double quotation marks. If the argument of the function were a variable, such as $fn or %5, you would not use the quotation marks.

The End command terminates execution of only the current project file. If a subordinate project file encounters an End statement, control is returned to the primary file.

The Stop Command

To stop the execution of all project files, regardless of their status as subordinate or primary, use the Stop command. When this statement is encountered, you are returned to the command level.

Format:	Stop
Example:	If [wage] < 0 then Stop

The Suspend Command

To suspend execution of a project file and temporarily pass control to the keyboard, use the Suspend command. (This command has the same effect as pressing Ctrl-Z.) While execution is suspended, you can perform any operation except Execute, which resumes the processing of the project file. Be careful not to disturb anything that was created or established by the project file. If you reorder a file, for example, the project file does not automatically return the file to the desired order when execution is resumed.

Execution Order Commands

This section presents the commands you use to control the sequence of execution of commands in the project file.

The Jump Command

The Jump command is used most often to transfer execution to a different line in the project file. The line at which execution continues is identified by a label.

Format: Jump l
            l = label

Example: Jump step3

In this example, *step3* is a label. When the Jump statement is encountered, execution transfers to the line labeled *step3*. If no line has that label, the error is caught during compilation of the project file. (Creation of labels is explained in the section entitled "Using Labels.")

The Jump command may, of course, be part of a conditional statement:

If [dept] = "ACCT" then jump depac

The Jump command can also be used to pass control to another application module, and, optionally, to begin execution of a new project file. If a new file is to be executed, the statement PROJECT-FILE must precede the file name. If any commands remain in the current project file, they are not executed.

Format: Jump a PROJECT-FILE f
            a = Smart application module, f = project
               file name

Examples: Jump Wordprocessor
            Jump Data-manager
            Jump Time-manager
            Jump Communications
            Jump Main-Menu
            Jump Spreadsheet PROJECT-FILE proj1

Using Labels

Label is not really a command, but the identifier of a line designated in a Jump command. The Label identifier and the label itself must be alone on a line; the label can be up to 20 characters in length. Any combination of letters or numbers is permitted, but spaces within the label are not accepted.

Format: Label l
              l = label

Example: Label step3

Label names are case-sensitive, so be careful. The command *Jump STEP4* will not locate a line identified with *label step4*. If you attempt to jump to a nonexistent label, your project file will not compile, and you will be given the opportunity to make the necessary correction.

The Call Command

Sometimes you need to execute the same set of instructions several times within a project file. You could, of course, type in the same lines over and over. A better way is to use a *subroutine*—a set of commands and statements that is written in only one location within the file, but is called from several different locations. The Call command is used to begin execution of a subroutine.

Format: Call p
              p = procedure name

Example: Call testit

For complicated project files, you can even have a Call statement within a called procedure; this nesting may extend to a depth of 20 levels. Commands for handling procedures are discussed in the next section.

Procedure and Return Statements

Like the Label statement, the Procedure statement identifies a line; in this case, the identified line is the beginning of a subroutine. The Return statement identifies the end of a subroutine.

Format: Procedure p
              p = procedure name

Example: Procedure testit

An entire procedure might be written as:

Procedure testit
Let $accum = $accum + [wage]
Lprint [first];[last];[dept];$accum
Return

Be sure that the "in-line" statements of the project file (the statements that are not part of a procedure) do not run into the procedure statements. The line before the Procedure statement must be one that transfers control, such as Jump or Transfer, or a termination statement, such as End or Stop.

The Command Statement

When you are at the command level or are executing Smart "by hand," you access DOS by pressing the quick key Ctrl-O, thus invoking a secondary command processor. The Smart System is temporarily interrupted so that you can execute DOS commands or other programs from DOS level. If you don't have enough available memory for executing DOS commands, you may need to use the -r option when you enter Smart at the beginning of a session. (The -r option is explained in the Introduction of this book.)

The Command statement provides DOS access from within project files. On a line by itself, Command invokes the secondary processor. Execution is transferred to the DOS level, where you can enter DOS commands. When you EXIT, Smart is restarted, and the processing of the project is resumed.

To execute a DOS command and remain within Smart, use the format

command /c CMD

where CMD is a DOS command. The /c must come before the DOS command.

This format may be preferable if you are building an application to be used by novice users. Remember that once the project accesses DOS and invokes the new command processor, the user has complete control of the computer.

A Peripheral Command: Lprint

The Lprint command sends data, text literals, and expressions to your printer. This command is much like the LPRINT command in BASIC.

Format:	Lprint
	e = expression
	l = literal enclosed in double quotation marks
Example:	Lprint "Last Name: ";[last]

If the Lprint statement ends with a semicolon (;), the print head does not advance to a new line after printing.

File Commands

Five file commands have been added with Version 3.0 of Smart. They can be used to read and write directly to external files in ASCII format. The types of files you can read and write are the same types you can edit with the Text-Editor or TYPE at the DOS command level. You cannot use these commands with Smart internal files, such as Data Base Manager files, Spreadsheet files, or Document files.

The Fopen Command

The Fopen command is used to open a file for reading or writing; this command must be issued before any other of these project-processing file-access commands can be used. After a file has been opened it is referenced by the file number.

Format:	Fopen f AS n
	f = file name, n = number
Example:	Fopen "account" as 1
	Fopen "%1" as 2
	Fopen "%2" as $div*$mo

Notice that parameters can be used to designate the file name and that the file number can be either a literal or an expression. If a file with the given name already exists, the Fopen command does not automatically erase the contents of that file. If you know the format of the file, such as its record and field lengths and the number of records, you can use the Fseek command to position the file pointer, which controls the position within the file at which data is read or written. Then you can use the Fwrite command to overwrite or add to the contents of the file.

The Fclose Command

Use the Fclose command to close a file.

Format: Fclose n
                 n = file number

Example: Fclose 5

Be sure to close every file you have opened. Otherwise, the data can be corrupted, or it can fail to be written properly to the file.

The Fread Command

The Fread command is used to read parts of an external file into a user-defined variable. The number of characters to be read can be specified by means of the LENGTH statement.

Format: Fread n INTO v
                 n = file number, v = name of user variable

Example: Fread 2 INTO $account

Format: Fread n LENGTH l INTO v
                 n = file number, l = length (number of
                     characters)
                 v = name of user variable

Example: Fread 2 LENGTH 6 INTO $account

The first example reads data from the current position in the external file; data is read up to but not including the next carriage return or line feed in the external file. The second example begins reading at the current position for a total of six characters. In both examples, the new pointer position is the character following the last character read.

Note that the "destination" of the Fread command must be a user-defined variable.

The Fwrite Command

Use the Fwrite command to write to an external file from the Project Processor. The file pointer indicates where the writing is to begin. This pointer is advanced to the next position following the end of the previous "write."

Format: Fwrite n FROM e
                 n = number, e = expression

Example: Fwrite 5 FROM $name

Format: Fwrite n LENGTH l FROM e
n = number, l = length, e = expression

Format: Fwrite 5 LENGTH 20 FROM $name

In the first example, the evaluated expression *e* is written to the file, followed automatically by a carriage return and line feed. The file pointer advances to the beginning of the new line.

In the second example, the expression is written to the file for the length specified. The pointer is advanced to the first character past the length, and no carriage return or line feed is issued. You would use this format if you were writing fixed-format external files.

The Fwrite command can be used to overwrite the contents of an existing file or to append data to the end of a file. You must know the format of the file, the lengths of records and fields, and the number of records. Use the Fseek command to position the file pointer.

The Fseek Command

The Fseek command is used with the Fread and Fwrite commands to position the pointer within an external file.

Format: Fseek n p
n = file number, p = pointer position

Example: Fseek 5 25

The example places the pointer of file number 5 at position 25. Remember to count each carriage-return, line-feed combination as two characters when you calculate the pointer position. Position numbers are relative to the beginning of the file, not to the current pointer position. In other words, you cannot position the pointer "ahead five positions"; you must specify the exact position.

If you know the format of the file, you can overwrite the contents of an existing file or append to the end of a file, using the Fseek command to position the pointer, and the Fwrite command to write the data.

Variable Assignment Commands

Variable assignment commands are used to enter values into a project-processing variable. User-defined variables are those you create; a *$* is always the first character of the variable name. The standard project variables of TEXT1 and TEXT2 (for text) and

VALUE1 and VALUE2 (for numbers) also are available. Parameters are numbered 0 through 9, and a percent sign (%) precedes the number.

The Input Command

The Input command accepts input from the keyboard, assigns the input to a project variable, and displays an optional message on the command line.

Format:	Input v m
	v = project variable name, m = message
	(optional)
Example:	Input $newsal Enter New Salary Amount:
	Input VALUE1 Enter the Account Number:
	Input TEXT1 Enter the State Abbreviation:

If a text message is not supplied, the name of the project variable appears as a prompt on the command line.

Using Parameters

Parameters are similar to project variables because both can contain values. Parameters are different, however, in that they are used to replace command-line options with variables. The format for entering a parameter value is different, as well.

Format:	%n m
	m = message
Example:	%1 Enter Target Wage:
	if [wage] < %1 then call subwage

The parameter numbers range from 0 to 9. Up to 25 characters, including spaces, may be entered into a parameter. You need not enclose the value in quotation marks, even if the value includes spaces.

Parameters cannot be used to provide destinations in Jump, Label, or Call statements. Don't use parameter variables in logical expressions, such as If or While. User variables should be used in those expressions.

The Input-Screen Command (5)

The Input-Screen command, found on command list 5 of the applications modules (see fig. 32.5), is another means of entering data into project variables or parameters. Not only is the input screen better looking than the screen you see when you use the Input or Parameters command, but also the Input-Screen command can be used to select from a list of alternatives defined by the application builder, in much the same way that you select options from a command list.

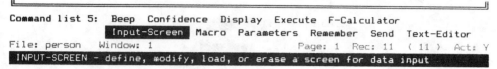

Fig. 32.5. *Selecting the Input-Screen command.*

The menu of the Input-Screen command prompts you to Define, Load, or Undefine an input screen (see fig. 32.6). As with other commands of this nature, you must first define a screen before you can load it.

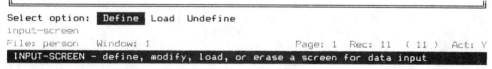

Fig. 32.6. *The Input-Screen menu.*

Selecting the Input-Screen Load command sequence initiates the execution of a previously defined input screen. Input-Screen Undefine deletes the screen definition from disk.

The definition screen looks very much like the definition screen you use to create screens in the Data Base Manager. Text, boxes, and lines can be included in the screen. A screen for entering values into variables or parameters is shown in figure 32.7.

The default order of input is top-to-bottom, but you can change the order by pressing F7; this screen allows more flexibility than do the custom screens. Notice that the function keys can be used to change the screen colors. The use of the screen is shown in figure 32.8. Text, values, and dates are being entered in system parameters; the prompt just below the screen border shows that data is being entered in parameter %4. Data can also be entered in system variables.

The Input-Screen facility can be used also to define a screen from which you select an item by moving a highlight block on a list of choices, just as you do with the command lists. While defining the screen, use the F5 key to define an area to hold the names of items

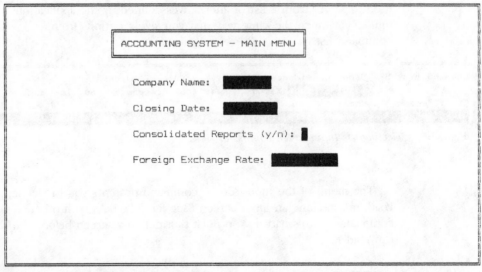

Fig. 32.7. *The Input-Screen definition screen.*

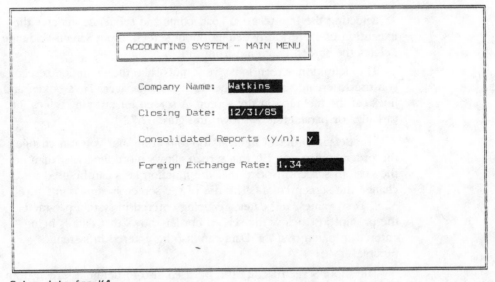

Fig. 32.8. *Entering data to the Input-Screen.*

to be entered in parameters. In the example in figure 32.9, you can
select a project file to be executed; the name is entered in a
parameter, such as %1. The two significant lines in the project file
would be

. . .

. . .

input-screen load repmen1
execute %1

. . .

. . .

```
                    WATKINS COMPANY, INC.

                     Report Menu  #1




          Detail Inventory :    DETINVRY
          Summary Inventory:    SUMINVRY
          Order Status:         ORDSTAT
          Backorders:           BACKREP
          Short Ships:          SHORTSHP
          Company Transfers:    COTRANS
          Damaged Goods:        DAMAGED
          Work In Process:      INPROCES
          Delayed Productions:  DELAYED
```

Select for %1 (use space bar)
F10 Finished   ^Z Cancel
File: person   Window: 1   Page: 1 Rec: 11 (11) Act: Y

Fig. 32.9. *Selecting a project file.*

The Input-Screen Load command causes the screen in figure 32.9
to be displayed. The user selects a project-file name from the screen,
and the name is entered in parameter %1, and the Execute command
begins execution of that file.

The Menu Statement
Menu statements can be used to input data in variables or
parameters, to draw boxes, or to print data. The Menu Print
command can be used to display the contents of a parameter on the
screen.

Format: Menu Clear fg bg No-Border
                 Menu Clear Box r c r c fg bg No-Border
                 Menu Draw Box r c r c fg bg
                 Menu Print r c fg bg m
                 Menu Input r c fg bg l v

In this notation, *r* is a screen row number, *c* is a column number, and *fg* and *bg* are foreground and background colors from 0 to 15. As in previous examples, *m*, *l*, and *v* stand for message, length, and variable, respectively. If you are using a monochrome monitor, specify 7 for *fg* and 0 for *bg*. The No-Border modifiers are optional.

Example: Menu Clear 7 0
                 Menu Clear Box 10 5 15 70 2 9 No-Border
                 Menu Draw Box 12 10 17 70 1 12
                 Menu Print 10 5 7 0 Enter Company Name:
                 Menu Print 20 10 7 0 Total is: %1
                 Menu Input 17 15 1 13 8 $doproj

The Menu Clear statement is typically used at the beginning of a series of Menu statements. The Menu Clear statement clears the screen and activates the specified foreground and background colors. If No-Border is specified, the border is not drawn.

The Menu Draw Box command draws on the screen a box in the specified colors. The first pair of row and column numbers specifies the upper left corner of the box, and the second pair specifies the lower right corner. Any screen display within the boundaries remains unchanged. To draw a box and clear the area within the box, use Menu Clear Box.

The Menu Print command prints text or the contents of project parameters on the screen. You cannot print the contents of user variables, however.

Menu Input accepts input from the keyboard and assigns the input to a project or user variable or a project parameter. Any accompanying text must be generated with the Menu Print command. Development of input screens is easier with the Input-Screen command on list 5 of the applications modules.

The Repaint Command

At the completion of a series of Menu statements, insert the Repaint command (with no options) before any other commands in the project file. This command restores the screen as it was before the Menu commands were issued.

The Repaint command can be used with the option *On* or *Off* to control repainting of the screen during processing. The normal mode is *On*, which causes the screen to be repainted as called for in the execution of the project.

If you want to leave a menu on the screen during processing, issue the command Repaint Off. Even if you do not want to leave the menu on the screen, the processing speed can be enhanced considerably by setting Repaint Off.

The Let Statement

The Let statement is used to assign a value to a project variable or parameter, a data base field, or a worksheet cell. The value can be a number, text, date, or any other appropriate data type. The result of the source expression (on the right side of the equal sign) is inserted in the target.

Format:	Let (target) = (source)
Example:	Let [wage] = [wage]*1.2
	Let r1c3 = sum(r1:3c7)
	Let $totwage = $totwage + [wage]
	If [wage] > $highwage then let $highwage = [wage]
	[sdate] = "06-30-86"
	Let person.[age] = $age

You do not have to use the Let command to assign values in this way; the command is optional, as you can see in the preceding examples.

Note that the last example applies only to the Data Base Manager. The target of the Let statement can be a field in a file other than the current file. The target expression in the last example refers to the Age field of the PERSON file. If the file is in a window, the record addressed is the current record. If the file is not in a window, the current record is record 1. The Let statement is the only command in which this feature may be used, and the alternate file designation can appear only on the left target side of the equation.

The Clear Statement

The Clear statement erases all or selected user-defined variables from memory. Project variables or parameters are not affected.

Format: Clear

Clear v,v

v = variable

Example: Clear $tot1,$tot2

A Clear statement by itself clears all user-defined variables. When variables are cleared, the computer memory formerly used to store them is made available for other uses.

Logical Decision Commands

The commands If and While control execution of the project file, depending on the contents of variables, fields, or cells.

The If Statement

The If statement is used to evaluate a condition and, depending on the result of the condition, execute a command. In figure 32.3, a simple If statement is used to determine whether the number of the current record (record) is equal to the total number of records in the file (records). The If statement has several formats, each with varying degrees of capability and complexity.

The simplest form of the If statement is

IF (logical expression) THEN (command)

This statement says, in effect, "If the logical expression is true, then execute the command." For example,

IF [dept] = "ACCT" THEN let $totact = $totact + [wage]

IF sum(r5:20c17) > 500 THEN call overbill

Notice that only one logical expression is evaluated, and one command is executed if the expression is true. (See chapter 30 for valid operators to use in expressions.)

When several commands are to be executed if the expression is true, use the following format:

IF (logical expression)

(command 1)

(command 2)

ENDIF

Note that the key word *then* is not used, and that the commands appear on lines by themselves. The key word *ENDIF* marks the end of the series of commands.

```
IF [dept] = "MKTG"
     Call markrep
     Lprint [last];" ";[first]
ENDIF
```

The command lines between *IF* and *ENDIF* are indented to make the lines more readable; the indentation serves no other purpose.

In the preceding two examples of the If command, the commands between the logical expression and the key word *ENDIF* are not executed if the logical expression is false; execution continues with the next statement in the project file; that statement is executed whether the logical expression is true or false. If you want the next statement to be executed only if the condition is false, use the Else construction:

Format:

```
IF (logical expression)
     (command 1)
     (command 2)
ELSE
     (command 3)
ENDIF
```

With this format, commands 1 and 2 are executed if the expression is true. Command 3 is executed if the expression is false.

Example:

```
IF [dept] = "DATA"
     call datrep
     let $tot = $tot + [wage]
ELSE
     let $newtot = $newtot + [wage]*1.1
ENDIF
```

Even more complicated conditional statements can be constructed with multiple expressions and the keyword *ELSEIF.*

Format:

```
IF    (logical expression 1)
          (command 1)
        ELSEIF (logical expression 2)
          (command 2)
        ELSEIF (logical expression 3)
          (command 3)
ELSE
          (command 4)
ENDIF
```

Example:

```
IF [dept] = "ACCT"
      let $totact = $totact + [wage]
ELSEIF [dept] = "MKTG"
      let $totmkt = $totmkt + [wage]
ELSE
      let $totrest = $totrest + [wage]
ENDIF
```

The While Command

The While command is used to loop within a project file while a logical condition is true. This is a special form of an If test and a Jump command.

Format:

```
WHILE (logical expression)
   (command 1)
   (command 2)
   ENDWHILE
```

Example:

```
WHILE record <> records
   let $totwage = $totwage + [wage]
   goto record next
ENDWHILE
```

The logical expression is reevaluated each time the ENDWHILE statement is encountered. If the expression is still true, the loop is executed again, beginning with the statement after the expression. If the expression is false, however, execution continues with the statement following the ENDWHILE.

Two special subcommands can be used with the While statement. Break exits the While loop immediately; Continue skips the remaining commands within the loop, but execution continues, if the While condition is still true.

Format:

```
WHILE (logical expression 1)
   (command 1)
   IF (logical expression 2) then CONTINUE
   IF (logical expression 3) then BREAK
   (command 2)
ENDWHILE
```

In this example, execution continues with the next line following ENDWHILE if logical expression 3 is true. If logical expression 2 is true, then the remaining lines before the ENDWHILE are skipped.

Project Execution Control

These project execution control commands will help with "debugging" and documenting your project files.

The Singlestep Command

If you are writing an extremely complicated project file, you may want to have the system pause before executing each statement, so that you can inspect what is happening. The Singlestep command is used for this purpose; single-step processing can be turned on and off during execution.

> *Example:* Singlestep On
> Singlestep Off

If you want to see the execution of the entire project file, place the Singlestep On command at the beginning. If you want to inspect just one routine, set Singlestep On at the beginning of the routine and set Singlestep Off at the end. You may want to Set Singlestep On according to whether a certain condition is true. You can easily do so by means of an If statement:

> If [DEPT] = "ACCT" THEN Singlestep On

If you want your project files to be executed always in Singlestep mode, change the setting to Yes in the parameters for each of the application modules.

If you set Singlestep On in a project file and do not set it off again, the next project file you run during the session will also be executed with Singlestep On. If you don't want this to happen, set Singlestep Off at the end of the project file.

The Quiet Command

If you have Singlestep On so that you can debug a project file, you'll probably want to have Quiet Off so that you can see the statements as they are being executed.

> *Example:* Quiet On
> Quiet Off

As with the Singlestep statement, the default condition can be set On or Off in the parameters settings of the application modules.

The Comment Statement

The Comment statement is used to make notations in the body of your project file so that you (or someone else looking at the project file) can better understand the file. The inclusion of comments in your project file does not slow execution, but a project file with many comments does take longer to compile.

Example: Comment Load the Invoice file here.
                        ' This is the end of the processing section.

A single quotation mark (') may be used in place of the Comment statement. In either case, you must allow at least one blank space before the comment itself.

Application Module Specific Commands

Certain commands pertain only to specific modules.

Data Base Manager Commands

The following commands apply only to the Data Base Manager.

The Update Only-One Statement. As you know, once you enter Update mode from the command level, you can change as many records as you want. Under the control of a project file, however, you may want to set a restriction so that a user can update only one record. The Update Only-One statement is used for this purpose. After the record is updated, Update mode is exited, and processing continues.

Example: Update Only-One

If the possibility exists that a key field will be changed during this Update, you should issue the Key Update command in the project file after the Update Only-One statement. No prompt asks whether the keys are to be updated, and the keys are not updated automatically. (Neither does the regular Update command issue the prompt when used within a project file.)

The Enter Blank Command. If you want to create a new record from within a project file, use the Enter Blank command.

Example: Let $last = [last]
Goto window 1
Enter Blank
Let [last] = $last

This statement is used when you have stored values in variables, and you want to create a new record with fields equal to these values. Again, be careful about your key fields. Keys are not updated automatically.

The Lock-Record Command. The Lock-Record command serves two purposes. If you are using Smart on a network, Lock-Record is used to prevent another user from updating the record on which you are working. If you are operating from the command level and using the Update command, such record locking will take place automatically. If you are using the Let command to update a data base field from a project file, however, you must handle the record locking with the Lock-Record command.

Even if you are not using Smart on a network, the Lock-Record command can still offer some significant advantages if you are using several Let commands to update the same record. Ordinarily, each time you update a field, the entire record is written back to the buffer. If you issue the Lock-Record command before you begin the series of Let statements, the record is not written to the buffer until you advance to the next record. This technique speeds processing when several Let statements are used with each record.

The current record is automatically unlocked when a different record becomes current.

Spreadsheet Commands

These commands apply only to the Spreadsheet.

The Cursor Command. The Cursor command is used in Spreadsheet project files to control the relative movement of the cursor or to prompt the user for input in a cell.

There are four commands for moving the cursor:

Cursor down
Cursor up
Cursor right
Cursor left

For data entry, the user can be prompted to enter any type of data as follows:

Format: Cursor m
                 m = message (optional)

Example: Cursor Enter number of dependents:

The data type of the cell is determined by the first keystroke, just as it is in Enter mode at the command level. A numeric character defines the cell contents as a value; an alphabetic character (or double quotation marks) defines the character as text; and the special characters @ or # may be used to define a date.

If you want to ensure that the cell contents are of the desired data type, use one of the following formats:

Cursor Text m
Cursor Value m
m = message (optional)

Even if you enter a number in response to Cursor Text, the character is stored as a text data item. (If you enter text in response to Cursor Value, there is no error message, and the cell contents are stored as zero.) You must press Enter to complete the entry.

The Enter Command.   Instead of prompting a user for a value or text, the cell contents can be derived from other cells, formulas, or project processing variables. The Enter command is used to create such an entry.

Format: @rxcy Enter t v
                 x = row number
                 y = column number
                 t = type (see the following example)
                 v = variable whose value is to be entered in cell

Example: @r15c7 Enter value $age

The types of entries that can be designated are Value, Text, Formula, and Date. The entry can come from a project processing variable, a user-defined variable, a parameter, or a literal.

Communications Commands

The following commands are used only in the Communications module.

The Break-Key Command.   The Break-Key command is used to send a break signal to the modem during transmission. Some computer systems use this signal to interrupt processing. This signal is similar to the one generated by presssing Alt-B.

The Empty Command. The Empty command should be used at the end of a project file in which data is being sent. To make sure that all the data has been sent from the buffer, the Empty command causes processing to pause until the buffer is empty.

Project Processing Functions

Some functions apply primarily to project processing. These functions are

ASC
ASK
CERROR
CHR
INCHAR
NEXTKEY

For a complete discussion of these functions, see Chapters 30 and 31.

Conclusion

The Smart project processing capabilities provide a means by which you can automate repetitive tasks and develop complex applications. If you are using the application yourself, you will find that project processing can save time and reduce mistakes. If others are to use the application, they do not need to know much about Smart to execute the project and perform complicated, detailed operations.

Project files can be entirely self-contained or can transfer control to other project files in the current module or in other modules.

Chapter 33

Using Smart's Common Commands

Certain common utility commands are available throughout the applications modules of the Smart system. These commands can enhance the appearance of your screen or make working with Smart easier, faster, and more comfortable for you.

The Autohelp Command (1)

The Autohelp command is found on command list 1 in each of the applications modules. The command is used to toggle the display of the autohelp line at the bottom of your screen. The autohelp line provides an explanation of the highlighted command.

The Beep Command

The Beep command turns off the computer's audible warning and attention signals. The command is a toggle; select Beep again to turn the sound back on.

The Border Command

To remove the border from around a window, execute the Border command. To replace the border, execute the command again.

The Confidence Command (5)

The Confidence command, found on command list 5 in each of the applications modules, is used to establish the mode of command execution. The default confidence-level setting can be established with the Parameters command for the main menu and for each module.

As you know, confidence level 3 displays the various command lists. If you are just starting to use the Smart system, you should use this level.

Confidence levels 1 and 2 also display the command lists, but not all available commands are displayed. If you are developing a system for others to use, you may not want them to be able to execute some of the more powerful commands used by system builders.

Confidence levels 4 and 5 do not display a command list at all. You see only the following prompt on the line where the first command list appears at the other levels:

    Command:

At these confidence levels, you are expected to know the commands. You shouldn't change to these confidence levels until you have had some experience with the Smart system.

Confidence level 4 is called the *Key-Word* level. This term means that when you type enough of the command for Smart to recognize, the system completes the command; then you press Enter, and the system executes the command. If you have mistyped the command, you can press Esc to terminate the execution of the command.

Confidence level 5, *Key-Word/Auto-Recognition,* is similar to level 4, except that the system does not wait for you to press Enter before beginning to execute the command.

Because each application module has commands that are the same and some that are different, the number of characters needed for the system to recognize a command can vary. This can cause some problems for you in command list 5 if you are not careful. For instance, compare the following:

Module	Abbreviation	Command
Spreadsheet	UNLOA	UNLOAD
Data Base Manager	UNLO	UNLOAD

In the Spreadsheet, one additional character is needed so that the system can distinguish between Unload and Unlock. If you are using the Data Base Manager at command list 5, however, and you type *UNLOA*, the system interprets this as the command Unload All, because the final A signifies the All option.

The Directory Command

The Directory command within the Smart system is similar to the DIR command in DOS. You can search for files by name or extension; even portions of names or extensions can be used to locate a file if you use wildcard characters. The asterisk (*) substitutes for "any characters in this position and to the right," and the question mark (?) means "any single character in this position."

For example, figure 33.1 illustrates the result of the Directory command. The search criterion was

   *.ws

This tells Smart to search for all worksheet files in the current subdirectory.

Unlike the DIR command at the DOS level, Smart's Dir command can be used to sort the display of file names in a number of different orders:

Key	Sort order
F2	File Name
F3	Date and Time, ascending
F4	File Size, ascending
F5	Special two-key sort: Name Extension Date / Time Size

In addition, pressing F6 causes Smart to print the directory. Press Esc to return to command level.

Filename	Ext	Date	Time	Size
BARDEMO	WS	19-Jan-1986	17:30	602
BILLS	WS	27-Jan-1986	13:16	2571
BUDGET84	WS	17-Jan-1986	11:07	418
BUDGET85	WS	17-Jan-1986	9:14	298
BUDGET86	WS	17-Jan-1986	9:14	298
CANADA	WS	29-Jan-1986	10:41	4739
COMPINT	WS	17-Jan-1986	13:22	4589
DECSAM	WS	19-Jan-1986	16:26	860
DEPSAL	WS	17-Jan-1986	9:21	298
DOMESTIC	WS	29-Jan-1986	10:41	4739
DOMGRAPH	WS	29-Jan-1986	22:33	4811
FILLSAMP	WS	29-Jan-1986	9:41	1068
INT11	WS	20-Jan-1986	16:04	4719
INT3	WS	17-Jan-1986	17:15	1121
INT5	WS	17-Jan-1986	21:34	4189
INT6	WS	18-Jan-1986	14:45	4149
INT7	WS	18-Jan-1986	15:02	4155

First ⟹

28 Files
Sorted by
Filename
Extension

F2 Sort by name   F3 Sort by date/time   F4 Sort by size   F5 Special   F6 Print
directory *.ws
File: book   Window: 1   Page: 1 Rec: 1 (1) Act: Y
DIRECTORY - list the files on a disk drive

Fig. 33.1. *Displaying a directory.*

The Display Command

The Display command is used to change from one type of display to another. You may want to use the different capabilities of your monitor at different times. If you have a monochrome monitor that can also display graphics, you may want to use Display Black/White most of the time but use Graphics mode in the Spreadsheet module so that you can see the different fonts. If you have a color monitor and are working in Color mode, the different fonts are displayed in different colors.

In all modules except the Data Base Manager, you can choose any of the following options of the Display command:

Black/White Color Graphics

Do *not* attempt to switch to a type of display that your system does not support.

The F-Calculator Command (5–F-Calculator, Alt-K)

The F-Calculator (formula calculator) command is found on command list 5 of each application module; the quick key is Alt-K. The formula calculator performs any calculations you might need, using all arithmetic operators and all the Smart functions; the results of the calculation can be placed in your work. The Ctrl-C quick key is used as follows to insert the results of the calculation:

Module	*Placement of results*
Data Base Manager	Current field in Enter or Update
Spreadsheet	Current cell
Word Processor	Current cursor location

In the Data Base Manager, your calculation can reference fields from the current record; in the Spreadsheet, the calculation can reference cells from the current spreadsheet.

Figure 33.2 shows the use of the F-Calculator in the Spreadsheet module. The screen has been split to show both the underlying worksheet and the F-Calculator screen.

The Average function has been used to calculate an average of the entries in row 3, columns 2 through 13 (r3c2:13). Pressing F2 causes the result to be displayed on the status line. Other function keys can be used to aid in editing a large formula. Press F10 to exit the F-Calculator.

Once you are back within your spreadsheet, you can move the cursor to any cell and, in Enter mode, extract the F-Calculator result from a buffer and insert it in the cell. Use the Ctrl-C quick key to perform this task.

Inserting the results of a formula calculation is similar in the Data Base Manager and the Word Processor. In either case, be sure that you are in either Enter or Update mode. The system retrieves the values as though they were typed from the keyboard. In this respect, inserting calculation results is much like using a macro.

Formulas in the F-Calculator can be as long as 1,900 characters. If you have many IF . . . THEN . . . ELSE statements, however, the total number allowable will be somewhat less. Keep your formulas within the boundaries of the screen, to enhance readability and to allow the maximum number of characters for the formula.

```
#1         1        2     3     4     5     6     7     8     9    10    11
1                        CANADIAN DIVISION
2                  Jan   Feb   Mar   Apr   May   Jun   Jul   Aug   Sep   Oct
3    Net Sales..  70.6  71.2  71.9  72.6  73.2  73.9  74.6  75.3  75.9  76.6
4    Gross Prof.  29.7  29.9  30.2  30.5  30.8  31.0  31.3  31.6  31.9  32.2
5                 -----------------------------------------------------------
6    G&A Exp....   2.8   2.8   2.8   2.8   2.8   2.8   2.8   2.8   2.8   2.8
7    EBIT.......  26.9  27.1  27.4  27.7  28.0  28.2  28.5  28.8  29.1  29.4
8    Int Exp....   2.2   2.2   2.2   2.2   2.2   2.2   2.2   2.2   2.2   2.2
```

```
╔═ F-Calculator ═══════════════════════════════════════════
║ average(r3c2:13)
║
║
║
║
║
║
╚═══════════════════════════════════════════════════════════
```

```
F1 Help        F3 Find        F5 Replace        F7 Insert line        F9  Repeat
F2 Calc        F4 Goto        F6 Define block   F8 Delete line        F10 Finish
Result: 74.2704530489                    Line:    1   Column: 17   Insert: OFF
 F-CALCULATOR - formula calculator
```

Fig. 33.2. *Using the F-Calculator command.*

The File Command (4)

The File command is used to perform three functions similar to those performed by the corresponding DOS commands:

Copy Erase New-Directory Rename

The File command is found on command list 4. The Copy, Erase, and Rename options prompt you for a file name; Copy and Rename also prompt for a second file name. The Erase option accepts the use of wildcards, but Copy and Rename do not. The New-Directory option prompts for a new directory name. Unlike its DOS counterpart, Copy does not permit copied files to overwrite existing files.

Depending on the application module, you may not be able to perform some functions. In the Data Base Manager, for example, you cannot erase files that are currently in use.

Most of the Smart system does not require the use of file extensions, so it is easy to forget about them. When using the File command, however, you must specify extensions; this command is like the DOS command in that respect. Refer to Appendix B for a complete list of file extensions.

To change your current directory without leaving Smart, use the File New-Directory command sequence. The prompt is

Enter new directory name:

Enter the path of the new directory, using backslashes (\) as appropriate. If the directory is located on a disk drive other than the default drive, you must enter the drive letter and a colon. Examples are

    \account
    A:\salary
    B:\canada\workplan

If you specify a directory that does not exist, the system will not catch the error at that time. Only when you issue a command to write to the disk will the error be caught. For instance, in the Spreadsheet, if you try to save a file to a directory that does not exist, you get the error message error creating file. Be careful with this File command option.

Active or loaded files are tagged with the identification of the original subdirectory, so that they are written back to that subdirectory even if you have changed to another subdirectory after loading the file.

Another method of changing your directory is by returning to DOS through the DOS Access facility, which you can invoke with the Ctrl-O quick key. You are then returned to DOS within a secondary command processor. Any DOS commands can be issued (including CHDIR). Many other programs can be run also, depending on the amount of memory you have reserved for DOS access. (Use the -r option when entering Smart to reserve a specified amount of memory.) To return to Smart from DOS Access mode, type *exit*.

The Help Command (F1)

The Help command is part of the Smart System's Help facility. The quick key for Help is F1; use this key at any time to display help screens pertaining to the current function, command, or operation.

To get help on any command, highlight that command and press F1. Figure 33.3 shows the results of pressing F1 when the highlight block is on the Delete command of the Spreadsheet.

```
          1        2     3     4     5     6     7     8     9    10    11
 1                         CANADIAN DIVISION
 2                 Jan   Feb   Mar   Apr   May   Jun   Jul   Aug   Sep   Oct
 3  Net Sales..   70.6  71.2  71.9  72.6  73.2  73.9  74.6  75.3  75.9  76.6
 4  Gross Prof.   29.7  29.9  30.2  30.5  30.8  31.0  31.3  31.6  31.9  32.2
 5            ------------------------------------------------------------
 6  G&A Exp....    2.8   2.8   2.8   2.8   2.8   2.8   2.8   2.8   2.8   2.8
 7  EBIT.......   26.9  27.1  27.4  27.7  28.0  28.2  28.5  28.8  29.1  29.4
 8  Int Exp....    2.2   2.2   2.2   2.2   2.2   2.2   2.2   2.2   2.2   2.2
 9  EBT........   24.7  24.9  25.2  25.5  25.8  26.0  26.3  26.6  26.9  27.2
10            ------------------------------------------------------------
11  Tax........   11.8  12.0  12.1  12.2  12.4  12.5  12.6  12.8  12.9  13.1
12  Net Income.  12.8  13.0  13.1  13.2  13.4  13.5  13.7  13.8  14.0  14.1
13            ------------------------------------------------------------

   DELETE - delete a block, or any number of rows or columns

   This command removes an area from the worksheet.  If, for example, a
   row is deleted, then the rows beneath the deleted row are moved upward.

Related topics:  Blank  Copy  Insert  Move  Vcopy
F1 Large help F2 Print help   F3 Help index   F10 Finished   Cursor keys
Worksheet: canada    Loc: r4c1                          FN:0    Font: Standard
 DELETE - delete a block, or any number of rows or columns
```

Fig. 33.3. *Using the Help command with F1.*

Pressing F1 again expands the Help window (see fig. 33.4); related topics are displayed on the command line. To get help on any one of those topics, move the highlight block to the topic and press F1. Press F3 to display the Help index shown in figure 33.5. Move the highlight block and press F1 to get help on any topic in this index.

The F2 key can be used to print the text of the help message. Although the help explanations are not a substitute for the manuals or this book, they can remind you of the main points of a command.

Press F10 or Esc to return to your prior "location" (command level or entry level).

The Index Command (Alt-A)

The Index command is used to display a list of the databases, worksheets, and documents that are currently loaded or active. The quick key for this command is Alt-A. The name, file, status, type, and size are shown for each current database, worksheet, or document.

```
          1      2      3      4      5      6      7      8      9     10    11
                         CANADIAN DIVISION
1
2               Jan    Feb    Mar    Apr    May    Jun    Jul    Aug    Sep    Oct
3   Net Sales.. 70.6   71.2   71.9   72.6   73.2   73.9   74.6   75.3   75.9   76.6
4   Gross Prof. 29.7   29.9   30.2   30.5   30.8   31.0   31.3   31.6   31.9   32.2
```

```
DELETE - delete a block, or any number of rows or columns

This command removes an area from the worksheet.  If, for example, a
row is deleted, then the rows beneath the deleted row are moved upward.

ROWS
  Delete rows beginning with the current row.

COLUMNS
  Delete columns beginning with the current column.

BLOCK
  Delete a block.
```

Related topics: Blank Copy   Insert   Move   Vcopy
F2 Print help   F3 Help index   F10 Finished   Cursor keys
Worksheet: canada   Loc: r4c1   FN:0   Font: Standard
DELETE - delete a block, or any number of rows or columns

Fig. 33.4. *The expanded Help window.*

```
Help Index
==> ACTIVATE - activate a worksheet
    AUTOHELP - remove/restore help line at bottom of screen (toggle)
    AUTO-RECALC - specifies when formulas will be recalculated
    BEEP - set error beeper on/off (toggle)
    BLANK - blank an area of the worksheet
    BORDER - remove/restore current window border (toggle)
    CLOSE - close the current window
    COLNUMBERS -  remove/restore column numbers (toggle)
    CONFIDENCE - change level of confidence
    COPY - copy an area of the worksheet to another area
    DELETE - delete a block, or any number of rows or columns
    DIRECTORY - list the files on a disk drive
    DISPLAY - alter display mode to B/W, color or graphics
    EDIT - edit a value, a formula, or text
    FORMULA-EDITOR - editor for entering or editing formulas
    ENTER - enter a formula, a value or text into the current cell
    EXECUTE - execute a project file
    E-NOTATION - change value cells to scientific or non-scientific notation
    FILE - copy, erase or rename a file
```

F1 Help for topic   F2 Print help   F10 Finished   Cursor keys

Worksheet: canada   Loc: r4c1   FN:0   Font: Standard
DELETE - delete a block, or any number of rows or columns

Fig. 33.5. *The Help Index.*

The Macro Command

The Macro command is used to establish a set of keystrokes that can be issued by pressing just one key. This feature can be a great time-saver if you have to perform repetitive tasks. When you execute a macro, the commands are executed as though you were entering them from the keyboard, so you must be careful to be in the right mode. Use command mode if the keystrokes are command keys, and entry mode if the keystrokes represent data to be entered.

Macro keys are dependent on the application. For example, you could assign one macro to Ctrl-Q in the Spreadsheet, and another macro to Ctrl-Q in the Word Processor.

The options of the Macro command are

Clear Define Load Remove Save View

The Macro Define Command

Your first step is to select Define. You are then prompted to

Press key to define macro for :

You need to enter a key that is to be used as "shorthand" for the other keystrokes. Don't choose a commonly used key, such as A or B; choose a Ctrl or Alt key combination that is not used for anything else in the application. You may want to try the key combination first, just to make sure it is not currently being used. Press the key (or key combination), but don't press Enter. The system immediately prompts you to

Enter macro for ^q :

For this example, I have used Ctrl-Q as the macro key. The caret (^) symbol stands for the Ctrl key.

Then enter the keystrokes you want to include in the macro. Unlike the Remember Start command, the macro facility does not have the capability to remember your keystrokes as you use them in the actual performance of the application. You may therefore have to write down the keystrokes before you begin defining the macro.

If you make a mistake, press Alt-F10 or Shift-F10. Alt-F10 is a "destructive backspace," and Shift-F10 erases the entire macro so that you can start again. Any other keys you press are included in the definition. Press F10 to save the macro.

Press F10 to save the macro. If you make a mistake, use Alt-F10 to back up or Shift-F10 to erase the entire macro and start again. Any other keys you press are actually included in the macro definition.

Once a macro has been defined, you can use it right away; you don't need to load it. Macro Define can be used also to edit an existing macro, but you must use the erasing keys Alt-F10 and Shift-F10 to move the cursor for editing. If you were to use the cursor keys or Ins or Del, those keystrokes would just be included in the macro. To enter an F10 in the macro, use Ctrl-F10; this combination can be useful for macros that change menu lists or macros that create definitions that require pressing F10 to exit and save the definition.

If you assign a macro to a key that is sometimes used for something else within the Smart system, you can still use the original function by pressing Shift-F10 before using the key. The original function of the key, rather than the macro function, will then be used for the next keystroke. The macro function is then invoked the next time you use the key.

The Macro View Command

To see a list of the active macros you have defined, issue the command Macro View. A sample is shown in figure 33.6. Press F10 or Esc to return to command level.

The Macro Remove Command

To get rid of one macro from the active list, execute Macro Remove. Type the macro key at the prompt. If the key had an original function within the Smart System prior to the macro definition, that function is restored.

The Macro Clear Command

To remove all macros from memory, execute Macro Clear. This command has the same effect as removing each macro individually.

The Macro Save Command

After you have defined a set of macros during one session, you may want to save them for use in subsequent sessions. To do so, select Macro Save. You are then prompted to

    Enter macro filename:

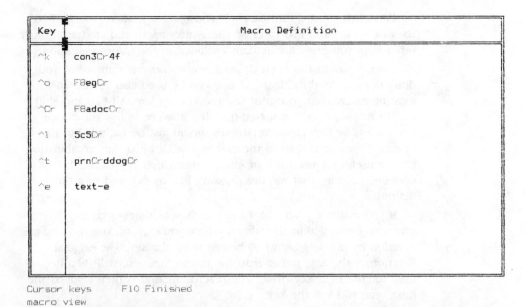

Key	Macro Definition
^k	con3Cr4f
^o	F8egCr
^Cr	F8adocCr
^1	5c5Cr
^t	prnCrddogCr
^e	text-e

Cursor keys   F10 Finished
macro view

MACRO - clear, define, load, remove, save, or view macros

Fig. 33.6. *Using the Macro View command.*

Type a name under which to save the macros. In the Word Processor and Spreadsheet modules, no pop-up menu is displayed to show the names of existing macro files. At the completion of the command, the macros that were in memory are written to a disk file; the macros in memory are not cleared.

The Macro Load command is used to load the macros back into memory during a subsequent session. Because macros can be saved in files, they are not tied to one spreadsheet or document. Macros can be used for any spreadsheet, for example, without having to be repeatedly redefined.

The Macro Load Command

To retrieve macro definitions you have saved in a file, execute the Macro Load command. A pop-up menu displays the names of the macro files in the current subdirectory; select the file you want to use and press Enter.

After you supply the name, the following prompt appears if you already have macros in memory:

Clear existing macros before load (y/n)

If you want the macros you load to replace the existing ones in memory, answer *y*. (Selecting this option is equivalent to selecting Macro Clear and then Macro Load.) If you want to add the macros in the file to the macros already in memory, answer *n*.

One key cannot have two meanings, so when conflicts occur, the most recently loaded macro takes precedence. To bypass the `Clear existing macros . . .` question, type a plus sign (+) before entering the name of the macro file to be loaded. This option can be especially useful in project files.

No explicit command is used to delete macro files from your disk; you can use the File Erase command to accomplish the task. File extensions are .MC1, .MC2, .MC3, or .MC6, depending on whether the macro was defined in the Spreadsheet, the Word Processor, the Data Base Manager, or the Communications module.

The Parameters command can be used to establish a macro file that is loaded automatically every time the applications module is entered. This capability is useful if you want to have the same set of macros available for every session with that module.

The Paint Command

The Paint command is used to change the color of the borders, windows, and other important screen features in each of the Smart application modules.

In the Data Base Manager, you can change the foreground color of the data, boxes and lines (graphics), and titles. In the Spreadsheet, you can assign different colors to each data type and to locked cells.

The Paint command can be used in the Word Processor to change both the foreground and background colors of a text block.

The Parameters Command (5)

The Parameters command, found on command list 5 of each of the applications modules, is used to establish the default settings of many of the options available within the module. These options have been covered in the relevant chapters of this book.

Remember that if you change any Parameter settings, the new options do not take effect immediately. They take effect the next time you enter the applications module. To make the change take effect within the same session, you must use one of the commands that are used to change a setting for the current session.

Using the Text-Editor (5)

A general-purpose text editor is available on command list 5 of each of the application modules. When you execute the Text-Editor command, you are prompted to

Enter filename:

No pop-up menu of file names is displayed, because you can edit a text or ASCII file with any name or extension. If the file has the .TXT extension, you don't have to enter the extension. Specify the full path if the file is in a subdirectory other than the current one.

The full set of cursor-control keys is available for use in the Text-Editor. In addition, the function keys can be used in the ways shown in table 33.1.

Table 33.1
Function Keys with Text Editor

F1	Displays Help Index
F2	Calculates. Similar to the F-Calculator
F3	Finds a text item
F4	Goes to a line number
F5	Replaces text items
F7	Inserts a line before current line. If you have previously deleted a line with the F8 key, the deleted line is inserted at the cursor position. This is a way to duplicate lines. If you have not deleted a line, a blank line is inserted.
F8	Deletes current line
F9	Repeats last Goto, Find, or Replace
F10	Saves work in current file and returns to command list. Note that there is no opportunity to supply an alternative file name.

The function keys in table 33.1 appear on the command lines below the Text-Editor screen. The following function keys do *not* appear, but can also be used:

Alt-F3	Reads a text file into the editor at the current cursor position. You must specify the extension, even for a .TXT file.
Alt-F2	Deletes all data in the editor
Ctrl-Y	Deletes the current line. Does not store line in buffer.
Esc	Exits the editor without saving the file

Smart Command Lists

Following are lists in alphabetical order of the commands for each module of the Smart system.

Data Base Manager Commands

Command	Command List	Quick Key	Description
Activate	4		Activates a file
Autohelp	1		Removes/restores help line at bottom of screen (toggle)
Beep	5		Sets the beeper on/off (toggle)
Border	3		Removes/restores the border of current window (toggle)
Browse	1	Alt-B	Activates/deactivates Browse mode (toggle)
Close	3	Alt-W	Closes the current window

Command	Command List	Quick Key	Description
Confidence	5		Changes confidence level
Create	1	Alt-C	Creates a new file or screen
Delete	1	Alt-D	Deletes or activates current record (toggle)
Directory	4	Alt-O	Lists the files on a disk drive
Display	5		Changes display mode to Black-and-White or color
Enter	1	Alt-E	Adds records to the current file
Execute	5	F8	Executes a project file
F-Calculator	5	Alt-K	Activates Formula Calculator
File	4		Copies, erases, or renames a file
File-Specs	2	Alt-F	Lists file specification of current file
Find	1	F3	Finds a record meeting the given criterion
Goto	1	F4	Goes to a file, a window, or a record
Help	1	F1	Help information
Index	4	Alt-A	Lists the currently active data base file(s)
Input-Screen	5		Defines, modifies, loads, or erases a screen for data input
Key	2	Alt-G	Adds, deletes, organizes, or updates key fields
Link	3		Links windows to display matching information

Command	Command List	Quick Key	Description
Load	4	Alt-L	Opens a data base file and prepares for processing
Lookup	2		Defines, indexes, loads, removes, and undefines lookup table
Macro	5	Alt-M	Clears, defines, loads, removes, and saves macros
Order	2		Changes order in which file is being accessed
Paint	3		Colors border, data, graphics, title, or window
Parameters	5		Changes system parameters
Print	1	Alt-P	Prints the current file, page, or record
Query	1	Alt-Q	Selects from a file records meeting criterion
Read	4		Reads ASCII or Smart files
Relate	2	Alt-N	Creates a file based on a relation between two files
Remember	5		Creates new project file or modifies existing file
Report	1		Prints or defines a table or form
Save	4	Alt-S	Updates disk without unloading file
Scroll	1		Scrolls through the file
Send	5	Alt-Z	Sends information to Spreadsheet or Word Processor

Command	Command List	Quick Key	Description
Sort	2	Alt-J	Sorts the current file and creates temporary index
Split	3	Alt-H Alt-V	Splits the current window into two windows (Alt-H splits horizontally, Alt-V splits vertically)
Text-Editor	5		Allows editing of a text file
Transactions	2	Alt-T	Performs file transactions between files
Unlink	3		Unlinks two windows
Unload	4	Alt-U	Deactivates a data base file
Update	1	Alt-I	Updates current record
Utilities	2		File utilities
Write	4		Writes data in ASCII, DIF, Smart, or text format
Zoom	3	F7	Zooms/unzooms the current window

Spreadsheet Commands

Command	Command List	Quick Key	Description
Activate	4		Activates a worksheet
Auto-Recalc	5	F5	Specifies the method to be used in formula recalculation
Autohelp	1		Removes/restores help line at bottom of screen (toggle)

Command	Command List	Quick Key	Description
Beep	5		Sets error beeper on/off (toggle)
Blank	1	Alt-B	Moves blanks into an area of the worksheet
Border	2		Removes/restores window border (toggle)
Close	3	Alt-W	Closes the current window
Colnumbers	2		Removes/restores column numbers (toggle)
Confidence	5		Changes confidence level
Copy	1	Alt-C	Copies an area of the worksheet into another area
Delete	1	Alt-D	Deletes a block or any number of rows or columns
Directory	4	Alt-O	Lists the files on a disk drive
Display	5		Alters display mode to Black-and-White, color, or graphics
Edit	1	Alt-E	Edits a value, formula, or text
Execute	5	F8	Executes a project file
F-Calculator	5	Alt-K	Activates Formula Calculator
File	4		Copies, erases, or renames a file
Fill	3		Fills row, column, or block with values
Find	1	F3	Finds a value or text item

Command	Command List	Quick Key	Description
Font	2	F6	Selects font for new items or changes font for existing items
Goto	1	F4	Goes to cell, named range, worksheet, or window
Graphics	2	Alt-G	Defines, generates, prints, plots, views, or edits a graph
Help	1	F1	Help information
Index	4	Alt-A	List the currently active worksheets
Input-Screen	3		Defines, modifies, loads, or erases a screen for data input
Insert	1	Alt-I	Inserts blank rows or blank columns at current position
Justify	3	Alt-J	Justifies cell contents left, right, or center
Link	3		Links windows that are to scroll together
Load	4	Alt-L	Loads a worksheet into the current window
Lock	2	Ctrl-L	Locks a single cell or a group of cells
Macro	5		Defines, removes, loads, or stores macros
Matrix	4		Performs statistical, matrix, or element operations
Move	1	Alt-M	Moves rows or columns
Name	1		Defines, undefines, displays, and edits user names

Command	Command List	Quick Key	Description
Newname	3	Alt-N	Renames the current worksheet or project file
Paint	2		Paints window, border, or cursor
Parameters	5		Sets spreadsheet parameters
Password	4		Attaches or removes a password for current worksheet
Print	1	Alt-P	Prints text or formulas
Read	4		Reads an ASCII data file
Reformat	3	Alt-Q	Changes format of numeric cells
Remember	5		Creates project file. Modifies, prints, or erases existding project files
Report	1		Defines or prints a report
Rownumbers	2		Removes/restores row numbers (toggle)
Save	4	Alt-S	Saves the current worksheet
Scroll	1		Scrolls through a worksheet
Send	5		Sends data to Data Base Manager or text to Word Processord
Sort	2		Sorts a block in a row or column
Split	3	Alt-H Alt-V	Splits the current window into two windows (Alt-H splits horizontally, Alt-V splits vertically)
Text-Editor	5		Allows editing of a text file

Command	Command List	Quick Key	Description
Text-Format	3		Defines justification for new text items
Titles	2	Alt-T	Fixes/removes titles
Unlink	3		Unlinks a window from group of windows that scroll together
Unload	4	Alt-U	Unloads a worksheet
Unlock	2		Unlocks cell or group of cells
Value-Format	3		Defines format for new value items
Vcopy	1		Copies values or text
Width	3		Changes width of one or more columns
Write	4		Writes a text file, document, or ASCII data file
Zoom	3	F7	Zooms/unzooms the current window (toggle)

Word Processor Commands

Command	Command List	Quick Key	Description
Autohelp	1		Removes/restores help line at bottom of screen (toggle)
Beep	5		Sets error beeper on/off (toggle)
Bold	2		Adds or removes boldface attribute on an item
Border	3		Removes/restores border of current window

Command	Command List	Quick Key	Description
Change-Type	4		Changes file type of current document (toggle)
Close	3	Alt-W	Closes current window or its footnote subwindow
Compute	2		Computes a sum or formula
Confidence	5		Changes confidence level
Copy	1	Alt-C	Copies a line, word, sentence, paragraph, or block
Delete	1	Alt-D	Deletes a line, word, sentence, paragraph, or block
Directory	4	Alt-O	Displays the files on a disk drive
Display	5		Alters display mode to Black-and-White, color, or graphics
Draw	3		Draws boxes, lines, or grids in graphics characters
Execute	5	F8	Executes a project file
F-Calculator	5	Alt-K	Activates Formula Calculator
File	4		Copies, erases, or renames a file
Find	1	F3	Searches for an item of text
Font	2	F6	Selects current font or changes font for existing item
Footnote	3	Alt-F	Inserts a new footnote or modifies existing footnote

Command	Command List	Quick Key	Description
Goto	1	F4	Goes to window, page, line, or user marker
Graphics	4	Alt-G	Inserts or removes graph from current document
Help	1	F1	Help information
Indent	2	Ctrl-N	Sets indent for new paragraphs
Index	4	Alt-A	Displays all current active documents
Input-Screen	5		Defines, modifies, loads, or erases a screen for data input
Insert	1	Alt-I	Inserts text from the copy buffer
Justify	2	Alt-J	Selects justification for new paragraphs
Load	4	Alt-L	Loads a file from disk into the current window
Macro	5		Defines, moves, loads, and stores macros
Margin	2	Ctrl-L	Sets margin for new paragraphs or releases left margin
Marker	3		Sets, removes, or displays user markers
Merge	4		Merges text from screen or file into current document
Move	1	Alt-M	Moves a line, word, sentence, paragraph, or block
Newname	3	Alt-N	Renames the current document
Newpage	2	Alt-E	Inserts forced page break before current line

Command	Command List	Quick Key	Description
Paint	3		Paints the current window, border, or marked region
Parameters	5		Sets Word Processor parameters
Password	4		Attaches or removes a password from document
Print	1	Alt-P	Prints a document or sets document options
Read	4		Reads a file from disk into the current document
Reformat	2		Reformats the current paragraph or entire document
Remember	5		Creates, modifies, prints, or erases a project file
Replace	1	F5	Replaces text
Ruler	3		Removes/restores the ruler in current window
Save	4	Alt-S	Saves a document
Scroll	1		Scrolls through a document
Send	5		Sends text to Spreadsheet or Data Base Manager
Spacing	2	Ctrl-V	Sets spacing for new paragraphs
Split	3	Alt-H Alt-V	Splits the current window into two windows (Alt-H splits horizontally, Alt-V splits vertically)

Command	Command List	Quick Key	Description
Tabs	2	Alt-T	Sets or resets current tab or decimal-tab stops
Text-Editor	5		Allows editing of a text file
Text-Sort	4		Sorts a block of text within the current document
Undelete	1	Alt-Q	Undeletes the previously deleted text
Underscore	2	Ctrl-U	Underscores or removes underscoring on an item
Unload	4	Alt-U	Abandons the current document without saving it to disk
Visible	2		Controls the display of special text characters
Write	4		Writes a portion of the current document to disk
Zoom	3	F7	Zooms/unzooms the current window (toggle)
Xlate	4		Converts documents to and from DCA format

Communications Commands

Command	Command List	Quick Key	Description
Answer	1	Alt-A	Answers phone after waiting for it to ring
Autohelp	4		Removes/restores help line at bottom of screen
Beep	5		Sets the beeper on/off (toggle)
Border	3	Alt-W	Removes/restores the border of current window (toggle)
Capture	1	Alt-V	Begins/ends capturing to buffer, printer, or disk
Confidence	5		Changes the confidence level
Dial	1	Alt-D	Dials a number
Directory	4	Alt-O	Lists the files on a disk drive
Display	5		Alters display mode to B/W or color
Duplex	2	Alt-U	Changes terminal screen to full or half duplex
Execute	5	F8	Executes a project file
F-Calculator	5	Alt-K	Activates Formula Calculator
File	4	Alt-F	Copies, erases, or renames a file
Filters	3	Alt-L	Edits the terminal or capture-filter tables
Format	2	Alt-E	Defines or removes a format definition for use with Send

Command	Command List	Quick Key	Description
Get	3	Alt-G	Gets a character or line for processing
Goto	2	F4	Switches phone connection to carrier or voice
Hangup	1	Alt-H	Hangs up the phone
Help	4	F1	Help information
Input-Screen	5	Alt-I	Defines, modifies, loads, or erases a screen for data input
Keyboard	2	Alt-J	Define/edits or undefines a keyboard definition file
Macro	5	Alt-N	Clears, defines, loads, removes, and saves macros
Match	3	Alt-M	Waits for a sequence of characters to be received
Output	3	Alt-C	Sends a sequence of characters
Paint	3		Paints border, window, or emulation
Parameters	5		Changes system parameters
Profile	2	Alt-P	Defines, edits, or undefines a communications profile
Receive	1	Alt-R	Receives a text or binary file
Remember	5		Creates new project file or modifies existing file
Send	5		Sends data to another application

Command	Command List	Quick Key	Description
Settings	1	Alt-S	Edits, loads, or saves communications settings
Text-Editor	5		Allows editing of a text file
Transfer-Time	4	Alt-Q	Calculates the time required to transfer a file
Transmit	1	Alt-L	Transmits a text or binary file

File Extensions

The Smart system relies heavily on the use of file extensions for identification of files. Most commands that prompt for a file name do not require that you enter an extension; the system provides the extension automatically. Following is a list of the extensions used within the Smart system.

Extension	Use and module
.BDC	Backup document files (Word Processor)
.BKY	Backup keyboard file (Communications)
.BP1	Backup project source file (Spreadsheet)
.BP2	Backup project source file (Word Processor)
.BP3	Backup project source file (Data Base Manager)
.BP6	Backup project source file (Communications)
.BTX	Backup text files (Word Processor)
.BWS	Backup worksheet files (Spreadsheet)
.CSF	Send format files (Communications)
.DAT	Special Smart format external files
.DB	Data base files
.DBS	Data base screen files
.DBU	Temporary data base update files
.DFL	Lookup definition files (Data Base Manager)
.DFQ	Query definitions (Data Base Manager)
.DFR	Report definitions (Data Base Manager)
.DFT	Transaction definitions (Data Base Manager)
.DFW	Summary definitions (Data Base Manager)

.DFX	Relation definitions (Data Base Manager)
.DFS	Sort definitions (Data Base Manager)
.DIF	Document Interchange File (Spreadsheet)
.DOC	Document files (Word Processor)
.DTM	Time management calendar file
.GDF	Graph definition files (Spreadsheet)
.IDX	Index files (Data Base Manager)
.IS1	Input screen definitions (Spreadsheet)
.IS2	Input screen definitions (Word Processor)
.IS3	Input screen definitions (Data Base Manager)
.IS6	Input screen definitions (Communications)
.Ixx	Key field files;*xx* = field number (Data Base Manager)
.KEY	Keyboard definition files (Communications)
.MBK	Macro backup file (All modules)
.MC1	Macro file (Spreadsheet)
.MC2	Macro file (Word Processor)
.MC3	Macro file (Data Base Manager)
.MC6	Macro file (Communications)
.PF1	Project source file (Spreadsheet)
.PF2	Project source file (Word Processor)
.PF3	Project source file (Data Base Manager)
.PF6	Project source file (Communications)
.PIX	Variable record location file (Data Base Manager)
.RDF	Report definition file (Spreadsheet)
.RF1	Project object (runtime) file (Spreadsheet)
.RF2	Project object (runtime) file (Word Processor)
.RF3	Project object (runtime) file (Data Base Manager)
.RF6	Project object (runtime) file (Communications)
.RFT	Revisable Text Format (Document Content Architecture) Word Processor
.SCL	Scaling file used to print graph (Word Processor)
.SCN	Graph screen file (Spreadsheet)
.TRN	Translation file for Xlate command (Word Processor)
.TXT	Text files (All modules)
.UCP	Communications profile
.WKS	Lotus 1-2-3 worksheet files
.WS	Worksheet files (Spreadsheet)
.WSP	Protected worksheet files (Spreadsheet)(Version 2)
.$$$	Temporary file (Example: QNOW.$$$ contains *Query Now* definition in Data Base Manager)

Index

More Computer Knowledge from Que

Que Order Line: 1-800-428-5331

All prices subject to change without notice.

REGISTER YOUR COPY OF
USING SMART

Register your copy of *Using Smart* and receive information about Que's newest products relating to integrated programs. Complete this registration card and return it to Que Corporation, P.O. Box 50507, Indianapolis, IN 46250.

Name _____

Address _____

City _____ State _____ ZIP _____

Phone _____

Where did you buy your copy of *Using Smart*?

_____

How do you plan to use the programs in this book?

_____

_____

_____

What other kinds of publications about integrated programs would you be interested in?

_____

_____

_____

_____

Which operating system do you use? _____

THANK YOU!

FOLD HERE

Place
Stamp
Here

Que Corporation
P. O. Box 50507
Indianapolis, IN 46250

Control Your Work Load With *Absolute Reference* And Get Your First Issue FREE!

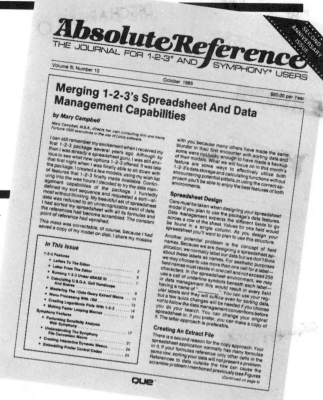

FOLD HERE

_____

_____

_____

_____

Que Corporation
P. O. Box 50507
Indianapolis, IN 46250

Place
Stamp
Here